SEAFOOD
AS WE LIKE IT

SEAFOOD
AS WE LIKE IT

ANTHONY SPINAZZOLA and
JEAN-JACQUES PAIMBLANC

Illustrations by Janet Cummings Good

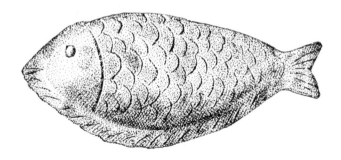

The Globe Pequot Press

Old Chester Road Chester, CT 06412

Manufactured in the United States of America
First Edition

Jacket and book design by Barbara Marks

Nutritional Analysis
by Frances Stern Nutrition Center

Library of Congress Cataloging in Publication Data
Spinazzola, Anthony.
    Seafood as we like it.

    Includes index.
    1. Cookery (Fish)   2. Cookery (seafood)
    I. Paimblanc, Jean-Jacques. II. Title.
TX747.S62 1985   641.6′92   85-9768
            ISBN 0-87106-862-1
10 9 8 7 6 5 4 3 2

Acknowledgments

■■

Some acknowledgments of gratitude must be expressed.

The authors were influenced by many who excited their concern for and appreciation of fine food, both first-hand and through their writings. To attempt to name them would be impossible, but to those who inspired, or taught, or showed, or shared with us — you are in these pages. We hope this book will allow others to share what we have learned of the pleasures that can be had by sitting down to eat honest food. And the joy that can come with preparing it.

Special thanks are required for the Berkowitz family of Legal Seafoods, in Allston, Massachusetts, from whose retail store in Boston we obtained almost all the seafood used in creating our recipes. To say that they and their employees were always extraordinarily helpful, is to say a great deal. More importantly — what we purchased was always fresh and of the highest quality.

Second, we owe gratitude beyond measure to two restaurateurs. Our thanks go to Lucien Robert of Maison Robert in Boston, and his chef, Pierre Jamet, for allowing us the use of the kitchen at Maison Robert during off-hours to develop and perfect these recipes. To Barry Kaplan and his chef, Bank Szerenyi, at the Gazelle Restaurant in Quincy, we owe equal thanks for similar hospitality. We used both kitchens and in both we were made to feel not merely welcome, but at home.

We rush to assure our readers at this point, that though we cooked in professional kitchens most of the time, we used standard household equipment and nothing that cannot be found in the average home kitchen.

Interspersed throughout the book you will find about a dozen and a half recipes provided by restaurateurs. We included them to give readers an idea of the dishes being created in today's restuarants. We have not tried in this to be all-inclusive or to seek only those that are avant-garde, haute cuisine, down-home, or ethnic. Without apology, we have merely tried to demonstrate in a small way how some restaurants of varying aims are using seafood. Among the vast array we might have chosen any other dozen and a half, but there is a limit to the space available, and we believe these will give readers an idea of how restaurant fare can be used in the home. We thank those restaurants who responded to our request.

We frequently bought seafood at retail outlets other than Legal Seafood, both to test the general availability of ingredients we were using, or because Legal did not have a certain item at the time when inspiration struck us. It is indicative of the Boston consumer's awareness of what fresh means in fish, and in the ability of these stores to provide it, that the Fish Market at Anthony's Pier 4 Restaurant, Boston; Wulf's Fish Market, Brookline; Frank Giuffre's Fish Market, Boston; and the Pines River Fish Market, Revere, never disappointed us in our purchases upon such occasions.

To work with one author is certainly a test of any editor; to work with two must be more than doubly difficult. We are certain that without seeking to, we tested the mettle of Cary Hull, our editor. We admit our special debt to her — her professionalism and patience were unflagging and supportive beyond measure. No small credit for the worth of this book also will be due to the design by Barbara Marks, whose graphics so clearly present what we set out to do. And Janet Cummings Good's illlustrations take readers to the heart of her subjects with a deft and sure hand. They have added so much to our original efforts.

Finally, to Charles Liftman, systems editor at *The Boston Globe,* we owe thanks for smoothing out the ways of computerdom, not merely with technical knowledge, but with understanding.

A l'ouazo

Contents

∎

Foreword

■

Some marriages, they say, are made in heaven. That must have been the case when Jean-Jacques Paimblanc and Anthony Spinazzola decided to get together to write this cookbook.

One, born in Lyon, France, the other in Boston; one a professional chef with the rigorous training of the Old World apprenticeship system, the other a professional journalist and editor whose hobby turned into a vocation. The chemistry between these two has been a pleasure to watch. It reminded me of my early years with the *New York Times* and Craig Claiborne. In spite of different backgrounds, their agreement on what they consider worthy dishes and worthwhile food has often made it seem as though they shared the same warm kitchen of childhood.

For many years my work has taken me to Boston as often as twice a month, more frequently in recent years with a daughter living in the area. During these visits, I came to know Tony Spinazzola personally and through his restaurant reviews in *The Boston Globe* and his general writing on food and wine. Many memorable evenings were spent following his suggestions of where to dine in the New England area. His no-nonsense, professional approach to the job of restaurant critic won him respect from his readers, his journalistic peers, chefs, and the restaurant industry at large. His contribution to the dining revolution that has taken place in Boston in the last decade has been immeasureable. When he began, nearly 20 years ago as the first serious critic in the city, Boston was not in the forefront of American cities in dining experiences. His contributions were undoubtedly a prime factor in raising the quality and sophistication of eating out in Boston to what it is today. The information and observations in this book are a credit to his journalistic ability and appreciation and concern for fine food.

It has been said that late bloomers are always the ones that provide the best flowers or the tastiest fruits. While they have been soaking up more sun and nourishment, the early bloomers are likely to have faded. For many years I have watched Jean-Jacques Paimblanc and knew the talent was there. He has studied and absorbed the kitchen arts since his boyhood through years in some of the most noted kitchens on two continents and now shares that knowledge in this work.

We first met when he was at Le Pavillon in New York, his first job in the

United States. Later, he joined me at the Howard Johnson Company, where we worked together for twelve years. Craig Claiborne and I had many opportunities to appreciate his quality as much as a friend as a chef.

I am happy to see that they have included recipes for lesser-used seafoods not often in American cookbooks in such quantity. They are a welcome addition to the growing curiosity and awareness of cooks in this country today.

When Jean-Jacques told me of his intention of writing this book with Tony, I knew that they would succeed. The result has been due to a mutuality of respect — for each other's palates as well as those of their readers. I am sure this work is the first of many to come.

PIERRE FRANEY
New York, New York

Introduction

■

This is a personal cookbook. We have cooked what we liked. We have tried to let our tastebuds, sound culinary practice, and the seafood before us determine the final dish. While acknowledging our debt to practitioners old and new, we have tried to steer a course between the 'good old days' and the fads of the moment.

We have not tried to prepare a complete handbook for cooking seafood, a kind of culinary catechism of the catch. You won't find a recipe here for baked stuffed lobster. You won't learn how to do a New England clambake on a deserted beach — or in a new heatproof rubbish barrel in a backyard in McCook, Nebraska. Figuratively as well as literally, there is a limit to what one can digest.

We have cooked just about everything "from scratch." We used nothing artificial and took only those shortcuts that prudence and prior use had taught were worthwhile.

Canned chicken broth, for example, is perfectly adequate for use as part of a recipe when you do not have homemade stock on hand and don't have the time to make it fresh. We have used instant couscous and commercial pasta, prepared horseradish and frozen puff pastry, and our vision is not so narrow that we can't imagine someone using canned or frozen crabmeat. Because we live in a colder climate, we have used dried herbs extensively when fresh were no longer forthcoming from the backyard, but we also sought out fresh herbs when we knew they were required. We drew the line at packaged breadcrumbs, however. With today's food processors and blenders, it takes only a moment or two to turn four slices of bread into a cup of fresh crumbs.

Good food needs the finest ingredients.

"The finest ingredients" does not automatically mean exotic and expensive ingredients. Freshness is the first quality of good food. Simple ingredients can make outstanding food. Once we were asked what were the four most important factors to a successful fish dish. Our answer was and still is:

1. Fresh fish.
2. Fresh fish.
3. Fresh fish.
4. A good cook and a good recipe.

If the quality or freshness of the fish you plan to cook is not satisfactory, do not expect to hide any deficiency by a fancy sauce; you may only aggravate your case. Give up while it is still time. Do yourself and your guests a favor — buy a chicken or a piece of beef!

Permit a digression, as modest as possible, about the authors, simplicity, and freshness.

One of the authors of this book, Jean-Jacques Paimblanc, grew up in Lyon, France. One of the first kitchens he worked in was in the restaurant, La Mère Brazier, an establishment that drew clientele from all over Europe who mostly came to dine on just one dish. What was this creation — pheasants' tongues in a secret sauce, perhaps, or thrushes stuffed with figs and roasted over the first-pruned vines of the Chambertin vineyard?

No, just a chicken — *volaille demi-deuil* — chicken cooked in a pot with water and leeks and carrots. Slices of truffles were slid under the chicken skin. The black and white effect gave the dish its name, "chicken in half mourning," and it was electric. A boiled chicken and two vegetables with slices of truffles.

"Well, of course," you say, "the truffles. . . !"

But truffles in that time and that place were not what they are today. An expensive ingredient, but they were to the France of that day about what a lobster is here today. The truffles perfumed the dish, to be sure, but it was the chicken that made it: A hen from Bresse, across the River *Saône* from Burgundy, a region celebrated for the poultry it raised. A free-ranging bird that had the run of some peasant's yard to pick at the food that it liked best, to grow flavorful, fat, and rich-meated. It was taken at that point in its maturity that would best serve its ultimate fate. Brought to the restaurant in the morning freshly killed and freshly plucked; in the pot by dusk. Probably feet and all, a rarity these days, the more to add body to the finished dish. And the same broth was used over and over during the day to poach other fowl, adding further to its enrichment.

The good madam, the owner of the restaurant, had worked at her celebrated dish and done it over and over until it was perfected, and it won her Michelin stars and made her famous in a country where such fame is not easily acquired.

It was in such an atmosphere that a young French chef learned the demands of bringing even a single dish to perfection, and the value of selecting the finest and freshest ingredients.

The second author of this work, Anthony Spinazzola, grew up in Greater Boston to a culinary scene much more varied if not so cosmopolitan. It was still a time when milk came in bottles and the cream floated to the top, when one could go onto any beach within the rim of Boston Harbor and dig a bucket of unpolluted clams, when consumers knew which potatoes to buy in which season and for what use. And there was clam chowder, creamy with the silken sheen that rendered salt pork gives, rough potatoes resistant and yet tender, and spoonful after spoonful of tender clams. A humble New England dish that undoubtedly was already classic before the country was born. Freshness, quality ingredients, and the perfection that simplicity alone brings were the keynotes of both dishes.

Good food need not be fancy nor expensive, merely fresh and treated properly.

You won't find "quick" recipes in this book (though many are quickly prepared), nor those that include ingredients so rare that only members of the food establishment can obtain them through professional sources. Our first rule was that if a seafood is not normally — or at least occasionally — available at retail shops from which most consumers buy, there is not much purpose to writing recipes telling how to cook it. Crayfish, for example, or scallops with roe intact; the pike, pickerel, and perch of the dedicated amateur fisherman are not to be found here.

We do, however, indicate in the appendix many fishes that can be substituted for the ones we cooked. After all, even a Gloucesterman will gladly give up his cod or lemon sole for a walleye he has just hooked.

Our viewpoint, from the beginning, has been personal, but not necessarily narrow nor, we hope, time-worn. We have purposely sought out and experimented with many of the underutilized species from the sea, but not to serve a messianic role for fishermen or the state and federal agencies involved with the fishing industry. Nor has it been to lead some charge of the avant-garde.

The reason for choosing many lesser-known species is practical: Overfishing and pollution have decimated many seafoods Americans have traditionally loved best. There is no question that in the coming years we will have to turn our attention more and more to marine foods that we never bothered with before. Even now, scientists of many countries are looking into a tiny Antarctic crustacean called *krill* as a future food source. It is not too distant in time that squid, sea urchin, and even sea slugs and other creatures will be finding their way to more and more tables. After all, humankind had to learn to eat the slippery, succulent oyster that hid within rock-like shells.

We deliberately set out to use not only underutilized species, but to explore new and different combinations, but not for the sake of being different. We have sought to apply traditional and well-known cooking techniques to traditional and well-known ingredients in new, but easily understood, combinations.

We have not presumed to define every way to cook this or that fish. We hope merely to have pointed the way, to have indicated some new treatments that can be applied easily to whatever seafood is at hand.

Seafood Basics

"Procrastination when serving meat is a misdemeanor; when serving fish, a felony."
— Howard Hillman in *"Kitchen Science"*

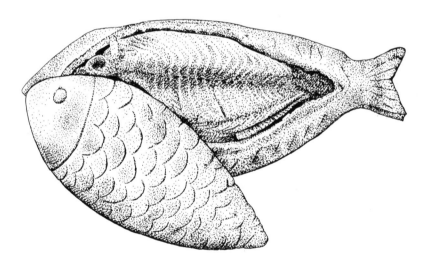

Porgy Baked in Salt-Dough Crust

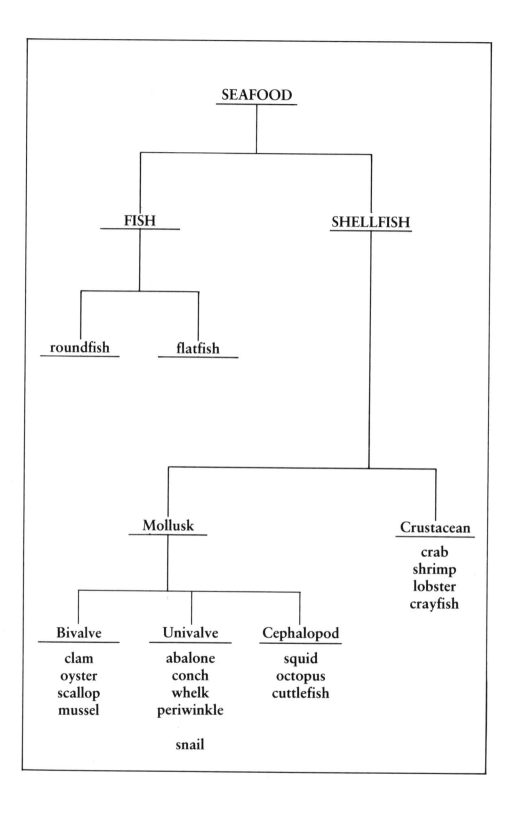

Families of Fish and Shellfish
■■

The biological classification, to the left, may help you to differentiate among the marine animals we commonly eat. A simplified rundown would be as follows:

Fish are the major category. Salmon, tuna, and striped bass are among the hundreds of round fishes; flounders, soles, and halibut are among the flatfishes.

Shellfish are the other major category. They are soft-bodied, hard-shelled creatures without a backbone. They have an external protective shell called an exoskeleton. It is a sort of a skeleton worn on the outside. There are three categories of shellfish, only two of which are shown: Crustacean and Mollusks. The third group is made up of Echinoderms (sea urchins and sea slugs).

Crustaceans have a firm outer covering. This is a broad grouping, with more than 35,000 species. Included are the crab, shrimp, lobster, crayfish, prawns, and barnacles.

The mollusks are divided into three subcategories of which the pelecypods, or bivalves like the clam, oyster, scallop, razor shell, sea dates, and sea truffles form an important food group for humans. The bivalves have the ability to concentrate in their bodies harmful bacteria and algae. Some of these, such as the "red tide," can be dangerous to human health. They are not removed by cooking. Bivalves should never be taken from waters of uncertain purity and never during red-tide emergencies in any waters.

The univalves, one-shelled mollusks, are another food group, though not as widely consumed. The snail, known best as food by the French word *escargot,* is the terrestrial member. Abalone, conch, and whelk consumption is widespread, but periwinkles, cockles, and limpets enjoy only limited attraction.

Cephalopods have elongated bodies with a fleshy mantle. Squid are the most widely eaten of the cephalopods. Only a rudimentary internal shell remains in the squid, a transparent piece of cartilage called the "pen" or sword. Squid have ten arms, as do cuttlefish; octopus have eight.

Buying Fish

In buying fresh fish, it is important to deal with a fish market that places great emphasis on obtaining and selling only the freshest fish possible. Fresh fish has a shelf life of about five days if it is handled properly. ("Shelf life" in this case is misleading, five days from the moment it is taken from the water is more accurate.) In a market, it must be protected from heat and drying. Fish should be kept on chipped or flaked ice in a cooler. The ice helps to maintain moisture. Make certain that you are getting fresh fish to begin with. In some cultures, fish is never bought except in the whole state, so that the buyer can be certain the fish is really fresh.

To determine a fish's freshness, look for the following signs:

a. Prime seafood is fragrant, even sweet-smelling, and does not smell "fishy."

b. The fish's eyes should be clear and full, not milky or sunken. A wall-eye, by definition, does not conform.

c. The flesh of a fresh fish is firm and elastic; when pressed it should not feel soft and your fingers should not leave an indentation.

d. Gills should be bright red, not muddy gray.

e. Skin color should be characteristic, with no red or other off-colors.

f. Steaks and fillets should appear moist and firm, clean-cut, with no yellowing or browning at the edges; nor should they appear dry.

Fresh fish is not obtainable everywhere at all times and there are occasions when your only choice will be to use frozen fish. **Someone has said that the opposite of fresh is not frozen, but stale.** A good frozen fish is better than a bad fresh one. Use frozen fish only if you must, but there are cautions to observe. A white cottony appearance, a brownish, leathery tinge, or any discoloration in the flesh of frozen fish indicates poor quality.

Fish are sold in a variety of cuts and forms, including the following:

Whole or round fish: These are just as they come from the water. In great fish eating countries, this is the way consumers prefer to buy their fish, as they can better determine freshness. In such countries fish often are cooked whole, with head and tail intact. This method guards against loss of flavor. Serious fish eaters are aware that some of the best meat is around the head of a fish. Whole fish must be scaled and eviscerated before they can be cooked. In many recipes, it is easier to leave the fins attached to the whole fish during cooking, as they can be removed more easily once the fish is

Market Forms of Fish

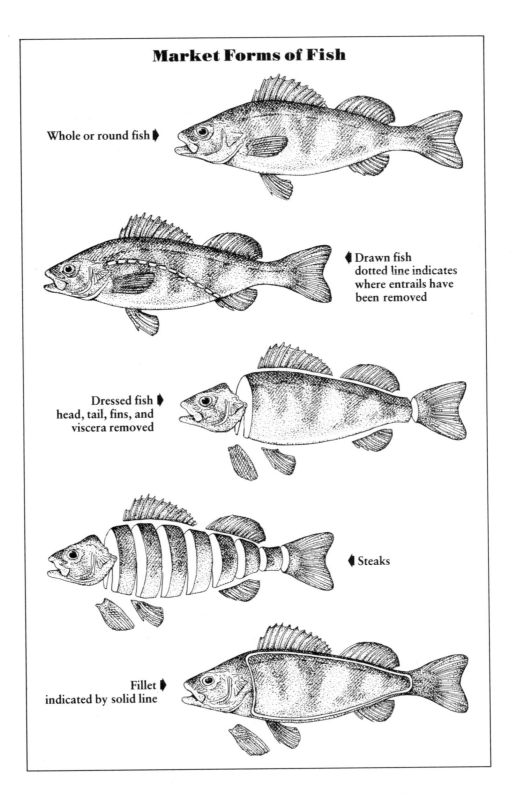

Whole or round fish ▶

◀ Drawn fish
dotted line indicates
where entrails have
been removed

Dressed fish ▶
head, tail, fins, and
viscera removed

◀ Steaks

Fillet ▶
indicated by solid line

cooked. Three-quarters of a pound makes 1 serving.

Drawn fish: This term applies to fish that have had entrails removed. The viscera spoil rapidly, so it is best to gut fish as soon as possible after they are caught. *Drawn* fish have longer storage life. They must be scaled; most often, but not always, the fins are removed before cooking. The yield of a drawn fish is about 50 percent; ½ pound makes 1 serving.

Dressed and pan-dressed fish: These fish have been eviscerated and scaled, and the head, tail, and fins may be removed. Smaller fish sold with head and tails intact are still termed pan-dressed. The yield is about 65 percent; 1 pound makes 2 servings.

Steaks: Steaks are cross-section slices of large dressed fish cut ¾-to-1-inch thick, though the thickness may be even greater depending on use. Normally the skin is not removed before cooking and serves to hold the flesh together. Halibut, swordfish, salmon, tuna, and eel are most frequently sold in steak form. A cross-section of the backbone is usually the only bone left in the steak. The yield is about 85 percent; 1 pound makes 3 servings.

Fillets: The sides of the fish taken lengthwise away from the backbone are called fillets. They are sold with and without skin attached and are practically boneless. Fillets are the most delicate cuts of fish and they can be cooked in numberless ways, but care must be taken in cooking so that they are not overcooked and do not dry out. They also tend to be fragile, especially when skinned. One pound makes 3 servings.

With flatfish such as flounder or sole, the fish can be filleted so that you obtain one whole fillet from the top side and one from the bottom. These two pieces are termed *crosscut fillets*. The two pieces of flesh, especially in larger fish, also can be cut out so that you obtain two fillets from the top and two from the bottom — the backbone along the center creating a natural division.

These are termed *quartercut fillets*. In this regard, the fillets of a flatfish may be thought of as being similar to a breast of chicken — you may use one whole breast, or each half. A flatfish, of course, has a top and a bottom "breast."

Butterfly fillets: These are pan-dressed fish that are opened flat like a book, with both fillets exposed. The bones, but not the skin, are normally removed, though this is not true for all species nor all recipes. The skin is used to keep the cut intact. In a butterfly fillet, the two pieces of fillet remain joined by the skin at the back. If they are joined by the skin of the belly, the cut is called a *kited fillet*. Such technical distinctions better serve the fish cutter than the fish consumer, perhaps, and your fishmonger will know what you want if you describe it or the eventual use. Shrimp are also frequently butterflied.

Fingers: To make fingers, the fish is filleted and the skin removed. The fillets are then cut into finger-length strips by slicing, sometimes in slanted or diagonal cuts, generally in pieces about ½-inch wide. Fingers are designed for deep-frying when coated with a batter, or for use in dishes such as seviche. Don't confuse them with fish sticks, which are commercial cuts taken from a block of frozen fish fillets. One pound makes 4 servings.

Centercut: Like a chateaubriand that is the heart of a beef tenderloin, a centercut of fish is the meatiest part. It is cut from just behind the *pectoral fins* (those on the sides of a round fish, about where the fish's shoulders would be) back toward the tail to the point where the fish begins to narrow. Deboned, this is the cut of salmon one would use to make *gravlax*. One pound makes 3 servings.

Halved fish: Pan-dressed round fish are often split down the backbone and sold with both the skin and bone attached, which makes them especially suitable for broiling. One pound makes 2 servings.

How Much Seafood Should You Buy

Type of Seafood	Amount to Buy per Serving
Clams, in the shell	6 to 8
Clams, softshell	12 to 20
Clams, shucked	½ pint
Crabs, cooked meat	¼ to ⅓ lb.
Fish, whole	¾ lb.
Fish, dressed and pan dressed	½ lb.
Fish, steaks(bone in)	½ lb.
Fish, steaks(no bone)	⅓ lb.
Fish, fillets	¼ to ⅓ lb.
Lobster, live	1 to 1½ lb.
Lobster, cooked meat	¼ to ⅓ lb.
Mussels, in the shell	1½ to 2 lbs.
Oysters, in the shell	6 to 8
Oyster, shucked	½ pint
Scallops	¼ to ⅓ lb.
Shrimp, headless	⅓ to ½ lb.
Shrimp, peeled and deveined	¼ to ⅓ lb.
Shrimp, peeled, deveined and cooked	¼ to ⅓ lb.
Periwinkles	¼ to ⅓ lb.
Sea urchins	6 to 8

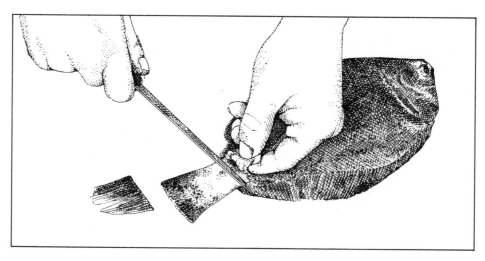

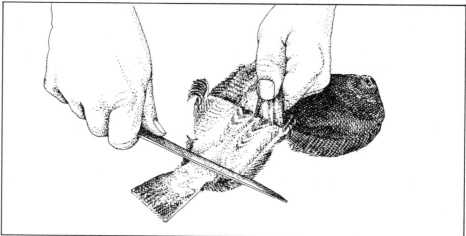

DRESSING A FLAT FISH TO COOK IT WHOLE

Top: After trimming the fish's tail with scissors, make a cut at the tail to create a tab of skin for gripping purposes.

Bottom: Lift the skin, using a knife to separate the flesh from the skin.

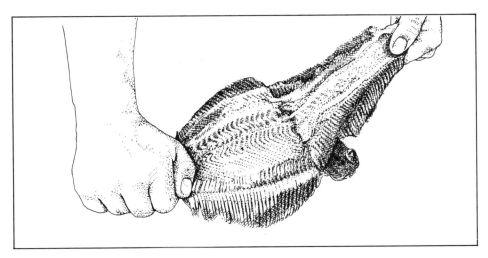

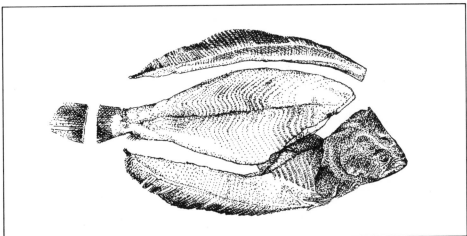

Top: Continue pulling the skin; it should easily pull free from the flesh.

Bottom: Trim the comb, the edge of small bones on each side of the fish. Note: Cut more deeply into the fish on the belly side so as to remove the head and viscera. The stomach cavity must be cleaned and thoroughly washed before you cook.

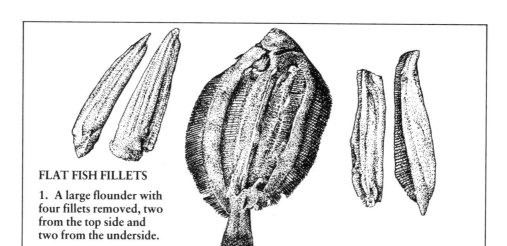

FLAT FISH FILLETS

1. A large flounder with four fillets removed, two from the top side and two from the underside.

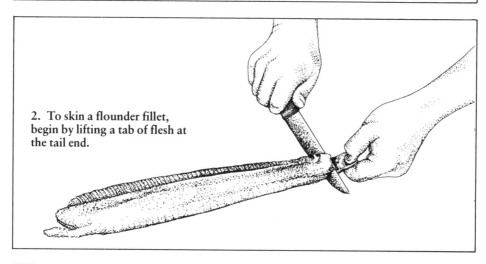

2. To skin a flounder fillet, begin by lifting a tab of flesh at the tail end.

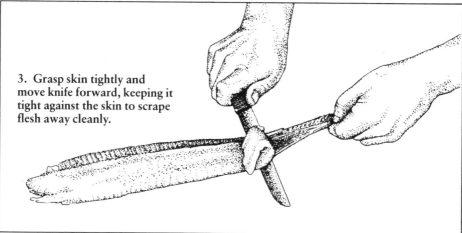

3. Grasp skin tightly and move knife forward, keeping it tight against the skin to scrape flesh away cleanly.

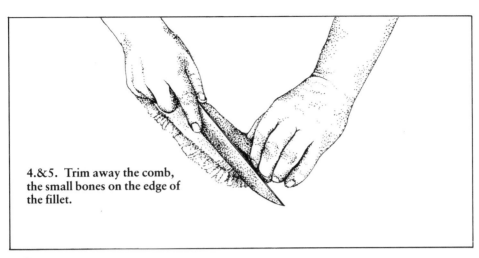

4. & 5. Trim away the comb, the small bones on the edge of the fillet.

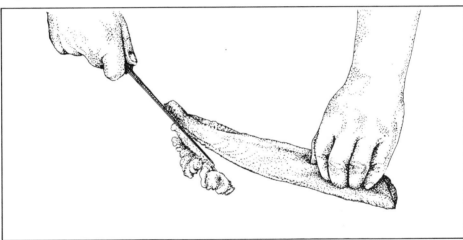

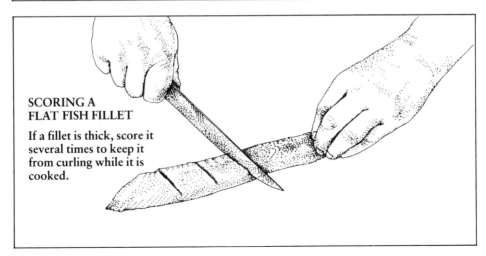

**SCORING A
FLAT FISH FILLET**

If a fillet is thick, score it several times to keep it from curling while it is cooked.

**HOW TO FILLET A
ROUND FISH**

1. Cut away the fins on the fish.

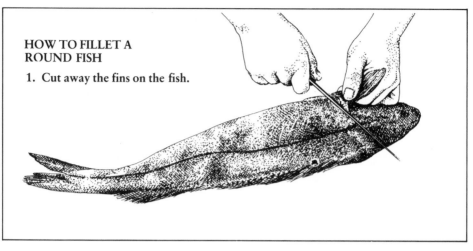

2. First score, then cut, along the backbone.

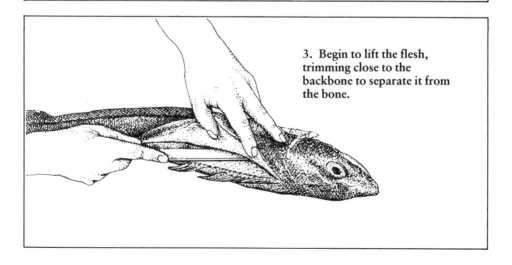

3. Begin to lift the flesh, trimming close to the backbone to separate it from the bone.

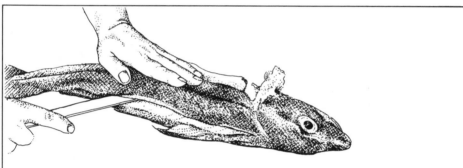

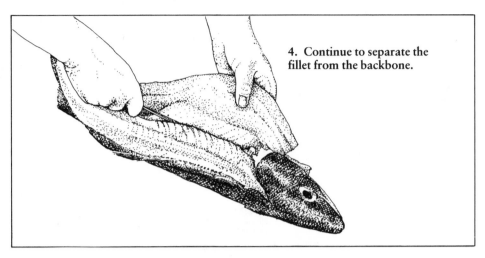

4. Continue to separate the fillet from the backbone.

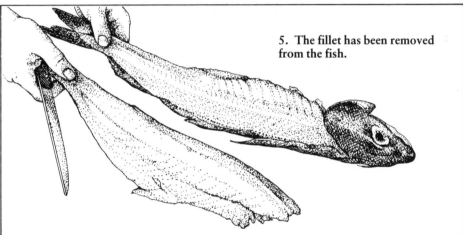

5. The fillet has been removed from the fish.

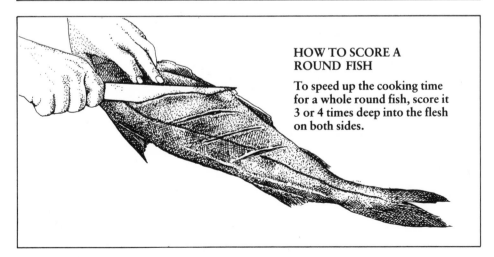

HOW TO SCORE A ROUND FISH

To speed up the cooking time for a whole round fish, score it 3 or 4 times deep into the flesh on both sides.

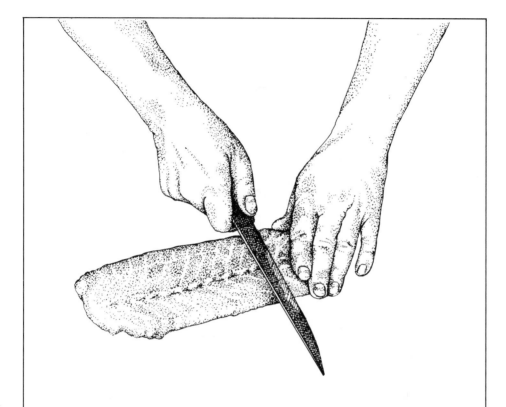

HOW TO CUT MEDALLIONS

1. A medallion is a coin- or medal-shaped piece cut from boneless fish fillets on a 45-degree angle to give it more cooking surface. Here a monkfish fillet is cut into 1½- to 2-inch-thick medallions.

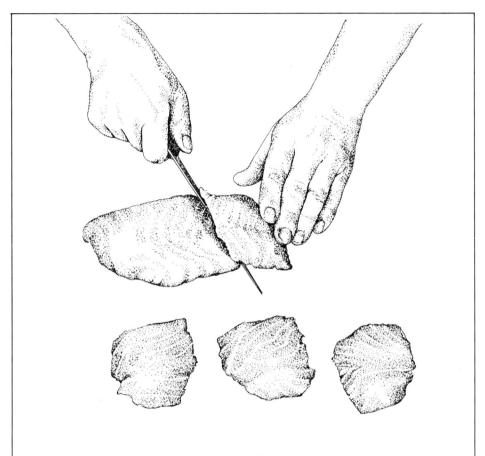

2. Note the angle of the knife as the medallions are sliced.

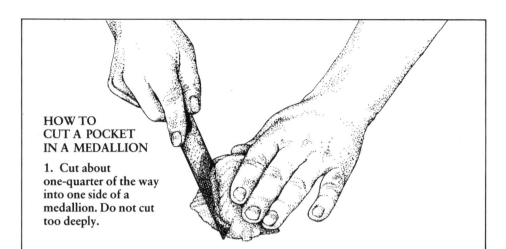

**HOW TO
CUT A POCKET
IN A MEDALLION**

1. Cut about
one-quarter of the way
into one side of a
medallion. Do not cut
too deeply.

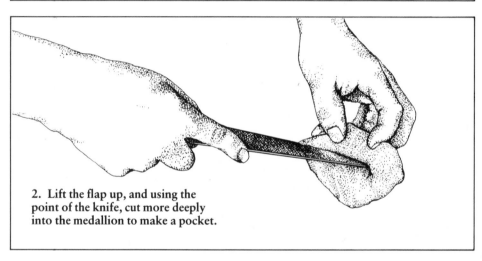

2. Lift the flap up, and using the
point of the knife, cut more deeply
into the medallion to make a pocket.

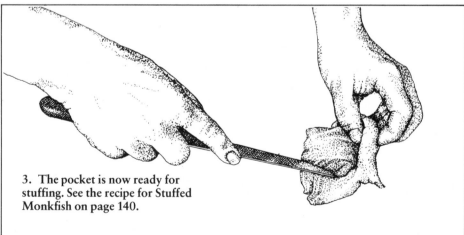

3. The pocket is now ready for
stuffing. See the recipe for Stuffed
Monkfish on page 140.

Keeping Fish

Now that you have acquired some fish, what do you do with it until you are ready to cook it?

One thing you do is decide not to keep it too long. You can assume that any fish you buy from a fish market is from one to three days out of the water, therefore you should cook fish you buy within a day or two, preferably on the day you buy it.

Fish must not only be kept cool, but moist as well. Maintain a temperature of 31 degrees Fahrenheit; a fish will remain fresh about twice as long at 31 as at 37 degrees. Keep your fish in the refrigerator atop a container of ice, if possible, until it is to be cooked. A wet dishtowel laid over the fish would be ideal.

Shellfish must also be kept moist as well as cool. Use wet paper towels to keep moisture within the package until you are ready to cook lobster, crabs, clams or mussels. Shellfish can tolerate storage at 33 or 34 degrees Fahrenheit.

Do not immerse shellfish or crustaceans in fresh water as it will kill them.

Eviscerating Fish

Whether dealing with fish you have caught yourself or with those bought from a dealer, you should know something about what will make a fish "go bad" before its time. Fish are highly perishable and usually are eviscerated almost immediately, since the intestines, liver, heart, and gills are the parts that deteriorate quickly and are the greatest possible source of bacterial contamination. The digestive juices in most fish are extremely powerful and these attack the walls of the body cavity if the fish is not dressed immediately. Most often this is accomplished by "gutting" the fish — making an incision into the belly through which the viscera is removed.

When cleaning the stomach cavity of a fish, it is important that you remove all traces of blood. Frequently there is blood along the backbone. Frequently, too, a membrane covers this portion of the backbone, and must be scraped away for you to wash the area completely of blood.

There are times when it is desirable to gut the fish, but not through the stomach. One way to accomplish this is by removing the backbone and then removing the viscera through the opening that is created (see drawing on page 230). Beginning near the head, cut close to and on one side of the backbone nearly to the tail. Repeat on the other side of the backbone. With the knife or strong kitchen shears, sever the backbone at both ends (and in several other places if necessary) and lift it free. The stomach cavity can then be emptied and washed through this topside opening. For some recipes it is necessary to keep the fish intact and the gutting is done through the gills.

In roundfish, the viscera are located where you would expect them to be, in the stomach at the bottom of the widest part of the fish. In flatfish, however, the visceral cavity is located in the front quarter of the body, just behind and below the gills.

Scaling Fish

You will need a fish scaler if cooking much fish, although many fish markets will scale fish for you if you ask. Many do it automatically. There is a wide variety available in kitchen stores and the like. The back of a knife or hacksaw blade bent into a u-shape will serve in a pinch.

A fish is generally scaled if it is to be cooked with the skin on. To scale a fish, scrape it with a fish scaler, or another implement from the tail toward the head. If you submerge the fish under water in a sink or large pot you'll keep the scales from flying all over the place. Rinse the fish well after all the scales have been removed.

Keeping a fish steady for scaling is easier to do if you can attach the fish securely in some way. A large clipboard with a powerful clip is an excellent way to handle the problem, if you can find one with a clip that is strong enough. They sometimes can be found in bait and tackle shops. If you can't find one, you probably can make one by attaching a strong clip to a piece of plywood or plastic.

Equipment

Two of the most important implements you might need when handling fish are more likely to be found in a home handyman's tool box than among kitchen implements. Nothing works as well for removing bones from fish than needle-nose pliers. Long thin bones in fish like salmon can be tenacious, and some grip as though barbed. Pointed pliers will repay their price in time and nerves saved the first time you use them. Machinists' or hobbyists' tweezers are also an excellent choice.

Snub-nosed or round pliers afford a better grip than almost anything else you can find when skinning a fish and, especially, an eel. Keep these tools only for use with fish.

Oyster and clam knives are useful, though many cooks find it easier to open oysters using a beer can opener. They insert the point at or near the hinge of the shells and pry upward.

A filleting knife is useful, but not entirely necessary. Its thin, flexible blade resembles a boning knife and is easily worked around all sizes and shapes of fish. A 9-inch blade is long enough to reduce work to a minimum. A standard boning knife or shorter chef's knife works just as well if you only have one or two fish to fillet.

Advice for the Fisherman

If you catch your own fish, dress it immediately and get it onto ice as quickly as possible. If you fish from a boat, you should have ice on board. Otherwise, keep fish out of the sun — a creel, basket, or other container that allows air circulation is best until you can get the fish onto ice. Newly caught fish should not be packed tightly in a creel or container. Seaweed, grass, ferns, anything that keeps the fish separated and allows air circulation, should be used between fishes.

If you freeze the fish you catch, it is best for all but the smallest fish to cut fillets from your catch — fillets freeze more thoroughly and faster than whole fish. Freezing the fillets singly, or at least in one layer, is also more efficient. You can make suitable packages of the fillets after they are frozen. Don't throw away the heads, bones, and trimmings. You can use these in making soups, stocks and sauces. They can be frozen if you can't use them immediately. Always remove the gills from heads, of course.

Although most experts recommend freezing clams and other shellfish after they are shucked, many clam diggers freeze quahaugs in the shell for short periods of time.

Fat fish (mackerel, bluefish, butterfish) will keep in the freezer two months; lean fish up to six months. All frozen foods begin to lose flavor after four months, however.

Properly frozen seafood can remain in the freezer for four to six months. Cooked seafood will last three to four days under proper refrigeration; two to three months frozen. Salted or smoked seafood will last several weeks in the refrigerator, but lox only three to four days, because it is lightly salted and the preservative effect is lessened. Dried and salted fish will keep more or less indefinitely, but once soaked it should be treated as fresh fish although some preservative effect remains.

Frozen seafood should not be thawed by allowing it to remain at room temperature — that will invite spoilage. Thaw seafood products either by leaving them in the refrigerator — allowing about 24 hours for a one pound package — or place them in running cold water — about one hour for a one pound package.

Cooking Fish

Overcooking is the major fault to be avoided when cooking fish. Since fish come in such a wide variety of species, sizes, shapes, textures, and cuts, precise cooking times have been difficult to pin down.

Cooking fish according to what has been called the "Canadian Method" has become widely accepted and guards against overcooking or undercooking. Developed by the Canadians, it eliminates a lot of the guess-work, is accurate in almost every instance, and is compatible with all cooking methods — broiling, baking, poaching, frying, even steaming.

The basic rule is to cook the fish for 10 minutes for each inch of thickness, measured at the thickest part of the fish or preparation.

The rule applies whether you are talking about a whole fish, a pan-dressed specimen, a steak, or a fillet. A whole fish, 2 inches thick, will take 20 minutes; a steak 1½ inches thick will require 15 minutes; a ½-inch-thick fillet will take 5 minutes.

Just lay the fish flat and measure it at its thickest point prior to cooking. The distance from the tip of your index finger to the crease of the first knuckle is approximately 1 inch.

If you are preparing a rolled fish or merely placing one fillet atop another with some ingredient between (as in our recipe for baked bluefish, page 194), the method still works. Measure the fish after rolling, stuffing, or combining. As an example, two ½-inch fillets with a thin stuffing laid lengthwise between them sandwich-fashion, might measure 1¼ inches. The cooking time would be 12½ minutes.

Some experts maintain that a doubling of the thickness of a fish requires more than a doubling of the cooking time, since the progress is geometric, not linear, and one should therefore quadruple the cooking time.

We did not find this to be accurate, but it is wise to bear the idea in mind when cooking whole fish or larger cuts — and test before removing from the heat.

A 10-pound bluefish, for example, measuring 5½ inches at its thickest point, was baked in an oven for 50 minutes; the flesh was still sufficiently undercooked for it to require another 10 minutes on each side over charcoal when barbecued according to our recipe for barbecued bluefish (page 195).

To test fish for doneness, flake with a fork. Lift a flake with a tine to see whether it is milky all the way through. Cooked fish flakes easily. If you were to separate the flakes of a raw fish, you would observe that the flakes are translucent throughout. As the fish cooks, the flakes turn milky and opaque in a progression from the outside in. When the flakes are milky and opaque to the very center of the portion, the fish is done.

Check bone-in steaks for doneness by inserting a knife or other pointed instrument into the center bone and rocking it back and forth. It will easily pull away from the surrounding flesh when cooked.

Other cooking hints:

1.   To be fussy about it, you should remove the fish from the heat when doneness is still a short distance from the very center or deepest part of the portion as the fish will continue to cook internally when you remove it from the heat. In that way you will have perfectly cooked fish.

2.   When using fresh fish, don't go directly from chilled state to cooking. Allow fish to just come to room temperature.

3.   Leaving the head and tail on whole fish while cooking helps to retain flavor. Even if you prefer not to serve whole fish that way, cook them without removing the head and tail.

4.   When baking whole fish or thick fillets, especially those with skin on, you can make them cook more quickly and evenly by cutting several gashes along the sides of the fish so that heat will penetrate. The gashes also will help to keep the fish from curling as skin shrinks during cooking (see the drawing on page 13).

5.   All fish shrinks somewhat during cooking, monkfish most noticeably; a factor to keep in mind where shrinkage might affect appearance.

6.   When cooking fish wrapped in foil or parchment, increase cooking time slightly to compensate for the enclosure.

7.   Often in cooking fish, the fish is covered and kept warm after cooking while you finish the sauce. Some liquid will drain from the fish as it sits. Don't waste it, pour this liquid into the sauce as you proceed. Don't add it at the very end of sauce-making, or you'll thin the sauce too much.

For specific cooking methods, follow the suggestions below:

Pan frying: Heat ¼-inch oil, butter, butter and oil mixed, or some other fat, such as bacon, in a pan until it is hot but not smoking. (Use a 375-degree setting on an electric frying pan or skillet. It also pays to check accuracy of electric thermostats with a hand thermometer from time to time.) Measure fish or portions. Dredge fish with flour, breadcrumbs, or dip it in a batter. Fry for half the time indicated; turn and complete cooking time. Dry on absorbent paper.

With very thin skinless flounder fillets, which are extremely delicate and likely to crumble or break, you must use a wide spatula and turn them with great care to avoid breaking portions. In most cases, it is not necessary to turn very thin skinless fillets, anyway. Cook on one side only and serve fish with the browned-side up.

If you are sauteing both sides of a fillet, cook with the dark side up first. Serve with the light side facing up.

Turning fish in a hot skillet or frying pan is an operation requiring care — the fat in the pan can easily spatter. Try doing it as follows: When the first side is done, tilt the skillet away from you so that fat collects on the far side. Keep fish on the high portion of the pan. Still keeping the skillet tilted, slide a wide spatula under the far side of the fish and turn it toward you. In this way, there will be no splatter. After turning, baste from time to time while the second side browns nicely.

Deep frying: Deep frying should be done from 350 to 375 degrees. A 360-to-370-degree range is even more precise, but with most thermostats and thermometers, it is generally easier to heat oil or fat to 375 degrees. Either use a thermometer, or test the temperature by tossing in a few cubes or pieces of bread — they should begin to cook immediately and brown completely within minutes.

Bread or batter the fish if the recipe calls for it. Completely submerge the fish in hot oil and cook for the time indicated. If you have a great deal of fish to fry, do it in batches rather than trying to fry it all at once. Too great a quantity will drastically lower the heat and require too much time to return to 375 degrees. The fish will become grease-soaked and not cook properly. When frying more than one batch, make certain the temperature has returned to 375 degrees before adding additional fish. Drain on absorbent paper when done.

Use a strainer or slotted spoon to remove any batter that has fallen into oil, as it will break down the oil more quickly and cause it to become rancid. Don't overuse the oil — change it when it grows dark or smells burnt.

Oven broiling: The thickness of fish will determine the distance you place it from heat as well as the length of cooking time. For thinnest fillets, place the broiler pan 2 inches from heat; place 1-inch-thick fish 4 inches from heat. Thicker pieces should be placed 5 to 6 inches away. Cook on one side for half the indicated time, turn and finish broiling. As in frying, really thin fillets need not be turned; serve so the side that faced the heat is up. Baste the fish with oil, butter, wine, or marinade once or twice as it cooks, if you desire. Lean fish, such as flounder and sole, tend to dry in broiling, so they should be frequently marinated and/or basted. Always preheat the broiler first.

Remember that fillets, such as those from flounder and sole, have a light and dark side. Cook so that light side is faced up when fish is served.

Grilling: Preheat grill, covered if possible, at least 15 minutes if gas or electric; up to 40 minutes (until an even white ash covers the fuel) if using charcoal or hardwood. Fish are more likely to stick if placed on a cold grill. Oil the grill bars lightly before heating and wipe off the excess.

Hardwoods like apple, hickory, and mesquite burn hotter than charcoal briquets and add their particular aroma and flavor to the food. If you are using hardwood chips simply for their aroma, rather than for cooking heat, soak them for 30 minutes or more in water before adding them to the coals.

Oil the fish before grilling it to prevent it from sticking. Almost all fish to be grilled is improved by marinating it first. Drain off excess oil or marinade to prevent flare-ups.

Lay fish across the grill, perpendicular to the bars. Fish shrink in grilling, and the edges might fall into the gaps between the bars and overcook.

Grill fish according to the directions for broiling. Try to turn the fish only once. Each time you handle it it is more likely to stick or break. Cooking times for grilling are not as precise as when broiling in an oven, so watch fish carefully. Test the fish for doneness by flaking with a fork.

Using a hinged metal fish grill is best for whole or pan-dressed round fish. Made of stainless steel, a fish grill resembles a thick wire cage hinged along one side so that it can be opened. The fish is placed in one side and the other side is closed over it. The grill should have a locking mechanism so that it doesn't open. The grill is placed directly in the coals, rather than atop the barbecue grill. It should have legs on both sides so that it stands up above the coals and can be turned over to cook fish on both sides. They come in at least two sizes.

A similarly styled hamburg or chicken grill can be pressed into service for smaller fish or sections.

Poaching: This is best done in a poacher with a fish rack, but one often can improvise, at least with fish 12 inches or less in length. It is a good idea to know the width of your largest pan so that you do not exceed that when buying a whole fish for poaching. Wrap it in cheesecloth, which helps to maintain the shape of the fish. If the ends of cheesecloth are tied to handles of the poaching rack or pot, removal of the fish from the hot liquid will be easier.

Boil sufficient water or court-bouillon (see pages 34, 35, and 36) to cover the fish. Allow it to cool. Place the fish in room-temperature liquid and return to a boil. When the water boils, lower the heat so that the liquid barely simmers — its surface should palpitate rather than be covered with bubbles — and begin timing. Remove fish if it is to be served hot, as is. For other preparations, especially those that are cold, allow the fish to cool in the poaching liquid.

Pan-dressed fish, steaks, and fillets also take well to poaching; they do not need to be wrapped in cheesecloth, however. Fatty or oily fish do not poach well.

Baking: The Canadian method calls for baking fish, uncovered, according to the 10 minutes-per-inch rule at 475 degrees. You may follow that generally, if you like, but for most baked preparations we provide specific cooking times and temperatures. Most of the baking called for in this book is with a cover of buttered kitchen foil or parchment to retain the moisture. Some recipes call for the cover to be fitted tightly, some loosely. We have found these requirements better suited to baked recipes.

Always preheat an oven to the desired temperature before putting the fish in.

Steaming: Seafood is steamed without coming in contact with the liquid. The liquid can be plain salted water, fish stock, or another aromatic liquid that will impart flavor.

Steam is not as good a conductor of heat as is water, but because it is at somewhat a higher temperature than boiling water, for practical purposes, you can follow the 10 minutes-per-inch cooking time rule.

Cooking "en papillote," enclosing the food to be cooked in parchment or foil, is a form of steaming even if the food is placed in a dry oven.

If you don't have a steamer, you can usually improvise one using a cake rack and roasting pan or other pot. Inverting an old pie tin in the bottom of a pot will also work, and if the tin is old enough, you can punch a few holes in it to provide better circulation.

Oily or fatty fish do not steam well.

Boiling: Fish is not boiled, of course, because violent boiling would eventually disintegrate it. Other seafood, such as mollusks and crustaceans, are often boiled, however, although it really isn't necessary to have a rolling boil throughout — simmering water is just as hot.

Notes Regarding the Recipes

All seafood used in the recipes is fresh.

Butter: We recommend you use unsalted (sweet) butter in all our recipes. The sodium computations for the recipes, however, are based on salted butter because that is what most people use.

There are two important reasons for our recommendation. The first is sound nutrition. A tablespoon of unsalted butter contains only one milligram of sodium. Salted butter contains 140 milligrams of sodium. That is an important consideration, whether you are on a low sodium diet or not. By using unsalted butter you can reduce the total sodium in any of the following recipes by 139 milligrams for each tablespoon of butter used. Divide by the number of portions to arrive at the sodium content of each serving.

The second reason for our recommending unsalted butter has to do with flavor. Cooking flavors are easier to control with unsalted butter. Unsalted butter is definitely required when ingredients such as salt cod, anchovies, almost all smoked seafood, caviar, and other salted products are used. In addition to cooking with it, it is especially desirable in hot butter sauces such as beurre blanc and in hollandaise and its derivatives.

Cream: Use the type of cream called for in the recipes. We prefer to use cream that has not been "ultra-pasteurized," which we feel gives some dishes a plastic feel on the palate and an unflattering flavor.

Herbs: It is only in an ideal world where one can find a ready supply of fresh herbs all the time. Consequently, in the recipes that follow, except where fresh is clearly indicated, the quantity given is for dried herbs.

Reduction: To reduce means to cook a liquid until some has been carried off by evaporation. When we write, "reduce until it coats a spoon," which we do in many recipes, we mean to reduce to about the thickness of medium cream. In this case, the liquid is generally the final sauce.

When we write, "reduce until it coats a spoon heavily" — as we do in a recipe for Navarin of Scallops — we mean reduce until liquid is the thickness of heavy cream. In the navarin, the liquid is neither a broth nor a sauce, just a thick liquid to moisten the dish.

Tomatoes: After more than a year of testing recipes, we have come to the conclusion that, except for that time of the year when truly garden-fresh tomatoes are obtainable, you are usually better off using canned peeled plum tomatoes imported from Italy.

Almost without exception, fresh tomatoes lack the color and flavor needed. Allowing them to ripen at home in a brown paper bag might make them softer and a shade deeper in color, but they still lack flavor — and by that time — often texture as well.

If you find you must use hothouse tomatoes, then we suggest you keep tubes or cans of tomato paste on hand and add a teaspoon or so of it along with your tomatoes to recipes.

Canned plum tomatoes from California are serviceable, but we found no particular brand that consistently yielded the intensity of color and flavor wanted.

"I don't like that fish": Too often a fish will be determined to be not to a diner's liking because it was less than fresh or was poorly treated in the kitchen.

The same person who continues to eat beef or veal or chicken, even after several bad experiences with tough beef, lackluster veal or dry or greasy chicken, will not give seafood its like due.

Do not necessarily discount a seafood because of one experience. Give it at least one more try. Many persons do not like scallops breaded and deep-fried, or detest steamed clams. But fried clams or scallops prepared some other way might be a pleasure unnecessarily avoided.

Give all manner of seafood a try when done differently from the way you recall you didn't like it — you may be surprised at your reaction.

Stocks, Sauces, Mousses

". . . With food, as with life's two other basic necessities, clothing and shelter, the simplest fulfillment of basic requirements has never been enough. People at all times and in all cultures have pursued an instinct for embellishment."
— Mimi Sheraton, in the "New York Times"

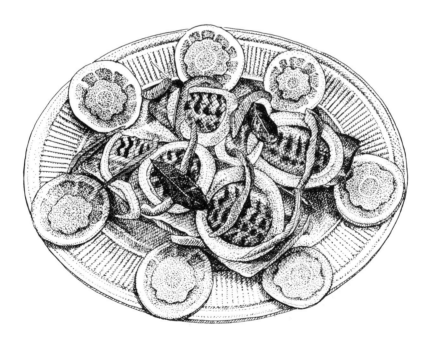

Cold Mackerel in White Wine

Stocks

Mention the word stock to most home cooks and they pale with thoughts of a pot bursting with meat, bones, vegetables, and aromatics slow-simmering for hours atop a stove. They envision a succession of straining and filtering operations.

Not so! Fish stocks take about 5 minutes of preparation time and no more than 30 minutes or so simmering. Three or four pounds of fish bones and trimmings, a few vegetables, a bit of seasoning, and that's it. You won't have to buy anything special. Most fish markets will gladly give you fish bones, carcasses, heads, and trimmings for the asking. Everything else you will need are ingredients that you undoubtedly have in the larder anyway.

And to what results. It is beyond the ability of words to describe what stock will do for your seafood cooking. You won't get a mere increase in flavor. You will be aware of a new round savoriness and smoothness to your food. But don't accept our word for it. Make a fish stock just once. Broil or bake two fillets with just a bit of salt and pepper. When cooked, serve one plain or with a pat of butter. On the other ladle two or three spoonfuls of fish stock that has thickened somewhat over heat. Taste and compare the two fish. The stock will be like adding a rich, homemade soup to your simple fish. It will taste sweeter, richer and, because of its delicacy, even more *of fish* without being *fishy*. Stock will give the same wonderful depth to seafood sauces, soups, and other preparations.

There is very little connective tissue in fish as compared to the meat of land animals; about 3 percent of its weight; compared to 15 percent for land animals. And what there is is very fragile and easily converted to gelatin — which is why one can make a fish stock in a great deal less time than a meat stock.

Some cautionary observations about fish stocks, or *fumet de poisson:*

1. We repeat, don't cook fish fumet too long. If you cook too long, the stock will acquire a pronounced flavor of fish bone. If you require a more concentrated stock, cook it with the bones for 30 minutes, strain, and then reduce it to what you want.

2. Use stainless steel or other non-corrosive pots when making fish fumets. The same can be said for the making of any stock that you do not want to have a darkened appearance. Acids such as those found in citrus

fruit juices, vinegar, and wine react with aluminum or iron in pots and darken the finished product.

3. Flounder, sole, whiting, haddock, cod, and fluke heads and bones are best for making fish stock, but any firm white fish will do. In New England, haddock is probably the easiest to obtain. Avoid oily fish such as mackerel or bluefish. Most fish dealers will be happy to give you the heads and bones you need. Some will even remove the gills for you. These carcasses are called "frames" or "racks" by the trade.

4. Flounder fillets have a line of small bones running down their length. You can feel them if you run your finger along a fillet. They must be removed, even when you are making stock, otherwise there is a danger that they will pass through the straining process and get into a final dish. Cut through on each side of the row of bones and discard (see page 87).

5. Remove the gills from the heads of fish you are going to use to make stock. Unless you have caught a fish yourself and it is only hours out of the water, it is always best to remove gills of a fish before using it. Gills are one of the first parts of a fish to deteriorate, and if not removed, they could adversely affect the flavor of the final product. Their presence makes stocks bitter.

6. Omit fish skins when making fumets. Skins give a gray cast to a stock and can also make it strong tasting.

7. Do not boil fish stock. Bring stock to a boil, but reduce heat once it has reached boiling point. What you want is a nice steady simmer with bubbles barely bursting on the surface. Boiling will make a stock muddy.

8. Do not store fish fumet in the refrigerator for longer than 3 days. If you must keep it another day or two, reboil it and return it to the refrigerator after it cools. Always reboil a stock that has been kept for more than two days before using it in a recipe.

9. Fish fumet freezes well. Store it in pint or quart jars. You will need about 2 cups to prepare dishes for 6 persons. Frozen fumet must be reboiled immediately after defrosting.

10. Avoid using strongly flavored herbs and other ingredients in fumets. While fumet is aromatic and robust, its rich delicacy can be overpowered by indiscriminate use of other strongly flavored ingredients. Bay leaf, tarragon, celery, and the like should be used in minimal amounts, if at all.

11. The exception is when making a fish stock to be used for aspic. The flavor of a cold preparation, such as aspic, is masked, and the basic fish stock must be made more highly flavored.

12. Be careful with salt. Remember the reduction of any seasoned liquid will intensify the seasoning. Do not exceed the salt recommended in the following recipes and remember that some chefs are inclined to leave it out entirely rather than risk having to make such a basic ingredient a second time.

13. Strain the finished fumet through a colander or other fine-meshed strainer. If you are going to use your fumet as a poaching liquid or in a sauce, you can press down on the solids to speed up the process and extract maximum flavor. But if the finished sauce is to be clear or if you are planning to make an aspic from the fumet, then you should let the draining be natural without help from you—pressing down will make the stock cloudy.

14. The simplest of fumets can be made from the court-bouillon (see below) that you poached a fish in. The exception would be that you cannot use court-bouillons that contain vinegar. Reduced to about half its liquid content, it would then be flavorful enough to function as a fumet, which is basically a more highly flavored court-bouillon made with less water.

White Wine Fish Fumet
BASIC FISH STOCK

4 pounds fish heads and bones
1 large onion, chopped
1 small carrot, chopped
1 tablespoon butter
2 cups dry white wine

8 cups water
small bouquet garni
½ teaspoon salt
6 white peppercorns

1. Remove gills from fish heads if they haven't already been removed. Discard skin. Wash fish under cold running water.

2. Saute onion and carrot in butter until soft but unchanged in color. Add fish bones and heads, along with any trimmings from the fish you are going to cook. Let it simmer, uncovered, over lowest heat for 10 to 15 minutes until smallest bones have begun to disintegrate and fall apart.

3. Add wine and water and bring to a boil. Add bouquet garni and salt. Cook over medium heat, so that pot barely simmers, for 30 to 35 minutes. Skim any scum that rises.

4. Peppercorns should be added during final 10 minutes of cooking so that their flavor is not too strong or bitter.

5. Strain through double thickness of dampened cheesecloth.

6. Use immediately or cool and store in refrigerator until needed.

Makes 1½ to 2 quarts. Approximate nutrition information per cup: Calories 370; protein 33g; fat 20g; carbohydrates 14g; sodium 1160 mg.

Red Wine Fish Fumet

RED WINE FISH STOCK

Do not think the amount of red wine in this recipe is incorrect. Red wine is less acidic than white wine, so you need more of it to break down the gelatin, calcium, phosphorus, and collagen in the fish bones. Red wine fumet has application where color is important in the final dish, in an aspic, for example.

4 pounds fish bones and heads	4 cups dry red wine
1 large onion, chopped	8 cups water
1 carrot, chopped	8 sprigs parsley, stems included
1 whole garlic clove	pinch dried thyme
2 tablespoons butter	½ bay leaf
¼ cup mushroom stems and pieces	½ teaspoon salt
	few whole peppercorns

1. Make the stock in exactly the same manner as the white wine fumet.

Makes 2 quarts. Approximate nutrition information per cup: Calories 370; protein 33g; fat 20g; carbohydrates 14g; sodium 1160 mg.

Fish Aspic

Aspic has many uses in fish cookery. It can be used to coat a large whole fish such as salmon or small fishes such as trout or Atlantic mullet that are to be decorated. Jelled in a thin layer in a flat pan, it can be cut into tiny cubes or diamond shapes, to be spread like so many jewels around a cold fish presentation. It also is invaluable in the making of terrines and pâtés. Aside from what aspic can do for the appearance of a dish, it also helps to seal in moisture in the preparations that it coats.

A fish aspic is made by clarifying a fish fumet. This procedure is used to make a fish stock that is perfectly limpid, where a cloudy stock would mar the appearance. The clarified stock should look like flat ginger ale, or the finest consomme, which is basically what it is.

Note: Instead of saffron, you can substitute 1 tablespoon of vermouth or madeira, for color and flavor. Or use 3 whole tomatoes instead of 1, which will provide more color.

4 cups fish fumet	½ cup sliced leeks, green part
2 envelopes gelatin (or 2 tablespoons)	1 cup dry vermouth
2 egg whites with shells	few turns freshly ground white pepper
½ cup chopped fresh parsley	small pinch saffron
1 whole tomato, crushed	

1. Bring fish fumet slowly to a boil in a non-corrosive saucepan. Dissolve the gelatin in the hot fumet and stir to mix thoroughly.

2. Test the fumet for consistency. Remove a tablespoon or two of the mixture and place it in the refrigerator in a small soup bowl. Within 10 or 15 minutes, it should be solidly jelled, but not hard and rubbery. If it remains soft, you will need to add more gelatin, a teaspoonful at a time, to the pot of fumet. Test after each addition until you are satisfied with the consistency. If it is too hard and rubbery, add liquid ¼ cup at a time.

3. Now, beat together egg whites, crumbled egg shells, parsley, tomatoes, leeks, and vermouth until the whites are foamy. Add some fumet to whites, then pour this back into fumet. Bring slowly to a boil — be careful not to let it boil over. At the first sign of boiling, reduce the heat and simmer for 10 minutes. Add the pepper and saffron, and correct the seasoning. It must be highly seasoned, because it will lose intensity when it is chilled.

4. Remove the pan from the heat and strain through several layers of dampened cheesecloth, being careful not to disturb the foam, otherwise the aspic will be cloudy. Cool to room temperature and use. Or, you may refrigerate for a future use; just reheat before using.

Makes approximately 4 cups. Approximate nutrition information per cup: Calories 370; protein 33g; fat 20g; carbohydrates 14g; sodium 1160 mg.

Quick Fumet I

In an emergency, or when pressed for time, or when fish trimmings and bones are not available, you can make a substitute fish stock using your own fresh or frozen or commercially bottled clam juice. Mussel juice also may be used, although its flavor is more emphatic. The finished product won't be as rich as a stock made with fish bones, but it will perform yeoman service. Add any trimmings from the fish you are going to cook to this fumet. Remember that since this is an uncooked stock, the alcohol in the wine will not have been evaporated. It is wise therefore, if using more than 3 or 4 tablespoons of wine, to simmer the wine for 2 or 3 minutes first to evaporate the alcohol before adding it to the recipe. Use no salt until you have tasted the fumet.

⅓ cup clam or mussel juice　　⅓ cup dry wine
⅓ cup water

1. Mix and use as called for in recipe.

Makes 1 cup. Approximate nutrition information per cup: Calories 30; protein 2g; fat trace; carbohydrates 5g; sodium 270 mg.

Quick Wine Fumet II

The flavor of this quick fumet will be closer to a true fumet. If you make a larger amount of this recipe, the ratio of clam or mussel juice to wine remains the same, but do not add more seasoning.

½ cup clam or mussel juice　　1 thick slice onion
½ cup wine (white or red)　　½ bay leaf
pinch white pepper　　⅛ teaspoon dried thyme

1. Simmer 10 minutes, strain, and use.

Makes 1 cup. Approximate nutrition information per cup: Calories 70; protein 6g; fat trace; carbohydrates 11g; sodium 260 mg.

Court-Bouillon with Wine

Court-bouillon, or "short-bouillon," is a quick bouillon that is used in poaching fish to add flavor to it. Don't be stunned by the large amount of salt in a court-bouillon — which makes the sodium count exceptionally high; the fish is only poached in it and will not contain all the salt.

This court-bouillon is useful when firming the flesh of fish is important. Ocean catfish, for example, is a soft-textured fish before it is cooked.

4 cups water	large bouquet garni
2 cups dry white wine	2 teaspoons salt
1 large onion, sliced	1 teaspoon whole white
1 carrot, sliced	peppercorns
1 leek, sliced	

1. To mixture of water and wine, add onion, carrot, leek, bouquet garni, and salt. Bring to a boil slowly and simmer for 20 minutes. Add peppercorns and simmer another 10 minutes. Allow to cool and strain.

Makes approximately 5 cups. Approximate nutrition information per cup: Calories 50; protein trace; fat trace; carbohydrates 12g; sodium 955 mg.

Clam Juice Court-Bouillon

This is an adaptation for a recipe in Madeleine Kamman's The Making of a Cook, *that takes advantage of readily available bottled clam juice (broth). Use it to poach shellfish, even shrimp, instead of using plain water, to add flavor to them. This recipe makes enough for 2 pounds of shellfish.*

4 cups clam juice	small bouquet garni, including
2 cups white wine	2 sprigs fresh thyme or ½
2 large onions, chopped	teaspoon dried
	6 whole white peppercorns,
	cracked

1. Simmer all ingredients for 30 minutes, adding peppercorns during the last 10 minutes. Let cool completely before using. Strain.

Makes approximately 6 cups. Approximate nutrition information per cup: Calories 35; protein 1g; fat trace; carbohydrates 7g; sodium 80 mg.

Milk Court-Bouillon

A milk court-bouillon is used where the recipe requires that the flesh of the fish be kept as white as possible. We recommend this bouillon for poaching the steaks in our recipe for Halibut with Tomato Mousseline (page 101) for just that reason.

4 cups water	⅛ teaspoon ground white
1 cup milk	pepper
1 teaspoon salt	

1. This preparation requires no cooking, just mix all the ingredients and use immediately.

Makes 5 cups. Approximate nutrition information per cup: Calories 40; protein 2g; fat 2g; carbohydrates 4g; sodium 395 mg.

Court-Bouillon with Vinegar

The increased amount of acid in vinegar over wine (5 percent in vinegar versus 2 to 3 percent in wine) makes this an especially good court-bouillon for use with softer-fleshed fish such as sole or ocean catfish since the increased acidity will firm the flesh even more.

4 cups water	large bouquet garni including
1 cup cider vinegar	2 sprigs fresh thyme or ½
½ cup carrots, sliced	teaspoon dried
½ cup onions, sliced	2 teaspoons salt
1 sliced leek	1 teaspoon white peppercorns

1. Combine water, vinegar, vegetables, bouquet garni, and salt. Bring to a boil slowly and simmer for 25 minutes. Add peppercorns and simmer for another 10 minutes. Let cool and strain.

Makes approximately 4 cups. Approximate nutrition information per cup: Calories 20; protein trace; fat trace; carbohydrates 5g; sodium 953 mg.

Marinades
▪▪

Marinades are used to preserve, to retard spoilage, to enhance flavor and to tenderize. The last, of course, is not necessary with fish. In fact, when applied to fish, the liquid is more to macerate than to marinate.

A marinade for fish can be made with a combination of oil, lemon juice, or wine with various flavorings added, depending on the effect wanted. Among the flavorings would be members of the onion family — shallots, leeks, scallions — or root vegetables such as celery and carrots; herbs like thyme and bay leaves, occasionally spices; or other ingredients like cranberries.

Depending on the results sought, the ingredients will differ greatly. For preserving, the liquid will be mostly water and salt (a brine). For enhancing, the liquid will contain a lot of strong flavorful ingredients.

One marinating technique widely used recently is one made with lemon juice, salt, and pepper, which is used on raw fish. The lemon or lime juice of a seviche is a kind of marinade.

Often a marinade is used for a short period of time before a fish is grilled or broiled. With lean fish, such marinades usually contain a fat such as oil or butter.

We use marinades in shark brochettes, salmon tartare, and other recipes.

Sauces
▪▪

One hears many Americans say that they don't like sauces. They call sauces "camouflage"; they say they spoil a dish; and some cooks say that they are too much trouble.

Yet the same Americans don't hesitate to dip their french fries into over-sweetened, over-salted, burnt-tasting ketchup; wouldn't think of eating fried fish or fried clams without a dollop or two of commercially prepared tartar sauce, and even demand that their roast beef be served swimming in *au jus,* even if it is made from a powder and water. We dip shrimp in a red glop called "cocktail sauce," splash hot pepper sauce onto clams on the halfshell, and dress up our raw oysters with a combination of both. Even the lowly ballpark hot dog gets its "sauces" of mustard and relish.

As accurate as the dictionary definition of a sauce might be ("Any flavorful soft or liquid dressing or relish served as an accompaniment to food"), Shakespeare understood it better: ". . . sharpen with cloyless sauce his appetite."

Sauces are the sophistication of civilization acquired through the millennia since our cave-dwelling ancestors first sunk their teeth into a half-cooked haunch of wild beast.

Sauces add flavor to a dish to be sure, and often the moistness that makes a food more palatable. What simple broiled meat or fish of whatever freshness or quality, whatever perfection in its grilling, is not made more wonderful still when accompanied by the velvety, piquant lushness of bèarnaise sauce?

Perhaps too many beef, chicken, and brown gravies lumpy with uncooked flour and afloat with unincorporated fat have dulled our appreciation; too many restaurant mornay sauces that tasted no different from the one in a chicken à la king have made us wary.

But such rampant mucilaginous mayhem need not dissuade — almost all foods are improved when accompanied with a properly made compatible sauce. In many cases, a plainly poached fish can seem to have been prepared solely to serve as the palette for its marvelous sauce. Use them often. Keep in mind that for most purposes, 1½ cups of sauce is sufficient for 6 to 10 servings.

We begin by presenting not a sauce *per se,* but a way to add color to your dishes. Many home cooks avoid the use of food coloring prepared from commercial dyes. The following are three natural food colorings you can make at home. They can be used to color many other food preparations: mayonnaise, a fish sauce, even a mousse.

Note: When making sauces, which typically require wine, lemon, vinegar and other acidic ingredients, always use a non-corrodible pan — stainless steel, enamel or the like and not aluminum, which can darken or color the sauce.

Natural Green Food Coloring

Here is a recipe for green food coloring using natural ingredients. Rather than color the food itself, of course, you can introduce color to a plate through the use of garnishes, which will often eliminate the need to color the ingredients themselves. But there are times when that won't do.

While this procedure reads like a lot of work, it actually isn't, and it is something you can do when greens are readily available and at their cheapest, or when you have other kitchen work planned that will keep you in the kitchen anyway. The coloring can be kept for future use.

All kinds of greens can be used — spinach, watercress, parsley, swiss chard — the more intensely colored, the better. The best results are obtained when more than one green is used.

30 to 36 ounces of greens

1. Wash greens thoroughly in several changes of cold water. Shake greens well, but allow any moisture that clings to leaves to remain. Chop coarsely and put into a food processor, in several batches if necessary. Puree completely.

2. If you do not have a food processor, remove every bit of water from greens. Place in a mortar, or heavy-gauge towel, and pound to a pulp with a pestle, meat tenderizer, or even a flat-bottomed pan.

3. In either case, place the pureed or pounded greens in the towel. Twist the ends of the towel in opposite directions, to squeeze out the liquid, continuing until the liquid no longer runs free. Reserve the liquid — you should get 4 or more cups. Scrape away solids that remain in the towel and discard.

4. Place the liquid in a double boiler and heat. The water in the bottom pan should not touch the bottom of the top pan; simmer at the lowest heat. The juice will coagulate as it warms, and the solids will rise to the top while the liquid becomes clear.

5. As soon as liquid is clear, remove from heat and pour contents of the pan through a dampened triple thickness of cheesecloth or a clean napkin that has been dampened and wrung out.

6. Scrape the solids from the napkin and either use immediately or place in a clean jar for storage. You should have about 1 tablespoon.

7. Float a thin film of vegetable or other oil on the surface of the food coloring (the more neutral-flavored the oil the better), cover with cap or foil, and refrigerate. Green coloring should last two weeks.

8. To use, begin by adding about ¼ teaspoon of extract to whatever

you want to color, stir well to incorporate, add additional coloring a little at a time until you achieve the desired result. Normal usage is about ½ teaspoon. Take what you need from the jar and allow the oil to drip away for a moment. Blot with a paper towel if oil will have an adverse effect on the food you are going to color.

Natural Orange Food Coloring

We use this carrot coloring in our recipe for Cod Crecy (page 121), as well as ½ cup of the liquid collected in making the coloring.

　2　pounds carrots

　1.　Scrub, but do not peel carrots. Cut in chunks and place in work bowl of food processor, in 2 or 3 batches if necessary. Add about 1 cup water to each batch. Work to a puree, scraping down the sides of the work bowl until you obtain as fine a puree as possible.

　2.　Place puree into a dampened clean kitchen towel and squeeze out as much liquid as possible, wringing the towel as tightly as you can. Catch the liquid in the top half of a double boiler. The double boiler should be stainless steel, porcelain, or other non-corrosive material. Discard pulp in towel or use it some other way, such as in a soup.

　3.　Slowly heat the liquid in the top of the double boiler (the water in the bottom half should not be in contact with the top half). As it warms, most of the solids in the liquid will collect on the top and the remainder of the liquid will become clear.

　4.　When the liquid is quite clear, and all the solids have accumulated at the top, strain through a clean, dampened linen napkin or triple thickness of dampened cheesecloth. Drain well. Place cloth on a flat surface and scrape the solids that collect on the cloth; you should obtain at least 2 tablespoons. This is your extract.

　5.　The extract you obtain will keep in the refrigerator. As with the green food coloring, you can keep it 2 weeks in a small container such as a baby food jar. Cover it with a thin film of oil.

Natural Red Food Coloring

2 medium beets, washed   ½ cup water

1. Wash beets, slice, and puree in food processor with water. Set puree to simmer over low heat. When reduced by about half (¼ cup), remove and strain. Use liquid immediately, or place it in clean jar, cover, and refrigerate for up to three or four days. Freeze up to 3 months.

Mayonnaise

A mayonnaise does not have to be stiff as is commercial mayonnaise; on the contrary, it should be soft and delicate.

If the mayonnaise is not to be used at once, you should stabilize it so that it will not break down. To do so, do not use vinegar in the initial preparation. Instead, boil the vinegar and add it hot at the end of the mixing.

Ingredients to be used in making mayonnaise should be room temperature when you begin.

To make colored mayonnaise, use our green, red, or orange natural colorings.

Flavoring mayonnaise requires only the addition of the flavor you want, such as anchovies, curry powder, more mustard, or a combination of mustard and curry. The mustard-curry combination is excellent with cold crustaceans: crab, lobster, and shrimp. Horseradish or herbs also may be used to flavor or color mayonnaise.

Mayonnaise
HAND METHOD

2 egg yolks
salt and pepper to taste
1 tablespoon Dijon mustard

1 tablespoon vinegar or lemon
   juice
1½ cups vegetable oil

1. Place egg yolks, salt, pepper, mustard, and vinegar in a mixing bowl. Stir vigorously with a wire whisk for 30 seconds.

2. Add the oil, drop by drop, whipping vigorously to incorporate each addition. As mixture emulsifies, you may begin adding oil in a steady stream, slowly, while continuing to whip. If you do not hurry the addition of oil, the mayonnaise will build properly without problem.

Makes approximately 1½ cups. Approximate nutrition information per tablespoon: Calories 126; protein trace; fat 14g; carbohydrates trace; sodium 30mg.

Mayonnaise
FOOD PROCESSOR METHOD

1 whole egg
1 egg yolk
1½ tablespoons Dijon mustard
salt and pepper to taste

4 tablespoons vinegar or lemon
   juice
1½ cups vegetable oil

1. Place egg, egg yolk, mustard, salt, pepper, and vinegar in the work bowl of food processor with either the metal or plastic blade.

2. Mix (pulse) for 1 or 2 seconds only, add the oil with motor running. Add the oil in a thin stream, but not too slowly. Refrigerate.

Makes approximately 1¾ cups. Approximate nutrition information per tablespoon: Calories 110; protein trace; fat 12g; carbohydrates 0g; sodium 32 mg.

Tartar Sauce I

■■

2 cups homemade mayonnaise
1 tablespoon drained, chopped
   capers

1 tablespoon minced fresh herbs
   (tarragon, chervil, parsley)

1. Mix ingredients to combine. Correct seasoning. Refrigerate.

Makes approximately 2 cups. Approximate nutrition information per 2 tablespoons: Calories 255; protein trace; fat 28g; carbohydrates trace; sodium 90 mg.

Tartar Sauce II

■■

2 cups homemade mayonnaise
1 tablespoon drained, chopped
   olives with pimientos
1 tablespoon chopped Greek,
   Sicilian, or Provençal olives
1 tablespoon chopped sweet
   pickles

1 tablespoon snipped fresh
   chives
1 tablespoon white wine or wine
   vinegar

1. Mix ingredients to combine. Correct seasoning. Refrigerate.

Makes approximately 2 cups. Approximate nutrition information per 2 tablespoons: Calories 260; protein trace; fat 28g; carbohydrates 1g; sodium 100 mg.

Sauce Gribiche I

Use Sauce Gribiche as you would a tartar sauce. It is very good with cold leftover fish.

1 cup homemade mayonnaise	1 tablespoon minced fresh parsley
2 tablespoons chopped sour gherkins or dill pickles	1 tablespoon snipped chives
2 tablespoons chopped capers	1 hardboiled egg, chopped

1. Blend all ingredients together. Refrigerate.

Makes approximately 1 cup. Approximate nutrition information per 1 tablespoon: Calories 90; protein trace; fat 10g; carbohydrates trace; sodium 40 mg.

Sauce Gribiche II

2 hardboiled eggs; separate yolks and whites and chop separately	1 cup oil
1 tablespoon Dijon mustard	2 tablespoons chopped sour gherkins
½ teaspoon salt	2 tablespoons chopped capers
pinch of pepper	1 tablespoon minced fresh parsley
4 tablespoons wine vinegar	1 tablespoon snipped chives

1. Separate the yolks and whites and chop separately.

2. Mash the chopped egg yolk into a smooth paste, forcing it through a fine-meshed sieve first to expedite the job.

3. Add mustard, salt, pepper, and vinegar. Mix well for 30 seconds and add oil slowly, as in making mayonnaise, add remaining ingredients and mix well. Refrigerate.

Makes approximately 1½ cups. Approximate nutrition information per 1 tablespoon: Calories 75; protein trace; fat 8g; carbohydrates trace; sodium 70 mg.

Sauce Vinaigrette

This sauce is used in Sauce Ravigote, as well as to season any salad.

Endless variations can be made using various aromatic vinegars (tarragon, basil, mint, etc.); lemon juice; various oils (corn, olive, walnut, hazelnut, grape seed, etc.) and herbs or other flavorings (garlic, shallots, scallions).

A general rule regarding the ratio in a vinaigrette is 1 part vinegar to 3 parts oil.

1 tablespoon Dijon mustard	½ cup oil
2 tablespoons red wine vinegar	white pepper to taste
1 teaspoon salt	

1. Blend together in a bowl, mustard, vinegar, salt and pepper. Slowly add oil while mixing with a wire whisk.

Note: We also make this vinaigrette ahead of time in larger quantities using a food processor. Place all ingredients except oil, plus 1½ tablespoons of cold water, in work bowl of food processor. Mix well and add the oil slowly. "This achieves an emulsion that is not very stable, but is very smooth and, to my taste, better than the hand-beaten type," Jean-Jacques says. The added water helps in the emulsion.

Makes approximately ¾ cup. Approximate nutrition information per 1 tablespoon: Calories 80; protein trace; fat 9g; carbohydrates trace; sodium 240 mg.

Sauce Ravigote
■■

Use this sauce as you would a tartar sauce. It is especially good on cold fish.

½ cup sauce vinaigrette, see
    recipe page 45
2 teaspoons minced fresh parsley
2 teaspoons minced fresh chervil
1 teaspoon minced fresh
    tarragon

1 teaspoon snipped fresh chives
1 teaspoon chopped onion
1 tablespoon drained chopped
    capers

1. Mix all ingredients thoroughly and allow to stand about 1 hour for flavors to meld.

Makes approximately ¾ cup. Approximate nutrition information per tablespoon: Calories 65; protein trace; fat 7g; carbohydrates trace; sodium 210 mg.

Sauce Mousseline, Cold
■■

A mousseline is much lighter and more neutral in flavor than mayonnaise alone, which often is precisely the flavor you seek. You may add extra seasoning, however, such as mustard, salt, or lemon juice to compensate for the cream. It is good with cold leftover fish.

1 cup homemade mayonnaise   ¼ cup heavy cream, whipped

1. Fold whipped cream into mayonnaise. Refrigerate.

Makes approximately 2 cups. Approximate nutrition information per 1 tablespoon: Calories 105; protein trace; fat 11g; carbohydrates trace; sodium 20 mg.

Aïoli

Aïoli, as with many preparations that were once laboriously made with mortar and pestle, can now be made in a food processor. Purists may frown, but the results are good even if they are not precisely the same texture as when ground by hand.

Use it where you would a mayonnaise, but where you want more flavor, especially of garlic.

4 garlic cloves
3 tablespoons lemon juice or
   vinegar
1 tablespoon Dijon mustard
1 teaspoon salt

pepper to taste
3 egg yolks
1½ cups olive oil
boiling water, if needed

1. In processor bowl, place garlic, lemon juice, mustard, salt, and pepper. Blend for 10 seconds. Scrape down garlic with a rubber spatula and blend again. Add egg yolks and blend for additional 10 seconds. Scrape down again and slowly add oil through the feed tube with motor running. Correct seasoning.

2. Aïoli should have the consistency of mayonnaise. If it is too thick, add 1 to 3 tablespoons of boiling water through the feed tube until it is the consistency you desire. Refrigerate.

Makes approximately 2 cups. Approximate nutrition information per 2 tablespoons: Calories 195; protein 1g; fat 21g; carbohydrates trace; sodium 150 mg.

Red Cocktail Sauce

■■

The red sauce served with oysters and clams on the halfshell in the vast majority of American restaurants and universally called "cocktail sauce," has been reduced in many cases to nothing more than ketchup with a little commercial horseradish, Worcestershire sauce, and a bit of lemon juice. A lot of restaurants have even eliminated the chili sauce that was once considered a mandatory ingredient. The store-bought kind generally has more of a chili sauce flavor and consistency, but it tends to be salty and sweet.

Our version offers fresh flavors and can be made in minutes using a food processor or blender. It will keep in the refrigerator for up to 2 weeks in a sealed container. It should be made at least 2 hours before using so that the flavors will meld.

1 pound canned, peeled Italian plum tomatoes with juice	1 tablespoon lemon juice
1 6-ounce can tomato paste	1 small clove garlic
¼ cup diced onion	1 tablespoon vegetable oil
3 tablespoons sugar	1 tablespoon Worcestershire sauce
2½ teaspoons salt	4 tablespoons horseradish
2 tablespoons vinegar	½ teaspoon crushed red pepper

1. Place all ingredients in the work bowl of a food processor and work until well blended.

2. Refrigerate.

Makes approximately 3 cups. Approximate nutrition information per 2 tablespoons: Calories 30; protein trace; fat 1g; carbohydrates 5g; sodium 310 mg.

Green Cocktail Sauce

■■

This sauce is alive with pungent sharp flavor. It is the one to use when you want a zippy sauce to accompany raw shellfish.

As with the red cocktail sauce, it will keep for up to 2 weeks in a covered container in the refrigerator. It also should be made at least 2 hours before you plan to use it. The salt, sugar, and horseradish may be increased if you prefer.

1½ cups pickled green tomato (jar)	2 tablespoons salt
1 cup avocado pulp	1 tablespoon Worcestershire sauce
¼ cup diced onion	1 tablespoon vegetable oil
½ cup sweet green pepper	1 small garlic clove
3 tablespoons prepared horseradish	⅛ teaspoon dry red chili powder
1 tablespoon sugar	1 tablespoon vinegar

1. Place all ingredients in the work bowl of a food processor and work until well blended.
2. Refrigerate.

Makes approximately 3 cups. Approximate nutrition information per 2 tablespoons: Calories 30; protein 1g; fat 1g; carbohydrates 4g; sodium 650 mg.

Sauce for Clams on Halfshell

1 cup clam juice	1 tablespoon minced fresh parsley
1 clove garlic, mashed	1 tablespoon butter

1. Combine juice from clams with bottled juice if necessary to make 1 cup.
2. Heat clam juice, add garlic and parsley. Reduce by about one-quarter — you should have ¾ cup remaining.
3. Add 1 tablespoon butter and blend. Correct seasoning.
4. Refrigerate and serve with cold raw clams on the halfshell. Or, spoon onto raw clams on the halfshell and slide under the broiler just to heat.

Makes enough for about 48 clams, when serving a teaspoonful on each. Approximate nutrition information per 1 tablespoon: Calories 15; protein 1g; fat 1g; carbohydrates 1g; sodium 90 mg.

Rouille

■■

This is a garlic sauce popular in Provençe. It is widely used as an accompaniment to soup, especially a bouillabaisse. It is a spicy rust-colored sauce redolent with garlic. Use it wherever you would want a garlic-mayonnaise.

Two adjustments can be made in this recipe. If you prefer a hot sauce, substitute one hot small fresh pepper for the sweet pepper. If hot fresh pepper is not available, you may use 1/4 teaspoon (more or less, according to taste) of hot crushed red pepper. It must first be soaked in water and be well drained.

Some cooks use bread in place of the hot potato. Dice 2 slices, about 1/2 cup, fresh bread, soak in water, squeeze dry, and proceed with the recipe.

1 medium potato	3 garlic cloves
1 sweet red pepper, roasted, peeled and seeded	salt and pepper to taste
	1 cup olive oil

1. Cook unskinned potato in salted water. Drain, peel while hot, and quarter.

2. Place in the work bowl of a food processor with all the remaining ingredients except the oil. Work into a very fine puree. With the motor running, slowly add the oil as in making mayonnaise. Taste, correct seasoning.

Makes approximately 2 cups. Approximate nutrition information per 2 tablespoons: Calories 255; protein trace; fat 27g; carbohydrates 3g; sodium 70 mg.

Tomato Mousseline, Hot

■■

This mousseline can be served hot or cold. It can be served with flavorful fish, such as bluefish, tuna, shark or swordfish, or against a milder-flavored fish such as halibut, which is the way we have used it on page 101.

2 garlic cloves
1 tablespoon minced fresh basil
1 tablespoon oil
½ cup coarsely chopped onions

1 pound can ground, peeled
   tomatoes, or 1 pound seeded
   and chopped fresh tomatoes
½ teaspoon sugar
salt
½ cup heavy cream

1. Mince garlic and basil together.

2. Saute onions in oil until soft but not browned. Add tomatoes, garlic, basil, sugar, and ½ teaspoon salt and simmer gently for 20 minutes, stirring often to prevent sticking or burning.

3. Pour into work bowl of food processor, in 2 batches if necessary, and puree until smooth.

4. Work through a fine strainer. Allow to cool.

5. Whip cream until it just thickens, add ¼ teaspoon salt, and whip until stiff.

6. Blend ⅓ of whipped cream into cooled tomato mixture. When well blended, fold in the rest of cream gently. Correct seasoning. Refrigerate, and serve chilled.

7. To serve hot, place atop cooked or nearly cooked fillets of fish and slide under a hot broiler just to brown.

Makes approximately 2 cups. Approximate nutrition information per 2 tablespoons: Calories 32; protein trace; fat 3g; carbohydrates 1g; sodium 110 mg.

Bechamel

■■

Technically bechamel is not considered a finished sauce, but what the French call a "mother sauce," from which other sauces may be made; for example, sauce nantua or mornay.

In times past, the making of bechamel was much more complicated than is common practice today. Today we think of bechamel as an all-purpose basic white sauce made of scalded milk, cold roux, and flavorings. Or hot roux and cold milk. The temperature contrast guarantees that there will be no lumps in a well-stirred bechamel. A mixture of milk and cream also may be used. When intended to be used in seafood preparations, fish stock or fumet can substitute for some of the milk.

¼ cup butter	salt
¼ cup flour	pepper
2 cups cold milk	nutmeg

1. Make a white roux by melting butter over low heat and adding flour all at once, stirring with a wooden spoon and cooking over low heat for 5 minutes. The roux should not take on color — it should be the palest straw color — and should not taste of raw flour.

2. Add cold milk, stirring with a wire whisk until lumps disappear and mixture is smooth. Bring slowly to a boil and let simmer for at least 10 minutes, or up to 1 hour. Add salt, pepper, and nutmeg to taste. Use in other recipes.

Makes approximately 2 cups. Approximate nutrition information per 2 tablespoons: Calories 50; protein 1g; fat 4g; carbohydrates 3g; sodium 80 mg.

Hollandaise Sauce

■■

BLENDER OR FOOD PROCESSOR METHOD

½ pound butter	1 tablespoon water
3 egg yolks	1 tablespoon freshly
½ teaspoon salt	squeezed lemon juice

1. Melt butter and keep it hot, but do not let it take on any color.

2. Blend together egg yolks, salt, water, and lemon juice in blender or work bowl of food processor until foamy. With the motor running, slowly add the melted hot butter. If hollandaise is too thick, add some hot water a teaspoon at a time to get the consistency you want.

Note: The water in this recipe can be replaced with parsley or carrot juice or even red wine to give you a colored hollandaise. Mustard, curry powder, or other flavorings also can be added.

Makes approximately 1½ cups. Approximate nutrition information per 2 tablespoons: Calories 150; protein 1g; fat 17g; carbohydrates trace; sodium 280 mg.

Hollandaise Sauce
TRADITIONAL HAND METHOD

3 egg yolks
⅓ cup water
½ teaspoon salt
1 cup, or ½ pound, hot clarified
   butter (see page 71)

1 tablespoon freshly squeezed
   lemon juice
white pepper to taste

1. Combine egg yolks, water, and salt in the top half of a double boiler. Using a wire whisk, whisk until foamy.

2. Bring water in the bottom half of the double boiler to a simmer. Place the top half into the double boiler, checking that the bottom of the top half does not come in contact with the simmering water. Heat, beating all the time. Continue until the mixture is thick and whitish. Be careful not to get mixture too hot or you will end up with scrambled eggs and it will lose its properties to make an emulsion.

3. Remove from heat. While still whisking vigorously, add, very slowly, the hot clarified butter. Add lemon juice; taste for salt; add white pepper if desired.

Makes approximately 1½ cups. Approximate nutrition information per 2 tablespoons: Calories 155; protein 1g; fat 17g; carbohydrates trace; sodium 280 mg.

Green Hollandaise

◼◻

1 tightly packed cup parsley
   stems and leaves
1 tablespoon water
2 egg yolks
1 cup hot clarified butter (see
   page 71)

1 teaspoon lemon juice, or
   more to taste
pinch salt
pinch white pepper

1. Work the parsley as fine as you can in a food processor. Then add 1 tablespoon water and work until it is a paste.

2. Using a rubber spatula, scrape the parsley into a clean kitchen towel. Squeeze out as much liquid as you can, twisting and wringing the towel tightly.

3. Discard the liquid and scrape the green pulpy extract off the towel. You should have about 1 tablespoon. Reserve.

4. Beat two egg yolks lightly with a fork, add the green extract, and beat to blend thoroughly.

5. Place yolks in the top of a double boiler making sure the water in bottom half of the pan does not come in contact with the top half. As they warm, whip yolks with a wire whisk until they become thick and creamy.

6. Off the heat, using a wire whisk, whip in the hot clarified butter a little at a time in a thin stream. Add lemon juice, salt, and white pepper. Continue to whip until it is smooth and thickened. Keep the hollandaise warm, but don't let it get too hot or it will break down. Holding it in a larger pan of warm water is the best method.

Makes approximately 1½ cups. Approximate nutrition information per 2 tablespoons: Calories 150; protein 1g; fat 17g; carbohydrates trace; sodium 280 mg.

Shellfish Butter

In regions where freshwater crayfish are not found, this preparation, made with lobster or crab bodies, will serve as the flavoring and coloring agent for a sauce nantua. Use crayfish bodies if they are available. Use this butter to enhance the flavor of a cream sauce, or a bit of it can be swirled into any sauce where the color and flavor would be compatible with the dish.

4 crustacean bodies — lobster, crab, or crayfish	½ cup diced onions
½ cup finely diced carrots	1 pound butter
	1 quart hot water

1. Remove outer carapace of lobster, it won't yield much in flavor though it will add color. Remove stomach sac. Break up small legs and other parts and either work in a food processor or put through a food grinder fitted with a ½-inch disk.

2. Saute onions and carrots in 1 tablespoon butter. Add ground lobster shells and the remaining butter and cook over low heat uncovered for 45 minutes to 1 hour. The heat must be kept very low.

3. Pour in hot water, stir, and mix thoroughly.

4. Strain through a coarse colander or strainer, pushing down with a large spoon to extract maximum flavor and color.

5. Chill until the top is solid; it will be hardened, colored and flavored butter. Remove this butter and discard the liquid.

6. Melt the butter over low heat. Strain through a fine sieve or a double layer of dampened cheesecloth. Store in a covered crock or jar in refrigerator as you would store clarified butter.

Makes 1½ to 2 cups. Approximate nutrition information per 2 tablespoons: Calories 214; protein trace; fat 23g; carbohydrates 1g; sodium 5 + mg.

Sauce Nantua

■■

This sauce is a warm rosy salmon-pink that is a marvelous backdrop to simply prepared seafoods. It is not only used with fish and shellfish, but is also often paired with eggs and chicken. The name comes from a town in east central France in the Department of Aine.

Its base is bechamel. Originally it was made with a beurre d' écrevisse, *a butter made from the pounded bodies of freshwater crayfish. Since crayfish are not universally available, the sauce can be, and often is, made with lobster or crab bodies. We combine the bechamel (page 52) with our shellfish butter on page 55.*

1 recipe for bechamel, about 2 cups	2 to 4 ounces of shellfish butter

1. Heat bechamel and stir in shellfish butter a tablespoon at a time until the sauce acquires the shade of color that you prefer.
2. Serve immediately.

Makes approximately 2 cups. Approximate nutrition information per 2 tablespoons: Calories 135; protein 2g; fat 12g; carbohydrates 5g; sodium 120 mg.

Béarnaise Sauce

■■

One of the great sauces of France, béarnaise is as enjoyable with meat as with many fish dishes, especially a simple broiled or baked fillet.

1 cup, or ½ pound, clarified butter, page 71	1 tablespoon white peppercorns, cracked
⅓ cup red wine vinegar	2 tablespoons minced shallots
½ teaspoon salt	1 tablespoon water
4 tablespoons minced fresh tarragon	4 egg yolks

1. Keep clarified butter warm, but not hot. Keep it over a pilot light, in a pan of tepid water, or in a turned-off oven until you are ready to use it.

2. In a non-corrodible top half of a double boiler, combine vinegar, salt, 3 tablespoons of the minced tarragon, peppercorns, and the minced shallots, and bring to a boil over low heat. Reduce until most of the liquid has evaporated and only a pool of 1 tablespoon or less remains in the pan.

3. Remove from heat and let the saucepan cool briefly.

4. Add the water and the egg yolks while stirring vigorously with a wire whisk. Put the top half of the double boiler over simmering water (don't let the water touch the bottom of the top pan). Continue to stir vigorously. Never stop stirring. When the yolks become thick and creamy, remove from heat and cool, continuing to stir all the while or the heat from the pan is likely to cook the eggs further.

5. You are now going to add the liquid clarified butter to the yolk mixture — both should be at approximately the same temperature. Dribble the butter in slowly, much as you would add oil to mayonnaise, beginning drop by drop and increasing to a thin stream as you incorporate it. You must continue to whip throughout.

6. Strain sauce through a dampened double thickness of cheesecloth.

7. Stir in the remaining 1 tablespoon of chopped tarragon.

Note: Fresh tarragon will provide much better flavor and should be used whenever it is available, but a fairly good result can be obtained with good quality dried tarragon. Replace the fresh tarragon in step 2 with 3 teaspoons of dried tarragon to make the basic sauce. After it has been strained, add 1 tablespoon of fresh chopped green herb, such as parsley or chervil, instead of the fresh tarragon.

Makes approximately 2 cups. Approximate nutrition information per 2 tablespoons: Calories 120; protein 1g; fat 13g; carbohydrates trace; sodium 210 mg.

Light Marinara Sauce

■■

This sauce can do yeoman service in the kitchen. With the addition of chopped pepper and onions that have been briefly sauteed, it can be poured over fish fillets and baked to make a haddock or cod pizzaiolo. We use it with Neapolitan Stuffed Squid (page 379).

½ minced clove garlic (about 1
   teaspoon)
4 tablespoons chopped onion
1 tablespoon olive oil
3 cups chopped imported canned
   peeled plum tomatoes

1 teaspoon salt, or to taste
freshly ground pepper
1 tablespoon chopped parsley
1 teaspoon dried basil (or
   oregano)

1. Saute onion and garlic in olive oil only until onion is soft and transparent but has not taken on color.
2. Add tomatoes, salt, and pepper and simmer for 20 minutes; add herbs and simmer 5 minutes more. Correct seasoning.

Makes approximately 2 cups. Approximate nutrition information per ½ cup: Calories 50; protein 1g; fat 2g; carbohydrates 7g; sodium 360 mg.

Rough Tomato Coulis

■■

This coarse tomato puree will keep for several days in the refrigerator, or it can be frozen, which makes it a handy staple to have on hand. You can add additional seasonings: garlic, onion, shallots, chives, basil, tarragon, thyme, or mint, and use it to garnish a variety of foods — fish, pasta, pâté, and meatloaf, to name a few. We use it with our Salt Cod Souffle, page 133.

2½ to 3 pounds fresh tomatoes
2 tablespoons butter
2 tablespoons olive oil
2 medium onions, diced
1½ teaspoons salt

freshly ground black pepper
pinch sugar
2 tablespoons minced fresh
   parsley leaves

1. Peel, seed, and chop tomatoes. Heat butter and oil, and saute onions about 6 minutes until translucent. Add tomatoes and the rest of ingredients. Cook over high heat a few minutes, stirring.

2. Lower heat to a simmer and cook until the mixture is quite thick, stirring often to keep it from sticking or burning. It is done when the juice gets thick and syrupy and the tomatoes begin to stick to the pan. Don't scorch or you will ruin it. Leave coulis coarse.

Makes approximately 2 cups. Approximate nutrition information per 2 tablespoons: Calories 20; protein trace; fat 1g; carbohydrates 2g; sodium 70 mg.

Tomato Concassée

Neither a tomato sauce in a strict sense, nor yet a vegetable accompaniment or garnish, this cooked and flavored tomato preparation is a perfect foil for many fish dishes.

1 tablespoon butter
1 tablespoon oil
¼ cup chopped onion
2 cups peeled, seeded and
      chopped fresh or canned
      plum tomatoes

1 garlic clove, minced
1 bay leaf
½ teaspoon dried thyme
salt and pepper

1. Melt butter in oil, add onion, and cook until transparent. Add tomatoes, garlic, bay leaf, and thyme. If concassée is to be served as a vegetable, salt and pepper it to taste. If it is to be used as part of a recipe, don't season until you complete the dish.

2. Cook 15 to 20 minutes until most of moisture has evaporated. Remove bay leaf. The sauce makes enough for 4 servings.

Makes about 2 cups. Approximate nutrition information per serving: Calories 85; protein 2g; fat 6g; carbohydrates 6g; sodium 140 mg.

Tomato Sauce for Seafood Ravioli

This recipe makes a thin sauce, which is the way many people prefer it with filled pastas, especially pasta filled with seafood. It is very good with our Crabmeat Ravioli (see page 417).

3 tablespoons butter
¼ cup minced onion
½ cup fresh or canned tomato
    puree
3 cups fish stock or quick fumet
salt and pepper to taste

1 tablespoon minced fresh
    parsley
½ teaspoon minced garlic
½ cup white wine
grated parmesan cheese
    (optional)

1. Melt butter in saucepan, add onion, saute lightly until transparent, and add tomato puree. Mix well and cook for a minute, stirring.

2. Add remaining ingredients, bring to a boil, and simmer for 20 minutes.

3. Pour sauce over filled ravioli; pass extra sauce and grated parmesan cheese.

Note: If you prefer a thick sauce, combine tomato puree, fish stock or quick fumet, and wine. Stir in 1 tablespoon of tomato paste and simmer over low heat until liquid is reduced by half. Then proceed with recipe. If you prefer it thicker still, after the initial cooking add one or two canned plum tomatoes squeezed of their juice or 1 small fresh tomato, peeled, seeded, and diced and squeezed of its juice.

Makes 4 cups: Approximate nutrition information per ½ cup: Calories 180; protein 13g; fat 11g; carbohydrates 7g; sodium 610 mg.

Red Wine Sauce
■■

We use this sauce with squid in two different ways, but it will serve just as nicely with shrimp or lobster meat with pasta.

FOR MIREPOIX:
½ cup carrots, cut in ⅛-inch dice
½ cup onion, cut in ⅛-inch dice
½ stalk celery, cut in ⅛-inch dice
1 slice bacon, chopped

3 tablespoons tomato paste
½ teaspoon dried thyme
1 bay leaf
1 cup dry red wine
2 cups fresh tomatoes, peeled, seeded, cut in ⅛-inch dice, or canned Italian plum tomatoes
1 teaspoon salt
pepper to taste

1. Saute bacon for 2 minutes; it will still be very soft. Add the vegetables and saute until the onions are transparent.

2. Add remaining ingredients, cover, and simmer for 30 minutes, or place in a 325-degree oven for the same amount of time. Correct the seasoning. The recipe makes about 3 cups, sufficient to be served with shrimp or lobster. Extra sauce may be stored in a covered container for 3 or 4 days in the refrigerator or be frozen for up to 3 months.

Makes approximately 3 cups. Approximate nutrition information per 2 tablespoons: Calories 18; protein trace; fat 1g; carbohydrates 3g; sodium 100 mg.

Pesto Sauce

Pesto is one of Italy's most popular pasta sauces. It is a basil-scented, unctu-ous green garlic sauce developed along the Riviera around Genoa. Pesto is now often used with seafood and other ingredients besides pasta. We use it in our recipe for Shrimp and Pasta Pesto, on page 422, or you may use it as a sauce on other shellfish.

Pesto used to be, and often still is, pounded in a mortar to achieve the smooth-rough oily texture that makes it adhere so well. In today's kitchen, the food processor makes short work of what would otherwise be a slow and laborious task.

2 cups tightly packed fresh basil leaves	½ cup parmesan cheese (or parmesan and romano)
3 tablespoons pine nuts	1 cup olive oil
2 cloves garlic	

1. Place basil, pine nuts, garlic, and cheese in the work bowl of a food processor and process until a near-puree is obtained.

2. Pour oil slowly through the feed tube while the motor runs and scrape down the sides of the work bowl with a rubber spatula once or twice. Run 20 to 30 seconds longer. Remove and reserve.

Makes approximately ½ cup. Approximate nutrition information per 2 tablespoons: Calories 140; protein 2g; fat 14g; carbohydrates 1g; sodium 70 mg.

Horseradish Cream Sauce

This sauce can be used as a dipping sauce for boiled shrimp or scallops. It also can be used to layer a casserole for shrimp, scallops, or small cubes of any lean white fish.

1 cup heavy cream	pinch ground nutmeg
salt and pepper to taste	1 teaspoon horseradish

1. Place ingredients into a wide saucepan and cook and reduce to about ¾ cup, until it is thick and coats a spoon heavily. Correct the seasoning and serve.

Makes 1 cup. Approximate nutrition information per 1 tablespoon: Calories 70; protein trace; fat 7g; carbohydrates 1g; sodium 50 mg.

Sweet and Sour Sauce

½ cup plus 2 tablespoons water	1 tablespoon minced sweet green pepper
½ cup sugar	1 tablespoon minced sour gherkins
½ cup white vinegar	¼ cup chunk pineapple
¼ cup chicken stock, homemade or canned	1 tablespoon cornstarch
1 tablespoon soy sauce	
½ teaspoon grated fresh ginger root	

1. In a small saucepan over low heat, dissolve sugar in ½ cup water.
2. Add white vinegar, chicken stock, and soy sauce, and blend well. Add remaining ingredients, except cornstarch, and heat through.
3. Dissolve cornstarch in 2 tablespoons water, add to other ingredients, and stir to thicken. Serve hot.

Makes approximately 2 cups. Approximate nutrition information per 2 tablespoons: Calories 85; protein trace; fat trace; carbohydrates 21g; sodium 270 mg.

Beurre Blanc

Although this sauce is of old and accepted use, it is not a classic as are such sauces as bechamel and nantua. A country sauce of the Loire valley; its origin is a housewife's sauce, quickly made, instantly served without much fuss.

In recent years, beurre blanc has been much used by nouvelle chefs who prefer its flour-less base and its lightness as a foil for their creativity. With that usage, beurre blanc has acquired something of a mystique — from the way it is often told, one would think that a seven-year apprenticeship is needed before one tackles beurre blanc. Not so.

All the sauce is, is a reduction of a very acid liquid (wine vinegar, white wine, or a combination) with butter whipped in. Some chefs use flavored vinegars such as tarragon or raspberry, but the basic formula is still the same. The acid is reduced to a mere puddle and then placed on the lowest heat and cold butter is whipped in piece by piece. The butter lowers the temperature with each addition as it melts into the growing sauce. As it disappears and the sauce warms up again, the addition of more butter brings it back to a safe temperature and the sauce making continues until all the butter has been added.

A beurre blanc should be soft, but not oily; a soft, whipped cream kind of consistency.

(Beurre noisette is a light brown color, sometimes with lemon juice added. Beurre noir is brown but not burnt; 2 tablespoons of wine vinegar are added, and sometimes capers and a little of their juice.)

The sauce should be made at the last minute, as it is not a good sauce for holding. If it must be held, it should be kept at less than 100 degrees and stirred from time to time. Serve it with all steamed or poached fish.

1 tablespoon finely minced shallots	¼ cup white wine or white wine vinegar or combination
pinch white pepper	½ to ¾ pound butter, chilled,
⅛ teaspoon, or less, salt	sliced into pats

1. In a small non-corrodible skillet or saucepan, combine shallots, pepper, salt, and vinegar or wine, and reduce to about 1½ tablespoons. You may strain the mixture at this point or not; some cooks prefer the texture the shallots provide, others do not.

2. With the pan over very low heat or on a heat diffuser, whisk in a pat of butter with a wire whisk. Continue to whisk until all the butter has been

incorporated before adding the next piece. Continue until all the butter has been added. Serve.

Serves 4–6. Approximate nutrition information per 1 tablespoon: Calories 105; protein trace; fat 11g; carbohydrates 1g; sodium 170 mg.

Red Beurre Blanc

BEURRE BLANC ROUGE

The flavor of this beurre blanc is more intense than that of the one above.

2 tablespoons minced shallots
¼ cup red wine vinegar
½ cup dry red wine
½ pound butter, softened

1 teaspoon fresh lemon juice (optional)
½ teaspoon salt
5 grinds fresh white pepper

1. Place minced shallots in a heavy-bottomed, non-corrosive saute pan. Add vinegar and wine. Reduce over low heat until liquid has nearly evaporated and there is about 1 tablespoon left in the pan. (The amount of reduction is not entirely critical, but the greater the degree of reduction, the thicker and less acidic the sauce will be.)

2. Remove pan from heat and add the soft butter, 1 tablespoon at a time, using a wire whisk. Whisk continuously to incorporate all the butter, making sure that one application has about disappeared before adding next. Rewarm pan gently as required, but don't get it hot or butter will separate. Taste and correct seasoning; add lemon juice if more acidity is desired.

3. Sauce may be strained to remove shallots. Hold in a warm place or over a double boiler (bottom of top pan should not touch the water, which should be barely simmering). If the temperature of the sauce rises above 145 degrees, the butter will separate and the sauce will break down. Serve about 3 tablespoons under each serving of fish.

Serves 4. Approximate nutrition information per 3 tablespoons: Calories 275; protein trace; fat 32g; carbohydrates 2g; sodium 550 mg.

Green Beurre Blanc

∎∎

BEURRE BLANC VERT

The procedure for this sauce is nearly the same, except that 1 cup of parsley and/or spinach is used to provide the color. You may use coarse spinach trimmings and parsley stems; you do not have to select finest leaves.

¼ cup white wine or white wine vinegar, or combination
1 cup firmly packed spinach or parsley or combination
1 tablespoon minced shallots
pinch of white pepper
⅛ teaspoon, or less, salt
½ to ¾ cup butter, chilled

1. Begin by placing vinegar or wine and greens in the work bowl of a food processor. Work to a puree. Strain liquid into a non-corrodible skillet or saucepan and proceed with the steps described for Beurre Blanc, above.

Serves 4 to 6. Approximate nutrition information per 1 tablespoon: Calories 110; protein trace; fat 11g; carbohydrates 2g; sodium 180 mg.

Compound Butters

∎∎

The following compound butters are easy to make, can be kept in the refrigerator or freezer until needed, and can add immeasurable flavor to simple poached, pan-fried, or broiled fish. Merely slice off a round and place it on each serving of hot fish. It will melt its goodness into the fish by the time you serve it.

After you have prepared the butter, place a strip of waxed paper or parchment flat on a work surface. Spoon mixture in a long sausage-like strip onto paper, leaving plenty of room at ends and on each side of mixture. Roll paper around mixture, coaxing it into a cylindrical shape. Wrap in aluminum foil and place in the refrigerator to set. If you must use it immediately, make sure the foil is tightly wrapped, and then drop roll into a bowl with cold water and ice cubes. It should set firmly in 15 to 20 minutes.

To use: Remove foil and paper, dip a small knife into hot water and slice a round approximately ½-inch thick (about a tablespoon) for each serving. For ease of handling after slicing, the round can be placed in ice water until ready to use. If your serving of fish is large, use two somewhat thinner rounds. Some cooks freeze the butter roll and take slices from it — frozen — as they require.

Compound butters may be kept up to two weeks in the refrigerator and up to four months in the freezer.

Cold Butter, Wine Merchant's Style

BEURRE FROID MARCHAND DE VIN

2 tablespoons finely minced shallots	5 grinds white pepper
⅓ cup dry red wine	2 tablespoons minced fresh parsley
2 tablespoons red wine vinegar	2 sticks softened butter
1 teaspoon salt	

1. In a small, non-corrosive saute or other wide pan, cook shallots over low heat with vinegar and red wine, reducing until the mixture is almost entirely evaporated and nearly a paste. The fine mincing will assure a better amalgamation later and the final color will be improved, as the shallots absorb more of the red color when finely minced. Cool completely.

2. Meanwhile, knead softened, but still solid, butter until it is easy to handle. Add the shallot mixture, salt, white pepper, and parsley. Mix thoroughly with a fork, stiff wire whisk, or your hands. Correct seasoning, remembering that the flavor intensity of the finished butter will be somewhat diminished when it is applied to fish.

3. Proceed as described above.

Makes approximately 1½ cups. Approximate nutrition information per 2 tablespoons: Calories 140; protein trace; fat 15g; carbohydrates 1g; sodium 180 mg.

Anchovy Butter
■■
BEURRE D'ANCHOIS

3 tablespoons flat fillets of anchovies; 3 to 6 pieces depending on size

½ cup soft butter

1. Make a puree of the anchovies, either in a mortar or by mincing extremely finely.
2. Mix pureed anchovies with soft butter.
3. Proceed as described above.

Makes approximately ½ cup. Approximate nutrition information per 1 tablespoon: Calories 85; protein trace; fat 9g; carbohydrates trace; sodium 130 mg.

Maître d'Hôtel Butter
■■
BEURRE MAÎTRE D'HÔTEL

2 tablespoons of minced fresh herbs; chervil and parsley or all parsley
½ cup soft butter

½ teaspoon salt
1 tablespoon lemon juice
⅛ teaspoon pepper

1. You can either mince herbs separately and then mix them by hand with the other ingredients, or you can place all ingredients in the work bowl of a food processor and blend.
2. Proceed as described above.

Makes approximately ½ cup. Approximate nutrition information per serving: Calories 100; protein trace; fat 11g; carbohydrates trace; sodium 270 mg.

Beurre d'Escargot

SNAIL BUTTER

The butter may be wrapped and sliced as a compound butter, but it is traditionally used to stuff snails in their shells. It may similarly be used with mussels or clams on the halfshell. See our recipe for Mussels with Snail Butter on page 331.

1 clove, about 1 tablespoon, minced shallot	½ cup loosely packed minced fresh parsley
2 medium garlic cloves, minced	½ cup soft butter
2 tablespoons sliced blanched almonds (optional)	½ teaspoon salt
	⅛ teaspoon white pepper

1. Place shallot, garlic, and almonds in work bowl of food processor. Work just to chop the ingredients. Add parsley and work, again just to chop. Add butter, salt, and pepper, and work once more.

2. Alternately, the butter may be made by hand. Chop each ingredient separately and then mix with softened butter.

Makes approximately ½ cup. Approximate nutrition information per serving: Calories 120; protein trace; fat 12g; carbohydrates 1g; sodium 275 mg.

Chive Butter

■■

Tarragon, thyme, and other minced herbs may be substituted for the chives in this recipe.

¼ pound soft butter
2 tablespoons finely minced
   chives

1 tablespoon lemon juice
½ teaspoon salt

1. Mix soft butter with chives, lemon juice, and salt.
2. Proceed as described above.

Makes approximately ½ cup. Approximate nutrition information per 1 tablespoon: Calories 105; protein trace; fat 12g; carbohydrates trace; sodium 300 mg.

Crème Fraîche

■■

In France, very heavy cream (crème double, *35 percent butterfat*), *when it thickens by the natural process of fermentation of lactic acid, becomes* crème fraîche. *It is similar to sour cream, but not so acid. Its flavor is also more nutlike, and it is much used in French kitchens. One reason is that, unlike sour cream, crème fraîche can be boiled with less fear that it will curdle. Today, crème fraîche can be found in many specialty food stores, at some dairies, and even in specialty sections of supermarkets.*

The recipe below makes a reasonable facsimile of a crème fraîche. It will not curdle, but will thin somewhat when it is cooked.

1 tablespoon buttermilk

1 cup heavy cream

1. Mix the buttermilk and the cream and let it sit out, partially covered, for 8 hours. Refrigerate. It will keep up to a week, though it will develop more acid as it ages.

Makes 1 cup. Approximate nutrition information per 2 tablespoons: Calories 100; protein 1g; fat 10g; carbohydrates 1g; sodium 10 mg.

Clarified Butter

Clarified butter has several important advantages over regular butter: It burns at a higher heat, so that it is less likely to smoke — the smoke point is raised from 250 degrees Fahrenheit to 350 degrees. It can be made in quantities of a pound or more and stored in the refrigerator for up to three weeks, and it can be frozen as well.

Since it is pure butterfat, no solids precipitate to the bottom when it is heated. It is these solids that give foods that are fried or sauteed in whole butter a surface with brown and black spots. Clarified butter used for sauteing and pan-frying will give your foods a clean-looking appearance.

Since clarified butter is butter with its protein removed, do not expect it or foods cooked in it to have the full, rich taste of whole butter.

1. Take the amount of unsalted butter you wish to clarify and cut it into small chunks. Melt it slowly, over a low direct flame or even in an oven-proof bowl set in a pan of water. Mostly you don't want to scorch the butter nor disturb it.

2. Leave the butter to melt — it will take from 20 minutes to an hour depending on the heat source and the amount of butter.

3. When melted, the butter will separate into three layers; a whitish top foamy layer, a yellow middle layer of butter as limpid as cooking oil, and a third layer of watery whitish sediment at the bottom. Carefully skim off the top foam with a spoon. Spoon or carefully pour the middle layer of deep yellow butterfat into a storage jar so as not to disturb the sediment. We save the top and bottom layers in a small jar or bowl to splash over vegetables at family dinners.

Servings and nutrition information cannot be estimated.

The Making of a Fish Mousse

If one translates the French word mousse, among the English words that apply would be froth, foam, suds, lather, whipped cream, and head (as on beer; the froth on a glass of champagne is also called its mousse in French).

Those are the cloud-like pictures that one should conjure up when contemplating this light and airy culinary creation.

A selection of mousses follows and we have included others in recipes throughout the book where they are required.

A mousse can be used in a number of ways:

1. Molded and cooked, it can be served as is with a sauce for a first course or a dinner entree.

2. It can be used in a terrine, as we have done in Seafood Terrine with Mousse Base, on page 223. Or two can be used in such a preparation. A layer of white fish mousse topped with a layer of another color, such as the pink of a salmon mousse or shrimp mousse, makes a very attractive terrine.

3. A mousse also could be used with one of the natural food colorings described on page 39 to contrast or blend with a sauce or garnish.

4. A mousse is also the basis for the French preparation called *quenelles,* described on page 78.

In the days before modern appliances, making a fish mousse was slow and laborious work. Kitchen hands had to cut, chop, and mince the fish and other ingredients by hand and then pound them in a mortar until a paste was formed. This was then worked through the finest of sieves, again by hand, scraping it back and forth across a muslin "tammy" or other screen. The fish was chilled, and only then could the cold eggs, cream, and flavorings be added to complete the mousse.

The food processor has put this delicate preparation within the repertoire of even the busiest of cooks, and no first-time attempt needs to end in failure today.

There are a few things to bear in mind about preparing a fish mousse.

Keep your ingredients cold. This applies to the seafood itself, the eggs (but not the egg whites to be whipped), the cream (if you're using it), and even the bowl of a food processor and its blade, if possible. The mixing of a mousse is best done in a metal or stainless bowl set into a larger bowl filled with ice, so that the ingredients are kept chilled while you mix.

You can use a food processor, a blender (though you might have to make your mousse in two or three batches), or a food mill. You also can make a mousse by hand, though that requires considerable work in hand-whipping and additional passing of the mixture through a fine-meshed sieve or strainer. One advantage of the food mill is that your mousse will have a smoother texture, and you can be very certain it will have no bones in it.

In using a food processor or blender, one danger is in overworking the mixture, which would break down the seafood's fibers too much and result in a mushy mousse. The danger in making a mousse by hand is that the mousse will not be worked enough. Whatever the method you use, follow directions carefully. It is better to underwork the preparation than over-work it, since you can test the mousse before the final cooking.

You must use truly fresh fish. The fish protein acts as a binder and does not work as well if it is getting stale and beginning to dry out.

We tried making mousses with various frozen fishes. Our recommendation is not to use them. The flat fishes, such as sole and flounder, don't bind well when thawed, and the moisture content is so high and variable that arriving at a formula is difficult. As frozen fish thaws, it leeches a great deal of flavor along with the melting ice crystals; so much flavor is lost that the resulting mousse will be flavorless. This is especially true of delicate fish such as flounder. We have found that even a fish with a relatively dense texture, such as swordfish and halibut, presents too many problems when it has been frozen to be used in a mousse.

Trim discolored areas of the fish. They are not harmful, but they will affect the color of the mousse. Cut the fish into pieces so it will be worked smoothly in the food processor or blender. Carefully check for bones. Bones are difficult to detect once the fish has gone through a processor or blender. (A food mill, however, will eliminate bones.) When using flounder, cut away the center portion of each fillet, since it contains small bones that are likely to go undetected.

Every mousse has at least one egg in it. You get lighter mousses by adding whipped egg whites. How you treat the ingredients, especially the egg whites, is essential to the quality of your mousse or mousseline.

Egg whites are protein; when protein cooks, it toughens. Don't be tempted to add more egg whites to a mousse than the recipe calls for. They won't make the mousse lighter; they will make it rubbery.

There must not be even a speck of yolk in egg whites to be whipped, and the bowl you use must be clean and dry. Egg whites should be at room temperature. Whip until whites begin to thicken. At this point, add the pinch of salt most recipes call for and continue to whip to soft peaks. Don't overbeat. Overbeating past the soft peak stage will make the mousse rubbery also, since the whites will set "harder" in cooking.

When adding beaten egg whites to the batter of a mousse (or any heavier batter, for that matter) you must work fast and gently. Rough handling will break down the volume of air you have worked into the whites and this will cause your mousse to be heavy. Begin by adding from one-quarter to one-third of the egg whites to the mousse batter, which should be at the bottom of a mixing bowl when you begin. Fold the whites into the batter with a rubber spatula, blending thoroughly. This will thin and lighten the batter and make the next step easier.

Proceed to work in the remainder of the whites. Again put the lighter whites on top of the batter. Cut through from top to bottom with the spatula, lifting up the heavier batter and placing it on the egg whites that you simultaneously work down into the batter. Continue this up and down blending, giving the bowl a quarter turn with each fold until no traces of whites can be seen.

If you are not familiar with making a seafood mousse, you should test the final mix before proceeding with the remainder of the recipe.

To test: Set a pan of salted water to simmering. Dip two standard kitchen tablespoons (pointed rather than rounded) into simmering water. Then scoop out a heaping spoonful of the mixture with one spoon and press it lightly with the second, rounding and turning the mixture into a compact egg shape. Slide one or two of these mousse balls — a French *quenelle* — into the simmering water and allow to poach for 10 minutes. The quenelles should turn in the water by themselves, but if they do not, turn them to cook evenly.

Taste them first for flavor — the flavor of a mousse will always be more delicate than the flavor of the fish from which it is made. Then test the texture — your mousse should be compact and smoothly blended, and light, not heavy or rubbery, crumbly or "sandy."

If your mousse appears too soft, you can stiffen it by adding the white of an egg (when proportions are similar to those in the recipe for Mousse I below). As stated above, however, the addition of whites is likely to make your mousse more rubbery. To make a mousse lighter, add ¼ cup of heavy cream.

Jacques Pépin recommends that salt be added at the end of the process of making a mousse: "It coagulates albumen (in the egg) and you don't want that to happen too early," he advises.

If the mousse is to be put into a mold, a fluted mold generally produces a more interesting result than a straight-sided one. Such considerations, however, are as much a matter of the final use and presentation of the mousse as of aesthetics.

A mold should be well chilled before you begin. It is then coated with soft butter and set to re-chill before filling.

Cover mousse with buttered parchment paper. It can be held at this stage in the refrigerator for 4 to 6 hours, but holding does risk the escape of incorporated air.

Preheat oven to 350 degrees and cook the mousse in a pan of water for approximately 35 minutes, depending on the size of mold.

Let stand for 15 minutes in a warm place before unmolding. It can be served with a sauce nantua.

White Fish or Salmon Mousse I

This recipe results in a mousse with good texture and subtle flavor. It is light but fairly firm and is good to use in a mold where you need some body. Salmon can be substituted.

12 ounces chilled firm white fish	pinch of nutmeg
½ teaspoon salt	pinch of cayenne
⅛ teaspoon freshly ground	1 chilled egg
white pepper	1 cup chilled heavy cream

1. Cut fish into 1 by 1-inch pieces, check for bones, and chill. In a food processor, work cold fish with salt, pepper, nutmeg, and cayenne just until it is pureed.

2. Add egg and process just until the ingredients begin to form a ball and pull away from the sides of the work bowl. It might be best to do this with on-off bursts. Add cream, pouring slowly through the feed tube with the motor running, and process an additional 15 to 30 seconds until smooth.

3. Test a spoonful of mousse in simmering salted water.

4. Proceed with rest of recipe.

Serves 4. Approximate nutrition information per serving: Calories 546; protein 35g; fat 43g; carbohydrates 3g; sodium 1366 mg.

White Fish or Salmon Mousse II

■□

This mousse is lighter than the one above. It has superb texture and is more delicate, and would be excellent for quenelles (see page 78). Salmon can be substituted.

12 ounces chilled firm white fish	pinch cayenne
½ teaspoon salt	1 whole egg, chilled
⅛ teaspoon fresh ground white pepper	1 egg white at room temperature
pinch nutmeg	pinch of salt
	1 cup chilled heavy cream

1. Cut fish into 1 by 1-inch pieces, check for bones, and chill. Work in food processor with salt, pepper, nutmeg, and cayenne until it is pureed. Add the whole chilled egg and process in bursts until the mixture forms a ball and pulls away from the sides. Work for 10 to 15 seconds. Add cream, pouring slowly through the feed tube, and work an additional 15 to 30 seconds until smooth.

2. Remove the mixture from the work bowl to a clean large bowl.

3. In a separate bowl, beat egg white until it thickens, add pinch of salt, and continue to beat to soft peaks. Combine one-third of the whipped white with the mousse mixture using a rubber spatula until blended. Gently fold in the rest.

4. Test a spoonful of mousse in simmering salted water.

5. Proceed with remainder of recipe.

Serves 4. Approximate nutrition information per serving: Calories 306; protein 18g; fat 25g; carbohydrates 2g; sodium 380 mg.

White Fish or Salmon Mousse III

The recipe that follows is ample for recipes for 4 to 8 portions, depending on the dish. To use half an egg, beat it lightly with a fork first and then pour off half.

1 pound chilled white fish fillets	pinch of cayenne
1 teaspoon white pepper	1 whole egg, chilled
¼ teaspoon nutmeg	2 egg whites
2 teaspoons salt	1½ cups chilled heavy cream

1. Cut fish into 1 by 1-inch pieces, check for bones, and chill.

2. Place half the fish into the work bowl of a food processor and process until it is pureed.

3. Add half the white pepper, nutmeg, and salt, half the chilled whole egg, and one egg white, and process until the mixture pulls away from the bowl in a ball. With the motor running, add ¾ cup cream through the feed tube and process 15 to 30 seconds. Scrape down the sides of the bowl with a rubber spatula and add the remaining cream slowly through the feed tube with the motor running until the mixture is smooth and well blended — about 10 to 15 seconds.

4. Transfer to a container, cover, and refrigerate. Repeat the operation with the other half of the ingredients. Blend the 2 batches gently; cover and refrigerate, allowing the mixture to rest and chill for 30 minutes or so before using.

5. Test at this point, then proceed with the remainder of recipe.

Serves 4. Approximate nutrition information per serving: Calories 438; protein 24g; fat 35g; carbohydrates 3g; sodium 1220 mg.

Quenelles

The original "quenelle de Lyon" is made with pike, beef suet, and a panade — a doughlike mixture made with flour, water or milk and used to give consistency to meat or fish forcemeats or stuffings. Today, a lighter version is made, still using pike but replacing the suet with butter.

The version we give is more like a mousseline; it is made from any of our basic fish mousse recipes. Our quenelles can be used as individual garnishes or a light first course.

1. To shape a quenelle, two methods can be used:

a. Dip 2 tablespoons (pointed, not rounded) in simmering water and scoop out a heaping spoonful of the mixture with one spoon. Press the mixture lightly with the second spoon to round and turn it into a compact egg shape. Lift the quenelle out of the first spoon with the second and slide it into water to cook.

b. Drop a spoonful (approximately 2 to 3 ounces) on a floured board and shape it into a cylinder form. Lift it from the board with a spatula and cook.

2. Poach quenelles in a shallow pan of simmering salted water. They will need about 10 minutes to cook, depending on size. They will rise from the bottom and automatically roll over in the water as they cook. Do not allow water to boil and do not cover.

3. Remove quenelles from water with a slotted spoon and drop into cold water. When thoroughly cooled, drain. Quenelles can be held at this stage for 24 hours, covered, in the refrigerator. Or you can use them now as a garnish.

4. Place quenelles in a buttered au gratin dish (do not overlap) and cover with a hot Sauce Nantua (page 56). Bake at 375 degrees for 20 minutes. They will double in volume and should be served at once.

Serves 4. Approximate nutrition information per serving: Calories 705; protein 37g; fat 58g; carbohydrates 8g; sodium 1490 mg.

Scallop Mousse

Whether you prefer sea or bay scallops in the following recipe is strictly a matter of taste, availability, or cost, or the use to which the mousse is to be put. Sea scallops will be more briny in flavor and leaner; bay scallops nuttier and richer.

12 ounces chilled scallops
½ teaspoon salt
⅛ teaspoon freshly ground
   white pepper
pinch nutmeg

pinch cayenne
2 egg whites whipped to soft
   peaks
1 cup chilled heavy cream

1. If the scallops are extremely fresh and you want an especially firm mousse, you need not add the egg whites. For a finer, lighter and more elegant mousse, fold in the egg whites, that have been beaten to soft peaks.

2. Proceed as with Fish Mousse I and II.

Serves 4. Approximate nutrition information per serving: Calories 230; protein 23g; fat 14g; carbohydrates 4g; sodium 540 mg.

Caviar Pillows

This is a rather elaborate recipe that uses a mousse, but if one is going to use caviar in other than its unadorned state, it deserves a proper setting. The lettuce-wrapped mousse will hide the caviar until a diner cuts in the pocket with a fork. A good party first course, much of the preparation can be done early, leaving only the sauce-making for the last moment. This dish uses radicchio, a red-tinged variety of wild chicory. If you can't find radicchio you can use other greens in this dish. Substitutes, however, will not give the sauce the pale blueberry-red cast that the radicchio will, and the unusual hue is what gives this dish its unique eye appeal.

You can use any caviar you prefer — or can afford — but the one you choose will have a bearing on how much you use. A first-rate Beluga, Osetra, or Sevruga would be especially suitable, since their flavor is rich but not overly salty. Salmon caviar from the American Northwest is also good in this dish. With these roe, you can use up to 1 teaspoon in each mousse. Other roe are likely to be saltier and their grain is likely to emphasize the saltiness, so that ½ teaspoon will suffice for each mousse.

Regardless of which variety of caviar you buy, sample a bit before using. The caviar should be a sharp and distinct accent for this dish, but it should not overpower everything else with its saltiness.

FISH MOUSSE:
1 cup sea scallops, chilled
½ teaspoon salt
freshly ground white pepper
1 chilled whole egg
½ cup chilled heavy cream

2 cups roughly chopped
    mushrooms

1 tablespoon butter
½ teaspoon salt
freshly ground pepper
2 heads radicchio
2 tablespoons minced shallots
¾ cup dry white wine or
    vermouth
4 to 8 teaspoons caviar
½ cup heavy cream

1. Make mousse: Drain and reserve liquid from scallops. Wash, drain, and pat scallops dry. Work them in a food processor just until smooth with salt and pepper. Don't overwork. Add chilled egg and puree about 30 seconds more. Add chilled cream and puree until smooth, scraping down sides of work bowl with a rubber spatula at least once. Don't overwork. Refrigerate until ready to use.

2. For the caviar-mousse packets: To prevent discoloration, immediately saute mushrooms in 1 tablespoon butter until very dry, about 5 minutes over medium heat, tossing or stirring frequently with ½ teaspoon salt and a few turns of the pepper mill. Reserve.

3. Separate the 2 heads of radicchio. You will need at least 8 of the largest and best leaves to make the pillows, but it is best to reserve more since you may have to use a double layer because of size or gaps in leaves. Your filled pillows are to be about 5 inches long.

4. Blanch leaves just 10 seconds in simmering water and immediately immerse them in cold water to prevent further cooking and to retain color. Lay out flat, pat dry, and reserve.

5. Wash remainder of radicchio and shred 1 cup, tightly packed. Reserve radicchio to use in sauce.

6. Arrange the 8 leaves of lettuce flat. Make a double layer if necessary. Add about 1 tablespoon of mushrooms to each leaf and spread nearly to the edges in a thin layer.

7. Place about 1 tablespoon of the seafood mousse in the center of each leaf. Don't use it all; save about 2 tablespoons.

8. Make a depression about the size of an acorn in the top center of

each portion of mousse. Using a demitasse or other small spoon, place ½ to 1 teaspoon of caviar in the depression. Use a small portion of the reserved mousse to cover the caviar. Round it off so that it forms a seal with the rest of the mousse.

9. Roll up the lettuce so that you have a bundle about 5 inches long. Repeat to make 8.

10. Butter an ovenproof pan or dish well. Sprinkle shallots over bottom and add the 1 cup of shredded lettuce to make a bed for packets. Lay in packets so that they fit loosely — an 8 x 8-inch baking dish should be ample. Season lightly with salt and pepper. Pour in ¾ cup dry white wine or vermouth.

11. Cover tightly with buttered kitchen foil or parchment. Refrigerate, if you wish, for a few hours until ready to cook.

12. Preheat oven to 375 degrees. Bake caviar pillows 12 minutes. Remove to a serving dish, cover, and keep warm.

13. To make sauce: Place contents of baking pan in a skillet with heavy cream. Cook until radicchio is tender. Place in blender or food processor and work until smooth but still retaining texture.

14. Return to skillet, add any liquid drained from the standing pillows, and reduce until the sauce is thick enough to coat a spoon. Adjust the seasoning and pour over caviar pillows in serving dish.

Serves 4. Approximate nutrition information per serving: Calories 445; protein 25g; fat 33g; carbohydrates 10g; sodium 815 mg.

Lean Fish

An old French fisherman's legend tells that St. Christopher decided to bless the fishes of the sea and to preach to them. All came except the flounder, who laughed and made faces, which annoyed St. Christopher. He cursed the whole family of flatfishes and condemned them forevermore to speak through twisted mouths.

Monkfish with Zucchini and Yogurt

The Flat Fishes

The Greeks and Romans named the sole, calling it "solea," or sandal, foot-wear no doubt for nymphs and sea sprites that lived in the sea. The description is apt: one large flounder caught off Montauk Point is known locally as the "snowshoe" flounder.

Despite what restaurant menus state about "sole," "lemon sole," and "gray sole," the chances are pretty slim that you have ever tasted a sole — at least not a true sole — if it was caught in the ocean waters of the eastern United States.

Just about everything that we call "sole" is a flounder.

There are only four true soles caught in the Atlantic waters of the United States, and these are small members of the Soleidae family and not of commercial interest.

That is of little matter, however, since the flounders of this side of the Atlantic are superb fishes that can be prepared in hundreds of ways and respond well to almost every form of cooking.

There are three families (Bothidae, Pleuronectidae, and Soleidae) of flatfish (Pleuronectiformes) in American waters on both coasts numbering more than 200 species. They range from small dabs to the Atlantic halibut, the largest flatfish, that can be up to nine feet long and 600 to 700 pounds in weight.

Flatfish are bottom feeders, some preferring sandy, stony floors, others mud, and others everything in between. Flatfish generally have a top color that is dark (olive, brown, gray, etc.) and a bottom color that is light (white, yellow, etc.). This coloration provides protection, for the dark top side is often mottled, making the fish nearly undetectable — by other fish as well as man — as they lie half-buried in the ocean floor hiding from enemies and waiting for prey.

Their shape can be somewhat round, as with most flounders; oval or elliptical, as with the Dover and some other soles; or even diamond-shaped, as with the turbot.

When born, flatfish have one eye on each side of their head, and other parts are in the normal fishy arrangement. As they grow and laze on the bottom, they lean to one side, the internal skeleton shifts and twists, and one eye migrates, bringing both eyes together on the uppermost side.

Flatfish can be either dextral, with eyes on the right side, or sinistral, with eyes on the left side. These arrangements have nothing to do with how they taste, and may not be of interest even to other flatfish.

Some other fish get confused with flatfish. Skates and rays also are flat, tend to feed on the seabed, and are also white on the underside, but that is their belly, not their side. Thin fish, such as the butterfish, John Dory, and pomfret, swim upright and appear to be vertical flatfish, but they are not. They are more or less treated as flatfish in the kitchen, however.

In Europe, the thick-bodied dextral Dover sole, with firm texture and excellent flavor, is considered the best of the family. Brill, the French barbue, and the turbot are also highly regarded. These occasionally come to this country frozen and even fresh (by air), but are not found in local waters to any extent.

On the Pacific coast, the English, petrale, rex, curlfin, and butter soles are all found, but they are flounders. The petrale is generally considered the best of these and is the one seen most often on restaurant menus on the West Coast.

The Atlantic species of the flounder you are likely to find in the marketplace are halibut, winter flounder, summer flounder, witch flounder, yellowtail flounder, and sand-dab.

Halibut

Halibut has long been the most desirable and most expensive of the white-fleshed flatfish. It is a true flounder. Weighing in at an average 10 to 60 pounds, it is also the largest. Females, the larger of the species, can run as high as 150 to 200 pounds. Halibut have been recorded at more than 700 pounds.

It is available all year, but is most abundant from March to August. Halibut usually is sold with the skin on so that consumers can be certain that they are getting what they are paying for. The skin of the halibut, like that of the John Dory, has a distinguishing characteristic, "the devil's thumbprint," which, together with a pronounced lateral line, serves as identification.

This flatfish is a right-eyed flounder in the Atlantic and a left-eyed flounder off the California coast. No one has explained whether that has political implications or not. You don't have to play politics with halibut, however; it is a solid citizen and excellent company at table. Its flesh is firm, tightly grained, bland, and sweet. Poached, baked, or broiled, halibut is excellent fare not needing much embellishment. It is most frequently sold in steak form.

Its name derives from the fact that in old England, flatfishes were called "butte." Considered the best of the flounders, this fish was served especially on holy days and other special days. Thus, it became "holy-day-butte," then "holy-butte" or "holi-butte," and eventually halibut.

Winter Flounder

This fish is also known as lemon sole (when it weighs more than 3 pounds), and blueback and blackback flounder (when it weighs less than 3). A dextral fish, it is most abundant in New England waters and the Georges Bank and as far south as New Jersey, though its range is from Labrador to Georgia. Lemon sole can weigh up to eight pounds. The smaller blueback is more abundant and more fragile than the larger lemon sole. Lemon sole is among the most delicately textured of the flatfishes and one of the most delicate in flavor. It is the thickest and meatiest of the North Atlantic flounders and its flesh is firm and white. It generally commands a premium price. This is the snowshoe flounder of Montauk Point.

Summer Flounder

This sinistral flounder gets its name from the fact that it moves inshore during the summer. Also known as a fluke, its average length is 18 to 24 inches, its average weight is 2 to 4 pounds. The fluke is a fine table fish with lean white meat. It is common on the retail market.

Witch Flounder

Better known as gray sole or pole dab in many areas, the witch flounder bears a similarity to the winter flounder, and most often commands the same premium price. It grows to about 25 inches long and can be distinguished from the winter flounder by the many deep indentations on its blind side.

Yellowtail Flounder

A right-eyed flounder with a prominent nose, the yellowtail flounder is also known as the rusty dab. It is an abundant member of the flatfish family, and is found from Labrador to Virginia, generally preferring inshore waters. Medium-sized, it averages 1 to 2 pounds in the marketplace. It is an exceptionally lean fish among the flounders, which average less than 1 percent fat.

Sand-dab

Also known as American plaice, sea dab, and long rough dab, the sand-dab can travel, as a food fish, as do many of the flatfish, as sole or flounder. The dab, which averages about 2 feet in length and 2 to 3 pounds, is noted for its rough scales. It is a good pan fish with distinctive texture and flavor and a minimum of bones. The European plaice is a different species.

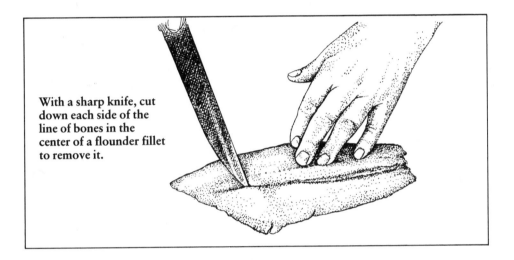

With a sharp knife, cut down each side of the line of bones in the center of a flounder fillet to remove it.

Cooking Flatfish

The flesh of flounder is extremely delicate and will not take rough handling in the kitchen. It is often best not to turn very thin, skinless fillets when pan-frying, sauteing, or broiling; cook one side and present that side facing up when served. The portion is normally thin enough to cook through without burning.

Before cooking the fillets or making them into a mousse, lay them on a flat surface. There is a line of small bones running lengthwise that you can feel if you run a finger along the fillet. Cut down each side of this bone line with a knife to remove it and divide the fillet in half. Don't use this piece in making stock or mousse — the tiny bones can be small enough that they might dislodge and then pass easily through a strainer.

We use the name sole interchangeably with flounder in our recipes.

Ocean perch and ocean pout make good substitutes for flounder, especially in recipes that call for rolling a fillet, which will not always work well with fillets from round fish.

Paupiette de Sole

◾◾

FILLETS OF SOLE ROLLED WITH ZUCCHINI

This dish is striking — a spiral of white sole surrounding a spiral of green-skinned zucchini set on a creamy-red sauce — and it is as easy to make as it is inviting to see. It makes a dinner entree for 4 or a first course for 8.

Fillets must be thin and about 1 inch longer than zucchini. Buy fillets as thin as you can; dabs or very small flounder would be best. You need eight. Failing that, you may have to slice each fillet in half horizontally along its length to get it thin enough.

Find a zucchini that is shorter than the fillets and about as wide. Cut the unpeeled zucchini end to end in paper-thin slices. This is easiest to accomplish if you have a mandoline slicer or a cold meat slicer. Don't rule out an adjustable knife or even a broad spatula-like cheese slicer, which can serve as an improvised mandoline for vegetables as soft as zucchini.

1 pound sole, in 8 thin fillets
4 tablespoons soft butter
1 zucchini, unpeeled, cut in 8
    paper-thin, lengthwise strips
salt and pepper to taste
½ shallot, minced
½ cup dry white wine
¾ cup heavy cream

½ cup peeled, seeded, finely
    diced fresh tomatoes or
    canned Italian plum
    tomatoes

GARNISH:
2 cherry tomatoes
4 sprigs parsley

1. Preheat oven to 350 degrees. Lay fillets out flat and lightly salt and pepper them. Using about 2 tablespoons soft butter, dot the fillets with small pieces. Lay a slice of zucchini on each fillet. Roll up the fillets so that they look like a jelly roll with the green zucchini skin showing along the sides. Fasten with a toothpick if necessary, though they should remain intact if they are placed seam-side down.

2. Butter an ovenproof pan with the remaining butter, sprinkle with minced shallots, lay in rolled fillets with seam down, season lightly with salt and pepper and pour in wine. Cover loosely with buttered foil or parchment. Place in preheated oven and cook for 10 to 12 minutes, or 10 minutes for each inch of thickness measured across diameter of roll. Don't overcook; thin sole cooks quickly.

3. Remove rolls from pan, set into a dish, cover, and keep warm.

4. Retain pan liquid to make sauce. Pour it into a saucepan and reduce by half or until there is about ¼ cup remaining. Add cream and reduce

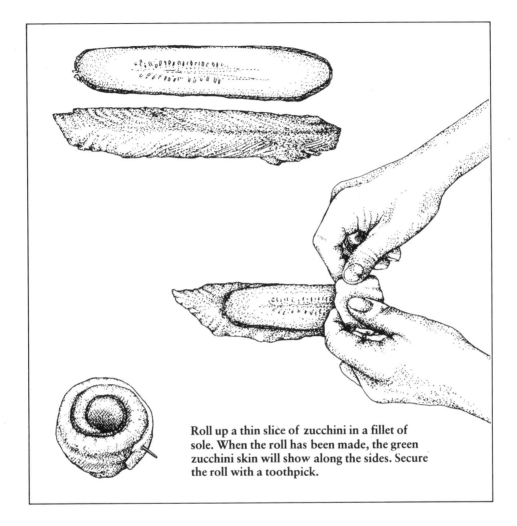

Roll up a thin slice of zucchini in a fillet of sole. When the roll has been made, the green zucchini skin will show along the sides. Secure the roll with a toothpick.

liquid to about ½ cup. Add diced tomatoes and cook for about 2 minutes. Correct seasoning.

5. Spoon 2 tablespoons of sauce onto the center of warmed individual serving plates, and set two rolled soles onto sauce. Garnish with half a cherry tomato set off with a sprig of parsley and serve.

6. If this is to be served as a dinner entree, boiled radishes make a good vegetable accompaniment. Just boil the radishes with a couple tablespoons of water, a little butter, and salt. When they are tender, toss the pan over the heat to let the water evaporate while you glaze the radishes.

Serves 4. Approximate nutrition information per serving: Calories 390; protein 20g; fat 28g; carbohydrates 15g; sodium 500 mg.

Sole Smelt-Style
GOUJONETTE DE SOLE

This dish is surprisingly light for coated and fried fish. This is because the fish is first cut into small fingers that remain light and tender in cooking.

In Europe, the Gudgeon (Gobio gobio) is a small freshwater fish seldom exceeding 8 inches in length, which often is eaten smaller than that. It is quite common in lakes, rivers, and streams. The flesh is very delicate and the fish is usually eaten like smelts: coated with an egg wash, dipped in fresh breadcrumbs, and fried. It is very popular that way in France, both as a dish in itself, and, with especially small goujonettes, as a garnish for other seafood dishes.

The sole in this recipe is handled the same way, or as the name we have given it indicates.

The fish can be gotten ready for frying and kept in the refrigerator for an hour or so before cooking.

1 pound fillets of any flatfish

EGG WASH:
1 whole egg
1 tablespoon oil
1 tablespoon water
salt and pepper to taste

Flour for dredging
¼ cup vegetable oil
¼ cup butter

BEURRE NOISETTE:
2 tablespoons butter
1 tablespoon lemon juice
1 tablespoon minced fresh
     parsley

OPTIONAL PROVENÇAL GARNISH:
1 whole garlic clove
½ cup peeled, seeded, and
     chopped fresh tomato

1. Cut fillets on the bias — diagonally across — into strips 4 to 5 inches long and ½- to ¾-inch wide. Salt and pepper the strips lightly.

2. Mix egg, oil, water, salt, and pepper in a bowl, beating lightly with a fork. Set out a second bowl with flour. Also set out a strip of foil or wax paper or a cookie sheet.

3. Dredge fish strips in flour. Shake off excess. Dip fish into egg wash and drain excess. Dredge fish again in flour, and pat so that it adheres. Shake off excess.

4. Roll the strips back and forth between the palms of your hands to coat strips thoroughly and to firm them. Do a few strips at a time, setting them on the foil or cookie sheet until all the fish has been coated. (Refrigerate at this point, if desired.)

5. Heat half of the oil-butter mixture in a 10-inch skillet until hot but not smoking.

6. You will be frying half of the strips at a time. Gradually add them to the pan so that you do not lower the temperature of the fat too abruptly. Turn them over when they're nicely browned on one side, and brown the second side. Place the cooked fish on a serving platter and keep warm. Add the remaining oil and butter, heat, and fry the second batch. Place on the platter with the first batch.

7. In a separate skillet, make beurre noisette: Heat 2 tablespoons butter until the color of a hazelnut, stir in lemon juice, and pour over fish on platter. Sprinkle with parsley.

Note: You also may serve the dish "à la provençale" with the addition of garlic and tomatoes. Brown a whole garlic clove and discard before frying fish. Peel, seed, and dice ½ cup fresh tomato, season with salt and pepper to taste, and saute for 2 minutes. Pour over fish.

Serves 4. Approximate nutrition information per serving: Calories 486; protein 32g; fat 38g; carbohydrates 3g; sodium 524 mg.

Flounder Country Style
◻◻
SOLE A LA PAYSANNE

This is a robust dish for hearty appetites — a whole pan-fried flounder surrounded by pearl onions, potatoes, and mushrooms.

Most often in this country, flatfish is sauteed or pan fried as fillets. This recipe calls for sauteing the whole fish. The choice is not whimsical — there is a big difference in texture and flavor between a sauteed or pan-fried flatfish fillet and a whole flatfish cooked the same way. For one thing, all flesh is more flavorful when cooked with the bone, and fish is no exception. The whole fish is also likely to be more delicately flavored and less oily. And the whole fish marries well with the sauteed vegetables in this recipe.

Ideally, it would be most dramatic to serve the whole fish on a platter surrounded by the vegetables. The fish would then be boned at table, not a difficult task. A fillet lies on either side of the backbone and two more lie in the same position on the underside. The idea is to remove these four fillets whole.

Begin by trimming away comb, the edgings of fin that surround the outside of fish, if it is still necessary. This should have been removed when fish was first pan dressed, but frequently some of the comb remains. Next, cut deeply from head to tail through the top center of the fish, down to the backbone. A fillet lies on both sides. Remove one by working your knife from the backbone toward the edge where the comb was, scraping along the rib bones to take the fillet off whole. Lift away the fillet and set it aside on a clean platter. Repeat on the other side of the backbone. You now should be able to lift the backbone and attached bones free from head to tail, usually in one interconnected piece. Separate the two fillets that lie beneath and lay them atop the first two fillets and serve.

The boning can also be done in the kitchen, if you prefer.

The presentation for this dish includes sauteed vegetables. When sauteing mushrooms, onions, or similar vegetables you want to brown, don't crowd them in a pan that is too small to hold them. Keep the vegetables in one layer in a hot pan. If the pan is too small, heat won't strike vegetables evenly and they brown unevenly and evaporate and waste moisture and flavor. Cook in two batches if necessary.

The preparation can be done ahead through step 5.

1 whole flounder, 1½ to 2 pounds	8 large mushrooms
3½ tablespoons oil	salt and pepper to taste
4½ tablespoons butter	milk for dredging fish
About 2 cups roughly cubed potatoes	flour for dusting
	1 tablespoon minced fresh parsley
	lemon wedges for garnish

To cook onions:
16 pearl onions
1 cup water
1 tablespoon butter
½ teaspoon salt
1 teaspoon sugar

1. See the drawings on page 8 and 9 on how to prepare a whole flat fish for cooking. Using large kitchen shears, trim the tail of the flounder so that about ⅓ of it remains. Allow the bottom skin to remain, but scrape it with a knife. Remove the top, or dark, skin cutting through it at the tail to afford a grip. Pull the skin toward the head; it should come free in one piece. Use pliers, if needed, to start.

2. Gut fish if this hasn't already been done.

3. Trim comb, the small edging of bones and fins along sides of fish. Cut off the head and stomach cavity by cutting on an angle down from the head.

4. With a knife, open a slit about 4 inches long at the thickest part of the fish on the skinned (top) side near the head proceeding toward the tail. Go through to the backbone. Score the fish 3 or 4 times crosswise on the top side. These gashes will help heat to penetrate more efficiently.

5. With a knife or large kitchen shears, break backbone in 2 or 3 places so the fish won't curl.

6. Melt 1½ tablespoons butter in 1½ tablespoons oil and get it hot. Add potatoes and saute until cooked and nicely browned. Remove, drain fat, and reserve potatoes.

7. Prepare onions: In a small saute or saucepan, over medium heat, place peeled and trimmed pearl onions, water, butter, salt, and sugar. Cover and allow water to simmer and slowly evaporate, shaking the pan occasionally to mix ingredients and cook the onions evenly. Remove the cover and shake the pan continuously as the water totally disappears to evenly brown and glaze the onions. Set aside.

8. Make mushroom caps by removing their stems. Reserve the stems for some other use. Saute the caps in 1 tablespoon of butter over medium high heat until they are evenly browned. Reserve.

9. Dip fish in milk, drain, and dredge in flour. Pat so that flour will adhere, and shake off the excess.

10. Over medium-high heat, warm 2 tablespoons butter and 2 table-spoons oil in a large skillet. Season fish with freshly ground pepper and brown it on the skinned side first. Turn over carefully and baste from time to time while the second side browns nicely. It should take about 5 minutes per side.

11. Discard the fat from the pan. Combine the potatoes, mushrooms, and onions in the pan and reheat thoroughly, tossing and shaking. There should be enough butter adhering to the vegetables so that you will not have to add any for the reheating. Sprinkle with parsley.

12. Set cooked flounder on large serving platter, or remove the fillets and reassemble the flounder, seemingly whole, on platter. Arrange the vegetables around the fish. Serve with lemon wedges.

Serves 4. Approximate nutrition information per serving: Calories 540; protein 40g; fat 31g; carbohydrates 28g; sodium 765 mg.

Fillets de Sole Duglére Froid

This is a unique cold summer variation of the classical dish created by Chef Adolph Dugléré at the Café Anglais in Paris. The sauce originally was a sauce poulette to which diced tomatoes were added. In cooking, it was enriched with butter. We have a recipe for Mussels à la Poulette on page 336.

The sauce in this case is simply a thick mayonnaise to which the cold fish broth reduction has been added.

The dish is served at room temperature.

30 ounces flatfish (5 ounces per serving)	MAYONNAISE:
1 tablespoon butter	2 egg yolks
salt and pepper	2 cups oil
2 tablespoons minced shallots	3 tablespoons lemon juice
¾ cup peeled, seeded, chopped fresh tomatoes or canned Italian plum tomatoes	salt and freshly ground white pepper to taste
¼ cup minced parsley	GARNISH:
1 cup white wine	lemon slices
½ cup fish stock (White Wine Fumet or Quick Fumet, page 30), or water	3 cherry tomatoes
	6 sprigs parsley

1. Butter an ovenproof dish. Sprinkle with salt and pepper, and minced shallots. Fold the fish fillets lengthwise in half, dark side turned in, and arrange in the dish. Don't crowd; they should fit snugly but not tightly. Add chopped tomatoes and half the minced parsley. Season the top of the fish lightly with salt and pepper, add white wine and fish stock, cover with buttered foil or parchment. If you wish, refrigerate the dish, covered with plastic wrap, until you're ready to finish it.

2. Preheat oven to 375 degrees. Bake, covered, for 15 minutes, or 10 minutes for each inch of thickness of folded fillets measured at thickest point; do not overcook.

3. Remove the fillets and as much of the chopped tomatoes as possible from the baking dish. Cover with a damp clean kitchen towel to prevent drying.

4. Place baking dish ingredients in a saucepan and reduce along with any liquid drained from standing fish. Reduce over medium-high heat until

most of the liquid has evaporated and is thick enough to coat a spoon. Cool completely.

5. Make the mayonnaise, following hand-method instructions on page 42.

6. Add the cooled fish stock reduction to the mayonnaise and mix well.

7. Correct seasoning; the dish should be tart, so use more lemon if necessary. Add remaining parsley.

8. Spoon sauce over each fillet, and garnish with a lemon slice, half a cherry tomato, and a sprig of parsley. Serve immediately.

Serves 6. Approximate nutrition information per serving: Calories 840; protein 29g; fat 78g; carbohydrates 5g; sodium 315 mg.

Halibut Terrine with Aspic

This recipe takes time, but it is best made a day ahead, and it is served cold. It is striking as a first course, cool with a piquant freshness provided by the parsley, dill, and tomato. It is light and could precede a rich dish.

The recipe calls for halibut, with a centerbone, that can be cut into a thick steak.

2¼ pounds halibut steak
1 small carrot
1 medium sweet red pepper
1 cup minced fresh parsley
2 tablespoons minced fresh dill
1 quart strong fish stock
1 recipe for Fish Aspic (see page 31)

¾ cup tomato concassée (see page 59)
salt and pepper to taste
bed of chilled greens
1 recipe Green Mayonnaise (see page 41)

1. The carrot and pepper are a garnish for the terrine. Slice the carrot extra thin. You want 9 slices. Fashion them with a cutter or by hand into a decorative design, such as a star, if you like. Blanch in simmering salted water for 10 to 15 seconds until tender but still firm. Remove and immediately refresh under cold running water.

2. Cut pepper into finely julienned strips. Blanch strips in simmering

salted water for about 30 seconds using a fine-meshed wire strainer to hold them. Place in cold water to refresh. Place pepper and carrot in refrigerator until needed.

3. Mince together parsley and fresh dill and reserve in refrigerator.

4. Remove the skin from the halibut steak and discard. Do not remove centerbone. Its gelatin will add to the stock and improve the aspic. Hold in the refrigerator.

5. Make fish stock, using 3 to 4 pounds fish trimmings, but not skin. You want an aromatic stock for this dish. Follow the recipe on page 30 for White Wine Fish Fumet, but double the amount of celery, carrot, parsley stems, thyme, and cracked pepper called for in recipe. Simmer the stock 30 minutes.

6. Allow the stock to rest so that the solids settle. Then ladle the stock — don't pour it directly — through a double thickness of dampened cheesecloth into a clean pot, being careful not to disturb sediment. Don't force it through cheesecloth, just use what falls through freely, as you want the finished fish stock as clear as consomme.

7. Poach halibut steak in the stock about 10 minutes for each inch of thickness. Don't overcook. Remove pot from the heat when the fish is done and allow it to cool in the stock.

8. When the stock has cooled to room temperature, remove the fish, and separate the flesh from the bones. Discard the bones and flake the fish into small bite-sized pieces and chill until needed. Strain the stock again through doubled thickness of dampened cheesecloth.

9. Meanwhile, place a 1½ quart mold or other suitable dish in the refrigerator to chill. An oval or rectangular mold would be best in terms of appearance.

10. Make fish aspic. Place the aspic in the refrigerator just to cool down, not set. To use, it should be chilled and thick, but pourable.

11. Meanwhile, make tomato concassée, draining it so that it is "tight" rather than runny or loose. Lightly blend ¾ cup of the concassée with 2 tablespoons of the aspic and salt and pepper to taste. Chill.

12. Remove mold from refrigerator and spoon in enough fish aspic to coat the bottom of the mold with a thin film. Pressing the blanched vegetables into the aspic, arrange an attractive lattice of the julienne strips of pepper in such a way that you can place a carrot slice in the center of each square formed by the pepper strips. Gently spoon a little more aspic atop the carrots and peppers. The peppers form a tic-tac-toe pattern and the carrots are the "Xs" and "Os."

13. Carefully return the mold to the refrigerator to allow the aspic to set, about 10 minutes. Remove and spoon in more aspic, sprinkle with one-third of the reserved parsley-dill mixture, and chill again in refrigerator.

14. Spoon more aspic into the mold and lay in half of the flaked fish. Cover with more aspic. Your mold at this point should be somewhat less than half full. Chill again.

15. Using a small spoon, lay a column of tomato concassée down the center of the mold's length. Being careful not to disturb the concassée, spoon in enough aspic to cover it, and chill again.

16. Spoon a thin layer of aspic in the mold, sprinkle with half of the remaining parsley-dill mixture, and allow to set again.

17. Lay in the remainder of the flaked fish and more aspic; the mold should be nearly full at this point. Chill.

18. Fill the mold with the remaining parsley-dill and aspic, cover with foil or plastic wrap, and refrigerate for at least 4 hours — or overnight.

19. To unmold the terrine, place it in a pan of lukewarm water only until the aspic pulls away from sides and bottom of the mold, and invert it onto a serving platter lined with chilled greens.

20. Serve with a green mayonnaise.

Serves 4. Approximate nutrition information per serving without mayonnaise: Calories 600; protein 74g; fat 25g; carbohydrates 23g; sodium 830 mg.

Sole au Plat

SOLE, ONE-PAN DISH

This one-pan dish can be prepared and cooked in minutes. It retains the delicate moistness of the fish, the mushrooms give it a pleasing texture, and the breadcrumbs give a crisp surface.

Although we use flatfish fillets in this recipe, small whole fish could also be used.

4 fillets of sole, 4 to 6 ounces each	2 tablespoons minced fresh parsley
7 tablespoons butter	2 tablespoons dry white wine
2 tablespoons minced shallots	1 cup fresh breadcrumbs
1½ cups sliced fresh mushrooms	
salt and freshly ground white pepper to taste	

1. Preheat oven to 350 degrees. Using 4 tablespoons butter, grease an oval au gratin dish or other ovenproof baking dish. Scatter shallots in dish. Lay fish atop shallots, top with sliced mushrooms, season with salt and pepper, add parsley, and pour in wine.

2. Dust with breadcrumbs. Using 3 tablespoons of butter, dot the surface with small pieces.

3. Bake for 10 to 12 minutes, or 10 minutes for each inch of thickness measured at the thickest part.

4. Serve directly from oven to table in dish in which it cooked.

Serves 4. Approximate nutrition information per serving: Calories 330; protein 29g; fat 21g; carbohydrates 5g; sodium 280 mg.

Flounder with Apples and Cider

■■

FILLET DE SOLE AUX POMMES

This is a dish for fall with the scent of Normandy — or anywhere that apples and apple cider are part of the fall scene. In this country, that can mean just about everywhere.

4 flatfish fillets, each 4 to 6 ounces, 1½ pounds in all
3 tablespoons butter
1 tablespoon minced shallots
salt and white pepper to taste
1 cup cider (hard, if available)
1 cup heavy cream

1 tablespoon Calvados or applejack
2 medium apples (Granny Smith or other firm variety)
2 teaspoons sugar
1 teaspoon salt

1. Preheat oven to 375 degrees. Using 1 tablespoon butter, grease an ovenproof dish, sprinkle with shallots and season with salt and pepper. Lay fish fillets atop shallots, add cider, and cover loosely with buttered foil or parchment. Bake 5 minutes.

2. Drain cooking liquid into a saucepan; reserve cooked fish, covered, and keep warm.

3. Reduce the liquid to ¼ cup, add cream, and reduce until thick enough to coat a spoon. Add Calvados or applejack and bring to a boil. Remove from heat and correct the seasoning.

4. Meanwhile, peel and core the apples and cut into 24 thin wedges. Melt 2 tablespoons butter in a saute pan, add apples, and saute until they are lightly browned. Add sugar and 1 teaspoon salt and continue to cook until apples are cooked, golden but still firm.

5. Arrange cooked fish in preheated serving dish or on individual preheated serving plates. Coat with sauce, arrange cooked apples around fish, and serve immediately.

Serves 4. Approximate nutrition information per serving: Calories 504; protein 30g; fat 33g; carbohydrates 22g; sodium 390 mg.

Halibut with Fennel

Celery-like fennel is not used much in American cooking, yet it is deserving of more attention. Its flavor is distinctive and it is available at the time of year when cooks are looking for different ingredients with which to enliven meals. It should be used while it is fresh, of course, but a couple of days in the refrigerator will do it no harm if it remains crisp. It is especially good cooked in a dish such as this. A large stalk of celery can be substituted for the fennel, if desired.

For another treatment of fish with fennel, see the recipe from Maison Robert restaurant in Boston: Monkfish with fennel, red wine and pistachios (page 141). We also use fennel with porgy on page 163.

20 ounces halibut fillets	pepper
1 fennel bulb	2 cups heavy cream
2 tablespoons butter	½ cup tomato concassée (see
1 tablespoon thinly sliced onion	recipe page 59)
1 cup dry white wine	¼ cup minced fresh parsley
½ teaspoon salt	

1. Slice the bulb, the white part of the fennel, into thin, crosswise pieces, to make about 1½ cups.

2. In a large, heavy, non-corrosive skillet, melt butter. Saute onion until transparent, add fennel and cook over medium heat, tossing until the vegetables pick up a little color.

3. Add wine, salt, and pepper, cover, and simmer over low heat until the fennel is tender, about 12 minutes.

4. Add cream and reduce over low heat until the liquid is thick enough to coat a spoon heavily.

5. Preheat oven to 375. Place half of fennel with its liquid in the bottom of a lightly buttered, ovenproof baking dish. Arrange fish fillets flat atop fennel. Strew remaining fennel on top of fish. Top with tomato concassée and then parsley. Correct the seasoning.

6. Bake for 12 minutes. Serve directly from baking pan. Buttered noodles make a nice accompaniment.

Serves 4. Approximate nutrition information per serving: Calories 605; protein 27g; fat 52g; carbohydrates 8g; sodium 550 mg.

Halibut with Tomato Mousseline

This recipe is for a halibut dressed in party clothes — a cloud of tomato mousseline is set atop a steak. The dish can be served hot or cold, as you wish, depending on the weather. If it is to be served cold, the fish can be poached up to 4 hours ahead of time, covered, and refrigerated. In either case, the mousseline can be prepared in advance through step 3.

We recommend this dish with halibut, but almost any fish can be used. If you serve this dish cold, you must use a non-oily fish (mackerel, bluefish, salmon, and the like are too fat and rich).

The preparation is performed in two steps: the tomato mousseline is made first and then the halibut is poached. In this case a milk court-bouillon is used for poaching, because it will keep the halibut marvelously white, an excellent contrast to the orange-red of the mousseline. If color is not a major consideration and the fish has soft flesh (if you are using bluefish, for example), use a white wine court-bouillon for poaching. It will help to firm softer fish.

4 halibut steaks, 5 to 6 ounces each	1 recipe for tomato mousseline (see page 51)
	milk court-bouillon (see page 35)

1. Make tomato mousseline. Refrigerate.

2. Meanwhile, poach halibut steaks in milk court-bouillon. The halibut and the court-bouillon both should be cold when you start poaching. Poach the steaks 10 minutes for each inch of thickness. Remove, drain, and pat dry with paper towels, or the mousseline might run because of the moisture.

3. To serve cold, refrigerate the fish and top with the chilled mousseline just before serving.

4. If the dish is to be served hot, do not allow the steaks to cool. After they have been drained and dried, top them with the mousseline and slide them under a hot broiler for 1 minute to glaze.

Serves 4. Approximate nutrition information per serving: Calories 330; protein 36g; fat 17g; carbohydrates 9g; sodium 650 mg.

Flounder Kiev

■■

The original Kiev was made with chicken breasts stuffed with chilled chive butter; some versions called for the inclusion of fresh truffles. Fresh truffles are virtually unobtainable by consumers in this country today; and when they can be found, the price is prohibitive, so the reference is academic. Truffles or not, this dish has a simple direct appeal both to the eye and to the palate.

This recipe calls for very thin fillets. It will be better if made with fillets from small flounder or dabs, rather than with fillets of larger flatfish. Small flounder or dabs are already quite thin. You cannot pound sole or otherwise flatten fillets and expect them to hold up to the cooking required.

The fish packages are pan-fried, which requires turning them in the cooking fat. To prevent splashing of hot fat while frying fish, or any food, tilt the skillet away from you so that the fat collects at the far end. Slide a spatula under the far side of the fish from you and turn gently toward you onto the "dry" side of pan. When they have all been turned, lay the skillet back on the burner and brown the second side of the fillets.

Read the recipe through so that you can envision what you are setting out to do, especially in the use of the butter. A great deal of mystique has been applied to the Kiev preparation, but this recipe is not at all difficult to make.

20 ounces flounder fillets: 8 pieces 2½ to 3 ounces each, as thin as possible.	EGG WASH: 1 egg pinch of pepper 1 tablespoon oil 1 tablespoon water
CHIVE BUTTER: ¼ pound soft butter 2 tablespoons finely minced chives 1 tablespoon lemon juice ½ teaspoon salt	flour for dusting salt and pepper to taste 2 tablespoons oil 2 tablespoons butter

1½ cups fresh breadcrumbs

1. Mix soft butter with chives, lemon juice, and salt. Chill until it begins to set but is still soft. Make 4 flattened patties using about 1 tablespoon of the mixture for each one. Make them oval-shaped to fit between two fillets. Also, make them somewhat thick so they won't melt too fast in cooking. Set patties on a small plate and chill well.

2. Make the fresh breadcrumbs in a blender or a food processor using about 5 slices of day-old white bread. Reserve.

3. Meanwhile, make the egg wash, beating the ingredients with a fork. Lay out a dish with flour and another with breadcrumbs.

4. Lay out 4 of the fish fillets on a flat surface. Place a butter patty in the middle of each fillet and lay a second fillet on top. Press edges to seal. Season lightly with salt and pepper.

5. Dredge each package in flour, and shake off excess. Then, dip each in the egg wash and drain. Dredge in breadcrumbs, patting and pressing on the surface to make sure the crumbs adhere. Place them in refrigerator to chill thoroughly. They may be held up to 4 hours.

6. When ready to serve, heat butter and oil in a skillet until hot, but not smoking. Lay the fish in the skillet and cook over moderate heat until it is brown. Turn carefully with a broad spatula and brown the other side.

7. When you remove the fillets from the skillet, they should be cooked and the butter filling just beginning to soften, but the core of chive butter should still be quite firm. Allow them to drain for a minute and serve while still hot. If cooked just right, the butter will be melted just as the dish gets to the table and should squirt out when the fish is pierced with a fork.

Serves 4. Approximate nutrition information per serving: Calories 520; protein 28g; fat 41g; carbohydrates 9g; sodium 815 mg.

Fillets de Sole Veronique
à notre manière
••
SOLE WITH SEEDLESS GRAPES OUR WAY

White seedless grapes make this sauce rich tasting and, when used as a garnish, add a distinctive note to the fillets of sole. Dishes garnished with grapes are usually called "Veronique."

8 fillets of sole (about 3 ounces each)
1 tablespoon plus 1 teaspoon butter
2 tablespoons minced shallots
1½ cups seedless white grapes, plus 16 to 20 for garnish
¾ cup dry white wine or dry vermouth

½ cup fish stock (see White Wine Fumet, page 30), or clam juice
½ teaspoon salt
freshly ground white pepper
1½ cups heavy cream
freshly squeezed lemon juice (optional)

1. Preheat oven to 375 degrees.
2. Butter a 12-inch ovenproof skillet and sprinkle with minced shallots. Fold fillets in half lengthwise, darker side turned in. Arrange 8 fillets pinwheel fashion in skillet with pointed ends toward center. Cover with 1½ cups of seedless grapes, pour in wine and fish stock or clam juice, and season with salt and pepper.
3. Cover with buttered foil or parchment and bake 8 minutes in preheated oven.
4. While sole bakes, prepare the grapes for garnish. Peel them if you wish. Saute in 1 teaspoon butter until they take on color, shaking and tossing so that they cook evenly. Retain them off heat in their skillet.
5. Remove the skillet from oven. Using a wide spatula, remove the fillets carefully as they are fragile and fall apart easily. Place in a warm dish, cover, and keep warm.
6. Atop stove, cook the grapes in the pan liquid over medium heat for about 5 minutes.
7. Add cream, and any liquid drained from standing fish, and continue to cook to reduce. When thickened enough to coat a spoon, remove from heat and work in a food processor or blender for about 30 seconds until smooth. Strain, reheat, and correct seasoning. If grapes have made sauce overly sweet, use up to 2 tablespoons lemon juice for balance.
8. Rewarm the garnishing grapes in their skillet, tossing them until they glaze.

9. Place 2 folded fillets on each of 4 warm serving dishes, pour sauce over them and garnish with sauteed grapes.

Serves 4. Approximate nutrition information per serving: Calories 570; protein 35g; fat 43g; carbohydrates 11g; sodium 575 mg.

Fillet of Sole Esterhazy
FROM FRICK'S RESTAURANT IN NEWPORT, RHODE ISLAND

Frick's is a small storefront restaurant in a more-or-less-Victorian house at the end of Thames Street in Newport, Rhode Island.

This simple recipe is a classic of Hungarian cooking. You may use sole or any firm white fish. If using cod or haddock, either use steak-cuts, or fillets cut into medallions. If using trout, however, cook with the skin on, place the fish skin-side down on the vegetables, and remove the skin before serving. For the julienne vegetables you may use carrots, leeks, turnip, celery (either stalk or root), parsnips, string beans, or whatever is in season. Select three, using contrasting colors for a better appearance.

5 to 6 ounces sole, per serving
1 cup mixed vegetables cut in
     julienne, per serving
3 ounces dry white wine, per
     serving
1 tablespoon paprika

½ teaspoon salt
pepper to taste
1 tablespoon butter for foil or
     parchment, per serving
2 tablespoons finely minced
     parsley, per serving

1. Clean the sole fillets, removing any dark flesh. Also remove the center line if you have bought a double fillet; discard.
2. Flatten the fillets slightly with a meat tenderizer, mallet, or the bottom of heavy saucepan. Fold fillets in half lengthwise so that the darker side is on the inside. All the folded fillets should be of the same thickness.
3. Blanch — individually — the julienned vegetables, immersing in simmering water for about a half-minute each, cooking them until about half done and still quite firm. Allow to cool.
4. In a thick-bottomed stainless steel or enameled wide, shallow,

flameproof pan, pour in the wine, salt, and pepper and paprika. Add the julienne vegetables and place on high heat.

5. As soon as steam rises, place fish on the vegetables and cover with buttered foil or buttered parchment and steam, covered, until fish is done (about 4 to 5 minutes for each half-inch of thickness). The vegetables should be done at the same time.

6. Remove fillets with a slotted spoon, and place them on warm serving plates. Lift out the vegetables and divide them into portions, setting them atop the fillets, without hiding the fish.

7. Meanwhile, reduce the liquid remaining in the cooking pot to about ½ cup, add finely chopped parsley. Correct seasoning and pour over the vegetables.

Serves 4. Approximate nutrition information per serving: Calories 200; protein 24g; fat 4g; carbohydrates 16g; sodium 450 mg.

Cod

With the settlement of Gloucester, Massachusetts, in 1623, the American East Coast fishing industry was born. Cod was the "beef" for the next 250 years, and fresh or salted, it was a mainstay of the diet in Europe, America, even the Caribbean and West Africa. Along the Atlantic seaboard its flaky, lean white meat was the basis for chowders, stews, fish cakes, and an endless variety of baked, boiled, poached, fried, and broiled dishes. It was stuffed, hashed, and put into soups. Codfish cheeks became a special delicacy (and still are to those who know them), and the tongue, bladder, and oil from the liver began to be used. In its dried form, cod migrated farther and farther inland. Codfish roe is served poached and smoked to this day, and Greek immigrants often found it an acceptable substitute for the mullet roes used in their homeland taramasalata, a forerunner of today's dips.

The American love affair with beef and other land animals; the advent of refrigeration that lessened the need for salt cod, and dropping cod catches, all have diminished the demand for cod in recent decades. But it is still one of the favorite fishes of this country and — unless pollution and over-fishing do it in — it will be here for another 250 years.

The cod is a whole family of fish that includes the Atlantic cod, haddock, cusk, pollock, and hake.

Fresh Atlantic Cod is lean, white, and firm with flakes that separate easily when cooked. It can be as heavy as 30 to 40 pounds.

In Scandinavia, a boiled (poached) cod fillet with boiled potatoes served with egg sauce and fresh dill is a worthy dish for family or guests. In this country the same dish might be served with parsley instead of dill and a light cream sauce instead of egg sauce.

The Pennsylvania Dutch have used cod to make a hash dish that had as an antecedent the popular red flannel hash made with beef. They make Shaker Red Fish Hash, using leftover poached cod, mashed potatoes, and sliced cooked beets with a cream sauce poured over all.

Haddock

Haddock run smaller than Atlantic cod and some find its white flesh softer, but the differences are not great. In cooking they are interchangeable. Fillets are usually sold with the skin on, as with cod.

Pollock

Also known as "Boston bluefish," the pollock could use a public relations firm — the consumer has never appreciated its value. While it might not appear as pristine as the cod or haddock when raw or plainly baked or broiled, the pollock has much in common with the other members of its family and much to recommend it. Its flesh is only somewhat softer, its flakes only slightly smaller, its flavor only a bit more assertive. When raw, it is slightly gray in color; it cooks white, however. It is a better fish than the public has yet to acknowledge and it works well in many recipes where it does not have to stand totally alone. Besides, it usually sells for about half the price of its cousins. Certainly use it without reservation in stocks, soups, stews, and similar preparations.

Hake

The small and slender hake has an off-white flesh that is coarser and softer and less bland in flavor than cod and haddock, but it is not a fish to ignore. A true cod, it is smaller than the head of the family and has fewer bones (a fact that recommends it highly). It averages under ten pounds in any of its subspecies; most often less than five. Its two long dorsal and anal fins and its long slender body give it an appearance more like that of the cusk than any other family members. It is much admired in the Mediterranean under variations of the name, *merluzza*. It is sometimes known by that name in this country. Other names used include the following: The silver hake (commonly called a whiting as well as New England hake); the white hake (also called Boston hake, black hake, mud hake, ling, lingue, and just hake); squirrel hake (also called red hake).

Whiting

What is called a whiting is most often the smallest of the hakes. It is also called silver hake, and the New England hake. Its average size is twelve to thirteen inches long and one pound in weight. The flesh is tender, though a bit coarser than its big cousins. Its size makes it especially useful as a whole fish, though fillets cook up just as well.

Cusk

This member of the cod family has a Latin name of *Brosme brosme* and a long history as an important food fish in New England. In 1983 in Maine, for example, 2.19 million pounds were landed, ranking it twentieth in dollar value and fifteenth in poundage in that state. More cusk was brought in than sea scallops, winter flounder, monkfish, alewife, wolffish (ocean catfish), mackerel, yellowtail flounder, swordfish, tuna, halibut, and skate. Still, it is not well known to the general public. It is sold primarily fresh or salted. It is vaguely reminiscent of cod; its white flesh is firm. Fillets have a center strip of bones that should be removed. It is often baked, broiled, or steamed and served in the ways that cod is served. A traditional dish for cusk is to steam it and serve it with a cream sauce.

The name "cusk" is also sometimes given to the burbot, the freshwater cod.

Tomcod

There are Atlantic and Pacific species of the tomcod. Small — about one pound — they are not important commercially, but occasionally appear in retail stores.

Scrod

Visitors to Boston are often told outlandish stories about scrod. It is often spelled "schrod" — and in the early days of pre-dawn Boston fish landing reports on radio, most often was pronounced that way. Spelled either way, it is the same thing. Scrod is not a species of fish, nor for that-matter, anything extraordinary in preparation or presentation, but it is excellent eating when fresh.

It is probably accurate that the word was a shorthand method first used to identify the market size of a small Atlantic cod — a 1½- to 3½-pound fish. But the cod family also includes haddock, hake, pollock, and cusk. And it is equally as likely that in dockside usage, the smaller members of some of these fish came to be called scrod as well.

Some authorities have asserted that the spelling "schrod" is used when one is referring to a young haddock and the spelling "scrod" when referring to a young cod. This is a possibility for which we have never found corroboration.

There is another story about the origins of the word scrod that should be included for the historical record.

It concerns that hoary hostelry, Boston's Parker House, which is also credited with originating the Parker House roll, lemon meringue pie, and Boston cream pie, among other noteworthy American favorites.

At some point in the past century, or so the story goes, the chef at the Parker House became annoyed each day having to await the arrival of the "catch of the day" to put his menu together. Since that particular menu item was invariably cod or haddock, he supposedly devised the word scrod to cover both contingencies, permitting him to get his menu printed early.

It is worth noting also, that until about World War II, scrod was considered a proper Boston restaurant luncheon dish, but not really worthy of a dinner menu. And, that the tail piece of cod used to be served as scrod, never the center cuts.

Today, at retail stores and in restaurants, a scrod is generally a fillet of either cod or haddock, and is considered a perfect dinner entree, by Bostonians, and, no less so, by visitors.

In the recipes that follow, any member of the cod family may be substituted for the stated fish.

Baked Scrod

Scrod, both fresh and frozen, is now seen in many markets beyond its Boston birthplace. If you want to enjoy it baked as they do in Boston, cook it this way: Buy scrod fillets with skin attached; plan on 4 to 6 ounces per person, or more depending on appetite and the rest of the meal. Preferably, do this within an hour or two before you plan to cook them. Freshness is what scrod is all about.

Place the scrod fillet in a buttered ovenproof dish or pan, season it, and drizzle melted butter over it. Bake at 375 degrees, or broil. Cook until the fish is easily separated into large flakes with a fork. The flesh, which was a translucent white, should now be milky and opaque throughout, but still soft and moist-appearing.

Remove from oven and drizzle 1 tablespoon melted butter onto each serving of fish, sprinkle it with 1 teaspoon minced fresh parsley, and squeeze lemon juice onto it. Serve immediately; pass lemon wedges.

Note: Don't be tempted to dust your scrod with paprika to give it color, as do many second-rate restaurant kitchens. For one thing, the flavor is all wrong, and for another, it is, as the poet said, "to gild the lily, to paint the rose." Serve it plain and simple.

Hake Hunter's Style
■■
MERLU CHASSEUR

The appeal of the French hunter style in cooking is universal and has made it a popular international preparation for generations — as appreciated in London as in Hartford or Atlanta. A member of the cod family replaces the more common chicken or veal in this recipe, but the combination of flavors is still straightforward and timeless.

20 ounces hake fillets, in 4
    portions of 4 to 5 ounces
¼ cup grated parmesan cheese
½ cup grated Swiss cheese
1 tablespoon olive oil
3 tablespoons minced shallots
2 cups sliced mushrooms

2 cups peeled, seeded, and diced
    fresh or canned Italian plum
    tomatoes
½ clove garlic, minced
¼ cup dry white wine
1 sprig fresh tarragon, chopped
    or ¼ teaspoon dry tarragon
1 teaspoon salt

1. Blend grated cheeses.
2. In a skillet, heat oil, add shallots and mushrooms and saute over medium heat for 3 minutes.
3. Add tomatoes, garlic, and wine and continue to cook, stirring frequently, for 5 minutes more. Add salt and tarragon and cook another minute. Correct the seasoning,
4. Butter a gratin dish lightly, spread half of tomato mixture in pan, and place the fish on top of it in one layer. Add remainder of tomato mixture. Top with grated cheeses. The dish may be refrigerated at this point, if desired, for several hours.
5. Preheat oven to 375 degrees while you bring the gratin dish back to room temperature.
6. Bake the fish for 12 to 15 minutes, until the top is nicely browned and the fish flakes easily. Serve immediately.

Serves 4. Approximate nutrition information per serving: Calories 335; protein 40g; fat 15g; carbohydrates 10g; sodium 780 mg.

Cabbage and Fish with Potatoes

This is hearty family fare in which the flavor of cabbage does not over-whelm and the bacon adds just the right note of fatty smokiness.

1 pound cod fillets	1 clove garlic, minced
3 large potatoes	4 cups cabbage, in ½-inch slices
4 slices bacon, chopped	1 teaspoon salt
1 cup sliced onions	1 or 2 turns of freshly ground
1½ cups peeled, seeded, and	pepper
diced fresh or canned Italian	3 tablespoons butter
plum tomatoes	

1. Boil unpeeled potatoes in salted water to cover until nearly done. Drain. When cooled, peel and cut into thick slices. You should have 1½ to 2 cups. Set aside.

2. Cut fish fillets in crosswise pieces. You will need 12 slices about 2 to 2½ ounces each. Set aside.

3. Preheat oven to 375 degrees.

4. In an ovenproof skillet, saute bacon to render its fat, but do not cook it too crisp. Add onions, tomatoes, and garlic and saute 2 minutes. Add cabbage, salt, and pepper.

5. Use 1 tablespoon butter to grease kitchen foil or parchment, and cover skillet with it. Place in oven and bake for 20 to 25 minutes or until cabbage is cooked but still fairly resilient. Toss to mix ingredients.

6. Using 1 tablespoon butter, grease a large ovenproof casserole or gratin pan and layer with potato slices. Cover potato slices with half of cabbage mixture, then lay pieces of fish on top. Cover with the remaining cabbage mixture. Using the last tablespoon of butter, dot the top. Cover loosely with foil and bake 12 to 15 minutes.

Serves 4. Approximate nutrition information per serving: Calories 460; protein 26g; fat 25g; carbohydrates 32g; sodium 890 mg.

Cod Irene

This is not an elaborate dish with complicated cooking, but a quick way to make a fish dish that is flavorful. At first glance, you might suspect that the mayonnaise emulsion would break down and separate, but it does not. And the flavor it imparts when mixed with sour cream is a delightful surprise. The recipe was suggested by Irene Maston, a friend of ours, and chef at Bumbershoots Restaurant, in Framingham, Massachusetts.

20 ounces cod fillets
1 cup mayonnaise
½ cup sour cream

¼ teaspoon salt
pinch of white pepper
1 teaspoon minced fresh dill

1. Cut the fillet on the bias into crosswise medallions. There should be 8 to 12 medallions, 2 or 3 for each diner.

2. Butter a cookie sheet or other ovenproof pan large enough to hold all the fish. Arrange each diner's portion in closely overlapping pieces, spaced about the pan so that each serving can be removed easily as a unit with a spatula.

3. Combine all the other ingredients and mix well. You may double the recipe for larger servings, but remember to keep the ratio of sour cream to mayonnaise at 2 to 1. Correct the seasoning of the sauce.

4. Refrigerate the pan and the sauce at this point for several hours, if desired.

5. Preheat oven to 425 degrees. Mound the sauce atop the fish. Keep it away from the edges, because if it runs onto the pan it will break down and burn on the hot metal.

6. Bake 10 minutes for each inch of thickness of fish measured at thickest point — a ¾-inch-thick piece will require about 7½ minutes. The sauce should acquire a mellow glaze.

7. Serve immediately on warmed plates.

Serves 4. Approximate nutrition information per serving: Calories 570; protein 26g; fat 50g; carbohydrates 3g; sodium 575 mg.

Warm Cod Salad

This is an excellent first course summer salad. Cod's ability to separate into large flakes makes it expecially suitable for a salad and the potency of the dressing is a good foil for the blandness of the fish.

You could prepare this dish up to two hours ahead of serving it. Rewarm the fish in a 225-degree oven. It should be served slightly warmer than room temperature so that its flavors can be fully appreciated.

1 pound cod or haddock (4
    steaks, 4 to 5 ounces each)
1 bunch watercress
1 small head soft lettuce (Boston,
    bibb, limestone)
1 small ear corn, about ½ cup
    kernels
½ cup dry white wine
½ teaspoon salt
good pinch of pepper

DRESSING:
4 tablespoons olive oil
2 tablespoons balsamic vinegar
1 turn of freshly ground pepper
½ cup sliced mushrooms
½ cup peeled, seeded, and diced
    fresh tomatoes

OPTIONAL GARNISH:
2 cherry tomatoes, halved

1. Wash lettuce and watercress, drain and reserve. Blanch corn and scrape off the kernels.

2. Preheat oven to 350 degrees.

3. Combine white wine, salt, and pepper in an ovenproof skillet over medium heat and poach cod steaks just until liquid is hot. Cover with buttered foil or parchment and place in preheated oven for 10 minutes, or for 10 minutes for each inch of steak thickness. Reserve the contents of the pan to make dressing.

4. Remove steaks. Flake, cover, and keep warm.

5. Make the dressing: Return pan liquids to fire and reduce over high heat to about 2 tablespoons. Add balsamic vinegar, olive oil, and pepper, stir, and remove from heat. Correct the seasoning; the mixture should be potent.

6. Mix two-thirds of dressing with corn, watercress, mushrooms, and diced tomatoes. Toss lightly. Reserve remaining dressing to moisten finished salad.

7. Refrigerate all the ingredients of the dish up to 2 hours, if desired. Just rewarm the fish in a 225-degree oven before continuing.

8. Spread a bed of lettuce on 4 salad plates. Divide three-quarters of the vegetables among the plates. Divide the flaked cod among the plates, piling

it in the center atop vegetables. Top the cod with remaining vegetables and drizzle some of remaining dressing on each serving.

9. Top with cherry tomato halves, if desired, and serve.

Serves 4. Approximate nutrition information per serving: Calories 255; protein 22g; fat 14g; carbohydrates 10g; sodium 484 mg.

Confit of Pollock and Leeks

A minimum of ingredients and a minimum of work, but the finished dish is a rich and flavorful combination that makes the best of cod's mild flavor.

20 ounces of pollock, hake, or cusk fillet(s)	½ cup dry white wine
2 tablespoons butter	2 medium leeks, white part only, sliced thinly, about 1 to 1½ cups
2 tablespoons minced shallots	
salt	1 cup heavy cream

1. Preheat oven to 375 degrees. Cut fish into 2 x 2-inch pieces.

2. Using 1 tablespoon of butter, grease an ovenproof pan. Sprinkle shallots over butter, add fish, season lightly with salt, and sprinkle with ¼ cup of wine. Cover with buttered foil or parchment and bake 10 minutes, or 10 minutes for each inch of thickness of fish measured at thickest point.

3. Meanwhile, in a wide skillet or pan, saute leeks lightly in remaining 1 tablespoon butter; do not color. Add remaining ¼ cup wine, cover, and simmer, stirring occasionally, until tender.

4. Remove fish from oven and set on serving platter. Cover and keep warm.

5. Add the baking pan juices to leeks and reduce to ¼ cup. Add cream and reduce to ½ cup. Before finishing the reduction, add to cream any liquids drained from reserved fish. Correct seasoning, pour sauce over fish, and serve.

Serves 4. Approximate nutrition information per serving: Calories 390; protein 27g; fat 29g; carbohydrates 6g; sodium 325 mg.

Fish with Pickled Vegetables

■■

This dish has quite a few steps, but the pickled vegetables may be prepared 4 or 5 days in advance, and the dressing may be made a day in advance. The last steps won't be terribly time consuming.

Cod or haddock fillets are suggested for use because of the way these fishes can be separated into large flakes. You can use either one large skinless and boneless fillet or several fillets that add up to 1 pound.

The vegetables listed here are only suggestions. You may use vegetables you prefer. Quantities are not exact, either. You are striving for variety in color, texture, and taste of more or less equal amounts of vegetables.

The vegetables are going to be placed in salted layers in a wide, deep container that will keep everything compact — a crock or large wide-mouth jar or plastic refrigerator jar will serve. It will have to be slightly larger than 6 cups. Salt each layer liberally; don't be afraid, you will eventually get rid of the salt.

1 pound skinless and boneless cod or haddock
1 cup onion, cut in vertical wedges ½-inch wide
1 cup broccoli flowerets
1 cup carrot sticks, ½ x ½ x 3 inches
1 cup celery, cut similar to carrots
1 cup zucchini, unpeeled, cut in thick wedges
1 cup sweet red pepper, cut in vertical strips
6 tablespoons coarse (kosher) salt, or more

¼ cup red wine vinegar
1 cup water
1 teaspoon salt

Dressing:
3 tablespoons Dijon mustard
white pepper to taste
1½ tablespoons lemon juice
1½ teaspoons minced fresh ginger
¾ cup oil

head of lettuce

1. Combine cut vegetables and toss to mix.

2. Place about one-sixth of the mixed vegetables in container, cover with at least a tablespoon of salt. Repeat layering and salting until vegetables are used up. End with a top layer of salt.

3. Put the covered container in the refrigerator overnight. Do not allow the vegetables to stand with salt for more than 24 hours or they will get mushy.

4. The next day, remove salted vegetables from refrigerator, place under cold running water and wash thoroughly, removing all loose salt.

5. Boil 2 quarts water, plunge vegetables into it, return the water to a boil. Drain immediately, but do not cool. Place in warm bowl.

6. Bring vinegar to boil and pour over warm vegetables in bowl. Toss and allow them to stand until cooled. At this point, the vegetables may be kept in the refrigerator for 4 or 5 days.

7. One day in advance of serving, you may make the dressing. Place mustard, pepper, lemon juice, and ginger in a blender or food processor with 1 teaspoon or so of oil and begin to whip. With the motor running, pour in the remainder of the oil slowly, as in making mayonnaise. Refrigerate, covered.

8. On the day you plan to serve the dish, place fish in 1 cup water with 1 teaspoon salt in ovenproof pan. Cover loosely with buttered foil or parchment. Heat atop burner until the water is at simmer. Then, bake in a preheated 375-degree oven until done and fish flakes easily when tested with a fork — about 10 minutes per inch of fish measured at thickest part. Remove fish from water and allow to cool.

9. Toss the vegetables with all but ¼ cup dressing.

10. Separate and wash lettuce. Pat dry and make a bed with whole leaves on a platter. Flake fish and mound it in center of platter. Arrange vegetables attractively around fish.

11. Chill completed salad if you like, a couple of hours.

12. To serve, spoon a bit of reserved dressing over fish and serve.

Serves 4. Approximate nutrition information per serving: Calories 530; protein 25g; fat 42g; carbohydrates 15g; sodium 1340 mg.

Whiting Colbert

Colbert is a classic and simple French style in which whole fish is boned through the back, dipped in egg wash, crumbed, and crisply pan-fried. A portion of seasoned cold butter is placed in the cavity created by boning to melt into the hot flesh.

Buy whole fish; you do not want fish eviscerated for this dish. You will remove the backbone and ribs from the top or back of fish. While this operation might sound difficult, it is not. It is much like deboning a chicken breast. See the drawing on the right, and also refer to the step-by-step drawings on pages 230 and 231.

4 whole whiting about 6 ounces each, or two 1-pound fish	2 cups fresh breadcrumbs
flour for dusting	1½ tablespoons vegetable oil
	2½ tablespoons butter
	8 slices cold maître d'hôtel butter (see page 68)

EGG WASH:
1 egg
1 tablespoon water
1 tablespoon oil
¼ teaspoon salt
pepper to taste

1. With large kitchen shears, remove fins from fish and trim away most of tail.

2. With a sharp knife, take out backbone. Begin just behind head (above gills) of fish, making an incision close to and on one side of backbone. Cut the back nearly to the tail. Do the same on the other side of the backbone, so that you have two parallel cuts down the length of the fish on either side of the backbone.

3. With the point of the knife, begin cutting deeper into fish, staying close to ribs, which extend down the sides from the backbone in an inverted "Y" shape. Keep the knife blade close to the ribs so as not to remove too much flesh. When you have exposed the skeleton, sever the backbone at head and tail with kitchen shears or knife. Lift out the backbone and rib cage. Clean out entrails and wash the stomach cavity well. Repeat with all fish.

4. Spread fish flat so that the cavity is open and oval-shaped.

5. In a bowl, mix egg, oil, water, salt and pepper.

6. Dust fish with flour, shake off excess, and then dip into egg wash. Drain. Dredge fish in breadcrumbs, patting so that crumbs adhere well.

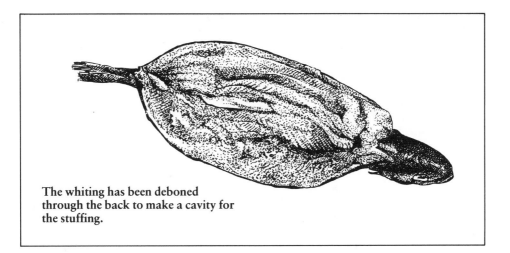

The whiting has been deboned
through the back to make a cavity for
the stuffing.

Shake off excess. Each step should cover fish thoroughly.

7. Heat butter and oil. Place fish, back- or open-side down (so that it
will be right-side up when it finishes cooking) into the hot skillet and cook
over medium heat until browned. Turn over and brown the other side,
basting. Cooking should take 4 to 5 minutes per side.

8. Remove to serving platter and place 2 slices of maître d'hôtel butter
in the cavity of each fish (about 1½ ounces depending on size). Serve immediately with lemon wedges.

Serves 4. Approximate nutrition information per serving: Calories 450;
protein 31g; fat 30g; carbohydrates 14g; sodium 370 mg.

Curried Hake

■■

This recipe produces a dish with mild curry flavor. If you prefer your curry with a more pronounced flavor you may increase quantity up to 2 tablespoons using either a commercial brand or your own favorite curry blend.

20 ounces of hake, cod, or
    haddock fillet(s)
½ cup finely chopped onions
2 tablespoons butter
1 tablespoon curry
1½ cups heavy cream

½ teaspoon salt
½ cup peeled, seeded, and
    chopped fresh or canned
    Italian plum tomatoes
1 tablespoon minced fresh
    parsley

1. Cut hake into pieces about 2 x 2 inches.
2. Saute onion in 1 tablespoon butter until it is soft and lightly colored. Add curry and cook for 1 minute while stirring.
3. Add cream and salt and cook for 2 minutes longer.
4. Preheat oven to 375 degrees. Butter an ovenproof dish or pan with remaining butter and lay pieces of fish on top. Cover with cream mixture. Bake 12 minutes. Remove fish to a serving platter, cover, and keep warm.
5. Pour the sauce from the cooking pan into a wide pan or skillet. Over high heat, stir in chopped tomatoes and reduce by half or until thick. Pour any liquid from the standing fish into the sauce before you have finished reducing it. Correct the seasoning.
6. Pour sauce over fish, sprinkle with parsley, and serve.

Serves 4. Approximate nutrition information per serving: Calories 500; protein 28g; fat 40g; carbohydrates 7g; sodium 470 mg.

Cod Crecy

In France, where such things are the subject of examination and debate, the district of Crecy just outside Paris is noted for the quality of its carrots — the finest of France. A dish bearing the name Crecy in its title therefore is certain to contain this root vegetable. Lovers of carrots will be especially fond of this recipe in that the very essence of carrot is collected first and used to color and enhance the flavor of the final dish.

20 ounces skinless, boneless cod fillet(s)	2 tablespoons minced shallots
2 tablespoons carrot extract	½ teaspoon salt
½ cup reserved carrot juice	3 to 4 turns freshly milled pepper
1 cup carrots cut in fine julienne	¾ cup dry white wine
2 tablespoons butter	1 cup heavy cream
2 tablespoons water	4 small sprigs parsley

1. Make carrot extract, as described on page 40, saving ½ cup of the liquid obtained in the last step of preparation.

2. Cut cod fillets crosswise into medallions about 1 inch thick.

3. Saute julienned carrots in 1 tablespoon butter for 1 minute. Add 2 tablespoons water, cover, and cook until tender. Then, remove cover and cook, tossing, until water has evaporated and carrots have a nice glaze. Cover and keep warm.

4. Preheat oven to 375 degrees. Using remaining tablespoon butter, grease the bottom of an ovenproof skillet and sprinkle with shallots. Add salt, pepper, carrot juice, white wine, and cod pieces. Heat atop the stove. Then, cover loosely with kitchen foil and bake in the preheated oven 8 to 10 minutes or until the cod is done when tested.

5. Remove the cod from the pan to a hot plate, cover, and keep warm.

6. Reduce pan liquids to about ¼ cup, add cream, and reduce over medium-high heat for 2 to 3 minutes, adding any liquids that have accumulated from the standing fish pieces. Reduce until the liquid has thickened to the point where it will coat the back of a spoon.

7. Strain, return to a clean skillet. Add the carrot extract, stir, and heat through. Correct the seasoning. You should have about 1 cup of liquid.

8. Place a pool of sauce on a warm platter or individual plates. Lay fish on top. Garnish with julienned carrots and parsley.

Serves 4. Approximate nutrition information per serving: Calories 410; protein 27g; fat 29g; carbohydrates 10g; sodium 410 mg.

Pollock with Scallops

■■

Americans don't make as much use of cabbage as do some other cultures, probably because we too frequently encountered it plain and boiled beyond redemption. In the land of the polka, mazurka, and polonaise, it is treated with more appreciation, and this dish with pollock, scallops, and cream would find a ready audience.

We recommend pollock or any cod, but you can also use ocean catfish, sole, or tilefish.

You can prepare this dish up to 6 hours ahead, up to the final baking, and keep it, covered, in the refrigerator. Allow it to come to room temperature while you preheat the oven.

8 ounces raw skinless pollock fillet	1 tablespoon butter
4 ounces raw sea scallops	¼ cup finely minced onions
2 tablespoons minced fresh parsley	½ teaspoon salt
1 small head of cabbage (Savoy if available)	freshly ground black pepper
	½ clove garlic, minced
4 slices white bread	1½ cups peeled, seeded, and diced fresh or canned Italian plum tomatoes
½ cup heavy cream	

1. Chop fish and scallops into bite-sized pieces. Do not use a food processor or food mill, as you want coarsely chopped pieces for this dish. Toss with parsley. Set aside or in the refrigerator while you proceed with the rest of recipe.

2. Separate the head of cabbage; wash; remove and reserve tough parts. Blanch the cabbage leaves in boiling water for 1 minute. Plunge into cold water to prevent further cooking and to set the color. Select the best leaves for stuffing; if they are small or oddly shaped, you may need 2 leaves for each packet. You will be making 8 packets.

3. Chop bread into ½-inch pieces and soak in the cream.

4. Chop enough of the less tough parts of cabbage to make ½ cup.

5. Saute onion in 1 tablespoon butter until transparent. Add the chopped cabbage and saute for 2 to 3 minutes more.

6. Allow onion-cabbage mixture to cool somewhat and add to reserved fish. Add softened bread and cream, salt and pepper, and mix.

7. Fill reserved cabbage leaves with the fish mixture and roll up. Set filled packets, seam-side down, in buttered ovenproof baking dish. Cover

with buttered kitchen foil or parchment. (If dish is to be baked later, cool and refrigerate at this point.)

8. Preheat oven to 350 degrees. Bring packets back to room temperature, then bake for 20 minutes. Mix tomato and garlic together and add to the pan around the cabbage, cover again, and bake 10 minutes more.

9. Remove cabbage packets to a serving dish, cover, and keep warm. Cook pan juices in baking dish, or in a clean saucepan, for another 10 minutes to reduce and thicken. Correct seasoning. The sauce should be liquid, but not at all soupy. Pour over the cabbage and serve immediately.

Variation: Add 1 tablespoon of minced scallions and 1 teaspoon of minced fresh ginger to the stuffing when you add the chopped cabbage to onion.

Serves 4. Approximate nutrition information per serving: Calories 312; protein 22g; fat 16g; carbohydrates 21g; sodium 560 mg.

Steamed Fish and Vegetables

There is no way to hide less than perfect ingredients when you steam foods — the process reveals and enhances whatever flaws the raw food incorporated. On the other hand, there is no better way to appreciate natural flavors. If you are going to prepare this dish, choose your ingredients with great care. Confine your choices to raw materials that are in season and unquestionably fresh.

The seafood you use is optional; plan 4 to 5 ounces for each serving. You may use cod or other lean fish; salmon or swordfish; shrimp, scallops, or mussels, to name just a few of the available choices. Cut fillets crosswise on the bias. They will steam more efficiently and look better on a plate. From ¾- to 1-inch of thickness is best for steaming.

When preparing vegetables for steaming, remember that the more tender the vegetable (tomatoes and zucchini, for example), the larger you should make the pieces; the tougher they are, the smaller the pieces (as with carrots and celery). This is especially true when you are going to steam a number of different vegetables and want them all to be cooked at the same time.

Before cutting up the vegetables, determine the steaming time for the fish by measuring it at the thickest part and allow 10 minutes for each inch of thickness. If fish is 1-inch thick and will therefore take 10 minutes to steam, you can cut each vegetable so that it will take about 10 minutes to cook.

If you are going to use two or three vegetables, plan about ¼ cup (or 3 to 4 slices or pieces of each) for each diner.

Carrots can be cut in fine julienne strips about ¼-inch square and 2 or 3 inches long. You can make them ⅛- or ½-inch square to regulate their cooking time. Celery, turnips, and similar vegetables should be cut in the same manner.

Sweet bell peppers should be cut in strips no thicker than ½-inch, but again, you can manipulate the steaming time by how you cut them.

Zucchini, depending on size, can be cut in pie-shaped wedges 2 to 3 inches long and up to ¾-inch thick at their thickest point. They also can be thickly sliced. Very small zucchini can be cut in stubby rounds 2 to 3 inches long. It is best not to peel zucchini or summer squash; the skin helps to keep the inner flesh intact and firm.

Cut tomatoes in half if small or into quarters or 6 wedges if very large. Mushrooms should be sliced; broccoli or cauliflower separated into small flowerettes.

Pea pods and string beans (if not too long) should be left whole. Cut fresh corn on the cob crosswise into 1-inch thick slices. Stick sturdy toothpicks into corn before steaming to make dipping into melted butter easier.

The water in a steamer should be boiling when you put the ingredients in; start timing at that point.

If you own two steamers, or a Chinese-inspired steamer of two or three tiers, you will be able to prepare your fish and vegetables at the same time with no difficulty. If you use one or two inexpensive collapsible steamers, make sure that when they are opened to their widest they fit snugly inside the pot or pots you are using. Colanders, strainers, and the like can often be used to make a makeshift steamer.

Arrange fish and vegetables on steamer rack, salt lightly, and bury seasonings among them. Steam until vegetables are cooked to the degree you prefer.

You need not have half the meal cold if you are forced to steam the ingredients in two batches. Remove the first batch of vegetables from the steamer, set them onto a warm plate, and cover with a clean kitchen towel wrung out in hot water. Keep the plate in a warm place or in an oven at its lowest setting (140 to 200 degrees) until the second batch is ready.

It is better to serve steamed dishes on a warmed platter "family style" if you are serving more than 2 persons, so that the time from stove to table is as short as possible and ingredients won't cool as quickly as they would if you arrange them on individual plates.

Serve with drawn butter, lemon butter, hollandaise sauce or green hollandaise (page 54.) If you must eschew butter, your meal need not be bland. You can season with herbs: a sprig or two of thyme, tarragon, chives, coriander leaves, parsley, basil, or mint. Using garlic, scallions, onions, or slivers of fresh ginger nestled among the vegetables or fish, will brighten the blandest of foods. Wedges of lemon also will provide more flavor.

Servings and nutrition information cannot be estimated.

Steamed Whiting with Mushroom Sauce

The steamed flesh of this close relative of the cod is especially mild and digestible and a perfect foil for the mushrooms and cream sauce.

You should have 8 whiting fillets in all, each weighing 2½ to 3 ounces. You may substitute fillets from other lean white fish such as flounder, ocean perch, or sea bass, in which case you may have only 4 fillets weighing about 5 ounces each.

See the above recipe for general information on steaming fish.

20 ounces whiting fillets
2 cups quartered mushrooms
1 cup heavy cream
salt and pepper to taste

2 egg yolks
1 tablespoon freshly squeezed
  lemon juice

1. In a food processor, work mushroom quarters only until they are coarsely ground, not pureed to a paste. The sauce must have not only the flavor of mushrooms, but some of the texture.

2. Boil the cream in a skillet, add mushrooms, salt, and pepper, and cook 8 to 10 minutes.

3. Remove from heat and vigorously whip in egg yolks with a wire whisk. Add lemon juice while continuing to whip. Correct seasoning. Reheat, but do not allow sauce to boil.

4. Meanwhile, steam whiting 10 minutes for each inch of thickness of fillets measured at thickest part. (Half-inch-thick fillets will require 5 minutes of steaming.)

5. Ladle a pool of sauce onto individual warmed serving plates and place fillets atop sauce. Serve immediately.

Serves 4. Approximate nutrition information per serving: Calories 475; protein 31g; fat 37g; carbohydrates 4g; sodium 240 mg.

Cod with Three Sauces

To a lover of seafood, it all looks beautiful. But there is something especially appealing about a whole steamed white fillet on a platter surrounded with vegetables, the rising heat wafting its sea-fresh aroma to waiting diners. It speaks of purity and wholesomeness; the goodness of a simple home-cooked meal.

The suggested sauces add needed piquancy or robustness to contrast with the blandness of the steamed fish.

Buy two skinless and boneless cod fillets of about 10 ounces each if you can or one large fillet. Do not use smaller pieces.

Potatoes should be whole, of a size for each to make a good portion for one person. Carrots should be peeled and washed and cut 2 to 3 inches long so that 2 pieces would be adequate for one diner. You may substitute or add leeks, cardoons, pea pods, celery, cooked chick peas, fresh peas, cauliflower, wedges of acorn squash, or whole shallots. If you wish to use a different sauce, you may substitute tomato concassée. All sauce recipes are found in the chapter on sauces.

20 ounces cod, haddock, or scrod

AN ASSORTMENT OF
INGREDIENTS SUCH AS:
4 eggs
4 medium potatoes
8 chunks carrot
8 pearl onions
1 cup broccoli flowerettes

4 white turnips, cut in half
1 cup string beans

¼ cup butter, melted (optional)
about ½ cup each of aîoli, green
   hollandaise, and
   anchovy-flavored
   mayonnaise

1. Steam the fish allowing 10 minutes for each inch of thickness measured at the thickest part. (Refer to the recipe for Steamed Fish (page 124) for general steaming information.)

2. Hardboil the eggs, and peel and quarter them. You'll probably want to steam the other ingredients, but the potatoes and carrots may be cooked in water. Steam as many of them as you can, matching their steaming time with that of the fish, as closely as possible.

3. Serve hot fish on a warmed platter surrounded by hot vegetables. Drizzle melted butter over ingredients. Pass sauces.

Serves 4. Approximate nutrition information per serving, without sauce: Calories 460; protein 38g; fat 18g; carbohydrates 36g; sodium 255 mg.

Dried Salt Cod

You needn't look down your nose at this staple that was used by European peasants from Scandinavia to the Mediterranean for centuries before the advent of refrigeration. The French use it to make their famous *brandade de morue* by pounding it to a paste with olive oil, milk, and garlic and serving it with fried bread. (Lydia Shire, chef at the Bostonian Hotel in Boston, combines *brandade de morue* with caviar and potatoes. The recipe appears on page 131.) The Portuguese are so fond of it they have devised more than 100 recipes for its use. In Spain it is most often seen prepared *à la vizcaina*, layered with tomatoes, onions, and red peppers, and baked. In Bermuda it is made into a traditional breakfast dish. In Italy, it is considered worthy of the Lenten Christmas Eve dinner.

We have incorporated it here not only because it is easily obtained all year, but because it can be used to make excellent and varied dishes with a unique flavor. We've even created a happy marriage between the bean and the cod in "Boston Cassoulet." It fits in with today's awareness of "sophisticated rustic" dishes — as owner-chef Moncef Madeeb of Boston's L'Espalier restaurant has termed them — that hark back not only to this country's early days, but also to the varied heritage of many Americans.

Not all salt cod is the same. For one thing the sodium chloride content is highly variable. Some forms are so lightly brined (4 to 5 percent salt content) that they are treated almost as fresh fish. Other cures are 17 to 18 percent sodium, and some more than that. The purity of the salt used in curing the cod is a factor in its quality. The trace elements and minerals in the salt affect the flavor.

There is a difference in the taste and texture of the boxed variety of flaked salt cod (so-called semi-dry) and the whole fish that is sold in ethnic markets as board-hard, flattened, triangular, kite-like slabs.

If you do not live near a market that carries the whole cod, you will have to make do with the boxed variety. While not quite the same as the whole cod, it has convenience on its side, since it comes already skinned and boned in small, easily managed pieces. In recipes where uncooked salt cod is called for, the boxed version is easier to work with, because peeling and boning uncooked whole salt cod, even after soaking, is difficult.

Both styles of salt cod must be soaked before cooking. The longer you soak either style, the less salty it will be. Six hours is the minimum for the boxed variety, and 8, 12, or 16 is better. For whole salt cod, 12 hours is the minimum, but some cooks immerse it for 24 or even 48 hours. The stiffer the fish, the longer its cure, and the longer it will take to get rid of the salt. (Sometimes the market where you buy the whole fish will have pre-soaked it. Ask the dealer how long he has soaked the piece you buy.)

The water should be changed three or four times during the soaking process. You will get better results if you allow tap water to run slowly for an hour into the container in which you are soaking the cod. Some people keep a thin stream of water running into the container throughout the soaking time.

Boxed salt cod increases somewhat in weight after soaking, from 16 to 18 ounces. The whole fish, however, loses weight, going from roughly 3⅓ to 1¾ pounds — 53 ounces to 26 — because of the elimination of skin and bones. Obviously, when buying boxed salt cod, you should buy approximately the amount called for in a recipe. For whole pieces, you will need twice as much dried weight to allow for waste.

When buying whole salt cod, look for white flesh with black skin attached. Soak with the skin side up so that the salt leeches down and out of the fish more efficiently. Try to buy the thickest sections. Yellow flesh is an indication of age; and the older the fish, the saltier.

After soaking either form, parboil the pieces of fish in fresh water. Some cooks like to add a bay leaf, a stalk of celery, and a sprig of thyme to the water. Bring to a boil, immediately remove the pan from heat, and allow the fish to stand in the water 10 to 15 minutes. Drain. Scrape off the fatty skin, and remove any bones. The fish is now ready to be used.

Stockfish often is confused with dried salted cod, but it is different. Stockfish is another cured fish that generally can be found in ethnic fish markets. It is air-cured, not brine-cured as salt cod is. To prepare it, cod, haddock, hake, or a similar white fish is gutted and split, washed and dried. It has its aficionados from Scandinavia to the Mediterranean.

Boston Cassoulet

■■

A MARRIAGE OF BEAN AND COD

And this is good old Boston
The home of the bean and the cod,
Where the Lowells talk to the Cabots
And the Cabots talk only to God.

Cassoulet is a specialty of southwestern France. It is a traditional dish of soaked beans, goose, and/or pork, mutton, or duck, sausages, onions, tomatoes, and garlic. There has been long chauvinistic dispute over which of several towns prepares the "true" or "best" cassoulet. Castelnaudry and the walled town of Carcassone are two of the more ardent contenders. As with the daube, *the name for the dish comes from the pot in which the cassoulet is cooked. It was originally made of clay and called a "cassol d'Issel."*

The connection is almost too obvious, but the challenge to play matchmaker for the two most outstanding culinary citizens of the "Athens of America" was irresistible.

This dish is hearty enough to serve as a one-dish family meal with salad.

1 pound soaked, cooked, skinned, and boned salt cod	½ cup diced onion
1 pound white navy beans	4 peeled, seeded, diced fresh tomatoes or one 1-pound can of whole Italian plum tomatoes
1 medium whole onion	
6 cloves	
1 celery stalk	3 cloves garlic minced, approximately 2 tablespoons
2 whole medium carrots	
½ teaspoon dried thyme	ground black pepper to taste
2 bay leaves	½ cup dry white wine
2 teaspoons salt	½ cup dry breadcrumbs
¼ cup diced salt pork, washed to remove salt	2 tablespoons butter

1. Sort beans, rinse several times, and then set to soak for 6 hours or overnight. Rinse presoaked beans under running cold water, drain, and place in a large pot with the whole onion stuck with the 6 cloves, celery, carrots, thyme, bay leaves, and salt. Cover with water and cook slowly until tender, about 1 to 1½ hours.

2. Alternately, put the sorted and washed beans in a large pot with 2 quarts cold water, bring to a boil, and cook, uncovered, for 1 minute. Re-

move the pot from heat, cover, and let stand for 1 hour. Add the vegetables and seasonings, bring to a boil again, reduce heat, cover, and simmer for 20 minutes.

3. As the beans cook, stir the pot occasionally to prevent scorching, and skim any foam that rises. Add water if the beans get too dry. Cool the beans when they are tender. Remove and discard bay leaves, celery, and onions. Remove carrots and cut them into ¼-inch-thick slices.

4. Spread salt cod out on a towel and flake into bite-sized pieces.

5. Cook salt pork over low heat until light brown, add onion, and saute until onion is soft and transparent. Add diced tomatoes, garlic, pepper, and wine and bring to a boil. Lower heat and simmer for 5 minutes. Add the sliced carrots and the beans. Mix well, but do not mash the beans. Correct the seasoning.

6. Transfer half the bean mixture to an earthenware or other oven-proof pot, arrange the cooked pieces of salt cod over the beans, cover with the rest of the bean mixture, smooth the top, and sprinkle with bread-crumbs. Dot the top with 2 tablespoons butter cut into small pieces. Refrigerate, if desired, several hours.

7. Bake in a preheated 350-degree oven for 30 to 40 minutes. Serve hot.

Serves 4. Approximate nutrition information per serving: Calories 700; protein 60g; fat 15g; carbohydrates 81g; sodium cannot be estimated.

Salt Cod with Caviar
■■
FROM SEASONS RESTAURANT, BOSTONIAN HOTEL, BOSTON

Lydia Shire is executive chef at the Bostonian Hotel, one of Boston's newest hotels. It is located across from Faneuil Hall Marketplace.

Seasons, the Bostonian's main dining room, is a bi-level, glass-roofed, chic setting for Lydia Shire's culinary creations presented on a menu that changes four times a year. The food reflects the growing confidence of young American chefs not only in their own ability and creativity, but in their ability to command ingredients tailored to their needs. Lydia Shire's food is eclectic, as the following recipe suggests, borrowing from the cuisines of Provence or New Orleans and adapting to the taste of her time and place. The French name for the preparation of the salt cod is Brandade de Morue.

1 pound salt cod with bone and skin or ½ pound boneless	salt and freshly ground black pepper to taste
1 small garlic clove, mashed	12 small, new pink potatoes
½ cup heavy cream	coarse salt
½ cup olive oil	1 ounce Osetra or other caviar
½ tablespoon finely minced or grated onion	

1. Make brandade: soak salt cod in cold water overnight or at least 12 hours. Skinless and boneless cod may be soaked somewhat less, but at least 8 hours. Change the water frequently.

2. Poach salt cod in simmering water just until done, about 15 minutes. Drain and flake carefully, removing skin and bone. Add mashed clove of garlic.

3. With a small electric mixer set on low speed or a food processor fitted with the steel blade (or, if you have a strong arm, use a sturdy wire whisk), add ½ cup each of warmed heavy cream and olive oil, working mixture constantly. Check that the consistency is light. Work in the onion. Season with freshly ground black pepper. Taste; add salt if necessary.

4. Meanwhile, preheat oven to 400 degrees. Coat potatoes with olive oil. Sprinkle with coarse salt and roast until soft inside and crisp outside, about 15 to 20 minutes.

5. As soon as the potatoes are ready, place 3 of them on each of 4 warmed salad plates. Spread the brandade on top, and top it with a dollop of fresh caviar. Osetra is expensive, but you may use any caviar your means allow. You also may add a little chopped hardboiled egg and chopped raw red onion as a garnish.

6. Serve this as a first course, or as an appetizer to be eaten with fingers.

Serves 4. Approximate nutrition information per serving: Calories 570; protein 23g; fat 39g; carbohydrates 32g; sodium cannot be estimated.

Salt Cod Souffle

This recipe raises homely dried salt cod as close to elegance as it probably can get. It is a smooth and creamy cloud of a dish set off by a tangy tomato sauce. The preparation through step 2 can be done up to several hours in advance.

8 ounces soaked, cooked, boned,
    and skinned salt cod
5 slices white bread
1¼ cups heavy cream
2 egg yolks
⅛ teaspoon pepper

salt
4 egg whites
softened butter and flour to coat
    mold
Tomato Coulis (page 58)

1. Chill the souffle mold.

2. Chop the bread, including the crusts, and soak the pieces in the cream for 15 minutes. If you are using crusty French, Italian, or similar bread, add an additional ¼ cup of cream.

3. Chop cooked cod into 2- or 3-inch pieces and work in the food processor for 30 seconds. Add pieces of bread and the cream they soaked in, and process just until blended. Add egg yolks and pepper and work until smooth, about 20 seconds. Taste and correct seasoning. Remove mixture from food processor and place in a bowl. (Refrigerate, if you wish.)

4. In a separate bowl, beat egg whites until thickened, add pinch of salt, and beat to soft peaks. With a rubber spatula, combine one-third of egg whites with salt cod mixture. When thoroughly mixed, gently fold in remaining egg whites.

5. Coat chilled mold with softened butter; dust with flour, and shake out excess. Fill with souffle mixture.

6. Preheat oven to 350 degrees. Cook for 35 minutes. Serve immediately with tomato coulis on the side.

Serves 4. Approximate nutrition information per serving: Calories 479; protein 26g; fat 33g; carbohydrates 19g; sodium cannot be estimated.

Morue à la Lyonnaise

SALT COD LYONNAISE

Americans know the Lyonnaise name best through Lyonnaise potatoes, which generally means with onions. Onions are in this dish, with potatoes and dried salt cod, a country-style combination with robust flavor.

1 pound soaked, cooked, and flaked salt cod
2 tablespoons minced fresh parsley
1 clove garlic
2 cups sliced onions
5 tablespoons butter

1 tablespoon oil
6 cups raw potatoes, sliced ⅛-inch thick
½ teaspoon salt
pepper
2 tablespoons red wine vinegar

1. Mince parsley and garlic together.
2. Saute onions in 1 tablespoon butter until brown.
3. Wash potatoes, drain well, and dry on paper towels. In a hot pan, saute potatoes for 20 to 25 minutes in 1 tablespoon oil and 2 tablespoons butter until brown on both sides.
4. Saute cod in remaining 2 tablespoons butter in another hot pan until lightly browned. Add potatoes, onions, salt, and pepper, toss, and add vinegar by pouring it into the side of the pan. Add parsley and garlic. Toss and heat through. Correct the seasoning.
5. Serve hot, right from pan.

Serves 4. Approximate nutrition information per serving: Calories 445; protein 37g; fat 19g; carbohydrates 32g; sodium cannot be estimated.

Cod Cakes Provençal

Codfish cakes were a mainstay of the American Atlantic coast diet since the earliest times. This recipe adds a touch of the flavors of Provence to that staple dish. It may be increased easily.

1 cup salt cod, soaked, cooked, skinned, and boned
3 medium potatoes
2 tablespoons melted butter
1 garlic clove, minced
white pepper
2 tablespoons chopped black olives

flour for dusting
3½ tablespoons butter
2½ tablespoons oil
lemon wedges for garnish
tartar sauce (see page 43)

1. Peel potatoes, cut in two. Place in pot, cover with water. Bring to a boil, cover, and cook until done. Drain extremely well at once. You want as much moisture removed from the potatoes as possible; dry them in oven at lowest setting for 10 minutes. Mash.

2. Break up cod into bite-sized pieces. Mix cod, potatoes, melted butter, garlic, and pepper, and blend thoroughly with a fork. Add chopped olives and mix.

3. Form into 8 patties, each one ½-inch thick and 2½- to 3-inches around. Refrigerate, if desired, a few hours until ready to cook.

4. Dust the patties with flour and fry them in butter and oil until one side is nicely browned; turn and brown the second side.

5. Serve at once with lemon wedges and tartar sauce. In this country, baked beans would be a traditional accompaniment.

Serves 4. Approximate nutrition information per serving: Calories 345; protein 10g; fat 25g; carbohydrates 22g; sodium cannot be estimated.

Morue en Choucroute
••
SALT COD WITH SAUERKRAUT

Boxed salt cod is the better and easier version to use for this dish, since the fish must be boned and skinned before it is cooked. Canned sauerkraut, or that sold in bags, is perfectly adequate unless you normally make your own. Don't have either the sauerkraut or the salt cod too bland because of over-soaking or over-rinsing, as this dish should be robust and assertive in flavor.

1 pound raw, soaked salt cod	1 cup dry white wine
2 pounds sauerkraut	3 or 4 whole juniper berries
½ cup thinly sliced onions	pinch of dried thyme
1 tablespoon butter	⅛ teaspoon cracked black
2 carrots, cut into sticks 1 x 1 x 3	pepper
inches	3 tablespoons butter, melted

1. Cut or shred raw soaked salt cod into bite-sized pieces.
2. Wash sauerkraut slightly.
3. Saute onions in butter in an ovenproof saucepan or other pan large enough to hold sauerkraut comfortably. When the onions are soft, not browned, add carrots, and saute 2 minutes. Add sauerkraut and toss lightly. Add wine, juniper berries, thyme, and pepper. Toss well. Preheat oven to 350 degrees.
4. Cover pan loosely with foil and bake 60 minutes in preheated oven.
5. Remove the pan from the oven and take out half the ingredients. Lay pieces of fish on the bed of sauerkraut in the pan and cover with the ingredients you removed.
6. Loosely cover pan with foil again and return to oven for 20 minutes. Correct the seasoning.
7. Place sauerkraut on warmed platter or warmed individual plates, and lay fish on top. Spoon warm, melted butter over fish. Boiled potatoes are a good accompaniment.

Serves 4. Approximate nutrition information per serving: Calories 325; protein 33g; fat 13g; carbohydrates 15g; sodium cannot be estimated.

Salt Cod Stew

BOUILLABAISSE DE MORUE

Fish stews are common to every coastal region of the world, and Bouilla-baisse Marseillaise is perhaps the best known of them all.

Inlanders, on the other hand, were unable to make fish stew until dried salt cod and other dried fish were available. The following stew uses dried salt cod, with a saffron-whiffed broth for a touch of sophistication.

This recipe is easier to make with boxed salt cod because the fish must be skinned and boned before it is cooked.

1 pound soaked salt cod
2 tablespoons olive oil
½ cup sliced onions
½ cup leeks, sliced crosswise
1 cup seeded and coarsely chopped, fresh tomatoes or canned Italian plum tomatoes
1 clove garlic, crushed
8 peeled potatoes sliced ¼-inch thick
½ cup dry white wine

1 cup fish stock (see White Wine Fumet, page 30) or 1 cup water
freshly milled black pepper
half a bay leaf
¼ teaspoon dried thyme
pinch of saffron
1 tablespoon minced fresh parsley
Rouille or Aïoli sauces (pages 47 and 50)

1. Cut salt cod into bite-sized pieces.

2. Place olive oil in a larger stewing pan, add onions and leeks, and saute over medium heat for 10 minutes, until onions are transparent, not browned. Add tomatoes and garlic and cook for an additional 5 minutes. Add the potatoes with half the cod, cover with wine and fish stock or water. (By putting in half the cod at this point and boiling rapidly, some of the fish will disintegrate and with the help of the potato starch, thicken the broth.) Add pepper, bay leaf, thyme, and saffron, and cook over high heat, uncovered, for approximately 15 minutes.

3. Add the remaining salt cod and cook over lowered heat for 5 minutes more.

4. Sprinkle with minced parsley.

5. Serve hot with crusty bread, accompanied by a rouille or aïoli.

Serves 4. Approximate nutrition information per serving: Calories 514; protein 72g; fat 10g; carbohydrates 31g; sodium cannot be estimated.

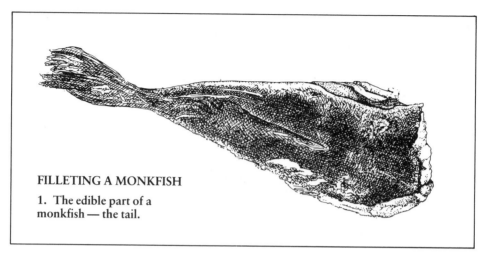

FILLETING A MONKFISH

1. The edible part of a monkfish — the tail.

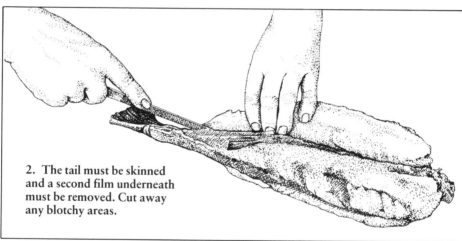

2. The tail must be skinned and a second film underneath must be removed. Cut away any blotchy areas.

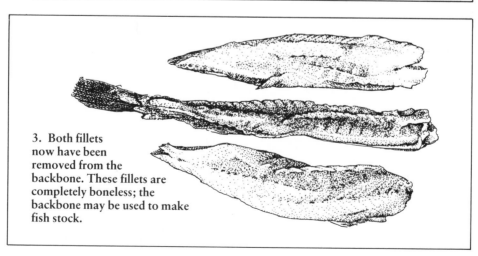

3. Both fillets now have been removed from the backbone. These fillets are completely boneless; the backbone may be used to make fish stock.

Monkfish

■■

The monkfish is also known as lotte, angler fish, goosefish, frog fish, and sea devil. One of its other names is bellows fish, and in the Carolinas it is known as the "allmouth." These names are for its large hinged mouth that enables it to swallow larger fish than would seem possible.

The monkfish is a bizarre creature. Its exceptionally wide mouth has a protruding lower jaw; it has a large rounded head that ends where the tail begins, prickly skin that is mud colored, and the tip of the first ray of the dorsal fin has an elongated bait-like fleshy tab that dangles over its mouth to attract victims.

No wonder fishermen on this side of the Atlantic have been throwing them back for generations.

Yet, it has long been prized by European chefs for its firm, bland, but delicately sweet meat. The color and texture of its flesh resemble that of a lobster, and if mixed with lobster will take on its taste. In fact, monkfish is a flavor carrier and takes on much of the flavor of other seafood with which it is combined — an excellent way to stretch more expensive shrimp or lobster, for example. It can be sauteed, broiled, poached, and baked, and is considered by many European cooks as an essential ingredient in paella and bouillabaisse.

The only part, generally, that is used is the tail section. The skin of the tail is removed by the fishmonger, as is the ugly head (no one would be likely to buy it, otherwise). You usually will have to remove the thin, tough membrane with which it is covered and trim away all discolored spots. (The trimmings save well in the freezer for future use in making stocks.) For this reason, it is always wise to buy more monkfish than what is called for in a recipe (say, 1¼ pounds when 1 pound is what you will need, trimmed).

It also will shrink more than other fish in cooking, especially when thick portions are being used. You should bear this in mind when it might be a factor in the finished dish.

Some chefs seek out the smallest whole monkfish tails of 7 or 8 ounces, which can be trimmed and then served in various recipes like a single fillet from other fish.

The queen triggerfish, which occasionally roams as far north as Cape Cod, is similar, with a flesh that is often compared to frogs legs.

Stuffed Monkfish

■■

This recipe uses thick medallions of monkfish fillet that are cut with a pocket, individually stuffed, and then quickly sauteed.

1½ pounds boneless monkfish
    fillet, skinned
¾ cups fresh breadcrumbs
½ cup heavy cream
4½ tablespoons butter
2 tablespoons shallots
1½ cups diced mushrooms

salt and pepper to taste
2 tablespoons minced fresh
    parsley
2 cups sliced mushrooms
flour for dusting
1 tablespoon oil

1. Trim dark blotch from monkfish fillet, and cut fillet into 8 1-inch-thick medallions, each weighing 2 to 2½ ounces. Cut a pocket in each medallion (see drawings on page 16).

2. Combine breadcrumbs and cream. Soak about 15 minutes.

3. Saute shallots in 1½ tablespoons butter until soft but not browned. Add diced mushrooms and cook 2 minutes. Remove from heat.

4. With a fork, blend breadcrumbs and mushroom-shallot mixture. Add salt, pepper, and parsley, and mix well. Taste and correct seasoning, if necessary.

5. Place 1 tablespoon filling in each pocket. Seal by pressing down on edges. (Refrigerate, if desired, for a few hours until close to dinnertime.)

6. Dredge stuffed fish in flour, pat, and shake off excess.

7. Saute sliced mushrooms in 1 tablespoon butter, season with salt and pepper to taste; this will be a separate garnish. Reserve off the heat.

8. In a large skillet, heat remaining 2 tablespoons butter and oil. Saute medallions until browned on one side. Turn and brown on second side. Saute about 5 minutes in all.

9. Serve 2 medallions to a person, surrounded with some of the sauteed mushrooms.

Serves 4. Approximate nutrition information per serving: Calories 475; protein 38g; fat 30g; carbohydrates 13g; sodium 650 mg.

Monkfish with Fennel, Red Wine and Pistachios

FROM MAISON ROBERT, BOSTON

Lucien Robert has operated a restaurant in Boston for more than three decades. His present location in the old City Hall on School Street in the heart of the city is his third. Each has been a move up to a more prestigious and elegant location; each has seen the restaurant's menu climb to a higher plane — but always in the most rigorous French tradition.

Lucien Robert, originally from Normandy, worked at Prunier's, in Paris, known for generations as that city's finest seafood restaurant, before coming to America. Having worked a stint in the Midwest, he came to Boston and opened Maître Jacques Restaurant in two rooms in the Back Bay in 1957. Later he moved to a modern setting in an apartment building in the city's first urban renewal project, Charles River Park. In 1971 he took over the basement and first-floor quarters in the old City Hall. Downstairs is Ben's Cafe, named in honor of Benjamin Franklin. It is a moderate priced bistro where diners may eat indoors or outdoors in the courtyard in good weather. Upstairs are the high-ceilinged formal dining rooms of the Bonhomme Richard.

If one word had to be found to describe Maison Robert's it would have to be the word "correct," at least as it applies to a French restaurant dedicated to haute cuisine. Although Maison Robert places emphasis on seeking perfection from among the classic repertoire, the following recipe by Chef Pierre Jamet demonstrates that Lucien Robert is keenly aware of the shifts in tastes and direction that are going on in food and seeks to provide his guests with a representation worthy of Maison Robert.

2 pounds monkfish, in one thick piece	1 fennel bulb, finely sliced
½ cup finely chopped peeled pistachios	½ teaspoon dried thyme
	salt and pepper to taste
3 cups red wine	½ cup crème fraîche (see page 70) or heavy cream
½ cup minced shallots	½ cup butter, plus 2 tablespoons

1. Prepare fish: Remove skin and dark blotches from monkfish. Cut into escallops, approximately 12 for 6 servings. Coat each escallop with chopped pistachios, and reserve.

2. Make sauce: Place wine, shallots, fennel, thyme, salt, and pepper in a saucepan. Cook slowly until wine is reduced and vegetables are cooked.

3. Place reduced contents of saucepan in the work bowl of a food processor and puree. Return to the saucepan, add the cream, and reduce until it is thick enough to coat the back of a spoon. Strain. Off the heat, add ½ cup butter while stirring vigorously with a wire whisk. Correct the seasoning.

4. Melt 2 tablespoons butter in a skillet. Saute escallops 2 minutes on each side on medium heat.

5. To serve, ladle a pool of sauce on each plate and add 2 escallops of sauteed monkfish.

Serves 6. Approximate nutrition information per serving: Calories 406; protein 24g; fat 30g; carbohydrates 9g; sodium 520 mg.

Monkfish Belle Meunière

◼◼

" But the plain Meunière is the best, and it is pleasant to think that it might have originated in the Miller's Wife (La Meunière) taking the little trout from her husband's hands, her own large and flowery from baking, throwing the fish into fresh butter, and then when they were cooked, sprinkling a little parsley over them; the lemon, I am sure, came later."
— Madame S.B. Prunier,
in Foreword to *Madame Prunier's Fish Cookery Book*

A meunière — miller's wife's style — as Madame Prunier suggests, is a quickly cooked dish in which the sliced fish is sauteed in hot butter and then served with a simple sauce of butter, parsley, and lemon juice. Madame Prunier knew something about the subject; she, and her father before her, were proprietors of Prunier's, the most famous fish restaurant of its era in Paris and, later, London.

You can use the same butter-oil mixture the fish cooked in to form the sauce, but we suggest you do not. It will have broken down and partly burned in the cooking process and the oil would probably make it too unctuous. Your finished dish will look and taste cleaner if you saute the fish, discard the cooking fat, and make the sauce with a fresh 2 tablespoons of butter. The difference will more than make up for the use of the additional butter.

Our recipe takes only minutes to prepare, but a marination of at least 30 minutes is required before you begin cooking.

14 to 20 ounces monkfish, in one
    thick piece

MARINADE:
fresh parsley
fresh coriander leaves
1 tablespoon fresh lemon juice
1 tablespoon vegetable oil

EGG WASH:
1 egg
1 tablespoon oil
1 tablespoon water
pinch of salt and white pepper

½ cup flour
4 tablespoons butter
2 tablespoons oil
1 lemon, cut in wedges

1. Trim the monkfish, then cut it crosswise on the bias into ½-inch slices.

2. Prepare marinade: Mince parsley and coriander leaves together, to make 2 tablespoons of each. Divide in half, reserving one half. Mix lemon juice, oil, and half the minced coriander-parsley. Toss fish slices in mixture to coat and marinate for 30 minutes or so in refrigerator.

3. Make egg wash: In a bowl, beat lightly with a fork, egg, oil, water, salt, and pepper. Place flour in a flat plate.

4. Remove fish slices from marinade and drain. Dip in egg wash and drain. Dredge in flour, pat into fish, and shake off excess.

5. Heat oil and 2 tablespoons of butter in saute pan until hot but not smoking. Saute fish 2 to 3 minutes on each side until nicely browned.

6. Place fish on a serving platter, cover, and keep warm. Discard cooking fat. Return pan to the heat and add remaining 2 tablespoons of butter and heat until nut-brown. Add lemon juice, then pour it over fish.

7. Sprinkle fish with the reserved minced coriander-parsley. Serve immediately with lemon wedges, and think pleasantly of the miller's wife.

Serves 4. Approximate nutrition information per serving: Calories 240; protein 25g; fat 12g; carbohydrates 6g; sodium 230 mg.

Monkfish Marsala

■□

Veal Marsala is well known. Monkfish works in this recipe because it has something of the same quality of veal — a mild and delicate flavor that takes on the flavor of ingredients it is cooked with. Tilefish would be a good substitute, if necessary.

There is one important caution: Make certain you use dry marsala, or the dish will be as cloying as veal marsala often is in second-rate restaurants, and your fish will taste as though it were cooked in maple syrup or butterscotch. Use more lemon juice, rather than less.

The dish is a basic quick saute that takes only minutes to prepare.

1½ pounds untrimmed monkfish fillet	½ cup dry marsala juice of 1 lemon
salt	1 tablespoon minced fresh
freshly ground black pepper	parsley (optional)
4½ tablespoon butter	
1 cup sliced mushrooms	GARNISH:
flour for dusting	4 lemon wedges
1 tablespoon oil	

1. Trim tough membrane and discolored areas from fillet. After trimming, the fillet should weigh a generous pound. Cut it crosswise on the bias into 12 even slices (medallions) about ¼-inch thick, each weighing about 1½ ounces. This will give you 3 slices, or 4 to 5 ounces, per serving. Press the slices with the heel of your hand to flatten slightly, and season them with salt and pepper.

2. Lightly season mushrooms with salt and pepper and saute in a small skillet or saute pan in 1 tablespoon of butter until browned. Reserve, cover, and keep warm in same pan.

3. Place flour in a flat dish. Dredge fish slices in it. Pat them and shake off the excess.,

4. Meanwhile, melt 1½ tablespoons butter and 1 tablespoon oil in a large skillet over medium-high heat. Get skillet hot, but do not let it smoke.

5. Lay the fish slices in the skillet and brown on one side, about 2 minutes. Turn carefully with a spatula and allow to just pick up color on second side — about 1 minute.

6. Add marsala. Allow fish to simmer another minute, remove, drain a moment and set onto warmed individual serving plates. Cover and keep warm.

7. Return the skillet to high heat and reduce until the liquid will coat a

spoon. Add 2 tablespoons butter and stir to smooth. Lift the skillet from the heat momentarily to prevent a flare-up, and squeeze lemon juice into it. Return to the fire to heat through. Correct seasoning.

8. Return skillet with mushrooms to fire and toss to heat through.

9. Pour the marsala sauce over the fish, arrange the mushrooms on the plates, sprinkle with parsley, and serve immediately. Garnish each piece with a lemon wedge.

Serves 4. Approximate nutrition information per serving, including optional mushrooms: Calories 300; protein 27g; fat 18g; carbohydrates 9g; sodium 790 mg.

Andouillette de Lotte
■■
MONKFISH SAUSAGES

In France, the andouillette *is — as the diminutive ending indicates — a small* andouille, *a form of sausage made largely from what we call chitterlings and tripe. Not a keeping sausage — they last about a week —* andouille *are of ancient origin. A country preparation, though they are enjoyed at all levels of French dining,* andouille *are not intended to be elegant in ingredients or appearance.*

Nowadays, chefs outside of France often give the name of another sausage, the boudin, *to what is really an* andouille. *The reason frequently is not lack of knowledge but a belief that* boudin *sounds more elegant and is easier to pronounce for non-French speaking people. The association of* andouille *with tripe and chitterlings doesn't help its image in this country, either.*

The following recipe, though made with fish, is in the style of the andouille.

The plastic wrap used in this recipe to form the sausages is safe to use in this manner. If you prefer, you may use natural sausage casings. The cooking procedure is basically the same, regardless of which you use.

Natural casings are sometimes available at supermarkets and butcher shops. Use the larger casings (Italian sausage or kielbasa size) for this recipe. Wash casings thoroughly, inside and out, as they have been packed in salt. Rewash in several changes of water. Place an open end over a faucet tap and flush the inside with running water. Natural casings can be tough;

you can tenderize them if you wish, by soaking for 24 hours in papaya or pineapple juice. Rinse after tenderizing.

Use a sausage funnel, or the like, to fill the casings. A pastry bag with a sausage nozzle (called "pig" or "lamb" stuffers) works well. Don't pack too tightly, or the stuffing will split the casing as it expands in cooking. Make sausages to whatever length you prefer — 4 to 5 inches is about right — by twisting casing into links and tying each link off. Prick sausages to allow air to escape.

You can prepare this recipe through step 8, and hold sausages in the refrigerator overnight, but temperature is important, and you must return the sausages to room temperature before proceeding.

1 pound monkfish fillet(s)
1 egg white
½ teaspoon salt
½ teaspoon freshly ground black pepper
1 tablespoon dry white wine or vermouth
1 tablespoon lemon juice
2 tablespoons minced parsley
2 sprigs minced fresh thyme (preferred, or ¼ teaspoon dried)

⅓ cup coarse fresh breadcrumbs
2 tablespoons melted butter
sausauge casings, if preferred

FOR COATING:
⅓ cup butter
1 tablespoon Dijon mustard
1 cup fresh breadcrumbs

Hollandaise-mustard sauce (see page 53)

1. Skin monkfish and trim. A 1-pound fillet should yield about 12 ounces of trimmed meat. Cut into slices about ¼-inch thick and then cut slices across into ¼-inch strips. Chill until cold.

2. Make sausage filling: Place cold monkfish strips in a mixing bowl. Add ½ teaspoon salt and egg white. Stir vigorously with a wooden spoon. Do not mash or beat. The stirring will extract some protein from fish that will combine with the protein in egg white and act as a binding.

3. Add wine, lemon juice, pepper, parsley, thyme, and breadcrumbs, and mix well. Add the melted butter that has been cooled to room temperature.

4. Marinate, chilled, 1 hour.

5. Set a pan of water to a low simmer.

6. To form sausages: Divide filling into 4 equal portions, about 4 ounces each. For each sausage you will need a piece of plastic wrap about 14 inches long (or one natural casing). Place a short end of plastic before you on a flat surface, the length stretching away from you. Lay one portion of filling 2 inches or so from the end nearest you and form into a rough sausage shape. Begin to roll upward, shaping and forming filling and keeping it

compact. When you have reached the far end and the filling is completely encased in wrap, twist the 2 ends of the wrap tightly in opposite directions. Tie a knot in one. Rework the filling within the wrap until you have a nicely shaped 2 x 5-inch sausage and tie the remaining twist of wrap. Complete operation with remaining 3 portions of filling.

7. Poach sausages in barely simmering water with 1 tablespoon salt for 8 minutes, handling them carefully so that the plastic wrap is not pierced or opened and water allowed to enter. Then, remove sausages from water with a slotted spoon and place immediately in cold water bath with ice cubes to "set."

8. Remove sausages when thoroughly chilled. Cut off the tied plastic ends with a scissor and carefully unwrap each sausage. Set on paper towels and pat dry. Natural casings should not be removed. Refrigerate sausages if desired, at this point.

9. Bring sausages to room temperature. Melt ⅓ cup butter, allow it to cool to room temperature, and then mix it with Dijon mustard. Set out a flat plate with the breadcrumbs.

10. Roll each sausage in mustard-butter. (If it is too cold it will be solid and unusable. It it is still too hot, butter will not adhere well.)

11. Roll sausages in breadcrumbs, patting and squeezing gently so that the coating is as even as possible.

12. Preheat oven to 375 degrees. Butter an 8 x 8-inch ovenproof pan and lay sausages into it, leaving space between them so that they will evenly bake and color. Bake 10 minutes until sausages acquire a deep golden brown color.

13. Serve warm with hollandaise-mustard sauce.

Serves 4. Approximate nutrition information per serving: Calories 330; protein 20g; fat 24g; carbohydrates 10g; sodium 820 mg.

Monkfish Stroganoff

The inspiration for this dish is obvious. Originally it was a dish of cubed or finely sliced fillets of beef browned in butter and served in a sauce of chopped onions, white wine, paprika, and sour cream. The name comes from the Russian general who is credited with inspiring it.

It is amazing how compatible the adaptable monkfish is to this recipe.

The freshness and flavor of your paprika may require more than our recipe calls for, so make certain that you taste the sauce along the way. Some paprikas are hot; our recipe, however, calls for sweet. If you prefer stroganoff spicy, you can add a pinch or two of cayenne to sweet paprika.

12 to 16 ounces monkfish
½ cup onions diced in ¼-inch
   pieces
2 tablespoons butter
½ cup sliced mushrooms
1 clove garlic, minced
2½ tablespoons paprika

1 cup dry sherry
½ teaspoon salt
pepper to taste
½ cup sour cream at room
   temperature
1 cup heavy cream

1. Cut fish into strips ⅜ x ⅜ x 3 inches.

2. Saute onion in 1 tablespoon butter until soft, but not browned. Add mushrooms and saute 1 minute, tossing. Add garlic, 1½ tablespoons paprika, and ½ cup sherry. Simmer a minute, remove from heat, and reserve.

3. Toss fish to coat it with the remaining 1 tablespoon paprika mixed with the salt and pepper.

4. Melt remaining 1 tablespoon butter in a clean skillet. When hot, add fish strips and saute, turning to brown all the sides, for about 3 minutes, or until tender. Remove fish, cover, and keep warm.

5. Into the same skillet, add the remaining ½ cup sherry, and reduce it until thick and slightly less than ¼ cup. Add cream and reduce until thick. Add sour cream, heat, and reduce once more until the sauce coats the back of a spoon.

6. Add the onion-mushroom mixture to the reduced sauce and stir to heat through. Correct the seasoning. Add the reserved fish to heat through.

7. Serve over warm noodles or with buttered noodles on the side. Spaetzel are a more traditional accompaniment, but rice also can be used.

Serves 4. Approximate nutrition information per serving: Calories 450; protein 22g; fat 35g; carbohydrates 14g; sodium 460 mg.

Monkfish Liver

Upon first consideration, this recipe might seem an avant-garde incursion from the kitchens of nouvelle cuisine. Not so. Our ancestors were too frugal to waste anything edible. Using "everything but the squeal" of the pig was fact, not fiction.

On the United States East Coast a century and two ago, cod was king, all of him: the tongue, the cheeks, the bladder, the vile-tasting liver oil, and the liver itself, which was usually poached in water acidulated with vinegar. In many cultures, skate liver is considered a delicacy, and shark liver is also eaten. Wherever the lobster is a native, its tomalley, or liver, is considered a special treat. Within the memory of some Bostonians, it was served up at about ten cents a bowl at the downstairs bar of the original Union Oyster House near Faneuil Hall. In any event, the livers of animals from the sea are no recent discovery, and monkfish liver is no exception. It is a frequently featured item at Manhattan's Lutece Restaurant.

Monkfish liver is not fishy, and does not taste like the liver oil one might have had to take as a child. It is served as you would calf's liver.

Those we obtained weighed about 30 ounces and were similar in general configuration to calf's liver. They were a lovely, chamois-soft rosy tan and pink, something like the texture of fois gras. *Monkfish livers are far from universally available, but as the species becomes more popular, they undoubtedly will be.*

1 monkfish liver	pepper to taste
flour	1 tablespoon lemon juice
4 tablespoons butter	1 tablespoon minced fresh
½ teaspoon salt	parsley

1. Trim away any dark or soft areas of liver. Slice on an angle just as you would calf's liver. Dredge in flour and shake off excess.

2. Melt 2 tablespoons butter in a frying pan on high heat. Fry liver in hot butter 3 minutes on each side, and season with salt and pepper. The cooked liver should be pink.

3. Remove liver from pan to a serving dish, cover, and keep warm. Discard cooking butter. Return the pan to the heat and add 2 tablespoons fresh butter and cook until nut-brown. Add lemon juice, pour over liver, and sprinkle with minced parsley.

Serves 4. Approximate nutrition information cannot be calculated.

Blanquette de Lotte aux Petits Légumes

■■

MONKFISH AND VEGETABLES IN CREAM

Blanquette de veau, *veal in a white cream sauce, is the best known of the preparations the French call by this name — "a sauce that coats thickly." Their distinguishing characteristic is subtle delicacy. Just as the veal, or another white meat, such as chicken or rabbit, creates a sophisticated understatement with cream, you will find the monkfish in this recipe performing the same function.*

It is not mandatory that you use the specific vegetables recommended. You can substitute broccoli flowerettes for the zucchini, for example, though the flavor of that vegetable can be dominating. Small white turnip also could be used.

1½ pounds untrimmed monkfish fillet(s)	1 cup dry white wine 1½ cups heavy cream
1-2 celery stalks	½ teaspoon salt
1-2 carrots	2 to 3 turns freshly ground white
1 small zucchini	pepper
green beans	2 tablespoons lemon juice
1½ cups sliced mushrooms	2 egg yolks
12 asparagus tips	½ cup peeled, seeded fresh or
3 tablespoons butter	Italian plum canned
2 tablespoons water	tomatoes cut in ½-inch dice
2 tablespoons minced shallots	

1. Cut celery, carrots, unpeeled zucchini, and green beans into baton shapes — about ⅜- or ¾-inch square by 1½- to 2-inches long to make ¼ cup of each.

2. Trim monkfish and cut it into crosswise medallions, 2 to 3 pieces, 4 to 5 ounces for each serving.

3. Cook vegetables first. Melt 1 tablespoon butter in a skillet. Add carrots, celery, and 2 tablespoons water. Cover and cook about 3 minutes. Add zucchini, cover and cook 1 minute, add mushrooms, asparagus, and green beans. Cover and cook over medium heat until vegetables are almost as tender as you like them, about 6 minutes, and the water has just about evaporated. Remove cover and evaporate the rest of the moisture, toss and shake the pan so that the vegetables cook evenly and develop a nice, even glaze. Cover and keep warm.

4. Melt 1 tablespoon butter in a separate skillet. Add shallots and cook over low heat 1 minute, add wine, and reduce until the liquid is thick enough to coat a spoon. Add cream, ½ teaspoon salt, white pepper, and fish pieces and bring to simmer slowly over medium-low heat. Cook 7 to 8 minutes, or until the fish is done. Remove fish, cover, and keep warm.

5. Over medium-high heat, reduce the liquid in which the fish cooked and pour in any liquid drained from the standing fish. Reduce to about 2 cups. Add contents of skillet to food processor or blender with 1 tablespoon butter, lemon juice, and egg yolks, and blend thoroughly. Return liquid to skillet, adding chopped tomato, cooked vegetables, and the fish. Heat thoroughly, but do not boil.

6. Set fish pieces onto individual warmed serving plates and pour the sauce and vegetables on top. Serve with parsley potatoes, rice, or noodles.

Serves 4. Approximate nutrition information per serving: Calories 635; protein 40g; fat 45g; carbohydrates 14g; sodium 990 mg.

Civet de Lotte
■■

MONKFISH IN RED WINE SAUCE

The name for this dish comes from an old European recipe, called, in French, civet de lievre, *in English, jugged hare. In the original recipe, the hare's blood was used as a thickener. About the only difference is that we have substituted monkfish for the hare, and, because it is fish, not cooked it so long. Although the dish looks long and complicated, it is the same basic procedure one would use in making a beef stew.*

Like most stews, this one gets better with age, so you can make it a day ahead and then reheat it just before serving. Note: If the stew is to be held, there is an important change regarding when you add the fish to the other ingredients that you must observe.

3 pounds monkfish, whole tail
   section

FOR ONION GARNISH:
16 small pearl onions
1 cup water
1 tablespoon butter
½ teaspoon salt
1 teaspoon sugar

FOR MUSHROOM GARNISH:
6 large or 8 medium whole
   mushrooms
1 tablespoon butter

TO SAUTE MONKFISH
MEDALLIONS:
1 tablespoon oil
1 tablespoon butter
salt and white pepper

FOR STOCK:
4 ounces salt pork (optional)
½ cup diced onions
½ cup diced carrots
2 tablespoons brandy
2 cups dry red wine
2 bay leaves
½ teaspoon dried thyme
6 parsley stems
3 cloves garlic, crushed
1 cup water
3 to 4 pounds lean fish trimmings, head, bones, but no
   skin

ROUX:
2 tablespoons butter
2 tablespoons, plus 2 teaspoons
   flour

1. Prepare first garnish; it will cook as you do other things. Into a small pan, placed peeled and trimmed pearl onions, water, butter, salt, and sugar. Cook, covered, allowing the water to simmer and slowly evaporate, shaking occasionally to mix ingredients and allow onions to cook evenly. Remove cover and shake continuously as the last of the water evaporates and onions glaze and brown evenly. Set aside.

2. Remove stems from mushrooms. Chop stems and reserve. Saute

caps in 1 tablespoon butter over medium-high heat until they are evenly browned. Reserve.

3. Wash salt pork, if you are going to use it (about four ¼-inch-thick slices). (In France, salt pork would be traditional in a stew, even in a fish stew that is based on an older hare stew.) Trim salt pork from rind, cut into half-inch dice, cover with cold water, blanch, and strain. Reserve.

4. Trim the monkfish and cut it into small medallions, each about 1¼ inches thick and weighing about 3 ounces. Reserve trimmings.

5. Season medallions lightly on both sides with salt and white pepper. You want medallions to sear quickly, so get a large saute pan or skillet hot before adding 1 tablespoon oil and 1 tablespoon butter. Brown medallions on one side, turn, and brown the other. They do not have to cook through. Remove and reserve, keeping them warm. Allow the fat to remain in pan.

6. In the same pan, over medium-high heat, saute onions until they pick up light color, add carrots, and toss until well browned. Pour off excess fat.

7. Deglaze pan over medium heat with brandy, scraping up browned bits with a wooden spoon. (It will be easier to do this if you remove the onions and carrots to a side bowl while you deglaze.) Add 1 cup red wine to the pan and continue scraping until you have loosened all adhering food particles and browned bits. Pour into a stock pot. Pour the second cup of red wine into the skillet to be certain all bits of food are loosened. Pour into stock pot.

8. Put onion and carrot along with reserved mushroom trimmings, bay leaves, thyme, parsley, garlic, water, the trimmings from the monkfish, and the fish trimmings into the stock pot. Add blanched salt pork if you are using it. Simmer 15 minutes, uncovered.

9. Add monkfish medallions along with any juices they may have released, make sure they are covered with liquid, cover the pan, and simmer 6 to 7 minutes. Remove only the monkfish medallions, reserve, and keep warm.

10. Reduce contents of pan over high heat to about half. You will need 2 cups liquid for the final stew, so it is better to end up with too much liquid at this point. Strain through a sieve into a clean saucepan, mashing ingredients to extract as much flavor as possible. Reduce the liquid to the final 2-cup measure.

11. Make roux: Cook flour in butter over very low heat for about 3 minutes. The roux should be a pale straw color.

12. Add 2 tablespoons of the roux to the 2 cups strained stock. Cook for a few minutes over low heat, stirring. The consistency should be that of medium cream. If it is too thin, add whatever roux remains, and stir again to incorporate. Correct the seasoning. Add the reserved pearl onions and

mushrooms, and simmer over low heat for 4 to 5 minutes.

13. Add monkfish medallions and heat through. Serve in a flat dish, making certain the steaks, onions, and mushroom caps are divided evenly.

14. If you are going to hold the civet overnight, turn off heat and allow stock with onions and mushrooms (step 12) to cool thoroughly before you add the monkfish. Cover with plastic wrap or foil and refrigerate. Heat through before serving.

Serves 4. Approximate nutrition information per serving: Calories 650; protein 40g; fat 45g; carbohydrates 18g; sodium 1150 mg.

Medallions of Monkfish in Cream with Pancetta and Fresh Lemon Verbena

FROM BLUEPOINT RESTAURANT IN PROVIDENCE

At 99 Main Street, in the center of Providence, Rhode Island, the Bluepoint Restaurant has captured the interest of sophisticated diners with innovative dishes like the following created by chef Maureen Pothier.

Pancetta is an unsmoked Italian bacon that is seasoned with pepper and rolled into a sausage shape about the size of a mortadella. It can be found in specialty markets, where you can buy thick slices cut from the round. It generally is used as salt pork is used, and, in fact, salt pork pressed with a little cracked black pepper is a good substitute. Pancetta is salted, but not overly salty in flavor. To approximate it, wash the salt pork, but do not blanch it.

Unless you grow your own lemon verbena, or have a friend who does, you may have trouble finding it. Thyme could be substituted, but even with a few drops of lemon juice, it won't be quite the same.

3 pounds of monkfish, in one
    piece
1 cup dry white wine
1 cup fish stock (see White Wine
    Fumet, page 30)
2 minced shallots
1 teaspoon dried thyme
½ bay leaf, crushed
3 to 6 parsley stems
zest of ½ lemon

2 cups heavy cream
¾ pound pancetta
2 tablespoons olive oil
3 tablespoons chopped fresh
    lemon verbena

GARNISH:
lemon verbena sprigs and lemon
    slices, optional

1. Remove all membrane, dark meat, and bone fragments from monk-fish. Slice into thin medallions on the bias, approximately ¼-inch slices.

2. In a skillet, combine wine, fish stock, shallots, thyme, bay leaf, pars-ley, and lemon zest, and reduce to approximately ¾ cup. Strain and set aside.

3. In another pan, reduce heavy cream to 1 cup. Set aside.

4. Dice pancetta in about ¼ x ½-inch pieces. Saute in olive oil over medium-low heat until lightly browned. Remove with a slotted spoon and set aside.

5. Quickly saute monkfish medallions, a few at a time, in the same pan until almost done — approximately 2 minutes each side. Remove to a plate and continue until all of the fish has been cooked.

6. Deglaze pan with wine reduction. Add reduced cream, pancetta, chopped lemon verbena, and monkfish along with any juices that have col-lected on the plate. Shake pan gently to heat all ingredients through.

7. Serve on a heated platter with optional garnish of lemon verbena sprigs and lemon slices.

Serves 4. Approximate nutrition information per serving: Calories 1000; protein 73g; fat 70g; carbohydrates 15g; sodium 480 mg.

Monkfish and Crab Salad

This recipe uses the same basic recipe as on page 183, except that the fish is removed from the roasting pan and allowed to cool. When it has cooled (it may even be chilled, making it easier to slice) it is used in a salad with crabmeat. It makes a superb summertime meal for company.

The sauce is handled in much the same way, except that the wine and butter of the other recipe are omitted and mustard and oil are substituted to create a mayonnaise-like dressing that marries well with the cool ingredients.

You may get ingredients — the dressing, crabmeat, fish, and lettuce — ready well ahead of serving and keep them chilled separately, but for maximum flavor, the dish should be served cool, neither cold nor warm.

If you'd like a dressing with texture, use a whole-grain mustard, such as those from France (moutarde de Meaux), Germany (Dusseldorf), or California.

5 pounds monkfish, weighed untrimmed with skin on, in one piece, bone-in	2 or 3 whole unpeeled shallots
	2 lemons, peeled, pith removed, sliced thinly
4 fresh crabs or 6 ounces fresh crabmeat	1 head of bibb or Boston lettuce
2 tablespoons soft butter	2 tablespoons Dijon or whole-grain mustard
salt and pepper to taste	1 cup vegetable oil
1 tablespoon oil	½ teaspoon salt
2 large or 3 small whole, unpeeled garlic cloves	pinch of white pepper
	1 large firm ripe tomato

1. Boil live fresh crabs in 4 quarts water with 4 tablespoons of salt. Cool, crack, and pick out meat. If crabs are purchased already boiled, crack and pick out meat. You can also buy fresh crabmeat. Carefully pick it over for bits of shell and cartilage. Chill until ready to assemble salad.

2. Preheat oven to 375 degrees. Skin and trim fish of soft or discolored areas. Leave backbone intact. Rub fish with 2 tablespoons soft butter lightly seasoned with salt and pepper.

3. Pour 1 tablespoon oil into 12-inch ovenproof skillet or roasting pan. Pan should not be too high-sided or ingredients will stew rather than roast. Place fish in pan and add garlic cloves and shallots. Distribute lemon slices around and on top of fish.

4. Bake 30 to 40 minutes, or 10 minutes for each inch of thickness measured at thickest point. Baste 2 or 3 times during cooking. Check fish

for doneness at the thickest point near backbone, and remove it from oven when done. Scrape lemon pulp from the fish into the baking pan. Peel garlic and shallots and return to pan.

5. Remove fish from roasting pan. Bone it and separate into 2 fillets, but do not slice. Allow to cool, then chill. Reserve pan juices and allow to cool, but don't chill.

6. Pour the contents of pan into a blender (preferred) or a food processor. Work until smooth. Add 2 tablespoons of mustard and continue to blend. With the motor running, add 1 cup oil in a thin stream, slowly at first, and then increasing the flow, much as you would when making mayonnaise. Add ½ teaspoon salt and good pinch of white pepper and complete blending. Correct the seasoning.

7. Separate lettuce to create a bed of greens on a plate 12-inches in diameter. Tear additional lettuce to make about 2 cups chopped or cut in thin chiffonade strips ¼-inch wide. Wash, roll in paper towels, and put in refrigerator to chill.

8. All the above steps may be done up to 4 hours ahead, or even the night before. Bring all the ingredients to room temperature before completing the preparation.

9. Cut the tomato from the top into 6 to 8 wedges; do not cut through, but leave about ½ inch at the bottom of wedges attached so that you can open tomato into a rosebud design. Scoop out most of the interior and spread wedges open.

10. Place the tomato in the center of a serving plate atop lettuce leaves. Place about ⅓ of the previously shredded lettuce into the bottom of opened tomato and strew the remainder over greens.

11. Toss crabmeat lightly with about 1 tablespoon of the dressing — don't smother it — and place into the tomato atop shredded lettuce.

12. Drizzle remainder of dressing atop lettuce around tomato. Cut monkfish fillets into slices ⅝- to ¾-inch thick and lay in overlapping shingle fashion atop dressing.

13. As you serve the salad, give each person a wedge of tomato with some of the crabmeat, lettuce, and some slices of monkfish.

Serves 4 to 6. Approximate nutrition information per serving: Calories 600; protein 41g; fat 45g; carbohydrates 10g; sodium 600 mg.

Monkfish with Zucchini and Yogurt

This dish not only has superb flavor, but it is an especially good choice for the diet-conscious person, who can eliminate the optional final tablespoon of butter. The trimming of the zucchini is not over-fastidiousness; the bright green peel gives the dish eye appeal.

1½ pounds monkfish fillet	1 tablespoon minced shallots
1 unpeeled, medium zucchini	1 tablespoon butter (optional)
¼ cup water	1 cup plain yogurt at room
1 teaspoon salt	temperature
2 tablespoons butter	4 egg yolks
1 cup dry white wine	

1. Trim the membrane and blotchy spots from monkfish. After trimming, you would have about 20 ounces remaining in one long sausage-shaped piece. Cut this crosswise on the bias into thick slices or medallions that resemble filet mignon or escallops of veal. They should be about 1 inch thick with 2 or 3 medallions for each diner.

2. Wash zucchini, but don't peel it. Trim the ends. Cut into thick rounds 2 or 3 inches long. Cut the rounds into lengthwise wedges ½- to ⅜-inch thick on the skin side. In this way, each piece will get the same portion of seeds and skin. If you cut the zucchini into thick slices, some pieces from the center will have no skin.

3. Place water, ½ teaspoon salt, 1 tablespoon butter, and zucchini in a sauce or saute pan. Cover and cook 5 minutes or until zucchini is nearly cooked the way you like it. Remove cover and cook further, tossing zucchini to evaporate remaining moisture and glaze pieces evenly. Remove from heat, cover, and keep warm. Rewarm them if necessary just before serving.

4. Preheat oven to 375 degrees. Grease an ovenproof pan with 1 tablespoon butter. Place monkfish medallions in the pan in one layer, sprinkle with ½ teaspoon salt, and pour in the wine. Cover pan loosely with aluminum foil and bake for 8 minutes. Remove fish and keep warm.

5. Drain pan liquids into a small skillet, add minced shallots and the optional tablespoon of butter, and reduce over high heat by about half; you should have a shade less than ½ cup. (If you wish to have a smoother, more elegant sauce, strain out minced shallots at this point and return the liquid to the skillet.) Bring to a boil and add yogurt, stirring constantly with a wooden spoon or wire whisk.

6. Beat egg yolks with a fork in a small bowl. Stir some of the hot liquid

into the yolks to warm them, and then pour the yolks into the hot liquid. Cook, stirring constantly, until the yolks have cooked and the sauce is thickened, about 2 or 3 minutes. Do not allow the mixture to boil.

7. Spoon the sauce onto one side of warm individual plates. Arrange the fish medallions in overlapping shingle fashion on the sauce. Arrange warm zucchini wedges in a fan shape on the other side with the bright skin-sides all pointing in the same direction. Serve immediately.

Serves 4. Approximate nutrition information per serving: Calories 310; protein 32g; fat 15g; carbohydrates 10g; sodium 910 mg.

Gigot de Lotte au Citron
■■
'LEG' OF MONKFISH WITH LEMON

This serving of monkfish is bathed with a delicious lemony sauce not unlike a thin hollandaise. A monkfish does not have legs, but since this fish is cooked with its backbone still in place, it resembles, if not a leg of mutton, at least a leg of lamb.

The bone is retained to add gelatin (body) to the finished sauce. You will have to order the monkfish that way in advance, since dealers generally de-bone the fish.

5 pounds monkfish, weighed untrimmed with skin on, in one piece, bone-in
1 stick plus 2 tablespoons soft butter
salt and pepper
1 tablespoon oil
2 large or 3 small whole, unpeeled garlic cloves

2 to 3 whole unpeeled shallots
2 lemons, peeled, pith removed, sliced thinly
½ cup dry white wine
1 tablespoon minced fresh parsley

1. Skin and trim fish of soft or discolored areas. Leave backbone intact.
2. Rub fish with 2 tablespoons soft butter lightly seasoned with salt and pepper.
3. Pour 1 tablespoon oil into a 12-inch ovenproof skillet, or roasting

pan. The pan should not be too high-sided or ingredients will stew rather than roast. Place fish in pan and add garlic cloves and shallots. Distribute lemon slices around and on top of fish. (This can be done ahead, if desired.)

4. Preheat oven to 375 degrees. Bake 30 to 40 minutes (or 10 minutes for each inch of thickness measured at thickest point), basting 2 or 3 times during cooking. Check fish for doneness at thickest point near backbone, and remove it from the oven when done. Scrape lemon pulp from the fish into the baking pan. Remove fish from pan, cover, and keep warm.

5. Peel roasted garlic and shallots, return to baking pan, and add wine. Reduce over medium heat until the mixture is thick and syrupy and coats a spoon.

6. Pour pan ingredients into a blender (preferred) or food processor and work until smooth; add the stick of soft butter a little at a time and continue working until butter is used up. A blender will give you a smoother, fluffier sauce than will a food processor. Correct seasoning, and keep warm.

7. Remove fish from bone; you should get 2 large fillets, one from each side. Slice portions on bias, ¾ to ⅝-inch thick — about 12 to 16 slices; monkfish shrinks a great deal in cooking.

8. Ladle a pool of sauce onto individual serving plates, place 3 or 4 pieces of monkfish in a circle near the center of plate atop sauce. Place an equal portion of minced parsley in the center of each serving.

Serves 4. Approximate nutrition information per serving: Calories 560; protein 52g; fat 35g; carbohydrates 10g; sodium 940 mg.

Porgy or Scup

Although these members of the sea bream family bear an all-American name derived from the coastal Indians, they are found throughout the world's oceans. The Narragansett Indians called them "mishcuppauog," a name that time shortened to "scuppaug," and eventually scup. "Porgy" derived from the same word. The names, scup or porgy, are used interchangeably today. Porgy, however, is the name for other fish of the same family. Therefore, when you are talking about the scup you are referring only to one fish; a porgy can be the same fish or two others. It's the same situation as cognac and brandy: all cognac is brandy but not all brandy is cognac.

For the budding ichthyologist, there are three members of the family that normally get to the American table:

Jolthead porgy: Running up to 8 pounds with an average of 2, the jolthead occurs from Rhode Island, south. It has good flavor.

Red porgy: This is the porgy of the commercial fisherman — it can weigh up to 12 pounds and more. Its habitat is from Long Island, south.

Scup (or porgy) is found from Nova Scotia to Florida, but most abundantly from Cape Cod to Cape Hatteras, especially from April to June. It is a late summer fish in the mid-Atlantic states. The scup is considered a good sport fish. Silver with blue and violet highlights, it can weigh up to 5 pounds but 1 pound is average. Its body is wider than it is long.

Given a choice, choose the larger fish when you can. The scup has many small bones, and a larger fish will contain proportionately more flesh than bones and the meat is therefore easier to remove. Its lean, coarsely grained, firm and flaky flesh has a mild, slightly sweet flavor that reacts best to simple preparations. It also has strong scales that adhere tenaciously; it is easier to scale when it is still wet.

Porgy Baked in Salt-Dough Crust

For this dish, a whole 2 to 2½ pound porgy is enclosed in a circle of rough, easily made dough — something like a turnover, but in the shape of the fish it encloses.

Why go through the trouble? Make it, and the aroma that rises when you open the dough will tell you.

Unlike a pastry dough, such as the puff pastry used to wrap a beef Wellington, this crust is not edible. It is a rough salt dough that serves only to enclose the fish while it cooks. The presentation of a fish cooked this way is more dramatic than fish cooked in parchment or foil, and not really that much more work, since the dough does not require the effort or time of other pastry. Do not salt the fish and do not attempt to eat the dough. It is incredibly salty, but the fish is not.

The fish is not scaled prior to cooking because scales keep the skin intact, making it easier to remove in one piece once cooked.

Black bass, red snapper, or seatrout may be substituted for the porgy.

1 whole porgy, 2½ to 3 pounds, gutted, head and tail intact, unscaled	4 tablespoons soft butter
	3 sprigs fresh thyme or 1 teaspoon dried
2 pounds coarse (kosher) salt	pepper
2 pounds flour	⅓ cup melted butter
2½ cups water	lemon wedges

1. Mix salt and flour in a large bowl. Add water all at once. Work ingredients until a rough dough is formed. It need not be smooth, merely well mixed and cohesive.

2. Roll out the dough quite thick, about ⅜-inch, and in a circle whose diameter is one-fourth again as large as length of fish.

3. Using 2 tablespoons soft butter, coat or brush both sides of the fish as well as the stomach cavity.

4. Preheat oven to 400 degrees. Lay fish on lower half of dough. Place 1 sprig of the fresh herb (or ⅓ of the dried herb) under fish, another sprig or one-third in the cavity, and top with the last. Bring other half over to cover fish. Seal edges and trim excess dough, leaving a 1-inch margin that follows the shape of the fish. Indicate the mouth by scoring the dough with the tip of a knife. Also indicate an eye and make horizontal scorings on the tail. Score scales over the fish. Place on a baking or cookie sheet and bake for 50 minutes. (See the illustrations on pages iii and 1.)

5. It will be more dramatic to remove the fish from the dough at the table rather than in the kitchen. Crack the dough and lift the fish out whole. Remove the skin carefully and separate the fillets. Divide among 4 serving plates, being careful to avoid serving the dough.

6. Serve with melted butter and lemon wedges on the side.

Serves 4. Approximate nutrition information per serving: Calories 516; protein 58g; fat 30g; carbohydrates 3g; sodium cannot be estimated.

Braised Porgy with Fennel

1 whole fish, 2 to 3 pounds, with
   or without head and tail
¼ cup olive oil
1 cup sliced onion
1 cup thinly sliced sweet green
   bell pepper
2 cups peeled, seeded, and diced
   fresh tomatoes, or canned
   Italian plum tomatoes

1 whole fennel bulb
1 garlic clove, minced
salt and pepper to taste
½ cup dry white wine or
   vermouth

1. Put half the oil in a saute pan, add onion, and saute until soft and transparent, but not yet showing color. Add pepper and cook until soft. Add tomatoes and garlic, season lightly with salt and pepper, and reserve.

2. Thinly slice the white part of the fennel bulb.

3. Clean, wash, and scale the fish. Preheat oven to 375 degrees.

4. Season fish inside and out with salt and pepper, rub with oil. Oil an ovenproof dish with remaining oil, arrange fennel slices on bottom, season lightly with salt and pepper, and place fish atop fennel. Pour onion, pepper, and tomato mixture over the fish, add wine, cover with buttered foil, and bake 20 minutes or 10 minutes for each inch of thickness of the fish measured at the thickest point. Baste several times during cooking.

5. Serve immediately.

Serves 4. Approximate nutrition information per serving: Calories 488; protein 56g; fat 24g; carbohydrates 10g; sodium 470 mg.

Porgy Boulangère

If you know your French, you know that a boulangère *is a baker's wife. In culinary parlance, a* boulangère *is a dish that was readily baked in an oven still hot from baking the day's breads.*

This dish is a kind of braise, a one-pot dish with substance and good flavor. Because it is a braise, nothing is lost in flavor if you decide you prefer to cook the fish without its head and tail.

1 whole porgy, with or without head and tail; cleaned, washed, and scaled	½ teaspoon white pepper
	½ garlic clove, finely minced
	½ teaspoon dried thyme
1 large onion, thinly sliced (about ¾ cup)	1 cup chicken stock, consomme, or water
3 tablespoons butter	3 tablespoons vegetable oil
5 medium potatoes, sliced ⅛-inch thick	2 medium or one large tomato, cut in thick slices
2 teaspoons salt	

1. Saute onion slices in 1 tablespoon butter until they take on a light color.

2. Preheat oven to 375 degrees. Grease an ovenproof dish or skillet with the remaining 2 tablespoons butter. Add sauteed onion, potatoes, salt, pepper, garlic, and thyme.

3. Add chicken stock, consomme, or water. Cook in preheated oven for 15 minutes, until potatoes are about three-fourths cooked.

4. Clean, wash, and scale the fish. Salt and pepper it inside and out and wipe with a thin coating of vegetable oil. You might use as much as 2 tablespoons. Lay the whole porgy in the pot on the potatoes.

5. Lay an overlapping strip of the thickly sliced tomatoes atop the fish and bake 8 minutes. Baste with remaining 1 tablespoon of oil, then bake an additional 20 minutes or so. When the potatoes are tender, the fish will be done and the dish is ready to serve.

Serves 4. Approximate nutrition information per serving: Calories 416; protein 26g; fat 23g; carbohydrates 25g; sodium 1440 mg.

Sea Bass

Although the sea bass or black sea bass frequently are called blackfish, that name more generally is applied to the tautog. The sea bass is a handsome fish with small scales in black and white that look like a herringbone weave. It is a fine table fish. The flesh is firm and white and delicately flavored. It is lean to medium-oily. It is a good pan fish, can be worked in a mousse or similar preparations, and bakes well. It is a favorite of Chinese chefs, who use it both as a whole fish for frying and as fillets. Although it can weigh up to 5 pounds, sea bass is marketed most often at 1½ to 3 pounds, which is a useful size for most home kitchens.

Tautog, somewhat firmer in texture (it therefore makes a good chowder fish), would be a good substitute, as would red snapper, seatrout, sea perch, grouper, or croaker.

Black Sea Bass with Rosemary Cream, Wild Mushrooms and Fiddlehead Ferns

••

FROM HARVEST RESTAURANT, CAMBRIDGE, MASSACHUSETTS

Fiddlehead ferns are a unique product of the American Northeast. They are the fronds of the Ostrich fern that are gathered in boggy areas in the spring before the ferns unfurl. Their flavor is most often likened to a blend of spinach and asparagus. They are available fresh as a specialty item in early spring; the season is almost always over by June 1. In this recipe from the Harvest Restaurant in Harvard Square, Cambridge, they are served with black sea bass.

2½ pounds black sea bass fillets
1 stick (¼ pound) butter
2 shallots, minced
sea salt and pepper to taste
1 cup fish stock (see White Wine Fish Fumet, page 30)
1 cup dry vermouth or dry white wine
1½ cups crème fraîche (see page 70) or heavy cream

1½ teaspoons fresh rosemary leaves
1½ pounds fresh wild mushrooms (morels, trompets, or shitake)
¾ pound fresh fiddlehead ferns, trimmed
6 fresh rosemary sprigs

1. Skin and bone the fillets and cut into six 6-to-7-ounce portions.
2. Preheat oven to 450 degrees.
3. In a casserole large enough to hold fillets, put 1 tablespoon butter in bottom and sprinkle with 1 minced shallot. Saute until shallot is transparent but not colored.
4. Salt and pepper fillets and place atop shallot.
5. Pour in fish stock to halfway up sides of fish and bake for 3 to 4 minutes, just until flesh is set. Remove fillets, cover and keep warm. (If fish stock is not enough to halfway cover fish, add wine as well.)
6. To liquid fish was cooked in, add wine, crème fraîche, 1½ teaspoons rosemary, and reduce over medium-high heat until the liquid starts to thicken.
7. Meanwhile, saute wild mushrooms in 1 tablespoon butter with the remaining minced shallot, salt, and pepper.
8. Also at the same time, blanch the fiddlehead ferns in salted water,

refresh them in ice water, and dry. Saute in 1 tablespoon butter with salt and pepper.

9. Finish the dish by adding remaining 5 tablespoons butter to the sauce to thicken it. Correct the seasoning and strain through a fine-mesh strainer.

10. Spoon a puddle of sauce onto the center of warmed serving plates. Arrange bass fillets, mushrooms, and fiddleheads on plates. Garnish with rosemary sprigs.

Serves 6. Approximate nutrition information per serving: Calories 620; protein 43g; fat 43g; carbohydrates 14g; sodium 700 mg.

Sea Bass with Spinach

1¼ pounds sea bass fillets, either 4 large or 8 small	2 turns milled pepper
20 ounces fresh spinach	2 eggs
5 tablespoons butter	10 tablespoons shredded Swiss cheese
1 small clove garlic, minced	4 tablespoons fresh breadcrumbs
½ teaspoon salt	juice of half a lemon

1. Stem and wash spinach and cut into strips ¼-inch wide. Over low heat, cook spinach in 1 tablespoon butter with garlic, salt, and pepper until moisture is nearly evaporated.

2. In a large bowl, beat eggs and add spinach. Mix in 6 tablespoons grated Swiss cheese. Correct the seasoning.

3. Using 2 tablespoons butter, butter either a large ovenproof casserole or 4 individual casseroles. Add spinach mixture and lay fillets atop mixture.

4. Season lightly with additional salt and pepper. Mix remaining 4 tablespoons cheese with breadcrumbs and sprinkle onto fish. Dot with pieces of remaining 2 tablespoons of butter. Squeeze a few drops of lemon over the casserole.

5. Preheat oven to 375 degrees. Bake 15 minutes and serve immediately.

Serves 4. Approximate nutrition information per serving: Calories 393; protein 41g; fat 22g; carbohydrates 10g; sodium 700 mg.

Sea Bass Shepherd's Pie

∎

Made with lamb or beef, shepherd's pie is an old favorite for family dinners. It is equally delicious with black sea bass and, with its vegetables, nutritious and hearty enough for a one-dish meal.

12 ounces sea bass fillets

MASHED POTATOES:
6 medium-large potatoes
1 tablespoon salt
1 tablespoon butter
½ cup cream
salt and pepper to taste

¼ cup carrots, cut in ⅛-inch
    dice
¼ cup onions, in ⅛-inch dice
¼ cup celery, in ⅛-inch dice

3 tablespoons butter
¼ cup water
½ cup mushrooms in small dice
¼ cup diced snow peapods
½ cup peeled, seeded, chopped
    fresh or canned Italian plum
    tomatoes
pinch of thyme
salt and pepper to taste
1½ tablespoons minced fresh
    parsley
¼ cup fresh breadcrumbs

1. Make mashed potatoes: Cut them in large pieces and place in cold water with 1 tablespoon salt. Cook until tender. Drain. Mash with 1 tablespoon butter, cream, salt, and pepper. Correct the seasoning.

2. Saute carrots, onions, and celery in 1 tablespoon butter for 1 minute. Add ¼ cup water and stew until tender and most of the liquid has evaporated. Add mushrooms, peapods, tomatoes, and thyme, cover, and continue to cook. Add fish, salt, and pepper. Cover and cook over medium heat just until fish is tender, about 8 minutes. Remove from heat.

3. Add parsley to fish and vegetables. Stir thoroughly, breaking fish into bite-size pieces. Correct the seasoning.

4. Coat an au gratin or other ovenproof mold or dish with 1 tablespoon of butter.

5. Preheat oven to 375 degrees. Line bottom of dish with half of the mashed potatoes. Spread fish mixture over potatoes. Top with rest of potatoes. Smooth the top with a spatula. Sprinkle breadcrumbs on top and dot with 1 tablespoon butter in small pieces.

6. Bake 30 minutes in preheated oven, and serve hot.

Serves 4. Approximate nutrition information per serving: Calories 375; protein 22g; fat 16g; carbohydrates 36g; sodium 1980 mg. (The sodium is high because of the salt used in cooking potatoes.)

Baked Sea Bass

There are many methods of setting whole portions of food within some kind of wrapper and cooking it. A classic Chinese dish, for example, is Beggar's Chicken, prepared by encasing the fowl in wet clay and baking it. The chicken is eviscerated but the feathers are not removed; they pull free with the hard-baked clay when it is cracked and removed.

The following recipe uses salt in a similar fashion. A whole fish is surrounded by well-soaked salt in a pot and baked. The result is a tender whole fish that is presented in all its glory. Surprisingly, the finished fish is not salty, providing you remove all traces of salt after removing it from its casing.

To bake the fish, it is best to use a heavy pot large enough to hold the fish from the tip of the head to the tail. The oval cast-iron pot with a tight-fitting cover that the French call a cocotte *is perfect. The fish also could be baked in a large cast-iron skillet if yours is deep enough to completely cover the fish, and then some. A deep roasting pan also will work. The pan should not be too much larger than the whole fish or a great deal of salt will be wasted unnecessarily.*

Red snapper or grouper may be substituted for the sea bass.

2 to 3 pounds whole sea bass, unscaled, gutted, with head and tail intact	2½ tablespoons freshly squeezed lemon juice
⅓ cup soft, not melted, butter	3 to 6 pounds coarse (kosher) salt
½ teaspoon salt	water, about 3 cups
pepper	½ cup melted butter
2 tablespoons minced chives	

1. Wash and dry fish well, but do not scale it. Cut away the fins and trim the tail by about two-thirds.

2. Mix soft butter, salt, pepper, chives, and 1½ tablespoons lemon juice, and stuff the fish cavity.

3. Line a baking pan with a layer of foil. Fill about ⅓ of baking pan with salt and sprinkle with about 1 cup water. Lay fish on its side atop the salt and cover completely with more salt. None of the fish should be exposed. Depending on the size of the pan, you will need from 3 to 6 pounds of salt.

4. Preheat oven to 400 degrees. Sprinkle salt with remaining water. The salt should be well soaked so that it will cake hard when baked.

5. Cover and bake for 45 minutes.

6. Remove from oven and allow fish to rest 15 minutes, uncovered. Turn over onto a flat tray or cookie sheet to see if you can unmold it all in one piece. If you cannot, turn right-side up again. Remove the salt from the top of the fish; if it is well-caked it should come away in one piece. The skin, or part of it, might pull away, too.

7. Using a wide spatula, lift fish free of bottom layer of salt and set on serving platter. Obviously, it will make a more dramatic appearance if the fish is presented whole, but it is not mandatory that it be served that way.

8. Whatever serving method you use, first brush or scrape away any residual salt that might adhere to fish.

9. With fish on a platter, skin the top side carefully. The skin should come away easily, since the scales help to keep skin together. Remove the fillet from the top portion and set it onto a fresh serving platter. Try to get it free in one piece, but no great harm is done if it is removed in sections.

10. Remove the backbone. Take up the bottom fillet by lifting it free of skin. Lay the bottom fillet atop the other.

11. Serve fish with lemon-butter, made by mixing the hot melted butter and 1 tablespoon lemon juice.

Serves 4. Approximate nutrition information per serving: Calories 607; protein 55g; fat 42g; carbohydrates 1g; sodium cannot be estimated.

Sea Perch or Ocean Perch

The ocean perch or sea perch is also called the rosefish, Norway haddock, and redfish. It has a handsome pink or rose skin with small scales that give it a crosshatched appearance. It is one of the rockfishes. In fact, it is the only rockfish in the western Atlantic, though they are a numerous species in the Pacific.

The normal range of the sea perch is from Labrador to the Gulf of Maine. Although it grows to 3 feet, the average size is 12 to 15 inches and ½ to 4 pounds. It is one of the most important food fishes of the Atlantic in terms of size of catch, often surpassing cod and haddock. It is abundant, fresh, from May to August, but a great deal of that is frozen.

A high-quality fish, the flesh is firm, white, and tender. The flavor is delicate and the flesh is excellent fried. In fact, it can be cooked in any way one might cook flounder, though the flesh is firmer and less likely to fall apart in a pan.

The skin of a sea perch is sandpaper-tough and should be removed whenever a recipe permits.

When the skin must be left on, so as to hold the fish flesh intact, especially with small fillets, present the fish with the skin down so that diners can leave it on the plate.

Tautog, black sea bass, scup, pollock, grouper, or red snapper may be substituted for ocean perch in most recipes.

Sea Perch with Cucumber or Asparagus

■■

This quickly-made recipe uses cucumber batons or asparagus tips as garnish, and their trimmings to flavor and thicken the sauce for the dish. Use the one that you prefer or the one that is in season.

If you are using small asparagus, you will need 6 per person, or 24 stalks. You may want only 2 or 3 asparagus tips if they are extremely large.

4 sea perch fillets, 5 to 6 ounces each	½ teaspoon salt
	freshly ground white pepper to taste
2 medium cucumbers, or 1 bunch asparagus	1 cup dry white wine
2 tablespoons minced shallots	1 tablespoon water
2 tablespoons butter	2 cups cream

1. Prepare either cucumber or asparagus as the garnish. You also will need some of the trimmings, so save them. If using cucumbers, peel, cut in half lengthwise to remove seeds, then cut halves crosswise into 2-inch lengths. Cut lengths into little "batons" about 2 inches long by ⅜-inch square. You will want 24 batons as garnish. Reserve. Discard skin and seeds, but save all the trimmings for sauce.

2. If using asparagus, peel the stalks and cut off tips. Cut off an additional 2 inches from the top of the peeled stalk to use in making the sauce. Discard the rest of the stalk.

3. Preheat oven to 375 degrees. Grease an oval au gratin or other oven-proof baking dish with 1 tablespoon butter and sprinkle minced shallots in the bottom. Add perch and cucumber or asparagus trimmings. Season with salt and white pepper and add white wine.

4. Cover baking dish with buttered foil or parchment and bake 10 minutes, or 10 minutes for each inch of thickness of fish measured at thickest part. Remove fish from baking dish, cover, and keep warm.

5. Meanwhile, in a skillet or small saucepan, melt 1 tablespoon butter and toss cucumber batons or asparagus tips while you saute them for half a minute over medium heat. Add 1 tablespoon water, cover, and cook over low heat, tossing occasionally for 5 to 8 minutes. When cooked, remove the cover and evaporate any water that remains, tossing the vegetables to glaze them evenly. Remove from heat, cover, and keep warm.

6. Transfer contents of dish in which the fish baked to a saucepan, add

cream and cook, stirring occasionally, until reduced by about half and liquid is thick enough to coat a spoon.

7. Pour into a blender or food processor and work until smooth and well incorporated.

8. Return sauce to the skillet to heat through. Correct the seasoning. Reheat cucumber or asparagus.

9. Put individual fillets on warm serving plates, nap with sauce, arrange 6 batons or asparagus tips on plates, and serve immediately.

Serves 4. Approximate nutrition information per serving: Calories 464; protein 32g; fat 32g; carbohydrates 12g; sodium 502 mg.

Sea Perch with Basil Butter

4 skinless sea perch fillets, 5 to 6 ounces each	freshly ground pepper
2 tablespoons butter	¾ cup dry white wine
2 tablespoons minced shallots	2 tablespoons chopped fresh basil (about 16 leaves)
¼ teaspoon salt	1 cup soft butter

1. Preheat oven to 375 degrees. Using 2 tablespoons butter, grease an ovenproof skillet or baking dish. Sprinkle minced shallots in pan. Lay fish fillets on top. Season with salt and pepper, pour in wine, and cover with buttered foil or parchment.

2. Bake 8 minutes, or 10 minutes for each inch of thickness. Remove pan from oven and remove fillets to a warm plate. Cover and keep warm. Retain pan juices.

3. In the same pan add basil, and reduce pan juices (over medium heat) until about 1 tablespoon remains. Simmer 2 minutes. Add soft butter a piece at a time until it is all incorporated. Correct the seasoning.

4. Set fish on individual serving plates, and spoon sauce over each serving.

Serves 4. Approximate nutrition information per serving: Calories 606; protein 27g; fat 54g; carbohydrates 6g; sodium 880 mg.

Perch Fillets à la Grecque

This is a recipe that will be better if made a day ahead and refrigerated so that the flavors have a chance to meld.
Either buy 4 fillets of approximately 5 ounces each, or 2 large ones.

20 ounces sea perch fillets, unskinned
2 tablespoons minced shallots
½ teaspoon dried thyme
1 bay leaf
½ teaspoon oregano
1 tablespoon cracked coriander seeds
1 large clove garlic cut in 6 pieces

1½ cups dry white wine
½ cup lemon juice
1½ teaspoons salt
¾ cup olive oil
1½ teaspoons black peppercorns, cracked
8 to 10 fresh button mushrooms, quartered
12 pearl onions

1. Cut fillets into ⅜-inch fingers, leaving the skin on.
2. Place all ingredients except the fish in a saucepan and bring to a boil. Lower heat and simmer 15 minutes.
3. Lay fish fillets in a deep ovenproof pan or casserole. Bring the ingredients in the saucepan back to a boil and pour over the fish. Cover tightly with foil and set over low heat. Poach 3 or 4 minutes.
4. Allow to cool, cover with wax paper, and refrigerate overnight.
5. Serve cold. Lift pieces out of the juice, set on serving dish, and spoon a little of the juice on top.

Serves 4. Approximate nutrition information per serving: Calories 543; protein 27g; fat 43g; carbohydrates 12g; sodium 920 mg.

Fillet of Sea Perch Murat

This is a classic way to prepare sole and other fish in France, but sea perch also works extremely well. You can prepare this recipe several hours ahead of serving — through step 5 — leaving only the final browning of the fish for the last moment.

1 pound sea perch fillets
2 fresh artichokes
1 lemon, cut in wedges
2 medium potatoes, cut in
    ½-inch dice
4 tablespoons butter
6 to 8 medium to large fresh
    mushrooms, quartered

½ cup milk
flour for dredging
2 tablespoons oil
salt and pepper to taste
1 tablespoon lemon juice
1 tablespoon minced fresh
    parsley

1. Remove skin from the fillets and cut them into pieces 4 to 5 inches long and ⅜-inch square.

2. Prepare artichoke bottoms. Remove all tough outer leaves until you get to tender, pale yellow-green heart. Rub with cut lemon and simmer in lightly salted water with the lemon pieces used to rub choke. Cook 20 minutes, or more, depending on size. Remove, allow to cool enough to handle.

3. Remove the hairy choke with a spoon, scraping the interior clean. Cut into ⅛-inch wedges.

4. Saute diced potatoes in 1 tablespoon butter until cooked through and crisp. Drain on paper towels and reserve.

5. In another skillet, saute mushrooms in 1 tablespoon butter just until they take on a browned edge. Add cooked artichoke pieces and saute 2 minutes more. Reserve.

6. Dip fish in milk and drain, then dredge in unseasoned flour and shake off excess.

7. Brown 1 tablespoon butter and 2 tablespoons oil in a large skillet. Add coated fish, season with salt and pepper, and brown, turning to crisp each side.

8. Tilt pan and remove excess oil. Add remaining 1 tablespoon butter and lemon juice.

9. Add sauteed potatoes, mushrooms, and artichokes, and toss to re-warm. Correct seasoning and serve immediately, sprinkled with parsley.

Serves 4. Approximate nutrition information per serving: Calories 410; protein 26g; fat 21g; carbohydrates 28g; sodium 400 mg.

Sea Perch Saltimbocca
■■

The inspiration for this dish is obvious—the small veal scallopine the Romans call "saltimbocca," or little "jump-in-the-mouths." In Rome, each scallopine is topped with prosciutto and a fresh sage leaf after one side of the veal has been sauteed. The second side is sauteed and the dish is brought to table with just the pan juices or a little meat glaze poured over.

Our version uses fish, naturally, but mozzarella is added to give the dish additional flavor and textural interest.

Sorry, but the sage must be fresh: dried sage won't do. If you do not have sage, a small sprig of fresh tarragon may be substituted.

4 sea perch fillets, 4 to 6 ounces each	3 tablespoons butter
4 slices mozzarella	salt and pepper
milk for dipping	4 slices prosciutto
flour for dusting	4 fresh sage leaves

1. Slice mozzarella about ¼-inch thick and then cut each slice into thirds.

2. Dip fillets in milk, drain, and then dredge in flour, pat to make it adhere, and shake off excess.

3. In an ovenproof skillet, brown fish in 3 tablespoons butter. If the skin is still on, brown with the skin-side up first. Turn fish over and brown second side. You do not have to cook fish, merely brown it. Season lightly with salt and pepper. Remove pan from heat.

4. Preheat oven to 375 degrees. Top each fillet with a slice of prosciutto. The prosciutto can overlap the sides a bit so that the edges will crisp somewhat while the dish cooks. Lay 3 pieces of mozzarella diagonally across the prosciutto, leaving a space between each piece. Top with a sage leaf.

5. Place in oven and bake about 4 minutes, or until the cheese begins to melt and the fish is cooked. Serve immediately.

Serves 4. Approximate nutrition information per serving: Calories 530; protein 29g; fat 35g; carbohydrates 22g; sodium 770 mg.

Seatrout or Weakfish

There is nothing particularly weak about this fish. The name comes from the fact that it has a fragile mouth structure that is easily torn by a fishhook. The Narragansett Indian name for the fish was "squeateague."

Seatrout are found from Massachusetts to Florida. The southern weakfish, common from Virginia to the Gulf of Mexico, is known as the spotted seatrout, or speckled trout in Louisiana. Seatrout are most abundant in summer, especially in the Mid-Atlantic states. They travel in schools, usually in shallow water over sandy bottoms in summer. The male produces a drumming sound that can be heard by fishermen.

They run from 1 to 3 pounds. Their flesh is as fragile as their mouth, so the fish should be iced immediately after being caught. Their flesh is lean, fine-textured, white, and sweet. They can be sauteed, baked, broiled, or poached, and work well in a mousse or quenelles. In general, use the fillets as you would flounder fillets.

Seatrout are not to be confused with sea trout (two words), a primarily European anadromous brown trout that spends part of its life in the sea.

"Daube" of Seatrout Baked in Salt Crust

■■

A daubière *is an ancient, French, raw baked clay cooking pot, glazed on the outside and usually large and round or oval in shape. Its cover was sealed tightly with a dough mixture so that the ingredients within — the* daube *— cooked slowly, practically vacuum-sealed. When first used, the interior was rubbed with garlic as a method of sealing the clay. This method of long, slow cooking worked well when stoves were fueled with wood and a pot could sit in or on the stove or amid the embers in a fireplace for up to 12 hours. Sealed thusly, a preparation held all its aroma until the daubière was opened.*

It is unlikely that you will find a daubière *in many homes today. This recipe is an attempt to create a similar utensil out of salt dough. We used a large, deep pie plate to hold the* daube. *You could use a deep ovenproof frying pan, skillet, or casserole, about 12 inches wide and 4 to 6 inches deep.*

This recipe is similar to the one for Baked Sea Bass (page 169), except that the fish is in pieces, and vegetables and flavorings are used. The appearance is not as striking, but the aroma is more captivating.

Do not salt, and do not attempt to sample baked dough. It is incredibly salty, but the fish is not.

1 pound seatrout, cut in large bite-sized pieces	½ cup onions, sliced about ¼ inch thick
2 pounds coarse (kosher) salt	8 thickly sliced tiny red potatoes
2 pounds flour	freshly ground black pepper
2½ cups water	1 tablespoon minced fresh parsley
6 tablespoons soft butter	¼ cup dry white wine
1½ cups celery, sliced crosswise as thinly as possible	6 tablespoons soft butter

1. Mix coarse salt and flour in a large bowl. Add water all at once. Work ingredients until a rough dough is formed. It need not be smooth, merely well mixed and cohesive.

2. Roll out dough quite thick, about ⅜-inch, in two circles, as for a 2-crust pie. One circle should be large enough to fill the pan and extend up and over the sides, and the other should be smaller, to serve as a cover.

3. Coat the pan using 1 tablespoon soft butter.

4. Place larger circle within pan; allow it to overlap the sides. Don't worry about minor tears in dough, merely overlap and squeeze dough to-

gether so that a good seal is formed. Moisten with water if necessary. Dough will be rather thick and harder to manipulate than pie crust or a similar dough.

5. Butter the inside of the dough with 2 tablespoons soft butter, spreading it evenly over the bottom and sides.

6. Preheat oven to 400 degrees. Lay celery slices onto bottom of daube, season with pepper. Place fish on top of celery, fitting into casserole in one layer or one overlapping layer. Place onions atop fish, add parsley, then potatoes and another couple of turns from pepper mill.

7. Using 1 tablespoon butter, coat smaller circle of dough and place atop filled daube, butter-side down. Press edges of dough together around top of casserole — moisten if necessary — and trim excess.

8. Bake 50 minutes.

9. When casserole has baked, remove from oven and invert while still hot onto a large round serving plate — the bottom will be easier to cut into; the top should have baked hard. With a sharp paring knife, cut a circle into bottom (now the top) of dough, leaving a margin around edge. Lift away cut portion of dough. Cut remaining 2 tablespoons of butter into small pieces and allow to melt into daube. When butter has melted, gently stir ingredients to combine.

10. Scoop out portions to serve on individual warmed plates.

Serves 4. Approximate nutrition information per serving: Calories 456; protein 27g; fat 30g; carbohydrates 19g; sodium cannot be estimated.

Chinese Cromesqui

Cromesqui is a Russian name for a croquette. In this country, this recipe probably would be referred to as fish cakes or fish balls.

This recipe is an especially good way to use cooked or raw leftover fish. Raw fish, however, should not be held uncooked for later use, but poached and kept wrapped in the refrigerator up to 24 hours. A few drops of the poaching liquid will keep it moist and fresh.

Use any firm and white fish: seatrout, cod, haddock, sole, ocean perch, halibut, hake, pollock, cusk, whiting, grouper, red snapper. You may use just one or a mixture.

You'll need to flake it as small as you can.

You may use either vermicelli or almonds as a coating for these fish balls. You will roll the balls in the pasta or almonds, or half the balls in each, so they should be in fairly small pieces.

Served with sweet and sour sauce, Chinese Cromesqui make a very good hors d'oeuvre.

1 cup cooked, flaked fish

FOR RICE:
½ cup rice
2 cups water
1 teaspoon salt

2 tablespoons chopped snow peapods
2 tablespoons chopped celery
1 tablespoon snipped chives
1 teaspoon minced or grated fresh ginger
¼ of a small garlic clove
1 tablespoon soy sauce (light soy, if possible)

pinch of salt
pinch of white pepper
¼ cup vermicelli
¼ cup almonds, slivered

EGG WASH:
1 egg
1 tablespoon water

flour for dusting
oil for deep frying
lettuce leaves
sweet and sour sauce (page 63)

1. Mix water, rice, and 1 teaspoon salt; bring to a boil and then simmer, covered, for 20 minutes. Drain well. Grind rice in a food processor until pasty.

2. In a bowl, mix thoroughly the cooked rice with the fish, peapods, celery, chives, ginger, garlic, soy sauce, salt, and pepper.

3. Moisten hands with water and roll the mixture between your palms

to form balls no larger than a walnut. You should have about 30. Place finished balls on a plate and chill at least 1 hour.

4. Break up vermicelli by snapping strands into manageable pieces about 3 or 4 inches long. Wrap them in a kitchen towel and roll with a rolling pin, or crush with your hands or the bottom of a small saucepan until you have pieces no larger than ¼ inch. Smaller bits are fine.

5. Likewise, you may use slivered or thin-sliced almonds, but the pieces should be fairly small. Mince them by hand or work in a food processor or blender to make them smaller. You may include 1 tablespoon finely ground almonds in the ¼ cup to give more even coverage.

6. Roll balls in flour, and shake off excess. Dip in egg wash and drain. Then roll them in vermicelli or almonds or half in each. Refrigerate until ready to cook.

7. Heat frying oil to 360 to 370 degrees. The oil should be deep enough to entirely cover the balls.

8. Drop a few balls at a time into the hot oil and fry until golden brown. Drain on paper towels and keep hot until all the balls are fried.

9. Arrange the hot balls on a bed of lettuce on a serving platter and serve as a canape with sweet and sour sauce.

Serves 4 to 8. Approximate nutrition information per fish ball: Calories 72; protein 2g; fat 5g; carbohydrates 4g; sodium 122 + mg.

Skate or Ray

Although different species, skates and rays are similar in taste, and their names are used interchangeably. Both prefer a diet of mollusks, which results in a fine tasting flesh with firm white meat. They are considered delicacies in Europe. The wings are the edible portion.

The wings contain long fibers or strands of meat, whose texture resembles crab and whose flavor is usually considered similar to scallops. One of the advantages of skate over other fish is that it does not contain bones, especially the little bones found in many fish. Many Americans may have eaten skate or ray without knowing it — "scallops" similar in size to large sea scallops are punched out of the wings by processors who do not always inform unwary consumers of what they are getting.

Because the wings are far removed from the visceral cavity, the flesh does not deteriorate as quickly as with other fishes and this extends the shelf life. A skate is one of the few fish whose quality improves if it is allowed to get somewhat "high" or "aged," but it should not be kept so long that it begins to smell "fishy." It can remain under refrigeration for 48 to 72 hours.

Retail markets sell skate wings either skinned or unskinned, but generally the skin is left on. Unskinned skate wings weigh about a pound or less. One wing is considered an adequate portion for one diner; a half pound of cooked meat will yield about 1 cup of flaked meat.

Wash skate wings and dry with paper toweling. Whether your wings are skinned or not, their eating quality will be improved if you first soak them in a saline or vinegar solution. Mix either 2 tablespoons salt or 2 tablespoons distilled white vinegar with 1 quart of water and immerse the fish in the bath for 2 or 3 hours. Remove and drain the wings. Skate are capable of re-forming a viscous surface coating for up to 10 hours after death, so it is advisable to wipe the skin thoroughly or to scrape it with a knife after it has been soaked to remove any remaining coating. Chill the fish until you are ready to use it.

It is generally agreed that poaching in a court-bouillon is the best cooking method for skate, and, as with salt cod, skate is always easier to skin after poaching. After the skin is removed, the flesh will easily slip off the cartilage. Cut along the lines of the fibers and then trim these pieces 1 inch long by 2 inches wide. Since the purchased wings are in a roughly triangular shape, you will never end up with perfectly even rectangles.

Skate Wings with Caper-Brown Butter

This recipe first poaches the fish and then bathes it with a highly flavored brown butter sauce.

4 skate wings

COURT-BOUILLON:
1 cup sliced onion
½ carrot, thinly sliced
1 bay leaf
1 teaspoon dried thyme
1 teaspoon freshly ground black
    pepper
¼ cup distilled white vinegar
1½ quarts water
1 tablespoon salt

SAUCE:
1 tablespoon capers
1 tablespoon diced lemon pulp,
    rind and white pith removed
1 tablespoon vinegar
1½ tablespoons butter
2 tablespoons minced fresh
    parsley

1. Prepare the court-bouillon in the non-corrosive pan in which you plan to poach the wings. Simmer for 15 minutes. (See page 34 for additional information on preparing a court-bouillon.)

2. Trim the soaked wings, and wash. Poach in court-bouillon for 10 minutes.

3. Turn off the burner, and remove the wings. When they are cool enough to handle, peel skin from both sides and return wings to court-bouillon until needed. Discard skin. This may be done a couple of hours before continuing the dish preparation.

4. Begin sauce by mixing capers, lemon pulp, and vinegar.

5. Reheat the court-bouillon to heat the wings. Remove them, drain on paper towels, and place on warmed serving dishes.

6. Cook butter in a small skillet until it acquires a rich hazelnut color. Add lemon-caper mixture — carefully, it may flare — and cook for a minute more on high heat. Pour butter over skate wings, sprinkle with parsley, and serve immediately.

Serves 4. Approximate nutrition information per serving: Calories 222; protein 43g; fat 6g; carbohydrates 6g; sodium 1900 mg.

Tilefish

Tilefish has long been ignored. To put things in perspective, this is partly because it was rare until the latter half of the 1800s when it was discovered in abundance by New England fishermen. Then it practically disappeared because of some climatic or oceanic catastrophe. It has been making a comeback since the early 1900s and has grown in availability and popularity in the last two decades.

This is a benthic fish, one that prefers the bottom at deep-ocean depths. It usually is found along the outer edge of the continental shelf in water deeper than 150 feet. Therefore, it is less accessible to sports fishermen than other fish.

A colorful fish, tilefish has a blue to olive-green back, with yellow or rose sides and a bright rose belly. Although some may grow to about 50 pounds, the average size is about 20 pounds. It is a slender, thick-meated fish with a thick body from top to bottom. Tilefish can be cooked by a variety of methods. It even makes excellent sashimi.

Until quite recently, culinary source books were relegating this exceptional marine citizen to a mere paragraph that usually ended describing the flesh as "coarse but edible." If you consider the lobster or scallop "coarse but edible," then the description is accurate, for those are the two seafood textures it most readily brings to mind. Its diet of crabs, shrimp, squid, and mollusks is reflected in its flavor, which many compare to the lobster. A goatfish, it is related to the Atlantic red mullet.

Tilefish with Mousseline

This recipe for tilefish with a mousseline made of tilefish makes a nice first course. Serve it with Sauce Nantua.

To make the mousseline, everything but the egg whites should be very cold before you begin.

18 to 20 ounces of tilefish fillet(s)	1 cup whipped cream
2 eggs, separated	2 tablespoons butter
salt	1 tablespoon dry white wine
freshly ground white pepper	1 recipe Sauce Nantua (page 56)

1. Cut 6 ounces of fish into 1-inch cubes. Chill. Cut the rest into thin slices so that 2 slices will total 3 to 3 ½ ounces, enough for one serving.

2. Make mousseline: Put the cold cubed fish into the food processor and puree. Add 1 teaspoon salt, pepper to taste, and cold egg yolks, and process just until mixture pulls away from sides of work bowl in a ball. With motor running, slowly add whipped cream through feed tube until smoothly blended, 15 to 30 seconds.

3. Beat egg whites until thickened, add a pinch of salt, and continue to beat to soft peaks.

4. Add ⅓ of egg whites to mousse mixture and incorporate thoroughly. Gently fold remainder of egg whites into mousse with a rubber spatula.

5. Preheat oven to 375 degrees. Butter the bottom of an ovenproof baking dish with 2 tablespoons butter. Lay fish slices on top. Lightly salt and pepper the fish.

6. With a large spoon, form mousse into egg-shaped quenelles large enough to nearly cover the fish slices. Cover fish slices with mousse.

7. Add 1 tablespoon dry white wine to moisten bottom of baking dish.

8. Make Sauce Nantua while fish bakes for 12 minutes. Remove dish from oven when mousseline begins to take on color.

9. Cover the bottom of serving plate with sauce, lay fish with mousseline on top, and drizzle a tracery of the sauce in a delicate pattern over all.

Serves 4. Approximate nutrition information per serving: Calories 290; protein 24g; fat 20g; carbohydrates 0; sodium 640 mg.

Tilefish au Gratin

20 ounces tilefish fillet(s)
2 tablespoons butter
3 tablespoons flour
1½ cups half and half
½ teaspoon salt
freshly ground white pepper to
    taste

nutmeg to taste
1 tablespoon capers
1½ tablespoons minced chives
1 egg yolk
1 tablespoon butter

1. Make a roux by melting the 2 tablespoons of butter in a saucepan over low heat and adding the flour all at once. Stir with a wooden spoon or wire whisk to incorporate. Cook 2 to 3 minutes; the roux should be pale straw in color.

2. Add half and half, salt, pepper, and nutmeg to the roux and bring it to a boil while stirring with a wire whisk to prevent scorching. Cook over low heat 5 minutes. Add the capers and chives.

3. Place the egg yolk in a small bowl. Stir a couple of tablespoons of hot sauce into the egg yolk. Then pour the warmed yolk into the saucepan of hot sauce and stir well.

4. Preheat oven to 375 degrees. Butter an ovenproof dish and place half of the sauce on the bottom and add the fillets. Top with the remaining sauce. Bake 12 to 15 minutes until the top has browned slightly. Serve immediately.

Serves 4. Approximate nutrition information per serving: Calories 340; protein 29g; fat 21g; carbohydrates 8g; sodium 560 mg.

Fillet of Tilefish with Garlic and Black Olives

■■

For this recipe you want a fish that cuts into a thick fillet. Sole or flounder won't do. Other choices include ocean perch or sea bass or seatrout.

For this dish, you want flavorful olives; avoid the pallid salad olives from a can. Use either Greek olives packed in brine or olives from Provence. Sicilian dried black olives would be too assertive, however.

20 ounces tilefish fillet(s)	1 clove garlic, minced
1 garlic clove cut into about a dozen slivers	salt and freshly ground pepper
2 tablespoons butter	3 tablespoons oil
⅓ cup chopped onions	¼ cup heavy cream
1½ cups peeled, seeded and chopped fresh or canned Italian plum tomatoes	flour for dusting fish
	black olives

1. Make small slashes into fillets much as you would in a leg of lamb and place a sliver of garlic in each.

2. In 1 tablespoon of oil, saute onions until soft and transparent. Add 1 tablespoon of butter, chopped tomatoes, garlic, salt, and pepper, and stew for 2 or 3 minutes.

3. Melt 1 tablespoon butter in a skillet or frying pan with remaining 2 tablespoons oil. Dip fillets in cream, drain, and dredge in flour. Shake off excess. Fry until golden brown. Remove, cover and keep warm.

4. Arrange the fried fish on a platter, and surround it with the tomato mixture and black olives.

Serves 4. Approximate nutrition information per serving: Calories 385; protein 27g; fat 23g; carbohydrates 15g; sodium 590 mg.

Tilefish Irish Stew

The flexibility of fish in being able to be used in many ways is demonstrated in this recipe for a classic stew that is usually made with lamb. We adapted and tempered it so that is will work with tilefish or any member of the cod family.

30 ounces of tilefish fillet(s)
½ medium cabbage, shredded (about 3 cups)
1 small leek, sliced (about ¾ cup)
1 medium onion, sliced (about 1 cup)
1-2 large potatoes, sliced (about 3 cups)
½ cup sliced celery
½ teaspoon dried thyme
1 bay leaf
salt and pepper to taste

1½ quarts fish stock (see White Wine Fumet, page 30)
1 tablespoon Worcestershire sauce

GARNISH:
24 chunks of potato or 24 *pommes parisienne*, see below
24 pearl onions
2 tablespoons minced green celery leaves

1. Cut fish into bite-sized chunks.
2. Place shredded cabbage, leek, onion, potato, celery, thyme, bay leaf, salt, and pepper into a large pot. Cover with 1½ quarts of fish stock.
3. Simmer 30 minutes, until everything is mushy. Remove the bay leaf, strain the liquid, and return all but about 2 cups of the strained liquid to the original pot. Reserve the 2 cups of liquid. Put solids through a food mill or work in batches in a food processor. Return the solids to the remaining liquid in the original pot and reheat. This is your stew base.
4. Meanwhile, place the tilefish in a skillet or another ovenproof pan with the 2 cups of reserved liquid and poach for 3 or 4 minutes. Remove fish.
5. Save up to 1½ cups of the stock used for poaching: you may need it to thin the stew after the cooking is complete. How much the potatoes and other ingredients will thicken stew is difficult to determine.
6. Prepare garnish: Either cut the potatoes into 1-inch cubes or, using a melon baller approximately the same size as pearl onions, turn out raw potatoes *parisienne*. You will need 1 or 2 potatoes if they are cubed, probably 3 potatoes if using a melon baller. Cook potatoes and onions in 3 cups salted water until tender.
7. Add poached fish to stew base. Add garnish and Worcestershire

sauce and correct the seasoning. Thin with reserved hot stock if needed.

8. Serve in heated bowls topped with a bit of minced celery leaves.

Serves 4. Approximate nutrition information per serving: Calories 600; protein 61g; fat 20g; carbohydrates 44g; sodium 1390 mg.

Tilefish à l'Orange

Why should only ducks receive this classic treatment? Fine-grained fish such as tilefish and monkfish work wonderfully well, and the dish is not at all difficult to make. Ocean catfish or flounder also work.

You may prepare the recipe through step 4 a couple of hours ahead of serving.

1 pound tilefish fillet(s)	¼ cup vinegar
2 oranges	1 tablespoon sugar
1 tablespoon butter	1 cup fish stock (see White Wine
½ teaspoon salt	Fumet, page 30)
2 tablespoons medium-dry sherry	½ cup butter

1. Using a potato peeler, peel one orange in wide pieces, making certain that you remove only the zest with none of the underlying white part (the pith) that can be bitter. Cut zest into finest julienne.

2. Blanch julienned rind by placing it in cold water and bringing it to a boil. Remove, drain, and reserve.

3. Cut two oranges into segments by cutting each wedge free from the membrane on either side, taking none of the white part. Collect any spilled juice — you will need ½ cup, add fresh juice from an additional orange if necessary. Reserve.

4. Cut fish into medallions by cutting the fillet crosswise on the bias. (To cut medallions, see drawings on page 14.) You will want 3 medallions totalling 4 to 5 ounces for each serving. (If using sole or flounder, buy 4 fillets of about 4 to 5 ounces each and use them whole.)

5. Preheat oven to 375 degrees. Butter an ovenproof skillet with the 1 tablespoon butter and lay medallions into it. Season lightly with ½ tea-

spoon salt. Pour in orange juice and sherry. Cover loosely with buttered foil and bake 8 minutes — or 10 minutes per inch of fish measured at the thickest part.

6. Drain the liquid from the pan and reserve. Cover the fish and keep it warm.

7. Combine vinegar and sugar in a small saucepan and reduce to 1 tablespoon. Add fish stock and the liquid that the fish cooked in and any liquid drained from the reserved fish. Reduce over medium-high heat until liquid is thick and syrupy and coats the back of a spoon.

8. Off the heat, add ½ cup butter, a piece at a time and whisk in, making certain that it is incorporated before adding more. Warm orange segments separately in a small skillet.

9. Place fish to one side of warm individual serving plates and spoon hot sauce over each serving. Garnish with the julienned rind. Arrange 3 or 4 orange segments attractively in a fan shape on the other side of the plate.

10. You can carry the similarity with duck further by serving this dish with cooked wild rice. The match has more than tradition to recommend it; the flavor combination is superb.

Serves 4. Approximate nutrition information per serving: Calories 460; protein 26g; fat 31g; carbohydrates 20g; sodium 1020 mg.

Fatty Fish

*"In the vast and sacred Samos you will see
extremely large tuna . . . buy some promptly,
no matter what the price."*
— Archestratus, as reported by Anthenaeus

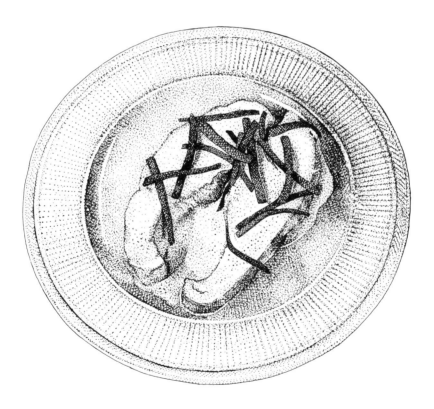

Salmon with Rhubarb

Bluefish

The bluefish, common from Florida to New England, and as far north as Nova Scotia in warm weather, is frequently maligned as a food fish. This is too bad, as it makes excellent eating, and its major faults are often the result of bad handling in the food distribution chain, or improper handling in the kitchen.

Probably the most voracious fish in the sea, bluefish will attack almost anything they find in their path, often decimating a school of fish without bothering to eat half of what they kill. The young are called "snappers" and adults "choppers." The names are accurate descriptions of their manners. The bluefish is also called the blue runner — among fish, it is a mover as well as a shaker. Because it is a fighting fish, and readily accessible, it is among the most popular with sports fishermen.

A fish that devours large quantities of whatever it finds in the sea must have a digestive system capable of handling such a diet — and the bluefish does. Its stomach enzymes are potent, and it should be gutted as soon after it is caught as possible, for deterioration begins quickly. The bluefish also has small scales and a thin skin. For this reason, scaling is more efficiently done when the bluefish is fresh from the sea and still wet.

It is for knowing such finer points and also for seeing that his suppliers observe them, that a good fishmonger is worth seeking out.

The average size for a blue is 3 to 6 pounds. The flesh of a bluefish is soft-textured with long flakes; moist and firm. It is quite mild in young bluefish; rich and flavorful in larger fish.

As with mackerel, tuna, and some other species, the bluefish is a fat fish with a high oil content and therefore does not freeze well. It is excellent when smoked, and smoked bluefish can be made into an excellent pâté. The oiliest portion of the blue is the dark stripe of flesh running along their sides. Some people find it too fishy or fatty for their taste. The dark stripe can be removed before cooking, or can be cooked with the fish — which will add to its flavor — and be removed later in the kitchen or by the individual diner.

Since it is so rich, bluefish does not need a lot of fat in its preparation; it reacts more advantageously to acidic embellishments, such as lemon, tomato, onions, and wine. Even the lactic acid of milk has a salutary effect on the flesh of a blue.

For a simple dish, bake bluefish in a pan with about a half inch or so of milk. Remove the bluefish to a serving plate with boiled potatoes and use the milk, with or without butter, to moisten the potatoes. The same idea works well with mackerel and finnan haddie.

Southern pompano, crevalle jacks, and mackerel make good substitutes for bluefish.

Bluefish with Mustard and Cream

The mustard and ginger in this dish add a piquant counterpoint to the rich bluefish flavor, and the cream unifies the dish into a pleasing whole. The final peppery notes add an additional, unexpected, layer of flavor.

20 ounces bluefish fillets	4 to 5 turns freshly ground black
1 tablespoon Dijon mustard	pepper
1 teaspoon minced fresh ginger	1 cup heavy cream
1/2 teaspoon salt	1 tablespoon lemon juice

1. Preheat oven to 375 degrees.

2. Place mustard, ginger, salt, pepper, and heavy cream in a lightly buttered ovenproof skillet, or other ovenproof pan. Lay in the bluefish fillets and bring to a boil on a burner. Then, cover with foil, and bake at 375 degrees for 10 minutes, or 10 minutes for each inch of thickness measured at the thickest part.

3. Remove fish to 4 individual serving plates, cover, and keep warm.

4. Reduce the liquid over high heat by about half, or until it is thick enough to coat a spoon. Correct the seasoning — you want the dish peppery. Add lemon juice at the last minute, remove from heat, and pour over the fish. Serve immediately.

Serves 4. Approximate nutrition information per serving: Calories 390; protein 32g; fat 27g; carbohydrates 3g; sodium 445 mg.

Baked Bluefish with Lemon

The soft, almost buttery-rich flesh of the bluefish is balanced by the tang of lemon in this recipe, and the anchovy flavor adds to its robustness. You can make your own anchovy paste using a half-can of flat anchovy fillets and a small clove of garlic. Mince and mash them together. You would still include the small clove of garlic called for in the main part of recipe.

2 bluefish fillets, unskinned, 16 to 24 ounces total
2 whole lemons
1 stick soft, not melted, butter
¼ teaspoon dried thyme
2 tablespoons anchovy paste
pepper

1 small garlic clove, finely minced
salt
2 tablespoons cold butter
1 tablespoon minced fresh parsley

1. Thinly slice the lemons. Mix together the stick of soft butter, thyme, anchovy paste, pepper, and garlic clove.

2. Place a large sheet of aluminum foil in an ovenproof baking pan and butter the foil. The foil should be large enough to enclose the fish.

3. Preheat oven to 400 degrees.

4. Line the foil with half the lemon slices. Place one fillet skin-side down atop the lemon slices. Spread the butter mixture over it and place the second fillet on top, skin side up. Salt and pepper lightly, and cover it with the rest of the sliced lemons. Close the foil by bringing the sides together and folding and crumpling it to form a sealed envelope.

5. Bake the fish for 20 minutes, or 10 minutes for each inch of thickness of both fillets and butter mixture measured at thickest part.

6. Remove from oven, open foil, and scrape the lemon slices from the fish. Remove fish to a serving platter, cover, and keep warm.

7. Strain the pan juices, including the lemon slices and other solids, pressing down with a spoon to extract maximum flavor.

8. Heat the strained liquid over high heat to reduce by half. Add the 2 tablespoons cold butter, one piece at a time, incorporating each addition before adding the next. Add parsley and correct the seasoning.

9. Skin the fish, divide the fillets in half, and place portions on 4 individual serving plates. Top with a tablespoon or two of sauce, and serve.

Serves 4. Approximate nutrition information per serving: Calories 435; protein 28g; fat 35g; carbohydrates 3g; sodium 1300 mg.

Barbecued Bluefish

NATHANIEL BENCHLEY'S NANTUCKET METHOD

Nothing fancy about this recipe; it just offers a delightful excuse to enjoy bluefish out-of-doors at the barbecue grill. The gin helps crisp the skin while cutting richness.

Buy or prepare fresh bluefish pan-dressed. Slash the fish 3 to 4 times on each side so that the marinade and heat will penetrate better. If the fish is thick also penetrate the flesh lengthwise along the backbone.

Preheat the broiler or barbecue grill: 10 to 15 minutes for a gas or electric grill; 30 to 40 minutes for charcoal to allow the fire to develop an even film of white ash that indicates it is at the right temperature.

We recommend a 2- to 3-pound fish. Large bluefish up to 10 pounds may be barbecued this way, but first must be baked until nearly done and then barbecued, which can be awkward. If your fish is between 4 and 7 pounds, you can compromise on the method. Place the bluefish in a barbecue grill that has a cover. Keep the grill hot, but the fish should be as far from the coals as possible. Cook, covered, and keep the fish from flaming. When nearly done, proceed to baste and flame crisp.

1 whole gutted bluefish, 2 to 3 pounds	½ cup melted butter for basting
milk for marinating, about 1 cup	¼ cup gin
salt and pepper	1 lemon, cut in wedges

1. Soak pan-dressed bluefish in milk for from 2 to 8 hours, turning occasionally.

2. Remove from marinade and dry thoroughly. Season with salt and pepper to taste.

3. Lay fish on hot charcoal or gas grill, basting it with melted butter, which will make coals flame and crisp the skin. Reserve 2 tablespoons of butter. Allow at least 5 minutes on each side for each inch of thickness of fish at thickest point. After turning, continue to baste with butter.

4. Mix the remaining 2 tablespoons of butter with the gin. Pour over the fish carefully; it will flame considerably. Cook a minute longer.

5. Serve immediately, with lemon wedges.

Serves 2 or 4. Approximate nutrition information per serving for 2 servings: Calories 711; protein 37g; fat 60g; carbohydrates 10g; sodium 460 mg. Approximate nutrition information per serving for 4 servings: Calories 355; protein 19g; fat 30g; carbohydrates 5g; sodium 230 mg.

Cold Baked Bluefish

This recipe can be made ahead and refrigerated for several hours, but allow it to come to room temperature before serving. Do not serve it chilled. Often, in dishes such as this, cold should not mean numbed.

Onions, tomatoes, capers, and vinegar offset the fish's natural richness.

Balsamic vinegar — aceto balsamico — is a wine vinegar made with aromatic herbs, and like wine, aged 5 to 7 years successively in barrels of different woods. Originating in Modena, Italy, it varies in flavor as well as quality from producer to producer. Its flavor is unique and just a drop or two is normally used in salads. On its home grounds it is often used with fresh berries for dessert. Use it with discretion, as it is potent and cannot be substituted indiscriminately for other wine vinegars. In this dish, its potency is exactly what is needed.

20 ounces bluefish fillets	2 fresh tomatoes cut in eighths;
½ teaspoon salt	or 2 cups imported peeled
3 to 4 turns of freshly ground	plum tomatoes, drained
pepper	1 teaspoon dried thyme
3½ tablespoons olive oil	1 crumpled bay leaf
1 cup thinly sliced onion	1 large garlic clove, minced
1 cup thinly sliced sweet green	⅓ cup capers
bell pepper	¼ cup balsamic vinegar
1 cup thinly sliced sweet red bell	1 tablespoon butter
pepper	

1. Salt and pepper bluefish. Reserve.

2. In an ovenproof skillet, or other ovenproof pan, saute the onion and pepper in 2 tablespoons olive oil until the onion is soft but not browned. Add tomatoes, thyme, bay leaf, garlic, capers, and vinegar. Continue to cook, stirring and tossing. Correct the seasoning.

3. In another pan, saute bluefish in 1½ tablespoons olive oil and 1 tablespoon butter to brown. Do not overcook.

4. Preheat oven to 375 degrees. Place fish atop the vegetables and bake, loosely covered with foil, for 10 minutes, or 10 minutes for each inch of thickness measured at thickest part.

5. Remove, baste with pan juices, and cool. Refrigerate for several hours if desired. Serve at room temperature with crusty bread and a green salad.

Serves 4. Approximate nutrition information per serving: Calories 330; protein 32g; fat 18g; carbohydrates 9g; sodium 600 mg.

Mackerel

The mackerel and the tuna are members of the same family — Scombridae. The Atlantic, or common, mackerel is the fish you are most likely to find at a table north of Fayetteville, North Carolina, since its range is approximately from Labrador to Cape Hatteras. South of the Carolinas, the Spanish and king mackerels dominate.

Mackerel are most abundant in May, June, and July in the North Atlantic. Half the mackerel sold in the United States is imported from Canada. Running from 14 to 18 inches, and averaging 1¼ to 2½ pounds, the flesh of the adult is oily, firm, and dark-fleshed. From 12 to 28 percent of the flesh can be red muscle, a relatively large amount. Its dark flesh and oily quality make it a prime candidate for marinating and grilling. While assertive in flavor, the meat can be sweet and light. Mackerel takes well to tart or acidic accompaniment; use it with lemon, tomatoes, and dry wine. For a change of pace, combine it with unsweetened cranberry sauce. Bluefish is often substituted for mackerel.

Tinker mackerel is the name loosely applied to immature common mackerel that run from about 6 to 10 inches in length. (The tinker, also known as a bullseye or chub, is a separate species that runs about a pound.)

The Spanish mackerel, with a minimum of red muscle, is a leaner and more delicate fish than its northern cousin.

Mackerel can be a bloody fish, so always thoroughly wash out the cavity before cooking it.

Maquereaux au Vin Blanc

COLD MACKEREL IN WHITE WINE

This dish is better the second day; it is good for a week or two if kept covered in the refrigerator.

4 mackerel, 7 to 8 ounces each	2 whole cloves
1 large onion, cut in rings	1 medium carrot, sliced
1 lemon, thinly sliced	1 tablespoon salt
2 bay leaves	10 cups dry white wine
½ teaspoon dried thyme	½ cup distilled white vinegar
1 teaspoon black peppercorns, cracked	½ sweet red bell pepper, thinly sliced

1. Wash and pan-dress the mackerel. Wipe dry.

2. Mix all the ingredients, except the mackerel, in a non-corrosive pan. Place it over medium heat, bring to a boil, and then simmer for 10 minutes. Remove from the heat and allow to cool.

3. Place the fish in an ovenproof dish — a glass dish is a good choice in this instance so that you can observe when the boiling begins. The fish should fit snugly, so a 9 x 12-inch dish should be adequate.

4. Add the vegetables and liquid. Cover loosely with buttered foil or parchment. Bring to a boil at the burner's lowest setting. When bubbles first begin to rise in the liquid, remove the dish from the heat, cover with a tight fitting lid or tightly fitted aluminum foil, and set aside to cool. Place the dish in the refrigerator if you're not serving it soon.

5. The dish should be served at cool, not cold, room temperature. Separate the 4 mackerel into 8 fillets. Serve each person one fillet skin-side down and one fillet skin-side up. Decorate with onion rings and bell pepper, and moisten with some of the cooking liquid. Serve with crisp bread.

Serves 4. Approximate nutrition information per serving: Calories 569; protein 45g; fat 28g; carbohydrates 32g; sodium 1610 mg.

Mackerel Gravad

This appetizer is an interesting variation on the more frequently seen salmon gravlax, and a lot less expensive, especially when mackerel are running and over-enthusiastic local sports fishermen are happy to give away some of their catch.

Mackerel should weigh about 2 pounds whole, deboned and skinned. Do not wash, pat dry with paper towels. You can marinate the fillets for 1 or 2 days, or 3 days if necessary.

4 mackerel fillets
1 tablespoon sugar
2 tablespoons salt
coarsely ground black and white
    pepper

3 tablespoons minced fresh dill
sprigs of fresh dill

1. Mix together salt, sugar, and peppers. Rub each fillet with this mixture and the minced dill. Reserve leftover seasonings.

2. Lay 2 fillets flat in a deep glass or china dish. They should fit comfortably, and should not be crowded. Cover them with sprigs of fresh dill. Lay the 2 remaining fillets on top, and cover with the remaining seasoning mixture and a few more whole sprigs of fresh dill.

3. Cover the fish with plastic wrap, then foil, and then a cover or small chopping board that will fit inside the dish. Place a weight on it, a half-pound can, rock, or anything else that is handy.

4. Refrigerate 1 or 2 days. Discard any liquid that accumulates during the first 6 hours. Turn fillets every 12 hours. Do not hold more than 3 days.

5. Serve cold with thin raw onion rings, cucumber slices, and crisp bread.

Serves 4. Approximate nutrition information per serving: Calories 209; protein 20g; fat 12g; carbohydrates 4g; sodium cannot be estimated.

Broiled Mackerel

This recipe will work with fish other than mackerel. Just keep the following suggestions in mind.

First, any fish to be broiled, whether whole and pan-dressed, or in steaks or fillets, should be at least 1-inch thick, otherwise it is difficult to control the cooking. One-inch-thick fish should be placed 4 inches from the broiler; thicker cuts should be moved farther from the heat, up to 6 inches, so that they cook through before over-browning.

The proportion of fat (oil) to acid (lemon) is correct in this recipe for fatty fish, such as mackerel, mullet, ocean pout, pompano, tuna, shark, or bluefish. For leaner fish — such as whiting or red snapper — add an additional tablespoon of oil and baste with the marinade more frequently to prevent the fish from drying out.

4 small or 2 large whole
    mackerel, unskinned with
    head and tail
4 teaspoons salt
freshly ground black pepper

juice of 4 lemons, about
    8 tablespoons
8 tablespoons oil
lemon wedges

1. Gut fish and wash visceral cavity well. Wipe fish dry with a damp cloth and paper towels. If fish are large, gash 2 or 3 times on each side so that the marinade and heat will penetrate.

2. Mix salt, pepper, lemon juice, and oil, and marinate the fish for at least 15 minutes or up to 2 hours in the refrigerator.

3. Place under broiler 4 to 6 inches from heat and broil 10 minutes for each inch of thickness, turning the fish once halfway through cooking. Baste with some of the marinade once or twice on each side. Lower the broiling rack if the fish shows any signs of charring.

4. Serve directly from the broiler with lemon wedges.

Serves 4. Approximate nutrition information per serving: Calories 453; protein 20g; fat 40g; carbohydrates 6g; sodium 2130 mg.

Mackerel with Roe Sauce

Occasionally, fresh whole mackerel, when bought or caught, will contain roe — two long sacs covered with a membrane. The roe will be marketed separately, as is shad roe in season. Look for compact, firm roe. It should be intact, and of uniform color with no cloudy or shriveled areas. Wash thoroughly, but handle carefully, as the roe is delicate.

The 2 mackerel roes in this recipe do not have to be precooked. They give the sauce a concentrated rich flavor along with texture.

4 mackerel fillets, 4 to 6 ounces each, unskinned	salt and pepper to taste
	½ cup dry white wine
1 tablespoon butter	1 cup heavy cream
1 shallot, minced	2 mackerel roes

1. In a wide shallow pan, melt butter, and add minced shallot, salt, pepper, and white wine. Reduce to 2 tablespoons.

2. Add the cream and simmer for 1 minute.

3. Add mackerel fillets and simmer over medium-low heat. Do not overcook. Remove the fillets when poached, 3 to 5 minutes, or 5 minutes for each ½ inch of thickness measured at the thickest part. Remove fillets, cover, and keep warm.

4. Add roes to poaching liquid and poach 3 to 4 minutes over low heat. Do not overcook or expose them to a high heat, or the eggs will toughen and the sauce will be gritty.

5. Place the poached roes and poaching liquid in a blender and work until smooth. Correct the seasoning.

6. Place the mackerel fillets on a serving platter and pour the sauce over. Serve immediately.

Serves 4. Approximate nutrition information per serving: Calories 500; protein 41g; fat 34g; carbohydrates 6g; sodium 200 mg.

Creamed Mackerel

◼◼

4 small mackerel fillets,   pinch of pepper
   unskinned   1 tablespoon Dijon mustard
1 cup heavy cream   2 teaspoons freshly squeezed
1 tablespoon snipped chives   lemon juice
1 teaspoon salt

1. Preheat oven to 350 degrees.

2. Score the skin-side of the fillets several times, crosswise, deeply if the fillets are thick. Lay the fish in an ovenproof baking dish.

3. Mix the remaining ingredients, except the lemon juice. Cover the fish with the mixture and bake for 15 minutes.

4. If the liquid is thin, remove the fillets and keep them warm. Place the liquid in a wide saucepan and reduce over medium-high heat until it is thick enough to coat a spoon. Add the lemon juice at the last minute. Correct the seasoning. Stir, pour over the fish, and serve immediately.

Serves 4. Approximate nutrition information per serving: Calories 409; protein 21g; fat 35g; carbohydrates 2g; sodium 599 mg.

Smothered Mackerel

◼◼

In this dish, the rich, soft flesh of the mackerel marries well with the tangy onions that give a sharp counterpoint of flavor. The dish is cooked with only the liquid exuded from the onion and the fish. In French cooking parlance, it would be called an étouffée, *a kind of cooking done under tight cover without much liquid. "To steam" or "stifle" or "smother" would be the closest English equivalents.*

If you wish, you could prepare this dish using whole mackerel or other small whole fish or fillets, such as bluefish fillets or whole butterfish. In that case you would not have to saute the onion slices, since the longer cooking time the fish would need would cook the onions thoroughly.

4 mackerel fillets, skinless, 4 to 6
    ounces each
1 onion
4 tablespoons butter
½ teaspoon salt
2-3 turns freshly ground pepper
¼ teaspoon dried thyme
1 medium bay leaf, crumbled
1 tablespoon freshly squeezed
    lemon juice

MAÎTRE D'HÔTEL SAUCE:
2 tablespoons butter
1 tablespoon freshly squeezed
    lemon juice
1 tablespoon minced fresh
    parsley

1. Slice the onion extremely thin, to make about 1½ cups. Saute the slices in 1 tablespoon butter until soft, without allowing them to color.

2. Using 1 tablespoon butter, grease a skillet or ovenproof casserole large enough to hold the 4 mackerel fillets. Put in the fillets so that they lie flat. Add salt, pepper, thyme, and bay leaf directly to the fish. Scatter the sauteed onion over the fish. Dot with the remaining 2 tablespoons butter. Sprinkle on lemon juice.

3. Preheat oven to 400 degrees.

4. If your casserole does not have a tight-fitting lid, you must make a cover for it. Place a layer of kitchen foil atop the skillet or casserole so that it overlaps the sides. Place a cover, or a cookie sheet and another pan over this. Place in oven and cook 12 minutes, or 10 minutes for each inch of thickness of thickest fillet.

5. Make maître d'hôtel sauce: Melt 2 tablespoons of butter in a small skillet, and add 1 tablespoon lemon juice and minced parsley.

6. Remove fish from pan to individual serving plates and pour on a little sauce.

Serves 4. Approximate nutrition information per serving: Calories 418; protein 28g; fat 32g; carbohydrates 4g; sodium 450 mg.

Mullet

Although the mullet has a range from Maine to Texas, about three-quarters of the American catch is from Florida. It is most popular in the South, but it is generally available in the North as well. The striped or gray mullet and the silver mullet are the species in American waters that get to the table. The silver mullet is leaner than the gray; both have white flesh that is mild with a nutty flavor. The striped mullet is the "Biloxi Bacon" of the South.

The mullet's firm, fat flesh is perfectly suited to the new American interest in smoking and grilling over woods, such as mesquite, grapevine prunings, hickory, apple, and other fuels. In France, it has long been a favorite for grilling over dried fennel. It also is good broiled, baked, and stuffed. A whole mullet is about 1 to 1½ pounds.

The mullet does not freeze well, and shouldn't be kept frozen for more than a week or two. The dark meat should be removed before the fish is frozen.

The mullet is often confused with a fish much admired along the Mediterranean and called, in translation, "red mullet." But that fish, the *rouget de roche* of France, marvelous when simply split and grilled with garlic butter or made into a pâté, is not a mullet at all. It is a goatfish and does not exist in American waters, although a mullet found here is called red mullet.

Like the roe of the monkfish, mullet roe is an underutilized product in this country, although there are many who appreciate its worth.

Baked Mullet

In this recipe, the gray mullet of the Atlantic is baked in a sealed foil envelope. The aroma that rises when the foil is opened at the table will set appetites at the ready. The marriage with lemon adds a crisp acid balance to the richness of the fish.

You can make your own anchovy paste by mincing and mashing one clove of garlic with 2 canned flat anchovy fillets. Do not eliminate the garlic in the recipe if you make your own paste.

Purchase an even number of fillets. This recipe can be made ahead, through step 4, and refrigerated several hours.

16 to 20 ounces mullet fillets,
    unskinned
2 lemons
8 tablespoons soft butter
2 tablespoons anchovy paste

pepper to taste
1 garlic clove, minced
¼ teaspoon dried thyme
salt to taste

1. Preheat oven to 400 degrees.
2. Slice lemon into thin slices.
3. Mix together soft butter, anchovy paste, pepper, garlic, and thyme.
4. Place a large sheet of kitchen foil in an ovenproof baking dish, leaving enough extended over the ends and sides to completely envelope the fish. Butter the foil well.
5. Line the bottom with lemon slices. Place one fillet, skin down, atop the lemon. Spread butter mixture over the whole fillet and place a second fillet over it, skin side up. Sprinkle with additional thyme. If using more than 2 fillets, repeat the operation with those remaining. Salt lightly. Place remaining lemon slices on the fish in shingle fashion to make an attractive presentation when the fish is cooked. Seal foil by folding and crumpling. Refrigerate at this point, if you wish.
6. Preheat oven to 400 degrees while you bring the fish back to room temperature. Bake the fish for 20 minutes.
7. Carefully lift the foil package from the baking dish and place it on a serving dish. Serve directly from the foil package at the table. Spoon any juices collected in the pan over the fish.

Serves 4. Approximate nutrition information per serving: Calories 469; protein 31g; fat 37g; carbohydrates 4g; sodium 1300 mg.

Mullet with Eggplant Sauce and Poor Man's Caviar

This is a dish for eggplant lovers, and a wonderful way to dress up a simple broiled fish. It has one further recommendation: It can be made a day ahead. The dish is served at room temperature.

You will want an eggplant that is likely to have lots of seeds. One that is large, and therefore older, is the one you want. Pick the biggest you can find. The seeds of an eggplant resemble roe, hence the name, poor man's caviar.

1 3-pound, or 2 1½-pound whole mullet; or 2 1½-pound whole mackerel; gutted, heads and tails intact	1 tablespoon lemon juice
	salt and pepper
	½ cup oil; half olive, half vegetable oil preferred
1 large eggplant	½ cup peeled, seeded and diced fresh tomato
3 unpeeled cloves garlic	
2 teaspoons Dijon mustard	4 sprigs of fresh parsley
3 hardboiled egg yolks	

1. Preheat oven to 375 degrees. Cut eggplant in half lengthwise. Score flesh deeply with cross-hatch gashes. Grease an ovenproof pan or baking dish with a little oil, place the eggplant flesh-side down, add unpeeled garlic cloves to the pan, and bake for 20 to 30 minutes. Turn pulp-side up and bake for 5 minutes more. Remove and allow to cool. Remove, peel, and reserve roasted garlic.

2. When eggplant is cool enough to handle, scrape the seeds from the center of the eggplant with a spoon. The seeds should pull away easily from the rest of the pulp. Mince them fine with a small, sharp knife. Cover and refrigerate.

3. Scrape the rest of the flesh from the skin of the eggplant and discard the skin. You should have 1 to 1½ cups of flesh.

4. Place eggplant pulp into the work bowl of a food processor. Add roasted garlic cloves, mustard, egg yolks, lemon juice, salt, and pepper, and work for 30 seconds. With motor running, slowly pour ½ cup mixed oils through the feed tube, as you do when making mayonnaise. The sauce should be thick, and almost, but not quite, pourable. Correct the seasoning. Cover and refrigerate overnight.

5. The next day, remove the eggplant sauce and seeds from the refrigerator and allow them to come to room temperature.

6. Wash the fish well.

7. Preheat oven broiler. Rub an ovenproof pan and the fish itself well with oil, and broil on one side until the skin blisters. Turn and crisp it on the second side. Reduce the oven temperature to 375 degrees so that the fish will bake. In all, the fish should broil and bake 10 minutes for each inch of thickness. A 2½-inch-thick mullet will take 25 minutes; a 1½-inch-thick mackerel will take 15.

8. Remove fish from baking pan and remove skin. Separate fillets, making 4 serving portions.

9. Season diced tomato with salt and pepper to taste.

10. Spoon eggplant sauce onto one side of each serving plate, dividing the mixture evenly; there should be about ¼ cup for each serving.

11. Arrange fish fillets opposite the eggplant, leaving a narrow space between them and the eggplant. Spoon 2 to 3 tablespoons of diced tomato into that space. Top the eggplant with some of the seeds and garnish the dish with a sprig of parsley.

Serves 4. Approximate nutrition information per serving: Calories 844; protein 72g; fat 55g; carbohydrates 13g; sodium 490 mg.

Salmon

The creamed salmon and peas traditional on July 4th not only served as a special holiday dish, but also marked the start of the prime salmon season, which, on the Atlantic coast, ran through summer and early fall in the days when salmon were plentiful.

That used to be the case, at least, before dams on New England rivers and pollution from textile mills, lumber operations, and municipal sewage wrecked the Atlantic salmon's spawning grounds. By the early 1800s, the Industrial Revolution was beginning to affect rivers in the Northeast where the anadromous ocean-living salmon returned to freshwater birthplaces to spawn. The Connecticut River was spoiled by 1815, the Merrimack by 1860; the Androscoggin, Kennebec, Penobscot, and St. John rivers soon followed.

The growing awareness of Americans that their harbors, rivers, and streams were becoming cesspools has brought about efforts to reverse the trend, and there are reports each year of salmon being able to get farther up such rivers as the Connecticut and Merrimack. But even with redoubled efforts, we are not likely to see conditions anywhere near what existed before man began to abuse natural resources.

Fishing for adult salmon off Iceland and Greenland also is reducing the number of fish that return to their native rivers to spawn. Discovery of these fishing grounds is fairly recent; for centuries, man did not know where the Atlantic salmon spent its time at sea.

Besides the Atlantic salmon, five other species are of interest: chinook, coho, sockeye, chum, and pink.

The chinook and coho are considered the best eating. The chinook usually weighs 10 to 20 pounds. Its flesh has very large flakes and is soft in texture. It is the fattest of the salmon. A coho has a finer texture than the chinook. The color of its flesh runs to shades of pink. It is relatively lean.

The deep orange-red color of the flesh of the sockeye salmon lives up to its second name of "Red." Firm textured with small flakes, it is rich. It is sometimes sold as "Blueback Salmon."

Chum salmon is a coarse-textured fish and has the lowest fat content of the five. Chum are the last Pacific species to make the run to freshwater spawning grounds. It is the orange-pink roes of the chum that are marketed as "Salmon Caviar."

**HOW TO CUT
SALMON STEAKS**

1. Cut through the fish,
beginning just behind the gills.

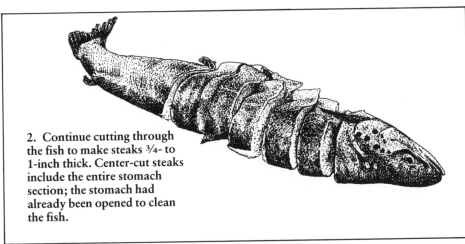

2. Continue cutting through
the fish to make steaks ¾- to
1-inch thick. Center-cut steaks
include the entire stomach
section; the stomach had
already been opened to clean
the fish.

The pink salmon is the smallest of the five. It is fine-textured with small flakes, and has a low fat content; its flesh is peach to rose in color.

Salmon is sold whole, as centercuts and other chunk sections, steaks, fillets, canned and frozen, and smoked. This is one of its most popular forms.

Scotch, Irish, and Danish smoked salmon are all sold in the United States. It can be cold-smoked Atlantic or Pacific salmon; native or imported. In spite of proponents for one or the other, all are quite similar, and their quality depends more on who did the smoking rather than where it came from, regardless of the price.

Lox is a salt-cured salmon that has been de-salted by soaking it in fresh water. Lox is a market name favored by delicatessens; it comes from "lax," the Scandinavian word for salmon, and is seen in "gravlax," and "rokt lax" or smoked salmon. It is almost always a Pacific salmon, mild-cured with sugar in a brine with a low salt content.

While lox is most frequently associated with New York's Jewish delicatessens and lox and cream cheese on bagels, it is not unknown elsewhere. *Lomi-lomi* is the Hawaiian name for salmon cured as lox is.

Nova is another delicatessen or market name for a cold-smoked salmon, most often a Pacific species, though some Atlantic salmon from Nova Scotia are treated in this manner.

Salmon must always be examined for bones before you cook with it. Though the fish does not have an inordinate number of bones compared to most fish, those that are there are usually securely imbedded. Pliers or machinists tweezers are the best implements with which to extract them.

Seafood Tartare

This is an appetizer using raw fish in the same manner as beef is used for steak tartare. It is a perfect dish when you are looking for a different hors d'oeuvre for summer entertaining.

The fish must be absolutely fresh, and should be well chilled throughout the assembling process. The tartare should be served in a dish set on ice or in some other way to assure that it stays cold. You can prepare it up to 3 hours before it is served, and keep it covered in the refrigerator.

The fish should be minced by hand into pieces no larger than 1/8-inch. A food grinder, food processor, or blender will not yield the correct texture for the dish.

For the garnish you may use less expensive roe from American sturgeon or salmon, lumpfish caviar, or the like. The color will not matter, since the half eggshell in which you set the caviar will set it off from the rest of the dish.

If you don't care to use caviar, set the chopped egg yolk into a depression in the middle of the fish. You also could use a hollowed-out small tomato to hold the egg yolk. Or use a cherry tomato alone, cut into quarters that are still connected at the bottom.

Blanched or roasted red bell pepper whipped into a puree in the food processor with a touch of wine, or pimientos treated the same way, also could be used as a garnish. Scallions, chives, a thick horseradish-cream,

French tapenade, *or Greek* taramosalata — *the list of garnish possibilities is limited only by your imagination. You will need several garnishes in all. Aside from the egg, any garnish chosen should have the acidic bite of something like capers to contrast with the mild fish flavor.*

Serve with plain crackers or party-size rye or pumpernickel bread.

½ pound fresh salmon fillet, minced
½ pound sea scallops, minced
1 tablespoon olive oil
1 tablespoon minced shallots
juice of 1 lime or lemon
⅛ teaspoon salt
freshly ground white pepper

FOR GARNISH:
caviar, capers, minced onion, minced parsley, and/or hardboiled egg.

1. In a chilled glass or stainless steel bowl, toss salmon, scallops, olive oil, shallots, and citrus juice. Add salt and a good pinch of freshly ground white pepper. Correct the seasoning.

2. Set the mixture onto a chilled 10-inch serving plate, mounding it in the center and leaving approximately a 2-inch border of clear plate for garnishing. Cover with plastic wrap or foil and place in the refrigerator.

3. Hardboil 1 or 2 eggs — 1 if you are going to use most of the garnishes recommended; 2 if you plan to use only a few. Reserve one half eggshell. Cool and chop whites and yolk separately.

4. Wash capers and allow to drain. Mince parsley and onion. You will need about 2 tablespoons of each one.

5. Remove fish from refrigerator and force the half eggshell into the center of the mixture. Fill the shell with caviar. Alternate the other garnishes as a border around the fish: An arc of chopped egg white, another of minced parsley, one of minced onion, one of capers, and one of chopped egg yolk.

Serves 6 as an appetizer; 4 as a light summer entree.
Approximate nutrition information per serving, without garnishes: Calories 219; protein 26g; fat 12g; carbohydrates 0.6g; sodium 217 mg.
Approximate nutrition information per serving, with garnishes: Calories 240; protein 28g; fat 13g; carbohydrates 1g; sodium 232 mg.

Steamed Salmon

This easily made dish with its delicate flavors of fresh ginger and dill not only tastes good, but is highly nutritious, low in calories and sodium, and has a good proportion of protein.

Romaine lettuce is suggested because it will hold its shape better when cooked and serves as a better wrapper, though it is somewhat coarser than soft lettuces. You may use bibb or other greens, if you prefer.

20 to 24 ounces boneless,
   skinless salmon fillet
1 tablespoon oil
2 tablespoons freshly squeezed
   lemon juice
2 teaspoons minced fresh ginger

2 tablespoons minced fresh dill
salt and freshly ground white
   pepper to taste
8 leaves romaine lettuce
2 tablespoons melted butter or
   beurre blanc

1. Cut salmon into 12 equal chunks.
2. Marinate fish for 45 to 60 minutes in oil, lemon juice, ginger, dill, salt, and pepper.
3. Set water in a steamer to simmer.
4. Wash lettuce well and choose the most tender center leaves. Remove most of tough ribs. With romaine use only the top third of each leaf.
5. Remove fish from marinade. Wrap lettuce about a chunk of fish — you can use 2 or 3 pieces of lettuce if they are small. Set seam side down in the steamer rack. Steam 10 minutes.
6. Serve 3 packets of fish to each diner and pour melted butter or a beurre blanc (page 64) over them.

Serves 4. Approximate nutrition information per serving: Calories 437; protein 36g; fat 30g; carbohydrates 3g; sodium 210 mg.

Quick Salmon Bake

In the place of the celery, in this dish, you may use chives, dill, tarragon, or another favorite fresh herb, if you wish.

1 pound salmon, thick boneless and skinless fillet
fresh parsley, to make 1 tablespoon minced
celery leaves, to make ½ tablespoon minced

3 tablespoons butter
1 tablespoon minced shallots
salt and pepper
2 tablespoons vermouth or dry white wine

1. Cut fillet crosswise into slices about ⅜-inch thick.
2. Mince the parsley and celery together.
3. Preheat oven to 375 degrees.
4. Using 1 tablespoon butter, grease an ovenproof pan or skillet. Sprinkle the bottom with shallots, and season lightly with salt and pepper.
5. Arrange the fish slices in overlapping fashion in the pan. Season lightly with salt and pepper. Add the minced parsley and celery. Cover with buttered foil or parchment.
6. Bake in preheated oven for 8 minutes or until fish is done. Remove from oven, remove fish from pan, cover, and keep warm.
7. On a medium-high stove burner, add 2 tablespoons butter to the baking pan, whipping in a bit at a time to incorporate thoroughly, adding any juices from the reserved salmon. Heat, but do not boil. Add ¼ teaspoon salt, and correct the seasoning.
8. Place the salmon on warm serving dishes, ladle a little sauce over each serving, and pass additional sauce.

Serves 4. Approximate nutrition information per serving: Calories 325; protein 26g; fat 24g; carbohydrates 1g; sodium 240 mg.

Salmon with Rhubarb

This is a superb marriage in which the tart, astringent flavor of rhubarb balances the suave richness of fresh salmon. Both arrive on the culinary scene at their freshest best at about the same time — as spring turns to summer. If you put up your own rhubarb in water or in a canning process equally as neutral, you can enjoy this dish at other times of the year. The dish works best, however, when the rhubarb is crisp.

Don't be tempted to peel your rhubarb the way you might peel a stalk of celery. You want as much of the rosy color of rhubarb as you can get.

Also, use a dry rosé wine. The tartness of the rhubarb might be overcome by a sweet wine, upsetting the flavor balance. It is better if you use a dry wine and, if necessary, add a touch of sugar or honey to the dish, rather than to begin by having a dish that is merely bland or downright cloying.

Since most of the pink wines you find on the market tend to be medium-dry or definitely sweet, check with your wine merchant. Rosé wines from Tavel in France, for example, are usually dry; Anjou wines are inclined to be sweet.

If he does not have a dry rosé, he might have a white wine from red grapes that is dry. Such California wines as White Zinfandel, or White Pinot Noir are usually in the market under such names as "blanc de noir" (white of black) or "eye of the swan" or some such designation. Such wines tend to be a light rose blush, pink or salmon-colored, and frequently are dry.

4 salmon steaks, 5 to 6 ounces each, bone in, skin on
1½ tablespoon butter
1 tablespoon minced shallots
1 cup dry rosé wine
2 cups thinly sliced rhubarb
salt and pepper
½ cup butter, soft, not melted
½ cup rhubarb, the reddest outside part, cut in fine julienne

1. Preheat oven to 375 degrees. Grease an ovenproof pan with 1 tablespoon butter. Sprinkle shallots in bottom of pan and place steaks atop shallots. Add wine. Strew sliced rhubarb about fish, season lightly with salt and pepper. Cover loosely with buttered kitchen foil or parchment.

2. Bake 10 minutes for each inch of thickness. You can check salmon steaks for doneness by inserting a knife or other pointed instrument into the center of the bone itself and rocking it back and forth. When the bone pulls free from the flesh, the steaks are done.

3. When steaks are cooked, lift from the baking pan, and remove the skin and centerbone. Discard. Cover steaks, and keep them warm.

4. Reduce liquid and rhubarb pieces in pan to 1 cup, adding any liquid that drains from the standing salmon steaks as the reduction continues.

5. Place the reduced liquid in a blender, in two batches if necessary, with the ½ cup soft butter; whip. Correct the seasoning.

6. Meanwhile, saute the julienned rhubarb just to wilt in the remaining ½ tablespoon butter.

7. Place the salmon steaks on warmed individual serving dishes, spoon a few tablespoons of sauce onto each steak, and garnish with rhubarb julienne.

Serves 4. Approximate nutrition information per serving: Calories 565; protein 32g; fat 46g; carbohydrates 6g; sodium 540 mg.

Salmon with Hazelnut Coating

This is a quick and simple recipe, and a marvelous and different way to use fresh salmon. Salmon's richness has a flavor that echoes that of the hazelnut and the combination marries extremely well. Don't be fooled by the simplicity — this is a rich dish.

Hazelnuts are most often sold without their shells, but with their inner brown skins covering the kernel. To remove the skins, place hazelnuts in a dry pan in a 350-degree oven and roast until the skins are crisp and dry. Rub the nuts between the palms of your hands and the skins will fall away. Repeat the roasting until you can remove the skins from all the nuts. This operation not only removes the skin, but also adds a wonderful roasted flavor to the nuts. The skins also can be removed by blanching, but roasting adds an additional quality for recipes of this kind.

Chop or grind the peeled nuts so that the finished product ranges from a powder to kernels the size of small peppercorns. The range of textures will give better adhesion and better flavor.

Using different nuts and different fish will provide an endless variety of dishes. Try walnuts, macadamia nuts, pecans, pine nuts, almonds, or any others at hand. Ocean catfish, ocean perch, members of the cod family, and all the flat fishes may be substituted for the salmon, especially if you seek a less rich dish.

1 pound boneless and skinless salmon fillet	1 tablespoon water
	salt and pepper
1 cup peeled, chopped hazelnuts	¼ cup plus 1 tablespoon flour
1 egg	3 tablespoons butter
1 tablespoon oil	lemon wedges

1. Cut the fillet into 8 medallions, about ⅜-inch thick.

2. Make egg wash with egg, oil, water, and salt and pepper to taste, and beat lightly with a fork.

3. Mix 1 tablespoon flour with the nuts and place in a flat dish.

4. Place ¼ cup flour in another flat dish.

5. Dredge fillets in flour and shake off excess. Dip in egg wash, drain, and then dredge in the nut mixture. Pat well so that nuts adhere.

6. Melt 3 tablespoons butter in a saute pan large enough to hold the fillets in one layer. Add the fish and saute on one side until golden brown. Turn over carefully and saute the other side. Don't rush the cooking; saute over medium heat so that the fish cooks, but the nut coating does not burn.

7. Place the fillets on warm serving dishes. Serve with lemon wedges. You don't need butter or other embellishments for this dish. The fattiness of the salmon and the oiliness of the nuts make it rich enough as it is, and the dish should be fairly dry.

Serves 4. Approximate nutrition information per serving: Calories 594; protein 32g; fat 45g; carbohydrates 14g; sodium 260 mg.

Noisettes de Saumon

◼◼

BONELESS SALMON "CHOPS"

In culinary parlance, noisette is used to describe a small, round, choice morsel of meat; lamb noisettes, for instance. In this recipe, a choice cut of salmon is prepared in much the same manner as one would prepare lamb.

The salmon steaks should be taken from a center-cut of salmon, so that as much as possible of the belly portion is included.

4 salmon steaks, about 24 ounces, bone-in	8 mushroom caps
5 tablespoons butter	2 tablespoons minced chives
1½ tablespoons oil	2 tablespoons freshly squeezed lemon juice
flour for dusting	

1. Make 8 noisettes weighing 2 to 2½ ounces each. With a sharp knife, cut away the backbone, taking a large piece of meat from each side of the steak; in effect, cutting each steak in half. They will look like a small pork chop. Tuck the "tail" of the chop around the center to make round noisettes. Secure with toothpicks so that they will retain their shape in cooking. Do not roll too tightly or heat won't penetrate efficiently. Just make a loose, round package of each noisette. (See drawings on the next two pages.)

2. Melt 3 tablespoons butter in a skillet and heat with 1½ tablespoons oil.

3. Dredge noisettes in flour, shake off the excess, and saute in the hot butter and oil until golden brown on one side. Turn and saute the second side. Remove from pan, take out the toothpicks, cover, and keep warm on serving plates.

4. Saute mushroom caps in same pan in which you cooked fish. Remove when nicely browned and place atop the salmon. Discard the butter in the skillet.

5. Add 2 tablespoons fresh butter to the skillet. Cook until nut brown in color, then add the chives and lemon juice. Pour over the fish.

6. Serve with lemon wedges. A bouquet of seasonal vegetables, such as asparagus tips, broccoli spears, green beans, or cauliflower, goes well with the noisettes. Small oven-roasted potatoes also would go well.

Serves 4. Approximate nutrition information per serving: Calories 293; protein 20g; fat 21g; carbohydrates 4g; sodium 90 mg.

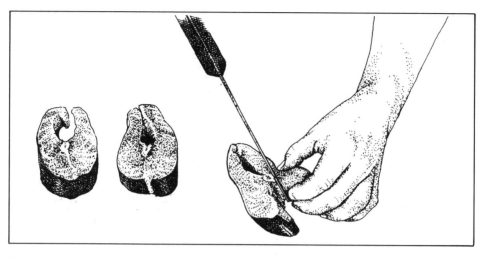

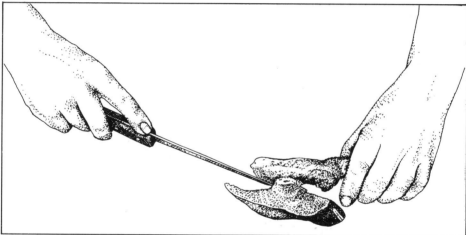

HOW TO MAKE SALMON NOISETTES

Top: Three salmon steaks will make six noisettes. Cut through the steak from the top to the backbone.

Bottom: Trim around the bone to separate the steak into two portions.

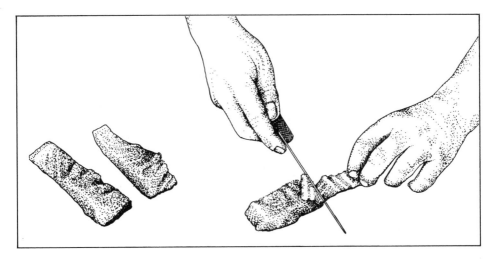

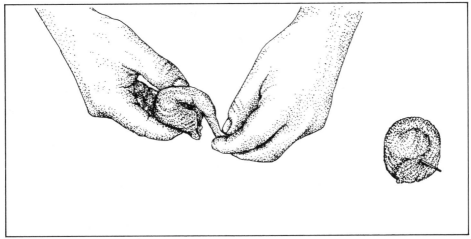

Top: Using a sharp knife, remove the skin from each piece.

Bottom: Wrap the "tail" end around the larger end of the piece of salmon, and secure it with a toothpick.

Salmon with Sorrel Sauce

Sorrel is an underutilized vegetable in this country, though it is much admired elsewhere, especially in France. It has been cultivated in Europe since classical times. In France, the bony shad is cooked with it. Sorrel's oxalic acid dissolves the shad's many small bones, making it easier to eat.

Sorrel has a pungent, acidic flavor that is almost sour. Americans with Russian, Polish, and other East Europe roots, Jews especially, use it in a soup, schav, *made with sorrel, onions, lemon juice, and eggs.*

In this dish, an adaptation of a dish made famous by the brothers Troisgros of Roane, the sorrel's tangy flavor contrasts with the mildly fatty, sweet flavor of the salmon. This dish has an added advantage: You prepare it through step 6 several hours ahead; in individual portions, in the dishes in which it will be served.

Watercress may be substituted for sorrel, using only the leaves.

1 to 1¼ pounds boneless, and skinless salmon fillet	2 tablespoons finely minced shallots
1 cup fish stock (see White Wine Fumet page 30)	2 tablespoons white wine
4 tablespoons melted butter	½ cup cream
salt and white pepper to taste	1 tablespoon freshly squeezed lemon juice
fresh sorrel to make 1 well-packed cup	

1. Make the fish stock.

2. For each serving, brush the center of individual, ovenproof serving dishes with about half the melted butter, and sprinkle lightly with salt and white pepper. Chill to set.

3. Cut salmon fillet into slices approximately ⅜-inch thick. Allow 3 or 4 slices per person, about 4 to 5 ounces a serving.

4. Arrange each salmon serving atop each buttered and seasoned plate, and brush the salmon with more of the melted butter. You want just a coating on the plate and fish, not a pool.

5. Hold the fish in the refrigerator until it is ready to be cooked.

6. Wash and trim the sorrel and shred or cut it into thin strips, about ⅛-inch wide. Measure 1 well-packed cup of sorrel. Set aside.

7. Preheat oven to 375 degrees. Make sauce: In a small skillet or saute pan over medium-high heat, cook together the shallots, fish stock, and white wine. Reduce it to approximately ¼ cup. Add cream and reduce by

half. The sauce should be fairly thick. Add the shredded sorrel, bring the sauce to a boil, and remove it from the heat. Season to taste, add lemon juice, and stir. Cover and keep it hot, but not boiling.

8. Meanwhile, salt and pepper the fish and bake 3 to 4 minutes until done. Remove the plates from the oven, and spoon the sauce around salmon, but not on top. Serve immediately.

Serves 4. Approximate nutrition information per serving: Calories 470; protein 42g; fat 30g; carbohydrates 6g; sodium 870 mg.

Darne de Saumon Genevoise

SALMON STEAKS IN GENEVA SAUCE

Let's see, the rule is white wine with fish, red wine with meat. Everyone knows that. Wrong. Red wine with seafood — even white-fleshed fish from river or ocean — is an ancient combination. Every country noted for its red wine has native dishes featuring seafood cooked in it. In the Mâcon, a region of southern Burgundy noted for its white wines today, a dish called sole mâconnaise *is a fillet poached in red wine. At one time, red wine was the predominant wine in the Mâcon.* Matelote *is the name given in French cooking to a fish stew made with red wine. There are endless examples.*

In this recipe, Genevoise *is the French word meaning "from Geneva." The sauce is a classic of the French repertoire usually made with salmon trimmings, red wine, herbs, and anchovies; occasionally meat glaze is added. And if you are a wine buff and know that almost all the wine made in Switzerland today is white wine, you should know that red wine was once predominant in several districts of the Alpine country, just as in the Mâcon. One school of thought maintains the name should be* Genoise, *denoting Genoa, where red wine and anchovies are more abundant than in Switzerland.*

No matter, the dish is just as wonderful regardless of ancestry.

For this recipe you will need 4 salmon steaks, or darnes, *cut from the center of the fish, if possible. Each should be 1¼ to 1½ inches thick and weigh 5 to 6 ounces. The sauce also works well with bluefish, scup, or halibut steak.*

4 salmon steaks

FOR FISH STOCK:
3 pounds salmon trimmings —
    head (gills removed), bones,
    no skin
2 tablespoons butter
¾ cup diced onions
½ cup diced carrots
3 cups dry red wine
2 cups water
¼ teaspoon dried thyme
1 bay leaf
6 parsley stems
½ teaspoon black peppercorns,
    cracked

2 teaspoons salt
1 clove garlic, crushed

FOR POACHING LIQUID:
1 cup fish stock
1 cup dry red wine

GENEVA SAUCE:
6 tablespoons soft butter
5 tablespoons flour
2 tablespoons anchovy paste
1 tablespoon chopped fresh
    parsley
salt (optional)
freshly ground black pepper
    (optional)

1. Make fish stock: Saute the onions and carrots in the 2 tablespoons butter until browned. Add all the rest of the stock ingredients, and cook for 30 minutes over low heat so that the pot just barely simmers. Skim carefully from time to time to remove any scum that rises.

2. Remove from heat and strain through a fine sieve and let the stock stand for approximately 10 minutes so that the fat rises to the top. Skim carefully; a paper towel dragged across the surface will help gather the last drops of fat. You should have about 4 cups of stock (*fumet*). Return to heat and reduce to about half over medium-high heat.

3. Preheat oven to 375 degrees. Poach salmon steaks: Butter a stainless steel, enamel or other ovenproof glass baking dish. Select a size in which the 4 steaks will fit snugly so that they don't lose their shapes. Mix 1 cup stock with 1 cup wine and pour over the steaks (reserving 3 cups of stock). The steaks should be covered completely; if not, add more red wine until they are. Cover with buttered foil or parchment and bake 12 minutes — do not overcook. To test steaks for doneness, poke a small knife into bone and rock knife back and forth. When bone moves easily and pulls away from flesh, fish is done.

4. While the steaks are poaching, begin making the Geneva Sauce. When the salmon steaks are cooked, lift them carefully from the poaching liquid and remove the skin around each steak. Remove the center bone of each steak by inserting a small knife at its center and tipping bone out of fish. Make sure that any smaller bones are removed. Cover and reserve

steaks, keeping them warm. Mix the poaching liquid (there should be about 1 cup) with the 3 cups of stock and reduce over medium heat to about 1½ cups while you complete the sauce.

5. Thoroughly mix 2 tablespoons anchovy paste with 2 tablespoons soft butter and set aside to be used in the sauce.

6. Melt 4 tablespoons butter in a heavy, non-corrosive sauce pan. Stir in flour and cook over low heat 2 or 3 minutes, stirring constantly with a wire whisk. Add the reduced 1½ cups stock together with any juices that have drained from the salmon steaks. Stir until smooth, and allow to cook over medium heat for 10 to 12 minutes. Stir occasionally to prevent scorching. Skim any fat or scum that rises. Remove from heat and strain sauce through a fine sieve. You should have 1½ cups.

7. Return the sauce to heat and boil for a second or two. Remove and add the reserved anchovy butter and stir in briskly with a wire whisk, making sure anchovy butter is thoroughly incorporated into sauce. Correct the seasoning, adding salt and pepper if you wish. The dish should be highly seasoned.

8. Place warm salmon steaks onto individual serving plates or onto serving platter, pour the sauce over them and sprinkle with chopped parsley.

Serves 4. Fumet, 1 cup: Approximate nutrition information per serving: Calories 345; protein 33g; fat 19g; carbohydrates 12g; sodium 1150 mg. Approximate nutrition information per serving: Calories 677; protein 37g; fat 46g; carbohydrates 25g; sodium 1890 mg.

Seafood Terrine with Mousse Base

A terrine and a pâté are similar preparations. Originally, a pâté was baked in a pastry crust, while a terrine was lined with pork and fat. Nowadays, the definitions blur.

Our terrine is a rectangular loaf that is lined with salmon slices and spinach and filled with mousse. When the terrine is sliced, a colorful center core of cooked whole carrot wrapped in spinach is revealed. Or, you may use a variety of vegetables in the center to achieve the same effect. Asparagus or fresh string beans may be paired with strips of bright red sweet bell pepper, either as is the carrot in this recipe or interspersed throughout the terrine. Kale, savoy cabbage, or other greens can be substituted for the spinach. A zucchini, unpeeled, cored, and blanched, which is filled with some of the mousse, would give a striking effect. Use your imagination in devising seasonal flavor and color contrasts that will make the dish attractive.

The terrine may be served hot or cold. It makes a nice, light summer lunch when it is served cold, or it can be used as a first course for a dinner. A tomato mousseline is a perfect sauce — light, flavorful, and contrasting in color.

1 pound fresh salmon fillet, in
    one piece
1 or 2 whole carrots
2 pounds fresh spinach

MOUSSE:
8 ounces chilled sea scallops
salt and pepper
pinch of nutmeg

1 chilled egg
1 cup heavy cream, chilled

¼ cup pistachios with skins
    removed or minced chives
    (optional)
Tomato Mousseline (see page 51)

1. Chill an ovenproof, oblong, 1-quart mold. Coat the bottom and sides with softened butter, and place it in the refrigerator to chill again.

2. Remove bones from salmon and slice it as thinly as possible, as you would smoked salmon. Chill until ready to use.

3. The carrot or carrots will be placed lengthwise down the center of mold. If you can't find a carrot that is about ½-inch shorter than the length of mold, you will have to use two or three. They should reach nearly from end to end, be of uniform thickness, and no thicker than about 1 inch. Cook in simmering salted water until tender but still firm.

4. Reserve water in which you cooked carrot to blanch spinach.

5. Wash and pick over spinach; trim tough stalks. Blanch spinach 10 seconds and refresh in cold water immediately to retain color. Lay out spinach leaves on paper towels, selecting the largest and most uniform, blot dry. Wrap carrot or carrots entirely within 2 layers of spinach leaves so that it resembles one long green sausage. Reserve it and the rest of the spinach. Discard water or save it for stock or soup.

6. Make mousse: Add cold scallops, salt, pepper, nutmeg, and pinch of cayenne to work bowl of food processor and work in bursts until mixture pulls away from sides of bowl in a ball. Add egg and process 10 seconds. Add heavy cream and process until smooth — 10 to 15 seconds. Chill while you proceed with next steps.

7. Remove mold and salmon from refrigerator. Line bottom and sides

of mold with salmon slices. The slices should extend over the sides and the ends of the mold so that when it is filled they may be folded part way over the top. Save a slice or two to cover the top of the completed mold. Press the salmon against the sides of the mold so that the butter will hold it in place. Salt it lightly.

8. Press the blanched spinach leaves flat against the salmon, in a layer about ¼-inch thick. Try to keep the thickness of the spinach uniform and have it extend over the top, but not as much as does the salmon. Reserve enough to cover the top to the same thickness.

9. Fill the mold ⅓ full with mousse and sprinkle a scant tablespoon of pistachios (or chives), if you are using them. Add more mousse to fill mold nearly half full. Set the carrot wrapped in spinach lengthwise down the center of the half-filled mold atop the mousse. Sprinkle a few more pistachios (chives) on either side, and add mousse until the mold is ⅔ full. Sprinkle another scant tablespoon of pistachios (chives). Fill the mold nearly to the top with the remaining mousse.

10. Lay the reserved spinach leaves flat atop mousse and bring overhanging spinach up and over top. Lay the reserved salmon slices atop spinach and bring original salmon flaps over atop this.

11. Preheat oven to 350 degrees. Set a 4-quart kettle or pan of water to simmer. Cover the mold with buttered foil or buttered parchment. Set it into a larger deep pan such as a roasting pan, and add simmering water halfway up the mold.

12. Set the mold in its water bath into oven and bake 45 to 50 minutes. Test the terrine to make certain it is cooked by inserting a metal skewer or small knife blade and allowing it to rest there for a few moments. When the skewer is withdrawn it should be warm — not hot or cool — along entire length that was inserted in the mold. Placing skewer or blade just under your lower lip immediately as it is withdrawn is the best way to test.

13. Remove mold and water bath from oven and take mold out of bath.

14. If you are serving it hot, allow to rest in a warm place at least 15 minutes before trying to unmold. Unmold and slice in kitchen, setting atop tomato mousseline on serving plate. Alternately, bring to table whole and slice, allowing each guest to pour his or her own sauce.

15. If you are serving it cold, cool in the mold and then set it in the refrigerator overnight. To unmold, you may have to set it into a warm water bath for a minute or two to loosen. Slice and serve on chilled plates.

Serves 4. Approximate nutrition information per serving without sauce: Calories 656; protein 50g; fat 45g; carbohydrates 15g; sodium 521 mg.

Rillettes de Saumon

POTTED SALMON

In a world too often populated by commercial dips and spreads more the result of chemistry than cooking, this recipe will be a revelation of clean fresh flavors. Rillettes *are an ancient French preparation using a shredded main ingredient blended most often with pork fat. Pork, chicken, duck, goose, and rabbit all are used.*

In this recipe, rich fresh salmon and flavorful smoked salmon are b'ended with cream cheese, mustard, and brandy. Don't mash everything too finely; the dish should have texture as well as flavor. Use it as an hors d'oeuvre, as a spread for crackers, toast points, or crusty bread.

You often can buy smoked salmon trimmings, which are less expensive and work just as well, so long as there are no bones, hard pieces, skin, or discolored portions.

You can make this a day ahead and keep it covered in the refrigerator.

4 ounces fresh salmon, cut into 1-inch cubes	2 tablespoons butter
4 ounces smoked salmon, cut into 1-inch cubes	1 teaspoon Dijon mustard
2 tablespoons white wine	2 teaspoons cognac or brandy
¼ teaspoon salt	freshly ground pepper
¼ cup cream cheese	

1. Cook fresh salmon in the 2 tablespoons wine seasoned with ¼ teaspoon salt, just until done. Allow to cool; cover and chill.

2. Put smoked salmon, cream cheese, butter, mustard, cognac, and a few turns of pepper into the work bowl of your food processor and work for 10 to 20 seconds. It should be pureed, but do not over-process. Correct the seasoning.

3. Flake and lightly mash the cooked and chilled salmon, using a fork. Again, don't break it down too much.

4. Using a spatula, combine the smoked salmon mixture with the fresh salmon, smoothing and blending evenly.

5. Cover with plastic wrap and chill.

6. Return the potted salmon almost to room temperature and serve as a spread.

Serves 4-6. Approximate nutrition information per serving: Calories 215; protein 13g; fat 17g; carbohydrates 1g; sodium 700 mg.

Trout

Although our interest in this book is fishes of the sea, the trout is so ubiquitous that it would be difficult to ignore it. At its best, trout is fine eating.

Trout and salmon have a common heritage; witness the salmon-trout. Trout also react well to the same kinds of preparations as are used for salmon—the simplest are best, but they also do well in complicated recipes.

Taken fresh from a clear, cold mountain stream and pan-fried, there are few fishes to match a trout. A living trout that you have selected yourself from a tank in a rustic dining room in Europe can be gastronomic fare of the highest order when it is cooked *au bleu*. Poached in vinegar and water enhanced with aromatic vegetables and herbs, it arrives a glistening blue at the table. Unfortunately, one cannot often visit bucolic riverside inns in the foothills of the Alps or icy, limpid Rocky Mountain streams to get trout.

Most often, the trout available to us is likely to be hatchery-grown, which, when rushed eastward fresh from Idaho or some other high ground, can be respectable eating. But such is not usually the case. Which is not to denigrate hatchery-grown trout — they can be of a high order. But which hatchery raised the fish is as important in this case as which house smoked the salmon when considering that table fare.

Just consider the circumstances of the trout's rearing; the temperature of the water (cold or lukewarm), the makeup of his home (was it filled with algae or too high in mineral content), his diet (if he fed on small oily fish like the alewife, his flesh is likely to be oily, too), and the amount of exercise he got in his lifetime (did he laze in a lake or battle the currents of a swift-flowing stream). There is even disagreement as to the eating qualities of the brook, lake, rainbow, and brown trout, just to name the best known.

Most of what is available at retail, at least from western sources, is frozen. The dictum we have laid down about all fish is especially true about trout: The opposite of fresh is not frozen, but stale. If you can't buy truly fresh trout, you will probably do better with one that has been properly flash-frozen.

Since obtaining all that knowledge about a foot-long, 1 to 2 pound spotted silver torpedo lying in a chiller at a fishmonger's store is darn near impossible, you will have to rely upon the fastidiousness of your dealer to see that you are well-served.

If we appear to belabor the trout, it is only because in most cases when he is far from his home his reputation is overblown and undeserved; his price too dear. Too often the trout is a mushy, flavorless specimen, with much of his essence leached or dried out by the time he is on a plate.

You might do better to consider the whiting, the ocean perch, or black bass for your supper, and wait for a trout snaggled from its local habitat by you or a generous fisherman friend.

One aspect of a trout, which makes it especially attractive, is the ease with which one can be boned, especially when cooked. The backbone and rib cage can be lifted out with a minimum of fuss, and this is one reason for the trout's popularity.

For the same reason, a trout is welcome in the kitchen when a recipe calls for stuffing it from the top or back. It is easily gutted by removing the backbone, rib cage, and viscera. See the drawings on pages 230 and 231.

Smoked trout usually is excellent — and, like smoked sturgeon and smoked eel — makes a wonderful and less common appetizer than smoked salmon.

Scallop-stuffed Trout

This dish will require less effort on your part if you can purchase your fresh trout already boned and eviscerated through the back. Otherwise you will have to do it. You may prepare this dish ahead of time, and do the baking just before serving.

4 whole trout, dressed and boned	1 tablespoon minced chives
8 ounces scallops	4 tablespoons soft butter
5 slices bacon	salt and pepper
	lemon wedges as garnish

1. Chop 4 slices of bacon coarsely. Reserve the fifth slice. Fry the chopped bacon until it is about ¾ done. Remove from pan, leaving rendered bacon fat. Crumble chopped bacon if pieces are too large.

2. In the bacon fat, saute scallops until lightly browned and firmed. Don't overcook them; 3 or 4 minutes should be enough. Remove scallops and drain on paper toweling. Retain the bacon fat. When the scallops have cooled, chop them coarsely.

3. In a bowl, mix chives with soft butter; add scallops and chopped bacon, blend, and reserve.

4. Using the retained bacon fat, lightly grease a baking pan large enough to hold the 4 trout. Rub trout with additional bacon fat and place in the pan stomach-side down. Open the cavity created by the removal of the backbone. Season lightly with salt and pepper.

5. Stuff each trout with one-quarter of the scallop-bacon stuffing. Cut reserved slice of bacon into 1-inch pieces and place these on the heads and tails of the trout to prevent them from burning.

6. Preheat oven to 400 degrees. Place baking pan in oven and bake for 10 to 12 minutes, or 10 minutes for each inch of thickness of trout measured at thickest part.

7. Serve immediately with lemon wedges as garnish.

Serves 4. Approximate nutrition information per serving: Calories 375; protein 45g; fat 21g; carbohydrates 1g; sodium 520 mg.

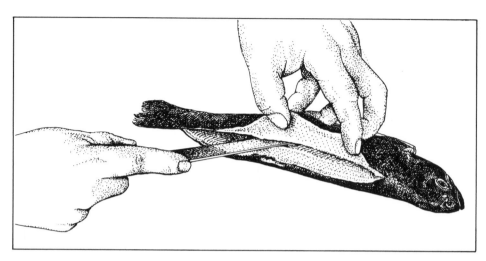

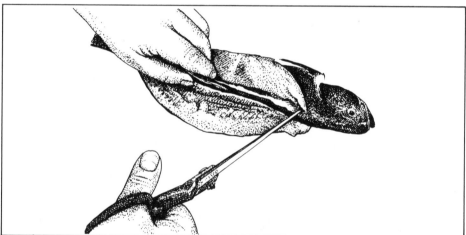

Top: To bone the trout through the back, make deep parallel cuts from head to tail along both sides of the backbone.

Bottom: Sever the backbone at each end with a knife or strong kitchen shears, and lift it out.

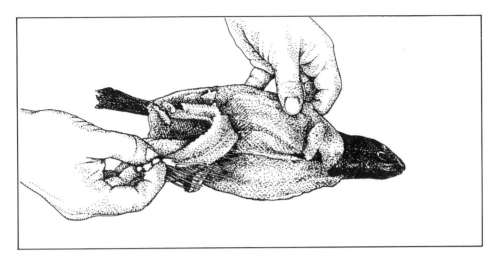

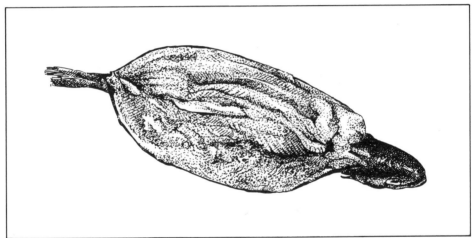

Top: If the trout has not already been gutted, remove the entrails through the back. Wash thoroughly. If you bought trout gutted in the usual way, you still can debone it through the back, but it will have no bottom under the stuffing. Getting it from the pan to the serving platter without dropping the stuffing would be tricky, if not impossible. One way around the problem would be to lay each trout on foil or parchment before stuffing them. After baking the trout and setting them on serving plates, slide the foil out from under them.

Bottom: You will place the stuffing in the cavity that you have created. The trout will bake lying on its belly.

Trout in Parchment

■■

TRUITE EN PAPILLOTE

*It is the duty of the cook to make a meal as pleasant as possible for guests —
and that includes the getting of the food from plate to mouth. To open a foil
or parchment envelope and then attempt to eat a fish off the bone amidst a
crinkly wrapping can be a trying feat.*

*Therefore, for this recipe you should do the work for your guests and
fillet the trout before cooking them.*

*Cooking in a package is an excellent method for cooking fish. Dry heat
from the oven and steam generated within the package cook the fish, yet
keep it succulent and moist. Each diner opens his own sealed envelope and
is met with all the marvelous aroma that has been trapped within. It will
work as successfully with flounder, whiting, and similar white fish fillets.*

*You will need 4 envelopes. Parchment paper works the best. Your next
choice would be brown butcher's paper, but not brown paper bags, which
are chemically treated. Foil also may be used, but it is your last choice for
aesthetic reasons — crinkly foil is not the most attractive thing to find on a
dinner plate.*

*Cut 4 sheets of paper. Each sheet should be 2 to 4 inches longer than
your fillets and roomily wide — you don't want to crowd the ingredients.
For 10-inch trout fillets, a sheet 12 to 14 inches wide by 16 inches long
would be adequate.*

*Fold the paper in half so that it is 12 by 8 inches. Trace half a heart on it,
beginning at the fold, and cut it out. You don't have to win an arts and crafts
medal with your effort; it will be fine so long as it somewhat resembles a
heart. Repeat with the other 3 pieces of paper. When the heart is folded, the
fish and other ingredients will go onto one lobe, the other will be folded
over the fish, and the edges will be sealed by folding.*

*The fish-filled envelopes can be held in the refrigerator for several
hours. Remove 30 minutes ahead of the cooking time so that they will come
to room temperature. Preheat the oven 15 minutes before cooking.*

4 whole trout
1 carrot
1 stalk of celery
1 leek
9 tablespoons butter
4 teaspoons minced shallots
salt and pepper

4 teaspoons dry white wine or
  vermouth
1 tablespoon minced fresh
  parsley
beurre blanc (page 64) or melted
  butter

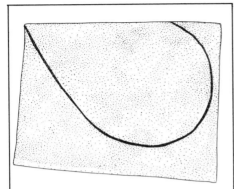

1. On a folded piece of parchment paper, draw one side of a heart.

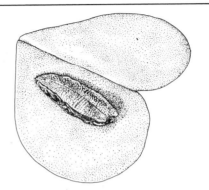

2. Open the paper and place the stuffed fillet of trout on one side, close to the fold.

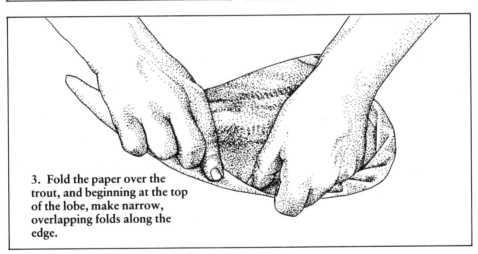

3. Fold the paper over the trout, and beginning at the top of the lobe, make narrow, overlapping folds along the edge.

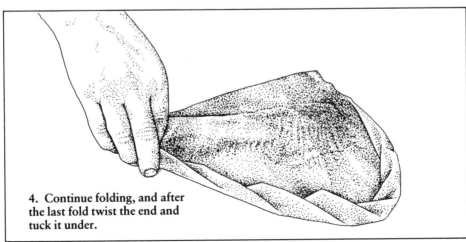

4. Continue folding, and after the last fold twist the end and tuck it under.

1. Cut two fillets from each trout, or have your fishmonger do it. Keep the 8 fillets cool until you are ready to use them.

2. Cut carrot, celery, and leek into julienne strips, about ⅛-inch wide by 2 to 3 inches long, to make ½ cup each. Place the carrots in a small saute pan with 2 tablespoons butter and a light sprinkling of salt and pepper. Saute over medium-low heat for 2 minutes, add celery, and in 2 more minutes add leeks. Saute until they all are cooked, but still quite firm. Remove pan from heat, cover, and allow vegetables to steam so that they will not toughen.

3. Butter one-half of the paper heart, using about 1 tablespoon butter per sheet. Season lightly with salt and pepper, and sprinkle 1 teaspoon shallots on each buttered half.

4. Place a fillet atop shallots, season lightly with salt and pepper, cover with one-fourth of the julienned vegetables, and place a second trout fillet on top. Season again with salt and pepper, moisten with 1 teaspoon of wine and dot with 1½ teaspoons of butter. Garnish with a scant teaspoon of minced parsley. Do this with each piece of paper.

5. Fold the second lobe of the heart over the fish. Beginning at the top of the heart where the two rounded lobes join, make narrow folds an inch or two in length around the perimeter. Each fold will serve to anchor the preceding one. The last fold can be double-sealed by turning the point of the heart up upon itself. Make 4 packages.

6. Butter a cookie sheet or other ovenproof pan with the remaining 1 tablespoon butter and set the 4 fish packages onto it. (Refrigerate packages a few hours at this point.)

7. Preheat oven to 375 degrees.

8. Bake packages for 12 minutes. Transfer to a serving plate with a wide spatula.

9. Serve with beurre blanc or melted butter.

Serves 4. Approximate nutrition information per serving: Calories 534; protein 34g; fat 44g; carbohydrates 4g; sodium 160 mg.

Trout Hawaiian in Parchment

Read the preceding recipe, as you prepare the trout fillets and the paper hearts in the same manner as in the above recipe.

8 trout fillets
¼ cup diced celery
¼ cup diced onion
7 tablespoons butter
¼ cup day-old white bread
     broken into small pieces
½ cup heavy cream
¼ cup diced apples
¼ cup chopped macadamia nuts

4 teaspoons minced shallots
salt and freshly ground black
     pepper
4 teaspoons dry white wine
1 tablespoon minced fresh
     parsley
beurre blanc (page 64) or melted
     butter

1. In a small saucepan, saute the onion and celery in 1 tablespoon butter over medium heat just until softened but not yet picking up color. Remove from heat, and allow to cool.

2. Place bread in a small bowl and add heavy cream. Work it with a fork and allow to soak.

3. Add chopped apples and nuts to onion and celery; mix. Incorporate bread and cream. Season with a turn of freshly ground black pepper and mix thoroughly.

4. Coat each paper heart with 1 tablespoon butter, season lightly with salt and pepper, and sprinkle with minced shallots.

5. Lay a trout fillet on one half of a paper heart, season with salt and pepper, and spread one-fourth of the apple-nut filling along its length. Top with second fillet. Sprinkle again with salt and pepper. Dot with 1 teaspoon butter; moisten with 1 teaspoon white wine; garnish with a scant teaspoon of minced parsley.

6. Seal package; complete the remaining 3 in the same manner. Place on buttered cookie sheet or baking pan, and refrigerate, if desired, a few hours.

7. Preheat oven to 375 degrees for 15 minutes. Bake packages for 12 minutes.

8. Serve with beurre blanc or melted butter.

Serves 4. Approximate nutrition information per serving without sauce: Calories 618; protein 37g; fat 52g; carbohydrates 7g; sodium 165 mg.

Shark

■■

Sharks, like the rays, skates, and some other edible sea creatures, do not have a bony skeleton, but, rather, are cartilaginous. Because they are cartilaginous, their yield of edible flesh is higher than that of bony fishes. Shark can be used in many recipes calling for swordfish, mackerel, tuna, bluefish, or even shad and mullet. Because some people hesitate to eat shark, its price is favorable. All those are good reasons to buy it, and once you have sampled shark, you will be certain to use it more often.

Shark flesh is not unlike that of swordfish. In fact, you probably have bought mako shark under the name swordfish, since it is sometimes substituted for that fish. Mako is excellent as a steak. It can be cubed and threaded on skewers or used in any barbecue variation. It also works extremely well in Chinese stir-fry dishes. It also is spelled maco, and sometimes is called mackerel shark.

The white flesh of the bull and blue shark closely resembles halibut, and, in fact, "harbor halibut" is a euphemism for shark in Maine. It also is often called "veal of the sea" for the same reason.

The spiny dogfish of the Atlantic, also called grayfish, is really a small shark. They average 3 feet in length and 7 to 10 pounds in weight, about half the size of a mako. The thresher, found in both the Atlantic and Pacific, is another shark species that is used as food.

Shark is more utilized in other countries than in the United States. The popular fish 'n' chips of England are commonly made from dogfish or other shark flesh. The Japanese are fond of shark meat and no serious Chinese banquet is complete without sharkfin appearing on the table in some way, often in the famous soup by that name. One species of shark is called the Soupfin, indicating it is the one used for that purpose by the Chinese, but, in fact, almost any sharkfin will do.

The most likely shark to be found on an American table, if any, is the mako shark.

Other than a human aversion to sharks because of their fearsome reputation, there is no reason to eschew the species gastronomically. Shark meat tastes good; it is firm, tender, and mildly flavored; many prefer it to swordfish. Its high yield, about 40 percent, roughly twice as much as that from bony fish, makes it economical.

It is also good nutritionally. It has more protein and less fat than beef, and also has fewer calories. It is low in sodium, but high in vitamins A and B, and contains generous amounts of minerals. Its liver oil is higher in vitamin A than cod liver oil.

There is one other aspect about shark that must be understood. Since they, like all fishes, live in an environment that is much saltier than their bodies, nature must provide a way of getting rid of the excess salt they take in. If they were not equipped to do this, they would give up too much water to their environment. Bony fish do this through a special adaptation in their gills that eliminates the excess. Cartilaginous fish do so by maintaining in their blood and tissues a high concentration of urea that maintains the proper balance of salt and water.

After death the amount of urea or ammonia increases. An ammonia smell is quite high immediately after cartilaginous fish are caught. This is natural. After some time, both the smell and the ammonia itself disappear, which is why it is recommended that such fish are better held a day or two before cooking. This gets rid of the excess ammonia and accomplishes it before other harmful deterioration has begun.

Some cooks soak ray and shark meat overnight to neutralize this tendency, or marinate it for at least several hours. Brine and milk are two marinades often suggested. We have cooked both skate and shark several ways without marination and have detected no strong ammonia smell before cooking and no undesirable smell or flavor after cooking. Most skate and shark meat that gets to retail fish markets is undoubtedly at least a day old before you buy it.

If the smell is present, however, you can wait 24 hours or more to make certain it has disappeared, and/or soak it in milk or brine before proceeding. There is nothing harmful about the flesh, however, except that the smell is offensive.

Smoked Mako Shark Vinaigrette

FROM PANACHE RESTAURANT, CAMBRIDGE, MASSACHUSETTS

Bruce Frankel is a young chef who opened his restaurant several years ago in a small storefront that lies within the shadow of MIT's main academic buildings. It was when nouvelle cuisine was still young and not yet known to many Bostonians. It was readily apparent that this was a dedicated, serious-minded chef who could meld a well-organized and knowledgeable staff. His food was fresh, of certain quality, his style clean to the point of severity. Frankel caught the new wave just as it began to swell, however, and Panache has been on upward course ever since.

This dish is in Frankel's tradition of using an ingredient, such as mako shark, which is not universally known and admired in this country, but beginning to catch on because of the work of chefs like Frankel. The brining followed by smoking is also an up-to-the-minute direction. The preparation technique is simple and straightforward, with no unnecessary complication, in spite of both brining and smoking.

1 pound mako shark, in 1-inch boneless steaks

BRINE:
1 cup hot water
2 tablespoons salt
3 tablespoons sugar or ¼ cup maple syrup
2 cups cold water

VINAIGRETTE:
1 finely chopped shallot

2 tablespoons sherry vinegar
freshly ground pepper and salt to taste
¼ cup olive oil
¼ cup vegetable oil
1 teaspoon chopped fresh tarragon or coriander leaves

2 tablespoons olive oil
2 tablespoons vegetable oil

1. Make the brine: Dissolve the salt and sugar in the hot water. Add the cold water and stir well. Place the fish in the brine and refrigerate for 36 hours. Remove the fish from the brine, dry well, and then let it sit uncovered for 2 hours before smoking.

2. Smoke the fish. Place the fish in a home smoker (L.L. Bean or Sears) and smoke it just for flavor by keeping it in for 20 minutes. Remove immediately and cool.

3. Make the vinaigrette: Combine the shallot, vinegar, salt, and pepper in a small bowl. Add the ¼ cup of both oils slowly, mixing constantly. Add the tarragon or coriander just before serving.

4. Cut the fish into strips 2 inches long and ¼-inch thick. Heat a large non-stick (Teflon) pan until medium-hot. Mix the two oils. Add half the quantity of oil and half the fish. Cook 10 to 20 seconds on each side. Place the fish on preheated serving plates. Repeat with the remaining fish and oil.

5. Mix the vinaigrette well and spoon over the hot fish. Serve immediatley as a first course.

Serves 4. Approximate nutrition information per serving: Calories 440; protein 23g; fat 35g; carbohydrates 10g; sodium 620mg.

Shark Brochettes

If you have liked swordfish this way, you should enjoy shark meat.

1 pound mako shark, cut into 2-inch cubes	1 tablespoon snipped chives
2 tablespoons oil	1 small onion
2 tablespoons lemon juice	1 medium zucchini
salt and pepper to taste	1 red bell pepper
	melted butter

1. Mix oil, lemon juice, salt, pepper, and chives, and marinate shark cubes in the mixture for an hour or so. Remove the cubes from the marinade and allow them to drain. Reserve the marinade.

2. Cut the onion into 8 equal wedges, and then cut each wedge in half. Cut the zucchini into crosswise chunks, or thick slices. Cut the bell pepper into wedges.

3. Alternate fish, onion pieces, sliced zucchini, and bell pepper wedges on skewers.

4. Grill over charcoal or broil under a gas broiler 4 inches from heat, basting frequently with marinade and rotating skewers to cook evenly. They should be done in 15 or 20 minutes.

5. Serve with melted butter, and lemon wedges.

Serves 4. Approximate nutrition information per serving: Calories 240; protein 25g; fat 12g; carbohydrates 7g; sodium 270 mg.

Stir-Fried Mako Shark

1 pound mako shark, cut into
    1-inch cubes
2 tablespoons light soy sauce
3 tablespoons dried black
    Chinese mushrooms, stems
    removed
¼ cup warm water
1 tablespoon cornstarch
1 tablespoon minced garlic
1 tablespoon minced fresh ginger
¼ cup onion cut into 1 x 1-inch
    squares
3 tablespoons scallions, white
    part only, cut into crosswise
    rings

1 green pepper
1 tomato
2 tablespoons dark soy sauce
pinch of white pepper
¼ teaspoon MSG (optional)
1 tablespoon Chinese cooking
    wine or dry sherry
1 cup chicken or beef broth,
    homemade or canned
1 tablespoon sesame oil

1. Marinate cubed shark in the light soy sauce for an hour or more, turning often.

2. Soak the mushrooms 30 to 60 minutes in ¼ cup warm water. Remove and coarsely chop. Set aside. Reserve 2 tablespoons of the mushroom-water and mix it with the cornstarch. Set aside. Stir the cornstarch mixture once more before you add it to the hot wok or skillet.

3. Prepare the garlic, ginger, onion, and scallions. Cut the green pepper and tomato into 6 wedges each, and then cut each one in half.

4. Drain the shark cubes. Heat 1 tablespoon peanut oil in wok or skillet. Add the shark cubes and saute them lightly. Remove the shark from the wok and reserve. Add garlic, ginger, onions, scallions, soaked mushrooms, and green pepper, and stir-fry until the vegetables are slightly cooked but still crisp. Add 2 tablespoons dark soy sauce, sherry, white pepper, shark, broth, and MSG. Bring to a boil, add tomatoes, cornstarch mixture, and sesame oil. Return to a boil and serve at once.

Serves 4. Approximate nutrition information per serving: Calories 265; protein 28g; fat 9g; carbohydrates 16g; sodium 1160 mg.

Swordfish

■■

Swordfish is a popular fish, both with sports fishermen and diners. It is a tropical fish that migrates as far north as Newfoundland. Its season is from June to October. The Latin name for the fish is the same root word as that for gladiator, *gladius*, the short sword carried by the Roman legions.

Swordfish flesh is off-white, sometimes pinkish with maroon markings, and is firm, medium-fat, and fine-grained. It is usually sold as crosscut steaks, and the centercuts are highly prized. It also is sold in cubes.

Anthony Athanas, of Boston's Pier 4 restaurant, and other fish-wise buyers make a distinction about the flesh of swordfish based on the way they are caught.

With the advent of world-roaming fishing fleets, the method of fishing for swordfish changed. For centuries the fish had been harpooned in waters fairly close to shore, which meant that whether caught on a single line or otherwise brought to boat, the swordfish was harpooned and most often brought aboard immediately.

The more efficient longlines of recent years introduced a new method in which fishing lines with multiple hooks are trolled behind the fishing boat. Swordfish strike the lines and are caught. The fish are not boated, however, until a sufficient number are hooked. It takes considerable time to get the miles-long lines aboard and back out again. This can mean that the first-caught fish can be dragged for hours behind the fishing craft — often dead for a considerable time.

Experts on swordfish say that rather than dying the more natural death by the harpoon, the longline swordfish are, in fact, drowned. This, they claim, results in a bloated, less-firm flesh. Almost all longline-caught swordfish are at least one day older when they get to market than those that were harpooned. Fish-wise buyers check that the swordfish they buy seems firm, not mushy.

A decade or so ago, sales of the species practically stopped in the United States when it was revealed that swordfish had far more mercury in them than the amount considered acceptable and safe for human consumption. There was some confusion at the time because it was not determined whether the high mercury level was due to some new manifestation of ocean pollution or was a natural attribute long common to the swordfish. The mercury poisoning scare abated, and swordfish consumption is back to near normal, since diners and scientists appear to have agreed that normal eating of the fish is unlikely to hold any danger and that the acceptable level of mercury was originally set too low.

Swordfish and Eggplant

Besides using swordfish in this recipe, you also may use tuna or mako shark.

14 to 16 ounces swordfish steaks
1 medium to small eggplant
2 tablespoons plus 2 teaspoons
   olive oil
2 or 3 large fresh tomatoes
2 cups thinly sliced onions

2 whole cloves of garlic
salt and pepper
pinch of dried thyme
½ bay leaf, crumpled
1 tablespoon minced fresh
   parsley

1. Remove and discard the bone and skin from the steaks. Cut fish on the bias into escallops, 2 x 3-inch slices, ¾-inch thick. Reserve.
2. Peel and cut eggplant crosswise, into slices about ¾-inch thick and roughly the same shape as fish slices.
3. Sprinkle eggplant slices with salt and set to drain for 15 minutes or so in a colander or on a slanted drainboard to draw off bitter juices.
4. Cut tomatoes in half and squeeze them to remove seeds and some liquid, and then slice into ¾-inch-thick slices. Reserve.
5. In a skillet over medium heat, saute onion slices in 1 tablespoon olive oil until lightly colored. Remove the onions and reserve.
6. In the same pan, saute 2 whole garlic cloves. Remove and discard the garlic when well browned. Saute the eggplant until it is nicely browned in the same skillet, using the additional 1 tablespoon olive oil if needed.
7. Preheat oven to 375 degrees. Spread the sauteed onion slices on the bottom of an ovenproof casserole lightly coated with olive oil.
8. Alternate slices of eggplant, tomato, and fish atop onion, overlap-

ping the slices by about one-third, until the ingredients are used up. Season with salt, pepper, thyme, and bay leaf. Drizzle 2 teaspoons of olive oil over all.

9. Bake for 12 minutes in preheated oven. Serve while hot, sprinkled with parsley. It also is good served cold.

Serves 4. Approximate nutrition information per serving: Calories 262; protein 22g; fat 9g; carbohydrates 17g; sodium 144 mg.

Serbian Swordfish
■■
FROM GAZELLE RESTAURANT, QUINCY, MASSACHUSETTS

Immediately south of Boston, in Quincy, Massachusetts, a young entrepeneur, Barry Kaplan, opened a restaurant named Gazelle on the top floor of a building in a complex of modern office structures. After having graduated from the University of New Hampshire, he had spent several formative years in the restaurant business, most recently in Las Vegas. Kaplan had acquired a reputation for restaurant design, both in terms of setting up dining areas and in providing a suitable kitchen to prepare the food. Overnight, Gazelle became a Greater Boston sensation.

The impressive and lavish modern decor of the dining room, with windows that provided views of the harbor and Boston skyline, won a first-place award in Restaurant Hospitality Magazine's *1984 interior design competition.*

To oversee the kitchen of his new restaurant, Kaplan hired master chef Bank Szerenyi, originally from Hungary, but with considerable experience in the United States and in Boston. He blends continental and American styles, classic and new cuisine in his inspired dishes.

Ask your fishmonger to cut two pounds of swordfish from the centercut portion of the fish into ½-inch slices. You may substitute salmon or halibut for the swordfish, if you like.

2 pounds swordfish in ½-inch slices, from centercut

4 extra-large baking (Idaho) potatoes

4 slices bacon, diced

1 medium yellow onion, finely diced

¼ cup butter

1 tablespoon sweet Hungarian paprika

3 cloves garlic, crushed

¼ cup fish stock or water

2 medium green bell peppers, quartered

1 medium red bell pepper, quartered

1 medium tomato, peeled, seeded, chopped

1 tablespoon tomato puree

2 scant cups sliced mushrooms

2 tablespoons chopped dill

¾ cup sour cream

¼ cup soft butter

½ cup fresh breadcrumbs

1. Scrub unpeeled potatoes and cook in lightly salted water for 30 minutes. Drain. Cool, then peel and slice about ¼-inch thick. Reserve.

2. Preheat oven to 375 degrees.

3. Saute bacon in ¼ cup butter until golden brown, add onions, and cook until it is translucent. Remove from fire. Stir in paprika, garlic, and stock. Add peppers, tomato, tomato puree, and mushrooms. Cook for 3 minutes, season with dill, and add ½ cup sour cream. Set sauce aside while you proceed with remainder of recipe.

4. Coat casserole with soft butter and then coat with half of breadcrumbs.

5. Layer dish with half of the potatoes, fish, and sauce, and then repeat.

6. Top with remaining sour cream and sprinkle with breadcrumbs.

7. Bake in oven 20 to 25 minutes. Serve immediately.

Serves 4. Approximate nutrition information per serving: Calories 925; protein 53g; fat 61g; carbohydrates 47g; sodium 610 mg.

Tuna

It is odd that when Americans think of tuna they think of it exclusively as a canned fish. That is rather unfortunate, since fresh tuna is very good eating and has been highly esteemed in other cultures for centuries. A tuna steak lathered with oil or butter, flavored with herbs or spices, and grilled over charcoal or wood is fine eating indeed. The flesh is compact and fine-grained, the flavor almost sweet. In some tuna, the raw meat resembles beef; cooked, it resembles veal.

According to archaeologists, tuna has been used by man since the Paleolithic age. In the Mediterranean, fresh tuna has been an important food since the time of the Phoenicians and Romans. Their knowledge of how to cut up a tuna has long been as important an art as butchering veal or lamb — and, as with pork, the "shoulder butt" was a defined cut in the tuna, a section with a particular texture and flavor, and cooking and eating properties. The belly meat of the tuna is as highly regarded in that part of the world as is bacon here.

The Japanese are fond of tuna and competition is fierce for the finer cuts. Several sections of the tuna are often served as *sashimi*, slices of raw fish. The various cuts, some sliced with the grain, some across, offer the same variations of color, texture, and flavor that one would appreciate in various beef cuts. A *sashimi* chef's reputation rests largely on the freshness and quality of his fish and his knowledge of how the cuts are to be treated.

Most Americans unfortunately only know tuna only in the forms in which six species come to market compacted and steamed in a can: (1) solid pack or "fancy," (2) chunks or "standard," and (3) salad or "flakes" — and white or dark meat. Fancy-style consists of large pieces of meat with no flakes. Chunk-style is packed with several large pieces of meat and enough flakes to make up the desired net weight. Flaked tuna consists entirely of small crumbs.

Six species of tuna come to market in cans. Of these six, the bigeye and the bluefin tuna are the ones you are most likely to find fresh in a retail market, but a third, the albacore, is a tuna worth knowing about, too.

Albacore is the most valuable because it cans best. The flesh is white and bland and only medium oily. Fresh albacore is delicious poached, broiled, baked, or smoked, and albacore steaks grill well on a barbecue and are also good pan-fried. "White-meat" tuna in the United States can come legally only from the albacore. Little albacore reaches the market fresh, unfortunately, since most of it goes to canneries, a lot never even gets to shore but is processed aboard ship.

With the bluefin, the bigeye is one of the most popular tunas in Japan; both also are preferred by quality fish houses in this country. The flesh of the bigeye is light colored, but not white like that of the albacore.

Also known as giant mackerel, leaping tuna, and school tuna, the bluefin is the largest of the tunas. The meat of the bluefin is darker than that of the bigeye — the color of raw beef. The Japanese say its flavor when raw is midway between cold raw beef and raw shellfish; it is considered among the best fish for *sashimi*. The flesh of larger bluefin tends to be darker and more oily. Our recipe for Braising Pan Tuna was made with the bluefin.

Other tuna are the yellowfin, skipjack, and little tunny or false albacore. Although you are not likely to find these fresh, they are used in canneries. Bonito, also known as the Atlantic bonito, is considered among the least valuable of the tunas. It has dark red, oily flesh, and a strong flavor.

While most species of tuna can be used interchangeably in cooking, the darker, more oily, and more strongly flavored flesh is generally better for eating if it is first marinated in lemon juice and oil or some similar combination of acid and fat.

Some authorities suggest soaking tuna in brine (1 cup of salt to 2 quarts of water), but we have not found it necessary in the way we have used the fish. (Soaking in brine will leach the blood from the flesh and whiten it; you may want to try this procedure with a favorite recipe.) For barbecuing, broiling, or roasting, we prefer the pronounced flavor and see no need to alter the color.

Fresh Tuna Salad
With Roasted Vegetables

This salad is as different from the everyday tunafish salad as a whale from a guppy. Smoky, savory, mellow vegetables are bathed with olive oil and paired with a broiled tuna steak — the size of a porterhouse of beef — flaked into bite-sized chunks. A splash of red wine vinegar pulls all the elements together.

This salad is basically prepared a day ahead and put together an hour or so before serving. Swordfish or mako shark may be substituted.

1 pound tuna steak, 1-inch thick	6 garlic cloves, unpeeled
1 large sweet red bell pepper	½ teaspoon salt
1 large sweet green bell pepper	freshly ground pepper
¼ cup olive oil	2 tablespoons minced fresh
2 medium zucchini, unpeeled	parsley
1 large onion	¼ teaspoon dried thyme
1 medium eggplant, unpeeled	½ cup olive oil
12 large mushrooms, or 8 largest	¼ cup red wine vinegar
shitake	1 head of bibb or Boston lettuce

1. Begin the dish the day before it is to be served. Skin whole bell peppers without removing stem by charring them over an open flame or by roasting them in a hot oven or under the broiler. When the skin is thoroughly blackened, place the hot peppers in a brown paper bag and seal it so that the peppers will steam in their own heat for 10 minutes.

2. Remove the peppers and peel away the skins under running water. They should rub off easily. Pat dry, remove stems, and cut the peppers in half. Scrape away seeds, remove interior white pieces, and slice in segments ½- to 1-inch wide. Place in a small sloped dish or other container with 1 teaspoon of olive oil. Cover, and store in refrigerator.

3. Still the day ahead, preheat oven to 375 degrees.

4. Cut the zucchini, onion, and eggplant into quarters; cut the mushrooms in half if they are very large.

5. Apply a thin coat of oil to a flat pan, such as a cookie sheet, with sides no higher than ½ inch. (If you use a deeper pan, the vegetables will stew rather than roast.) Toss the cut vegetables and the unpeeled garlic with what remains of the ¼ cup of oil. Set them on the pan and roast 20 minutes or more, turning occasionally, until everything is nicely browned with edges just beginning to char.

6. When done, remove and reserve the garlic cloves and allow the vegetables to cool.

7. With a tablespoon, carefully remove the pulp of the zucchini and eggplant, trying to scrape it away from skin in one or two whole pieces. Place pieces on a plate or platter.

8. Peel the cooked garlic cloves and place them in the work bowl of a food processor with salt, pepper, parsley, thyme, ½ cup olive oil, and vinegar, and work until smooth. Spoon this dressing over vegetables, but don't toss or mash vegetables. Cover and refrigerate at least 4 hours or overnight.

9. Final preparation: At least 1 hour before you plan to serve the salad, take the vegetables from the refrigerator to allow them to come to room temperature. Broil the tuna steak 4 inches from the heat for 5 minutes on each side. Flake while it is still warm.

10. Separate and wash the lettuce; blot dry. Choose the 6 best leaves and lay them on one end of a large oval or oblong serving platter of neutral color. Chop the rest of the lettuce and strew it over the whole leaves. Mound fish on top. Spoon a tablespoon of dressing collected from the vegetables over the fish.

11. Arrange the vegetables in a fan shape on the remainder of the platter, alternating for color and textural contrast.

12. Serve with crusty bread.

Note: If your platter is dark colored, use a leaf of lettuce under each portion of vegetable so that it will stand out attractively. If your platter is round, the tuna should be centered on it.

Serves 4. Approximate nutrition information per serving: Calories 440; protein 34g; fat 26g; carbohydrates 19g; sodium 300 mg.

Braising Pan Tuna

THON FRAIS EN COCOTTE

It is difficult to say which tastes best in this dish, the tender braised meat of the tuna or the fragrant, robust, and tangy sauce. Raw tuna may resemble beef in color, but when the tuna in this dish comes from the oven, it looks like the richest, pale veal. Larding with anchovies keeps the tuna from drying out, which a piece of fish such as this is apt to do.

Use one piece of tuna, about 4 inches thick, without bone or skin.

You will need a low, wide pan with a close-fitting lid, what the French call a cocotte. *Any oval or round ovenproof casserole large enough to hold the tuna will serve. Don't crowd, you need space around the fish.*

2½ to 3 pounds thick cut, boneless fresh tuna
1 can flat anchovy fillets packed in oil
4 tablespoons butter
1 tablespoon olive oil
salt and pepper
1 onion, diced
1 cup peeled, seeded, diced fresh tomatoes or canned Italian plum tomatoes

2 garlic cloves, crushed
1 bay leaf
½ teaspoon dried thyme
½ cup dry white wine
1 tablespoon minced fresh parsley

1. Blot tuna dry. Drain anchovies well. You may want to reserve their oil. Using either a larding needle or a small, pointed knife, insert pieces of anchovy throughout the tuna as you would put slivers of garlic into a leg of lamb. Use all the anchovies. To make the dish with even a stronger anchovy flavor, you could coat the fish with the reserved anchovy oil, or add up to 1 tablespoon of it to the next step.

2. Melt 2 tablespoons butter in the casserole and add the olive oil. Lightly brown one side of the tuna over moderate heat. Lightly salt and pepper the upper side of the tuna. Carefully turn the tuna over and brown the other side. Salt and pepper the browned side lightly.

3. Preheat oven to 375 degrees.

4. Add the onion, tomatoes, garlic, bay leaf, and thyme alongside, not atop the fish. Cover tightly and set in oven. Braise for 20 to 25 minutes. Don't overcook. The time we've given, slightly less than the general rule, results in the best serving. With browning time, a 4-inch-thick piece will cook 35 minutes in all.

5. Carefully lift the fish from the casserole and place on a serving dish; cover and keep warm. The fish should have rendered some of its moisture; approximately ½ cup of liquid should remain in the dish. Remove the bay leaf and discard.

6. Place the casserole over high heat, add the white wine, and reduce by half. Correct the seasoning, whisk in the remaining 2 tablespoons butter, and add minced parsley.

7. Cut tuna into slices ½-to ¾-inch thick. Pour the sauce over the fish and serve.

Serves 4. Approximate nutrition information per serving: Calories 335; protein 41g; fat 17g; carbohydrates 4g; sodium 273 mg.

Tuna-stuffed Eggplant

In this recipe, flaked tuna, eggplant pulp, cooked rice, and seasonings are placed in a baked eggplant shell and topped with breadcrumbs before a final baking. All the preparation can be done ahead, up to the final baking.

This is a recipe that can use leftover cooked fish. Swordfish, mako shark, bluefish, or mackerel may be substituted for the tuna.

1 pound raw tuna, or 2 cups cooked fish	½ cup chopped onion
2 medium eggplant	1 clove garlic
5 tablespoons olive oil	1 tablespoon minced fresh parsley
salt and pepper	¼ cup fresh breadcrumbs
½ cup cooked rice	
½ cup, homemade or canned, chicken stock, or water	

1. Bake the tuna in a preheated 375-degree oven for 8 minutes. Remove and flake it to make 2 cups.

2. Turn oven down to 350 degrees. Cut eggplant in half lengthwise. Score pulpy flesh with a sharp knife, cutting about ½-inch into the flesh, but staying ⅜-inch away from the sides. Season lightly with salt and pepper and drizzle about ¼ teaspoon olive oil onto the 4 halves.

3. Lay eggplant skin-side up on a lightly oiled ovenproof cookie sheet or roasting pan. Bake 20 minutes. It is cooked when the flesh and skin are soft, but the skin still retains its shape. It is important that you do not overcook the eggplant, as it must hold its shape when it is hollowed out.

4. Meanwhile, cook rice using ¼ cup long-grained raw rice (which is best for use as a stuffing or molding) in ½ cup chicken stock or water. Cook, covered, 20 to 25 minutes, and remove from heat. If rice is too moist, leave it uncovered over the pilot light or on a flame tamer so that it will dry somewhat as you proceed with rest of recipe.

5. Remove pulp from eggplant shells, but leave a ⅜-inch margin of flesh so that the eggplant will hold its shape. Coarsely chop eggplant pulp.

6. Saute onion in ½ tablespoon oil until it is transparent and just beginning to change color. Add the chopped eggplant and saute 1 minute to dry it. Reserve, off the heat.

7. Mince parsley and garlic together.

8. Mix the flaked fish, rice, parsley-garlic, and eggplant. Season with ½ teaspoon of salt and pepper. Toss well to blend. Correct the seasoning. Stuff the skins. Sprinkle with breadcrumbs. Refrigerate at this point, if you wish, for several hours.

9. Preheat oven to 350 degrees. Bake the eggplant 15 to 20 minutes until it is heated through.

Serves 4. Approximate nutrition information per serving: Calories 245; protein 28g; fat 6g; carbohydrates 20g; sodium 520 mg.

Crustaceans

*"The additional cracking of the (lobster) claw
should be done slowly, so that the juice does not
squirt when the shell breaks."*
— Emily Post

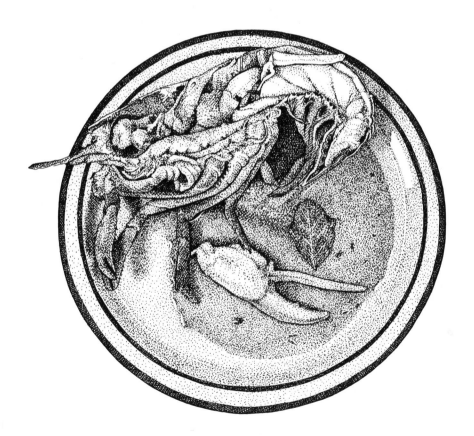

Lobster of the Sun

Crab

Crabs are members of the same family as the lobster and shrimp — Crustaceans with hard exoskeletons.

The blue crab is the most common of the species found on the East Coast, although, because of the overfishing of the blue, deep-sea dredges more and more are bringing in other species — the Jonah, cancer, and red crab.

The blue crab occurs from Massachusetts to Florida, occasionally as far north as Nova Scotia and as far south as the Bahamas, but it is most abundant from New Jersey to Cape Hatteras, especially in Chesapeake Bay.

Hardshell blue crabs are sold alive, boiled, or steamed in the shell. The best morsel is the backfin lumpmeat. The meat from the steamed crab also is picked from the shell and packed in containers to be sold as refrigerated fresh crabmeat. It must be kept refrigerated until used. The meat is packed, in a descending order of value, as Lump Meat (large pieces); Flake and Lump; Flake Meat; and Meat and Claw Meat.

Traditionally, at least in the crabbing centers of Maryland's Eastern Shore, crabmeat was picked by hand, but more and more, machines are doing the work.

Softshell crabs are from Maryland and Virginia. They are blue crabs that have just emerged from their old hard shells and have new, soft, pliable shells. The idea is to catch them just as they molt. They must be placed immediately into freshwater since saltwater hardens the new shell quickly. Softshell crabs are normally sauteed and eaten more or less whole, softshell and all. Because they are highly perishable, they are rarely offered fresh at retail outside the greater Chesapeake Bay area, but they can be obtained frozen.

Other American crabs, almost all of which are not available fresh in the East, include the Alaskan King crab, the Snow crab, the Dungeness, and the Stone crab. Only the latter is sometimes available fresh in East Coast markets.

The stone crab comes primarily from Florida. Its shell is exceedingly hard, something like the tough ceramic nose cone of a spaceship. The crab is caught in traps and only one claw is removed, along with the knuckle, and is immediately cooked. The crab is returned to the water, where it will regenerate another claw within a month — a sort of self-perpetuating crab farm of its own. The meat is excellent. The crab is shipped, chilled or frozen, and is served cold with melted butter or a flavored mayonnaise and lemon.

Unless you live in a coastal area, you usually will be offered crabs at the fish market that already have been boiled or steamed. As with all seafood, you will have to depend on your fish dealer for assurances that the crabs he is selling were cooked when absolutely fresh and that they have not been around too long.

When buying whole crabs, pick up several to gauge their weight. The heavier a given size, the more meat it will contain. In most cases, you will be seeking to remove the white meat from crabs, the backfin lumpmeat under each "wing" of the shell, and the meat from the large claws.

Most guides compute the yield from a crab at about 20 percent, so that 1 pound of crab in the shell should provide a little more than 3 ounces of meat. We have seldom obtained that much. We have found that a boiled, medium-to-large blue crab yields about 1 ounce of crabmeat if both the body meat and the meat of large claws and knuckles are collected.

But there is much more to a crab — almost all of it except the stomach and gills, can be utilized. (The gills are spongy growths that are called "dead man's fingers.") Some recipes require the use of the creamy "butter" and other parts of crab, which you will have to collect as you clean each crab. This can be wiped from the interior of shells with a finger.

Some recipes call for the use of the liquid in a crab. In such cases, crack crabs and collect body parts in a fine strainer over a mixing bowl to catch the natural liquid. Press down on crab parts to extract liquid.

Empty and broken shells, creamy parts, odd pieces of usable meat, and unused small legs can be used to make a crab stock (though the flavor will be emphatically crab), a sauce, or a mayonnaise-type dressing. You also can use them in making Shellfish Butter (see page 55).

Other recipes call for saving a shell for stuffing, much the same as is done with scallop shells. Separate the shells as you clean them and save the top shell. If shells are to be stuffed, you have to remove the "wings," or the flaps from the underside of the top or carapace shell. You can cut these away with heavy kitchen shears, so that the shell is completely open to its edges like a small oval casserole.

You also can save crab shells for future use in much the same way that scallop shells are saved. If you clean them thoroughly, you won't have to freeze or refrigerate them. Wash, scrape, and brush the shells in hot water, letting them soak in the water between brushings if necessary to make sure that all residue is removed. Store them in a plastic bag in a cool place until you want them. They can be used several times over, but they must be washed each time. Their red color will begin to fade over time, but by the

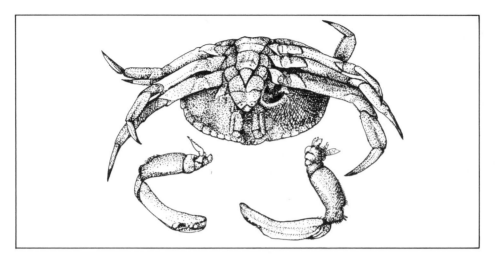

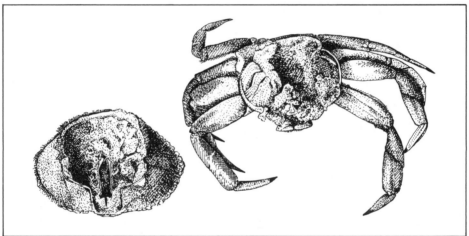

Top: Remove the crab's large claws by breaking them off at the body. Don't pull the meat out of the sockets, or you will make the interior lump meat more difficult to remove.

Bottom: Pull off the top shell. The stomach cavity and spongy gills that lie on either side are now exposed.

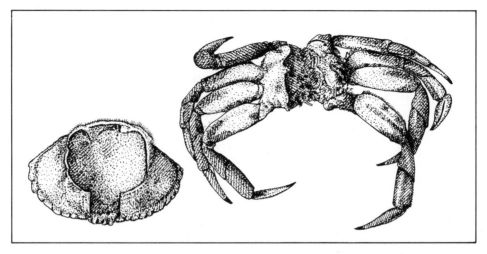

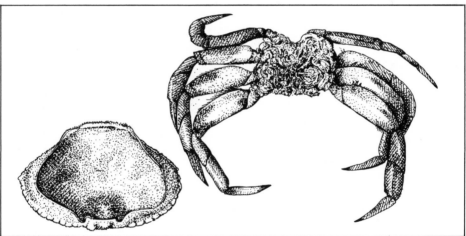

Top: The top shell has been cleaned and the mouth parts and gills removed and discarded. The chambers holding the body meat on either side are covered with a white, opaque, cartilaginous membrane.

Bottom: The membrane has been cut away from the body chambers. The remaining legs now may be cut off close to the body, and the meat scooped out. The top shell has been trimmed with scissors to hold a stuffing.

time they are pale, a true crab lover should have found several excuses to acquire fresh ones.

Live crabs are boiled or steamed in plain or flavored water until they change from their natural color to red. Remove them from the heat at this point and allow them to cool in the cooking liquid for up to 15 minutes to absorb flavor. Crabs that are overcooked will be mushy. Do not use crab boil or other seasonings except when you plan to eat the crabs out of their shell, or where you want the resulting strong flavor for a dish such as curry.

Wash the crabs, using a brush if necessary. Crack the shell, as illustrated, and be sure to pick over the meat carefully to remove all bits of shell and transparent cartilage.

Six medium-large blue crabs should yield about ¾ to 1 cup crabmeat; ¼ cup body parts, squeezed dry; and ¾ to 1 cup liquid.

Crab Cakes

Sweeter and richer than cod cakes, these crab cakes can make a good luncheon dish, a first course, or a meal in themselves.

1 pound crabmeat
½ cup diced sweet green pepper
½ cup diced sweet red pepper
1 tablespoon butter
⅓ cup tartar sauce (see page 43)
2 teaspoons Worcestershire
   sauce

2 teaspoons minced fresh parsley
1 egg
4 crumpled saltine crackers
salt and pepper to taste

To fry:
½ cup vegetable oil
⅓ cup butter

1. Pick over crabmeat for bits of shell or cartilage.
2. Saute peppers in 1 tablespoon butter until tender. Cool.
3. Mix together all the ingredients with a fork. Do not overwork, as you want to retain the crabmeat texture.
4. With your hands, mold mixture into about 16 flat patties approximately 2½ inches wide and ½-inch thick. If you wish, these may be made ahead and refrigerated a few hours.
5. In a large skillet suitable for frying, heat the butter and oil over medium heat. Fry cakes on each side until golden brown.
6. Serve at once with additional tartar sauce and french fried potatoes.

Serves 4. Approximate nutrition information per serving: Calories 725; protein 22g; fat 68g; carbohydrates 6g; sodium 490 mg.

Crab in Corn Husks

This recipe uses one of America's favorite summertime foods — corn on the cob — in a different way. The result is a marvelous marriage of familiar flavors that have a caramel-like mellowness when cooked over charcoal or in a broiler. The presentation is different and sure to prove a surprise when the ear of corn is opened at the table.

The ears of corn are removed from the husks and the husks kept whole and undamaged so that they look like green canoes. Crab, corn, vegetables, and seasonings are then mixed and used to stuff the husks, which are then roasted. Chopped leftover firm lean fish, such as tilefish and monkfish, or lobster, or scallops may be substituted for the crabmeat. Grilling on charcoal is the preferred cooking method, although the canoes can be broiled.

Preheat broiler or barbecue grill; 10 to 15 minutes for a gas or electric grill; 30 to 40 minutes for charcoal to allow the fire to develop an even film of white ash that indicates it is at the right temperature.

8 ounces fresh lump crabmeat	1 teaspoon salt
4 large ears corn on cob	turn of freshly ground black
1 cup of one or more vegetables,	pepper
such as lima beans, diced	¼ cup soft butter
string beans, fresh baby peas	¼ cup minced fresh parsley
2 tablespoons butter	½ cup melted butter
½ cup minced onions	
1 cup minced sweet red bell	
pepper	

1. Remove the tassels from the corn. Slit the husk lengthwise with a knife — do not attempt to pull or tear it. When the ear of corn is exposed, cut it from the husk by forcing a knife through the base of the ear to sever it. Try not to damage or puncture the husk. If you do, take 1 or 2 leaves of husk from another ear to make repairs. Remove all traces of tassel. Reserve the husks and wash the ear of corn.

2. Scrape the kernels from the ears of corn; you should have 2½ cups. Reserve the kernels.

3. Precook 1 cup of vegetable in salted water, drain, dry on paper towels, and reserve.

4. Saute onion in 2 tablespoons butter until soft and transparent, not colored. Add chopped red pepper and corn kernels. Cook until the corn is

as tender as you prefer it. Add salt, pepper, crabmeat, and the precooked vegetables. Cook 1 minute.

5. Remove from heat and allow to cool. Fold in the soft butter — it should not melt, but act as a binder — so that mixture adheres. Add the minced parsley and blend. Correct the seasoning.

6. Spread open the emptied husks. It is easier to accomplish this by tying the tassel end tight with kitchen twine before filling. Reserve one or two leaves of husks to cover the opening. Fill the corn husks with the mixture. Place the reserved strips of husk over the openings to completely enclose the filling to make a sealed package. Tie filled husks in several places so that they remain closed while cooking. The string will undoubtedly burn away on grill, but will remain long enough to do its job.

7. Refrigerate filled husks up to several hours, if desired. Remove them from the refrigerator while you preheat the grill or broiler.

8. Place the filled husks on the barbecue grill with the opening facing up. The filling does not really have to cook much; it merely has to heat through for the flavors to blend. Grill until the bottom is charred but not burnt. If using a broiler, place the husks 6 inches from heat and cook until the top is charred. Remove carefully with spatula and tongs so that the husks do not open.

9. Serve one corn boat to each person, suggesting that they remove all but the end strings to open the husk. Pass the ½ cup melted butter for guests to pour into their opened boat.

Serves 4. Approximate nutrition information per serving: Calories 540; protein 12g; fat 42g; carbohydrates 28g; sodium 1230 mg.

Cold Stuffed Crab

Home cooks frequently hesitate to make a new dish because its recipe appears at first look to be "too complicated." Most often it isn't. If a recipe is broken down into its parts and the dish understood that way, it won't appear so formidable. This dish is a case in point.

In the dish, crab shells are stuffed with a fish mousse. Half a lemon is inserted in the mousse, and the mousse is baked. When the lemon is removed a depression is left to hold a seasoned stuffing. The presentation is different, a contrast in colors, flavors, and textures, all within the original crab shell. It makes a lovely summer meal.

Use whole, fresh, boiled or steamed crabs. You should obtain sufficient crabmeat from the boiled crabs to provide 6 ounces of crabmeat for the remainder of this recipe. If you prefer to not go through the trouble of picking all the crabmeat from the shell, buy 6 ounces of crabmeat. You must reserve the liquid and creamy parts from the crabs, however, to use in making the filling.

Save the top shell of each crab. Wash them thoroughly. Using scissors, trim shells evenly at edges.

All the work may be done in advance.

4 large blue crabs	¼ cup chili sauce
1 recipe for fish mousse (fish mousse No. 1, page 75)	1 tablespoon minced shallots
	1 tablespoon lemon juice
2 lemons	½ tablespoon horseradish
	1 tablespoon minced parsley
FILLING:	¼ cup sweet red bell pepper, cut in ¼ inch dice
1 tablespoon Dijon mustard	
¼ cup vegetable oil	
pinch of salt	bibb lettuce
½ cup minced celery	

1. If they are not already cooked, boil crabs in salted water. When cool enough to handle, remove meat from body and large claws, and reserve. (You should have 6 ounces crabmeat. If not, supplement with more.) Reserve separately the juices, creamy parts, and any bits of crabmeat. Prepare 4 shells for stuffing as described at the beginning of this section.

2. Make the fish mousse: If possible, use salmon for the mousse to give the finished dish a soft pink color. Test the mousse in simmering water before proceeding. It will be placed raw in crab shells to be baked.

3. Wash the lemons, dry, and cut them in half lengthwise.

4. With a spatula, fill the 4 crab shells with the uncooked mousse. Butter the rinds of the halved lemons. Press a lemon into each mousse, cut-side up, forcing it down, and rounding the mousse about it.

5. Preheat oven to 375 degrees. Crumble kitchen foil into a baking pan large enough to hold the stuffed crabs. The foil will serve as a bed that will keep crabs from tipping. You also could use rock salt, but foil is handier.

6. Add ¼ cup water to pan — pouring it under foil, so as not to wet the crabs or mousse. Place the crabs atop foil. Cover loosely with additional foil and bake 15 minutes.

7. Remove crabs when they are cooked, and allow them to cool.

8. Meanwhile, make the filling: Strain the liquid and creamy parts taken from the boiled crabs into a large mixing bowl. Add Dijon mustard and any bits of meat taken from the crabs and stir thoroughly with a wire whisk. You should have ½ cup of mixture. While whipping, slowly pour in the oil, as in making mayonnaise. Continue to whip and add salt, celery, chili sauce, shallots, lemon juice, horseradish, parsley, and sweet red pepper. Mix thoroughly.

9. Reserve and chill half of the sauce.

10. Pick over the reserved crabmeat carefully for any bits of cartilage or shell. Add it to the remaining sauce, breaking up the large pieces.

11. Remove the lemon half from each crab and discard.

12. Fill the hollows with the crabmeat and sauce mixture. Chill up to several hours.

13. Serve each crab on a leaf of bibb lettuce and serve the additional sauce on the side.

Serves 4. Approximate nutrition information per serving: Calories 721; protein 60g; fat 57g; carbohydrates 9g; sodium 1626 mg.

Lobster

■■

In New England, *Homarus Americanus* — the American lobster — is taken seriously. Since 1941, Massachusetts has had a law on the books, which is sort of a Yankee appellation of origin. It is the kind of law that the French first propounded to guarantee the source of wines and some other products; other countries, including the United States, also now use such laws delimiting the source of their wines. But Massachusetts did it first regarding the lobster.

It is the major reason why you never see rock lobster tails from South Africa, Australia, or elsewhere on a restaurant menu in the Bay State — restaurateurs can't figure out what to call a lobster that isn't.

The operative section of Chapter 598 of the General Laws of Massachusetts protecting the good name of the American lobster reads:

"No person shall sell, or represent for the purpose of sale, any lobster as a native lobster unless the same shall have been originally caught or taken in the coastal waters; nor shall any person sell, or represent for the purpose of sale, any crustacean as a lobster unless the same is of the species known as *Homarus Americanus*; nor shall any person sell, or represent for the purpose of sale, any meat as lobster meat unless such meat is wholly from crustaceans of such species. Violation of any provision of this section shall be punished by a fine of not less than ten nor more than fifty dollars."

A 1945 opinion of the Attorney General of the Commonwealth further determined that:

"The sale of canned lobster meat derived from crustacea of the species *genus palinurus*, labeled with various trade names, and with the word 'lobster' preceded by the word 'rock,' is a violation of this section."

The Great and General Court of the Commonwealth went even further in 1982 when it decreed that all barrels, boxes, or other containers containing lobsters or lobster meat taken from the shell must be plainly marked "Lobsters" or "Lobster Meat" followed by the permit number under which the lobsters were taken. The law permits interstate shipment of other lobsters under federal regulations, but those taken from Massachusetts waters must be so labeled and, therefore, must be *Homarus Americanus*. The fine is not less than five hundred nor more than one thousand dollars.

In Massachusetts when you say "lobster" there can only be one species you are talking about.

It is incredible to think that there was a time when New England farmers would pull up to beaches after a northeast storm and gather wagonloads of lobsters to be used as fertilizer. Incredible, also, that fishermen used lobster for bait to fish for cod and striped bass.

Lobster today is one of the most costly seafoods in the world — outranked only by caviar.

Like the crab and shrimp, *Homarus Americanus*, the American, or sometimes Maine, lobster is a crustacean. Its cousin, *Homarus vulgaris*, or the European lobster, is similar but smaller.

The lobster has a jointed body, two large pincer claws, four other pairs of walking legs, swimmerets, and a hard exoskeleton. One claw is larger than the other and is used for crushing. The second is lighter, more streamlined, and quicker in movement. It is used for catching its prey, which, with the lobster, may be just about anything. Lobsters are not only scavengers, but cannibalistic, and will eat smaller members of their own kind. That is why their claws are pegged in captivity. A lobster that has lost one claw is called a cull at market and is cheaper than a two-clawed lobster.

Almost all of a lobster is edible. The meat is firm and sweet. It is in the tail, knuckles, claws, and body; many consider the body meat the sweetest. The liver, or tomalley, is considered a special delicacy. It is contained as a soft green strip in the body. It is eaten as a spread on toast or crackers, or is used in sauces. The orange-red coral, or roe, of the female, a strip that parallels the liver but runs from the body and into the tail, also is eaten as is, is used in sauces, or, as we do in our recipe for Seafood in Angel Hair Nests, minced as a bright garnish. If you want a female lobster for such purposes, the dealer can differentiate. For that matter, so can a layman. In lobsters of equal size, the female will have a comparatively broader abdomen and tail than the male, and its first pair of swimmerets will be smaller and more flexible.

The walking legs in a lobster also are eaten. They are cracked or broken at each knuckle and the meat sucked out of them. The creamy "butter," which can be wiped off the inside of the shell with your finger, may be called for in a recipe.

The stomach of the lobster, called the "sand sac," must be discarded. It is small, gritty, translucent, and pouch-like, and lies in the head, just beneath and behind the eyes. It is easily removed. The intestinal tract also is removed. This usually is a thin dark line running from the stomach to the tail. The spongy gill tissues, corresponding to the "dead man's fingers" in a crab, also are not eaten. They are in the body walls close to the walking legs.

The lobster's shell, greenish-blue or reddish brown in its natural state, turns bright red when cooked. The entire body together with the shell and other uneaten parts, can be broken or ground, and used to make stocks, soups, bisques, sauces, and gravies. (See our recipes for Lobster Bisque, page 394, and Shellfish Butter, page 55.) The hard carapace — the part of the shell that covers the body, like the carapace of a crab — does not contain much nutritive value or flavor, but it does give up its pigmentation to color a sauce or bisque and should be used for that purpose. Fish dealers who boil or steam lobsters just for the meat often sell the lobster bodies for cooking purposes.

The lobster has to shed its shell and put on a new one to grow. Molting usually takes place in the summer. It must shrink its body somewhat to get out of its old shell and then grow into its new one. It does this by absorbing a lot of water and a softshell lobster is watery and not particularly good eating.

Lobsters are graded commercially by size, or weight. You can order a "chicken" lobster (the smallest, about 1 pound), "quarter" (1 to less than 1½ pounds), "large" (1½ to 2½), or "jumbo" (more than 2½). However, the normal procedure at retail is to order a lobster by weight, rather than by a name, except for the chicken. Lobsters nowadays are brought in from 1 to 5 pounds; 1½ to 2 pounds is the most popular size.

There are many lobster-wise New Englanders who insist that the best way to cook a lobster is to boil or steam it in seawater. Unless you live where you can dip into the unpolluted ocean, that method is not available and you will have to compromise. Find a pot large enough to hold the number of lobsters you are going to cook. The water must cover the lobsters. Use several pots if you have that many, or cook them in batches. Place fresh water in the pot and add 1 tablespoon of salt for every quart of water. Cover with a lid and bring to a rolling boil. Drop in the live lobsters head first, one after another. The water will stop boiling; keep the heat high. Begin timing when the water returns to boil. Cook a 1-pound "chicken" lobster for 10 minutes. Cook a 1¼-pound lobster 12 minutes; a 1½-pound lobster 14 to 15 minutes; a 2-pounder 16 to 18 minutes. In spite of opinion to the contrary, larger lobsters are not necessarily less tender than smaller lobsters.

Lobsters also may be steamed with about 3 inches of water in a kettle. Piling lobster one on top of another, however, creates problems, since those on the bottom will cook sooner. Use more than one pot rather than crowd the lobsters. The time for steaming is the same as for boiling — counted from the emission of fresh steam after the lobster have been put in the pot.

Lobster meat is more easily removed from a cooked lobster than a raw one.

In recipes where you are required to saute or fry raw lobster pieces in the shell as a first step in cooking, saute for just a minute or so after the lobster has completely turned red. Otherwise there is a danger of overcooking when you perform a second cooking operation.

If you hesitate to boil or cut up live lobsters for humane reasons, you can make them insensitive to pain by plunging a knife in the underside at the junction between the tail and the carapace. This is supposed to kill the lobster's nerve system. (See the drawing on page 268.)

Several facts about lobsters are worthy of mention, but you are not likely to encounter one of these even once in a long lifetime of lobster eating. In spite of their rarity, to encounter them unprepared can ruin your appetite.

Occasionally people put away in the refrigerator a cooked lobster or part of one, intending to eat it later. Going back to it, they discover that it appears to glow. This is a natural, though extremely rare, phenomenon that can occur with many forms of sea life. It is caused by a natural phosphorescent bacteria, and is in no way harmful, according to a marine biologist in Maine to whom we have spoken. Go ahead and finish the lobster — just omit the candles.

Even less often, one might come upon a boiled lobster with a thick, black, tar-like substance that runs through the center of the body from stomach to tail. The immediate assumption is that the lobster might be "bad." It isn't. The black substance is the sign of immature or otherwise undeveloped roe — what would normally be the orange coral. Discard it and eat the rest.

Some large lobsters are occasionally attacked by an organism that attacks the flesh and turns it mushy. The spores responsible are harmless to man, but such a lobster is unappetizing and would have to be discarded.

Generally, 1 small lobster or half a large lobster makes 1 serving. A 1¼ to 1½ pound lobster will yield about 1 cup of cooked lobster meat.

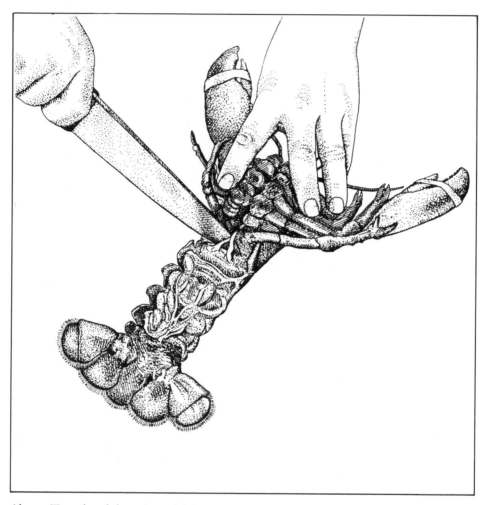

Above: To make a lobster insensitive to pain, sever its main nervous system by inserting a knife where the body and tail join. The narrow tail and inflexible first pair of swimmerets (visible over the blade) indicate this lobster is a male.

. Right: The lobster has been split in half from the head through the tail. The arrow on the right points to the liver, or tomalley, an edible part of the lobster. The arrow on the left points to the stomach, which is inedible.

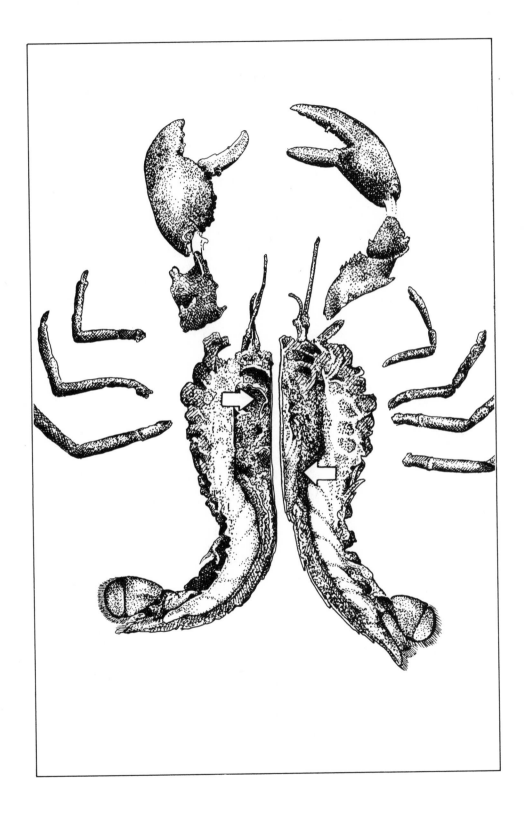

Homard à l'Americaine

■■

Don't let the length of the list of ingredients dissuade you from attempting this recipe. It is a classic of the French repertoire, is marvelous by itself, and also can be used as the basis for other dishes — as in our Lobster Chartreuse that follows.

The name of the recipe has been the source of continuing dispute. Spelled as above, it supposedly indicates that the dish was first created for some unidentified American visitor to France. Spelled "Amoricaine" it supposedly indicates the ancient name for a part of Brittany on France's northwest coast, a region where the lobster is plentiful.

Pick the story you like best and spell it as you wish, but do try making lobster in tomatoes, brandy, and wine at least once.

The live lobster is cut up in the shell before cooking. If you hesitate to do this, perhaps your fishmonger will. You also can deaden the lobster to pain by severing its nerve connection by inserting a knife at the joint between body and tail.

2-pound live lobster
¼ cup vegetable oil
¼ cup onion, in ¼-inch dice
¼ cup carrot, in ¼-inch dice
2 tablespoons shallots, in ¼-inch dice
¼ cup cognac or brandy
4 fresh red-ripe tomatoes, peeled, seeded, coarsely chopped; or one 12-ounce can Italian peeled plum tomatoes
½ teaspoon dried thyme, or 1 sprig of fresh

½ bay leaf
1 clove garlic, minced
1 cup dry white wine
2 tablespoons tomato paste
salt and pepper to taste
½ teaspoon dried tarragon, or a good sprig of fresh
1 cup fish stock (see White Wine Fumet, page 30) or water
2 tablespoons soft butter
2 tablespoons flour
1 tablespoon minced fresh parsley

1. Cut the tail and claws from body of live lobster. Cut tail section crosswise into 4 or 5 medallions. Cut body in half, lengthwise, and remove the sand sac from head, the tomalley, and the roe. Chop the roe and reserve it and the tomalley for use in finishing the sauce. Discard the sand sac. Crack claws and knuckles and chop the walking legs.

2. In a large, heavy saucepan, heat the oil and add the cut-up lobster pieces. Stir and cook on high heat until the shells have turned red and the

meat is well seared — crisp-edged, but not too brown. Remove from the pan and set aside.

3. Add the diced onions, carrots, and shallots to the oil, lower the heat to medium, and saute until they are soft and transparent but not colored.

4. Add the sauteed lobster and cognac. Allow to warm, and carefully ignite the cognac. Shake the pan until the flame dies. Add tomatoes, thyme, bay leaf, garlic, white wine, tomato paste, salt, pepper, tarragon, and fish stock or water. Bring the mixture to a boil and cook, covered, 15 minutes. Remove the lobster tail pieces, knuckles, and claws. Remove meat from the shells and keep warm. Let the sauce cook for an additional 10 minutes.

5. Strain the sauce into a saucepan, pressing down to extract as much flavor as you can from the remaining lobster pieces and other ingredients. Bring the strained sauce to a boil and reduce until it is slightly thickened.

6. Using a fork, mix together in a bowl the tomalley, roe, and soft butter, add the flour, and incorporate well. Add the butter mixture to the boiling sauce a bit at a time while stirring with a wire whisk. Cook a minute or two, lower heat and add lobster pieces, simmer to warm through. Correct seasoning.

7. Sprinkle with the parsley and serve hot with rice.

Serves 4. Approximate nutrition information per serving: Calories 535; protein 53g; fat 28g; carbohydrates 16g; sodium 1088 mg.

Lobster Chartreuse

A chartreuse is any dish prepared in a mold whose ingredients are arranged attractively, especially if vegetables or other ingredients are used as a wall to enclose other ingredients. We take some liberty in naming the dish — originally chartreuse referred to a preparation for pheasant, partridge, or quail, usually with vegetables. In the Middle Ages, Chartreuse referred to the wilderness where St. Bruno established the Carthusian Order in 1094. The word also is used to describe a specific consomme and the famous liqueur produced by the Carthusian monks.

This dish incorporates the Lobster Americaine above. Its excellent flavor and attractive appearance make it a perfect dinner party entree. You will need a 1-quart round mold with straight sides in which to make it. It is baked in a bain-marie, a water bath. The mold is set into a larger pan (a roasting pan will do) containing simmering water that comes one-third of the way up the sides of the mold. Although the preparation appears formidable, it isn't really, since everything through step 9 can be made several hours ahead. The remainder is mostly assembly. The result will be worth the effort.

1 recipe for Lobster Americaine, above
1 recipe fish mousse (Mousse Number 1, page 75)
carrots, cut into about 20 ¼-inch sticks
asparagus, about 20 peeled stalks
1 additional carrot, sliced very thinly
1 sweet red pepper
½ stick butter, soft, not melted
1 tablespoon melted butter

    1. Prepare the recipes for Lobster Americaine and fish mousse. Chill both in the refrigerator. Also set the mold into the refrigerator to chill.

    2. The carrot sticks and asparagus are to be used standing vertically, like a stockade fence, to line the sides of the mold. They should be slightly shorter than the height of the mold. The exact count is difficult to determine, but you will need 16 to 20 pieces of each.

    3. Cut the carrot slices. These will go into the bottom of the mold before you fill it, and will become the decoration on the top of the finished dish when it is unmolded. If you prefer, you may cut the slices into a star, diamond, or another shape. Trim the sweet red pepper into thin julienne, about ⅛-inch thick. They will form the rest of the decoration.

    4. Blanch the trimmed vegetables in 2 cups of simmering water to which you have added 1 teaspoon salt. Cook the thin-sliced carrots and the

julienned pepper first, for about 10 seconds. Remove. The carrot sticks and asparagus will take longer. Cook only until *al dente*; they must be firm. Refresh the vegetables under cold running water as soon as you remove them from the hot water; chill.

5. Remove mold from refrigerator and coat bottom and sides thickly with softened butter. Rechill.

6. Remove the mold from the refrigerator and arrange the blanched carrot slices and sweet red pepper strips on the bottom. You want to create a tic-tac-toe pattern with the pepper strips. Place a slice of carrot into each empty square.

7. Line the sides of the mold with alternating asparagus and carrot sticks, pressing them into the butter so that, as best as you can, there are no spaces between them.

8. Carefully pour a 1½-inch layer of mousse into the mold atop the carrot and pepper design. Make a depression in the center of the layer of mousse.

9. Remove lobster pieces from the reserved cold Lobster Americaine, one piece at a time, using a fork — you want to carry some of the cold sauce with the lobster meat. Set all the lobster into the depression and top with 1 tablespoon sauce; reserve the remainder of the sauce. Pour in the remaining mousse, which should come about ¼ inch below the top of the mold — it will expand in cooking. Cover the mold with buttered foil or parchment paper. Refrigerate the mold for several hours at this point, if you wish.

10. Preheat oven to 350 degrees. Simmer a pan or kettle of water to use for the *bain-marie*. Remove the mold from the refrigerator.

11. Pour an inch or two of simmering water into the *bain-marie*. Center the filled mold in the bath and add simmering water to bring its level one-third up the sides of the mold.

12. Place the mold and the water bath into the oven and bake for 45 minutes.

13. Remove the mold from the bath. Set the mold in a warm place for 15 to 20 minutes.

14. Meanwhile, heat the reserved Lobster Americaine sauce.

15. Invert and unmold the chartreuse onto a warm serving platter and brush the sides with 1 tablespoon melted butter so that the exposed vegetable border glistens.

16. Spoon warm sauce around the perimeter of the chartreuse — not on the top — and serve immediately. Pass additional sauce separately.

Serves 4. Approximate nutrition information per serving: Calories 631; protein 44g; fat 44g; carbohydrates 13g; sodium 1414 mg.

Savoy Cabbage with Lobster and Caviar
■■
FROM FOUR SEASONS RESTAURANT, NEW YORK CITY

If there is a more chic restaurant in the United States than the Four Seasons in the midst of competitive, sophisticated midtown Manhattan, it would be difficult to name. If there are two more aware restaurateurs than Paul Kovi and Tom Margatai, the genial operators of the Four Seasons, they would be hard to find.

Although Four Seasons cuisine had won wide acclaim because of the restaurant's attention to seasonal changes, plus its high standards and its creativity, the partners broke new ground when they introduced "Spa Cuisine," food with flavor and style that also paid attention to such nutritional considerations as sodium and cholesterol content, calories, proteins, carbohydrates, and other aspects of diet.

This recipe was created by chef Seppi Renggli. It calls for caviar; you may use Beluga, red salmon, or golden American. Fresh caviar is recommended.

You will need a total of 3¼ cups of fish stock for this dish. See page 30 for White Wine Fish Fumet.

The savoy cabbage leaves for this dish must be blanched to be soft enough to roll without breaking. Bring a large pot of salted water to a boil. Have ready a large bowl of ice water. Cut out the core of the cabbage and discard. Remove tough outer leaves. Put cabbage in boiling water, turning it so that all the leaves cook. Remove in about 2 minutes. Peel off the outer leaves and plunge them into the ice water. Pat dry. You will need 5 pretty leaves. Trim them so that the stem end is no thicker than the rest of the leaf; you may use just half a leaf or so.

1 2½ pound lobster	¼ cup fish stock
freshly ground black pepper	1 recipe fish sauce, below
5 pretty cabbage leaves,	4 teaspoons caviar
blanched and pared	

1. Bring a large pot salted water to boil. Add lobster. When the water boils again, lower heat to simmer, cover, and cook 18 minutes. Drain and cool the lobster.

2. Remove meat from tails and claws. Cut claws in half. Cut tail crosswise into 8 pieces. Sprinkle lobster pieces with freshly ground black pepper.

3. Place 4 cabbage leaves on work surface, outside down. Divide the lobster pieces evenly among them and place them in a pile in the center of

the leaf so red of lobster is down. If there is roe in your lobster, divide it among the packages of lobster meat. Gather each cabbage leaf around lobster to make packages. Place one at a time on a dry kitchen towel. Wrap the towel around and squeeze to eliminate excess liquid.

4. Place packages, seam side down, on a plate. Cover them with the fifth cabbage leaf to keep them moist and sprinkle with ¼ cup fish stock.

5. Put the plate in a steamer over simmering water. Cover and cook to heat through, 3 to 5 minutes. Remove and discard cabbage leaf cover. Lift packages from plate and gently pat dry. Place one package on each of 4 warmed serving plates. Spoon fish sauce around.

6. Top each with a teaspoon of caviar.

Fish Sauce

3 cups fish stock
1 cup heavy cream

¼ pound lightly salted butter,
     cut into 1-inch pieces
juice of ½ lemon

1. Put the stock in a wide saucepan and reduce to 2 cups. Bring it to a boil, remove any scum that rises, and reduce to 1 cup.

2. Add cream and boil over high heat until reduced to about half, about 5 minutes. Whisk in butter a piece at a time. Stir in lemon juice. Correct seasoning.

Use hot.

Serves 4. Approximate nutrition information per serving: Calories 850; protein 52g; fat 65g; carbohydrates 16g; sodium 1740 mg.

Lobster Salad with Vegetables
••
SALADE DE HOMARD AUX LÉGUMES

Too often, unfortunately, a lobster, crab, shrimp, or even tuna "salad" turns out to be some of the main ingredient tossed with an overabundance of chopped iceberg lettuce, and held together with a thick mortar of bottled mayonnaise or salad dressing. Sometimes chopped celery is added, more for volume than flavor or texture.

One sampling of this salad, with its fresh natural flavors, is likely to turn you away from the former kind of salad forever.

The dressing recipe calls for vegetable oil. Do not use olive oil, because its flavor will dominate. The preparation may be done ahead, through step 10.

TO STEAM LOBSTERS:
2 lobsters, 1¼ to 1½ pounds each
2 cups dry white wine
1 teaspoon cracked black peppercorns
½ cup chopped onions
12 parsley stems

VEGETABLES FOR SALAD:
1 large potato
celery
string beans, green or yellow
carrots
zucchini
summer squash
red onion

DRESSING:
juice of 1 lemon
2 tablespoons Dijon mustard
½ cup vegetable oil (not olive oil)

1 tablespoon minced parsley (or chervil or other available fresh green herb)
salt and pepper to taste
1 head of soft lettuce
lemon wedges

1. You will need a pot with a tight-sealing cover large enough to hold 2 lobsters. Put wine, pepper, chopped onion, and parsley stems in the pot. When it comes to a boil, set the live lobsters into the pot, cover, and seal tightly. Cook the lobsters 12 minutes.

2. Remove lobsters from pot and allow them to cool. Chill them in the refrigerator. Reserve the pot juices; they will go into the dressing.

3. Boil the unpeeled potato in salted water until it is tender. Drain, peel, and chill.

4. Cut celery, string beans, carrots, zucchini, and summer squash,

into julienne strips about ⅜-inch thick, to make 1 cup of each. Cut the potato into julienne strips of the same size. Cut red onion into slices about the same thickness to make ½ cup of slices. Blanch the celery and carrots in salted water for 2 minutes, add the zucchini, summer squash, and red onion and cook for 1 minute longer. Refresh under cold running water. Drain well. Chill all vegetables.

5. Break lobsters by bending them backward where the tail joins the body. Do this over a container to catch juices, not only from the tail and body, but the claws as well. Remove all the lobster meat from the shell and cut it into bite-sized pieces. Keep the claw meat whole. Chop coral if present. Chill lobster meat, claw meat, tomalley, and coral.

6. Pour the lobster pot liquid into a small skillet or saucepan. Add juices from lobsters. Reduce to about 2 tablespoons, until it is nearly a paste.

7. Prepare dressing: With a rubber spatula scrape the ingredients that have been reduced to paste into a mixing bowl. Add lemon juice and mustard, stir to blend, and add tomalley and coral. Add oil, pouring slowly at first, and then in a thin steady stream, as you constantly whip with a whisk, much as you would in making mayonnaise.

8. Add the lobster pieces (not the claw meat) and toss to coat with the dressing. Chill.

9. Separate lettuce, wash and blot dry with paper towels. Lay out whole leaves to form a bed on a large chilled plate or platter.

10. Toss all the vegetables, except potato, with 1 tablespoon of parsley or other minced herb. Add the julienned potato and fold gently, so that it does not crumble. Add salt and pepper to taste, and chill up to 4 hours.

11. When ready to serve, spoon the lobster pieces and dressing into the center of the lettuce, set the meat from the 4 claws attractively on the plate, and garnish with lemon wedges.

Serves 4. Approximate nutrition information per serving: Calories 490; protein 26g; fat 29g; carbohydrates 30g; sodium 400 mg.

Lobster Sausage with Cabbage

FROM RESTAURANT JASPER, BOSTON

Jasper White already had attained a good measure of acclaim in other establishments when he opened his own, Restaurant Jasper, about two years ago. His restaurant registered almost instant success. He is another of the young American-trained chefs with a knowledge of classic cuisines and methods, and an appreciation of the necessity for quality ingredients and attention to detail that has always marked the finest kitchens. With several other young Boston chefs, he has been on the cutting edge of what is new among aware, sophisticated diners.

This recipe for Lobster Sausages makes about a dozen large sausages, a perfect size for a first course or main course. Use pork casings for this size sausage. One other advantage of these casings is that they show the colors of the sausage more dramatically.

Smaller sausages may be used as an appetizer. You also can use miniature sausages as a garnish in soups and seafood stews (it would make our elegant Lobster Consomme on page 399 a more filling dish, for example). Instead of natural casings, you can wrap the forcemeat in cabbage or lettuce leaves, or in leeks. You also may use the procedure the authors have used of enclosing the forcemeat in plastic wrap before poaching. See Monkfish Sausages, page 145, for information on using natural casings and plastic wrap casings.

When increasing this recipe, do not increase the garlic in the same proportion as the other ingredients, use less.

SAUSAGE FORCEMEAT:
3 2-pound lobsters
1 red pepper, roasted, peeled,
    and cleaned (see page 247)
6 ounces lightly salted butter
1 teaspoon finely minced garlic
1 stalk celery, peeled and finely
    minced
½ medium carrot, finely minced
3 teaspoons finely minced
    parsley and chervil (or just
    parsley)

salt to taste
freshly ground black pepper to
    taste

TO SAUTE FINISHED SAUSAGES:
2 tablespoons butter

FOR CABBAGE:
6 cups shredded raw cabbage
1 tablespoon butter
salt and pepper to taste

1. Break off the tails of 2 of the lobsters, and remove the raw meat from the shell. Puree the tail meat with the roasted pepper in a food processor.

2. Cook the whole lobster and the remaining claws and bodies of the 2 other lobsters about 7 to 8 minutes in boiling water.

3. Split the cooked lobsters and crack the claws so that the meat cools quickly.

4. Remove every speck of edible meat and cut into ¼-inch dice.

5. In the 6 ounces of butter, slowly heat up the garlic, celery, and carrot until the butter is foamy. Do not overcook the vegetables; their crunchiness will give character to this sausage. Allow to cool a bit.

6. When the vegetable mixture is at room temperature, fold it into the puree of raw lobster and roasted pepper.

7. Mix this with the parsley and cooked lobster meat. Season with salt and pepper. Correct the seasoning.

8. Using a pastry bag with a sausage nozzle, stuff the forcemeat into the casings. Pack loosely to allow for twisting the casing into links. This sausage does not shrink; it expands. Chill the finished sausages for an hour or two.

9. Lightly poach the sausage in simmering lightly salted water, about 3 minutes for smaller sizes, 5 minutes for larger. Drain.

10. Melt 2 tablespoons of butter and saute sausages, turning them just enough to crisp the skin and add additional flavor.

11. Meanwhile, blanch the shredded cabbage for 30 seconds in boiling salted water. Drain well. Saute for 2 to 3 minutes in 1 tablespoon butter, season with salt and pepper, and toss well.

12. As a first course, serve one large sausage accompanied by the cabbage. As a main course, serve 2 sausages per person.

Serves 12 as a first course, 6 for dinner. Approximate nutrition information per first course serving: Calories 225; protein 17g; fat 16g; carbohydrates 4g; sodium 410 mg.

Lobster in Puff Pastry

This recipe concentrates the lobster's flavor and creates a luxurious first course or entree. Flaky puff pastry marries incomparably well with the sauced lobster. You may use your own recipe or purchase one of the frozen versions now available. Follow package directions for handling.

If you are serving the dish as a first course, you will need 8 bite-sized, 2 x 3-inch rectangles that you will open as you would a sandwich. For a main course, make pastry cases about 4 x 5 inches in size. With the tip of a knife, score the pastry case with a ¼-inch border all around, to create a basket effect when it bakes. The pastry cases can be prepared a few hours ahead.

We have cooked this dish with as many as four 2-pound lobsters without losing a whiff of flavor. Simply double the recipe for each additional 1½- to 2-pound lobster.

1½ pound live lobster	pinch of dried thyme
1 sheet puff pastry, at least 16 x 20-inches, ⅛-inch thick	12 parsley stems
	1½ cups dry white wine
1 egg	½ cup water
1 tablespoon water	freshly ground black pepper
	¼ cup butter
To cook lobster:	
½ cup diced carrot	1¼ cups soft butter
½ cup diced celery	1½ tablespoons butter
¼ cup diced shallots	2 tablespoons brandy

1. Preheat oven to 400 degrees. Brush the sheet of pastry with 1 egg mixed with 1 tablespoon of water, and cut it into desired shapes. Bake 10 to 12 minutes until puffy and nicely browned. Remove from the oven. If you are using the recipe as a first course, split the 2 x 3-inch puff pastry cases open in the middle like a book. Make a depression with your thumb in one side of the open book to hold the lobster mixture. A larger rectangle should have been baked into a basket effect, as described above. You can accent this by pushing down in center with your thumb if necessary. Set these aside.

2. Place carrot, celery, shallots, thyme, parsley stems, white wine, water, 3 or 4 turns freshly ground black pepper, and ¼ cup butter into a pot large enough to hold the lobster.

3. Cook, covered, for 8 to 10 minutes, or until the vegetables are soft and the mixture has developed a rich aroma.

4. Add the lobster, cover, and cook for 12 minutes. Remove the lobster,

reserving the pot liquid. Allow the lobster to cool sufficiently and then break it up, collecting all juices. Remove as much lobster meat as you can, plus tomalley, coral if any, and creamy parts from claws and body. Discard shell. Cut lobster meat into bite-sized pieces and reserve.

5. Combine the juices from the lobster, plus the tomalley, coral, and creamy parts with liquid in which the lobster cooked. In a wide pan, reduce the mixture over high heat. It is important that the reduced liquid becomes quite thick and mayonnaise-like, as it has to act as a binder. You should have 1 cup or a little less.

6. Off the heat, whip the 1¼ cups soft butter into the reduced liquid a bit at a time, making certain each addition is incorporated before adding more. You also may do this in a blender — the sauce will be fluffier.

7. Meanwhile, melt 1½ tablespoons butter in a separate skillet over low heat. Add the cut-up lobster meat and allow it to warm over low heat. Add brandy, heat, then ignite and toss until the fire goes out.

8. Reheat the puff pastry a few minutes in a 250-degree oven to make it crisp.

9. Combine lobster meat with sauce, stir, and spoon into the puff pastry shells. Leave the larger pastry cases open; top the small cases with one side of the "book." Serve immediately.

Serves 4. Approximate nutrition information per serving: Calories 1200; protein 37g; fat 102g; carbohydrates 37g; sodium 552 mg.

Lobster of the Sun
■■

This is an excellent recipe for a hot weather first course, especially during August or September, when native tomatoes are red-ripe, fresh basil is plentiful, and the cool piquancy of the sauce is a perfect foil for the richness of the lobster — and the weather.

The dish is refreshingly easy to make, and can be made the night before through step 3, leaving only the final short and cool assembly before dinner.

The lobster meat is removed from the claws and knuckles, but each diner gets a half lobster in its shell, with the tail meat loosened for easy eating, and accompanied by claw and knuckle meat. As a first course, half a chicken lobster would be enough. As a main course, you could serve each guest two halves of a small lobster, or half a 1½-to 2-pounder.

This recipe is adapted from a dish created at the Locanda d'Angelo, in Amelia, Carrara, Italy. The owners of that highly regarded inn, Mr. and Mrs. Angelo Paraccuchi, prepared the dish at a special dinner at the Castle Restaurant, in Leicester, Massachusetts, several years ago, following their appearance in the visiting chefs' program at the culinary division of Johnson and Wales College in Providence, Rhode Island. The style is that of Italian nouvelle. It is what chef Roger Verge, owner of the Moulin de Mougins and a leading exponent of French nouvelle, would call a "dish of the sun."

The adaptation is ours, of course; credit for the inspiration belongs to the Paraccuchis.

This dish works best with truly ripe fresh tomatoes. The orange juice must be freshly squeezed. Reserve 4 of the largest basil leaves for garnish. Use a 6-to 8-cup non-corrosive saucepan for the first step. The dish should be eaten just slightly chilled, not ice cold.

2 live chicken lobsters	1 teaspoon salt
fresh oranges	8 fresh basil leaves
6 fresh, ripe, medium tomatoes	salt
½ cup extra virgin olive oil	freshly ground white pepper
2 tablespoons lemon juice	

1. Grate the rind of 1 orange and reserve. Squeeze the oranges to make 2 cups of juice, saving as much pulp as possible. Discard the seeds and skin.

2. Cut tomatoes in half, squeeze over a strainer to retain the juice, but discard the seeds. Chop the tomatoes coarsely and measure 2 cups. Put the tomatoes and their juice, plus the orange juice in a pot. Add all the remaining ingredients, except the lobsters and the basil. Stir to mix.

3. Bring to a boil and cook at low simmer for 1 to 1½ hours. (The time is not critical.) Add 4 chopped basil leaves. You should have about 1½ cups. Cool, cover, and chill overnight or at least 4 hours in the refrigerator to meld flavors.

4. Meanwhile boil or steam the 2 chicken lobsters. Cool, cover with plastic wrap or foil, and chill for 6 hours or overnight.

5. About 1 hour before serving, remove sauce from the refrigerator and correct the seasoning. Puree in a food processor or blender, in batches if necessary, until the ingredients are well homogenized. Strain through a fine-meshed sieve or doubled layer of dampened cheesecloth. Whir in the blender or food processor once more. Reserve.

6. Split the lobsters lengthwise. Remove and discard the stomach sac. Remove the meat from the knuckles and the claws, preferably in one piece. Loosen the tail meat from each half of the lobster, but leave it in the shell. Wipe lobsters with a dampened cloth or paper towel.

7. Spoon about ¼ cup of sauce onto half of each of 4 chilled serving plates. Lay the half lobster in its shell next to the sauce, decoratively adding the meat of one claw and knuckle meat to plate. Garnish with a leaf of fresh basil. Pass a bowl with the remaining sauce.

Serves 4 as an appetizer. Approximate nutrition information per serving: Calories 425; protein 22g; fat 29g; carbohydrates 18g; sodium 900 mg.

Saupiquet de Homard au Poivron et l'Huile d'Olive

FROM JULIEN RESTAURANT, MERIDIEN HOTEL, BOSTON

The Meridien Hotel in Boston is a sister establishment to the Parker Meridien in New York. The Boston property is located in the heart of the city's financial district in what was formerly the Federal Reserve Bank. What is now the main dining room, the Julien, was once the bank's main counting room.

The food in Julien is nouvelle cuisine in style, uncompromising in execution, and polished professional in presentation. Executive chef Michel Pepin is from the Beaujolais region of France in that stretch along the Sâone from Lyon to Dijon that is often considered the homeland of French cui-

sine. Overall direction of the menu for Julien is provided by French chef Gerard Vie, owner of Les Trois Marches in Versailles, who makes periodic visits to update the menu. The following salad of lobster with a red pepper sauce and an olive oil dressing is a favorite at the restaurant. It is served at room temperature, on chilled plates.

2 lobsters, 1 to 1¼ pounds each	salt and pepper to taste
2 cups loosely packed, washed spinach, stems removed	1 sweet red bell pepper
	¼ cup olive oil
1 tablespoon cherry vinegar or other fruit vinegar	1 tablespoon freshly squeezed lemon juice
2 tablespoons peanut oil	caviar or truffle (optional)

1. Steam lobsters for about 10 minutes, drain and cool. Keep the claw meat in whole pieces, and slice the tail meat. Reserve. Remove meat.

2. Drain spinach and dry on paper towels.

3. Make dressing: Mix peanut oil, cherry vinegar, salt, and pepper. Reserve.

4. Make sauce: Cut the red pepper in half and remove seeds and white membrane. Cook 3 minutes in simmering salted water. Drain. Puree in food processor or blender. With the motor running, add olive oil slowly as you do in making mayonnaise. Add lemon juice, blend well, and correct the seasoning.

5. Toss spinach with dressing.

6. Cover the bottom of two chilled plates with the red pepper sauce. Place spinach in the middle, atop the sauce, on each plate. Place the sliced lobster tail around spinach and the two claws facing each other atop spinach.

7. Decorate with caviar or truffles between the lobster slices.

8. Serve immediately or hold in refrigerator if necessary, but not more than about 30 minutes, or the flavors will begin to dissipate.

Serves 2. Approximate nutrition per serving: Calories 600; protein 41g; fat 44g; carbohydrates 10g; sodium 740 mg.

Lobster Fricassee

Fricassee is a descriptive French word indicating that white meat or poultry — or in this case, lobster — has been cooked like a stew in a sauce of white wine, cream, and seasonings with vegetables.

2 live lobsters, 1 to 1½ pounds each

FOR MIREPOIX:
¼ cup celery, in ¼-inch dice
¼ cup carrots, in ¼-inch dice
¼ cup onions, in ¼-inch dice
1 tablespoon butter
pinch dried thyme
1 bay leaf
salt and pepper to taste

1 cup dry white wine
4 cups heavy cream
1 medium carrot
1 medium stalk of celery
18 asparagus tips or ½ medium zucchini
½ cup fresh peas

BEURRE MANIE:
1 tablespoon butter
1 tablespoon flour

1. Make mirepoix: In a pot large enough to hold 2 lobsters, saute diced celery, carrots, and onions, with 1 tablespoon butter and pinch of thyme, bay leaf, salt, and pepper. Cook, stirring often, until vegetables are softened. Do not be tempted to add a larger quantity of vegetables, or their flavor will be too pronounced.

2. Add white wine, bring it to a boil, and add the lobsters. Cover, turn heat down to medium-low and steam 12 minutes.

3. Remove the lobsters and cool. Retain other ingredients in pot. Remove the meat from the lobster shells over a container to catch their juices. Reserve the juices and meat separately.

4. Pour the liquids and vegetables from the lobster cooking pot into a smaller pot; add the lobster shells. With a potato masher, break up and mash the lobster shells. Add the cream. Shake and cook over medium heat. Cook and reduce slowly to about half the original quantity to extract the maximum flavor from shells.

5. Strain first through a colander and then through a fine-meshed sieve. You should have about 2 cups of liquid. Return to a clean saucepan and reserve off the heat.

6. Trim carrot and celery (and zucchini, unpeeled, if you are using it) into baton shapes — pieces about ⅜-inch square and 2 inches long. You will need 4 to 5 pieces of each for each serving.

7. Bring lightly salted water to boil in a pot. Cook carrots and celery 3 minutes, add asparagus tips, cook 2 minutes longer, add peas (and zuc-

chini) and cook for 2 minutes more. Drain, and refresh under running cold water. Drain well.

8. Combine the tablespoon of butter and tablespoon of flour to make the beurre manie. Return the cream mixture in the saucepan and add beurre manie a piece at a time, stirring in each addition with a wire whisk until it is well incorporated. This will thicken the sauce to the desired consistency.

9. Add the blanched vegetables and cook for 2 minutes more. Add the lobster meat and heat through. Correct the seasoning.

10. Serve in warmed soup bowls.

Serves 4. Approximate nutrition information per serving: Calories 1070; protein 29g; fat 97g; carbohydrates 20g; sodium 350 mg.

Roasted Lobster

If we are going to have to stretch our lobsters because of lack of availability and price, this is the kind of recipe that will permit us to do so — without giving up the flavor. The dish is rich enough so that one lobster will do where two small boiled or steamed lobsters would be served. You may double the recipe if necessary.

The lobster in this recipe should be placed into the oven alive. If you wish, make it insensitive to pain by inserting a knife into the underside at the joint where the tail meets the body or carapace.

You also may steam the lobster for 15 minutes. The resulting flavor will not be as intense and you will have to include ½ cup fresh or bottled clam juice to make the sauce.

If you discard the sand sac and other inedible parts, you can freeze the rest of the lobster body for some future use after taking the meat. Place the chopped walking legs and the body shell in a doubled plastic bag and freeze up to four months.

1½-pound live lobster	1 tablespoon minced shallots
1 bunch of watercress	½ cup heavy cream
1 tablespoon vegetable oil	2 turns freshly ground white
1 tablespoon butter	pepper

1. Preheat oven to 400 degrees.

2. Wash and dry the watercress. Select a dozen of the largest leaves to use as a garnish. Chop and reserve the remainder. Place the selected leaves into a strainer and blanch them in simmering water for 10 seconds. Refresh under cold running water and set flat on paper toweling to dry while you proceed with the rest of recipe.

3. Place the lobster in a roasting pan, drizzle it with the oil, and roast it for 15 minutes. Immediately upon taking it out of the oven, drain off the accumulated pan juices and reserve.

4. Cool the lobster enough to handle. Over a bowl or other container, break it in half where the tail and body join, and then break off the claws. Reserve the juices.

5. Place the lobster on a cutting board to remove the meat from tail, claws, and knuckles. Cut the lobster tail into medallions about ½-inch thick. Cover all the meat, and keep it warm in a low oven. Add all the juices you obtained from the lobster to the reserved pan juices.

6. Saute the shallots over medium heat in the butter until soft but not browned — about 2 minutes.

7. Puree the reserved chopped watercress in a food processor and add it to the saute pan with shallots for a few minutes to eliminate any moisture. Add reserved lobster juices and cook over medium heat about 5 minutes until the mixture is thick and syrupy.

8. Add cream and reduce the sauce over medium heat until it is thickened and will coat a spoon. Add white pepper. If you roasted the lobster alive, the lobster flavor is quite intense and you should not add salt. Correct the seasoning.

9. Set a pool of sauce onto warmed plates and add lobster pieces. Garnish with blanched watercress leaves.

Serves 2. Approximate nutrition information per serving: Calories 430; protein 21g; fat 37g; carbohydrates 3g; sodium 330 mg.

Shrimp

Shrimp are called prawn in some places, and prawn are called shrimp in others; both commonly are known as shrimp in the United States.

And, as finicky writers enjoy pointing out, so-called American "shrimp scampi" is a total misnomer.

The Italian scampo (of which scampi is the plural) is not a shrimp at all, but a lobster — or to be more correct a lobsterette, technically a nephropid. *Nephrops norvegicus* is its Latin name. You can translate it as Norway lobster. It's also called a Danish lobster. Obviously, scampi are lobsters.

Except that those brought in by Irish fishermen have always been called Dublin Bay prawns. And the French and more southern European countries tend to call them *langoustine* or some variation of that name. And those members of the Adriatic branch of the family are called scampi by the Italians.

A favorite way to cook scampi is broiled and basted with garlic butter. We Americans take a large Gulf shrimp and prepare it the same way and call it "shrimp scampi," which is in the tradition, after all, of how dishes often get named in the first place. It is shrimp as scampi are prepared — and that's shorter and more alliterative than "shrimp alla scampi." So, there's really nothing wrong with calling the dish "shrimp scampi," especially since the thing is a prawn to some, a lobster to others, and a langoustine to still more.

Speaking of shorter, in this book, at least, the plural of shrimp is shrimp, not shrimps.

Garlic butter or not, the shrimp is America's favorite seafood and so well known it seems unnecessary to provide much description as most consumers have long acquaintance with them in the many forms they are marketed: fresh, frozen, canned, dried, breaded (both cooked and uncooked), as paste, semipreserved, as soups, bisques, newburg, and other prepared dishes, whether frozen or canned. They can weigh up to 5½ ounces each or be as tiny as 300 or so to the pound.

Fresh shrimp, also called "green" shrimp, sometimes are marketed with their heads on, especially when sold close to where they are taken, though many gourmet restaurants as far north as New York, Boston, and Chicago now seek these out for the guarantee of freshness and added flavor they provide in many dishes. Consumers removed from the Gulf states are not likely to find shrimp with heads on in retail markets as the highly perishable crustacean is even more perishable when it hasn't been decapitated. Since only the tail is eaten anyway, the loss to consumers is not great.

Technically, a shrimp is a decapod crustacean. The decapod means he has 10 legs (5 pairs) and crustacean means he wears his skeleton — an exoskeleton — on the outside like the crab and the lobster.

Most of the shrimp you find in fish markets in the North have been frozen, whether they appear to have been or not. They are sold in the shell as well, peeled, and deveined; often cooked, peeled and deveined. In the trade they may be sold by weight. Names such as extra colossal, jumbo, large, medium, small, and tiny (with steps in between) are often attached to the various sizes of shrimp, but the public seems to go by that nomenclature when buying shrimp as much as it does when buying olives.

Shrimp also are sold by the count — so many to the pound. If you want shrimp solely for their impressive size, get U-10s, under 10 per pound. You stuff and bake these or barbecue them to make the biggest impression. Some shrimp imported frozen from the Orient are in the super colossal size, about 2 to a pound.

Shrimp from 10 to 15 and 16 to 20, the next two sizes, are quite large and can be used in any preparation where size is a consideration. After these divisions, shrimp run 21 to 25 to the pound, 26 to 30, 31 to 35, and so on. Those 51 to 60 are called small in some charts, and more than 70 are considered tiny. The larger the shrimp, the higher the price.

Maine Shrimp

The Maine shrimp may not be as well known as other shrimp in this country. Coming at them from different places and at different times before this work was begun, the authors independently discovered the outstanding qualities of the so-called "Maine" shrimp. When we began this book, we were sure our shrimp recipes were going to advance the cause of this northern crustacean — primarily because we knew, having eaten them for more than a dozen years, that they were available fresh and that their flavor was excellent; delicate, nutty, sweet, and fresh-tasting. Being small — approximately 80 to 120 count, or less than the size of a quarter when peeled — they make a wonderful appetizer deep-fried; they can be popped into the mouth like popcorn. And they work well in recipes.

Our motivation was not chauvinistic. Our enthusiasm will probably best be understood by shrimp lovers from states bordering the Gulf of Mexico, who know of their shrimp firsthand-fresh.

Investigation and emerging reality since have tempered our commitment for this time and this book, but our hopes have not been dashed for the future. We include in our recipes allowances for the Maine shrimp, but quality Gulf and other shrimp may, of course, be used.

The story of the Maine shrimp, generally unknown even within 10 or 15 miles of their breeding grounds, is an interesting one. It is worth telling, at least in part, at a time when new or underutilized species of marine life are being sought for food.

The shrimp's scientific name is *Pandalus borealis*. It is also known as the northern shrimp, pink shrimp (especially in Alaska), and northern prawn and deep water prawn in Europe. It is nearly Arctic in habitat and circumglobular. It is a small shrimp, measuring about 4¾ inches at best, and only half of that is the part that is eaten.

The Gulf of Maine, at a latitude of about 40 degrees north, is its southern limit. Nowhere else is it found south of 45 degrees north latitude. It strays south as far as Martha's Vineyard, off Cape Cod, though it occurs in greatest abundance from Mt. Desert Island in Maine to the Stillwagen Bank off the northern tip of Cape Cod. It occurs in depths from 60 to 2700 feet.

It is bright red when alive. When it is trawled for in deep water, as the Scandinavians do, it is generally cooked at sea. The Scandinavians are its most ardent pursuers. They use a lot of it themselves, as well as export it, frozen, to this country. The shrimp is also sought by Massachusetts fishermen, who, like the Scandinavians, tend to seek it at greater offshore depths in summer.

In Maine, however, the shrimp is sought inshore. During the winter, mature females come in close to spawn, and that is when fishermen seek them out. It is essentially a winter fishery. The season begins with moderate catches in January. In February and March, fishing is at its height and the season slacks off again in April and May.

The shrimp were noted in abundance in 1884, but were not fished extensively because of the limitations of gear. Fishing for the shrimp began seriously in 1938, according to Alden P. Stickney and Lorraine L. Stubbs; most of the data we cite were taken from their 1983 monograph for the State of Maine Department of Marine Resources.

In the more than 40 years since, there have been only two major periods of abundance: in 1944 and 1969. There are two major forces at work: the shrimp's environment at the southern edge of its limit, and the fishing itself. There seems to be a correlation between high water temperature and the decrease in shrimp abundance. Whether the warmer water adversely affects the shrimp themselves or positively affects their predators; whether it is the adult shrimp, the eggs, or the juveniles that are most affected, scientists can't say, because there aren't enough facts.

Like the even tinier krill that Russian and Japanese scientists are studying in the Antarctic, *Pandalus borealis* may or not be one of our foods for the future. If she is, the dainty lady of the northern seas is a delicious one.

We are optimistic. At this writing, the population of Maine shrimp appears to be in a cyclical upswing, and if it continues they might be more generally available, at least in the next few years.

In years of abundance, the shrimp are available fresh, whole; cooked, whole; cooked, peeled; cooked, peeled, and frozen; raw, peeled, and frozen; and peeled and canned.

If you buy Maine shrimp frozen, you must thaw them thoroughly and drain them. Wrap them in a dry kitchen towel or several layers of paper towels before you cook them to remove excess moisture; the moisture can be considerable and is likely to make your dishes soupy if not removed.

Amateur as well as many professional cooks tend to overcook all shrimp. As is true with most seafood, the Japanese have taught the world that shrimp can be eaten raw, so there is no need to cook it for a long time.

If using fresh or frozen Maine shrimp, be aware that they cook extremely fast. Follow the same procedure as for smaller shrimp given immediately below, but do not allow the shrimp to cool in their own heat or they will toughen. Drain and use them immediately.

For raw, unpeeled, shrimp, 30 to a pound or more, bring enough water to cover them to a boil. Add 1 tablespoon salt for each quart of water and add the shrimp. As soon as they change color, turn off the heat, and drain off the cooking water. Allow the shrimp to cool in the dry cooking pot in their own heat until they are cool enough to peel.

For larger shrimp, proceed in the same fashion, but do not drain the shrimp. Remove from heat and let them cool in their own cooking water.

Should you peel shrimp before cooking?

If meat and fowl tastes better when cooked with the bone, so does seafood. Unless there is some reason for not doing so, always buy unshelled shrimp and cook them with the shell. The resulting broth, by the way, can also be used as a stock — though it will be strong — and the ground up shells can be used as the basis for a shrimp bisque and other dishes. Be cautious when using the shells, however. High iodine or other mineral content and other factors can make the resulting dish bitter. Taste the mixture whenever you cook shells in this fashion to make certain that you won't spoil a dish.

Is it necessary to devein shrimp? No, they are not harmful eaten that way, but for aesthetic reasons (in a shrimp cocktail, for example) they are often deveined. Like the belly of a clam, it's a matter of personal choice.

Shrimp Creole

There are hundreds of variations on the creole theme, some of them quite complicated. This version is simple and direct and uses everyday ingredients to develop the flavors that make Louisiana cooking so popular.

Jalapeño peppers are now almost universally available. If you cannot find them, use any hot pepper. Since the hotness of peppers varies widely, it is wise to begin with only half a pepper and add more as desired.

It also is wise to be careful in chopping or slicing hot peppers. The airborne esters can burn your eyes. Always wash your hands and the knife after working with hot peppers, and keep your hands away from your face. It also is a good idea to wipe the chopping board with a damp cloth when you are through.

Other than the cooking time involved, the preparation time of this dish is no more complicated than making a salad.

1 pound peeled raw shrimp	1 tablespoon minced garlic
onion	½ teaspoon dried thyme
sweet red bell pepper	1 small bay leaf
sweet green bell pepper	½ teaspoon salt
1 jalapeño pepper	freshly ground black pepper
celery stalks	½ cup stock (fish or chicken) or
fresh tomato	water
½ cup canned tomato puree	

1. Cut all vegetables into ½-inch dice. You will need 1 cup of diced onions, both peppers, celery, and tomato.
2. Saute the onion until lightly colored. Add sweet peppers and saute 2 minutes. Add jalapeño pepper and celery and saute 2 minutes. Add chopped tomato, puree, garlic, thyme, bay leaf, salt, pepper, stock or water, and simmer for 30 minutes.
3. Add shrimp. Cover and cook 7 minutes. Correct the seasoning
4. Serve with boiled rice.

Serves 4. Approximate nutrition information per serving: Calories 245; protein 35g; fat 3g; carbohydrates 17g; sodium 850 mg.

Stir-fried Shrimp

Set out all your ingredients ahead of time, and the actual cooking of this flavorful dish can be done in 10 minutes or less.

1 pound peeled raw shrimp
1 tablespoon cornstarch
⅓ cup dry sherry wine
3 tablespoons peanut oil
2 teaspoons minced garlic
2 teaspoons minced fresh ginger
½ cup sliced water chestnuts
1 cup Chinese cabbage cut in
    thin strips

1 cup green peppers in wedges
20 snow peapods
3 tablespoons soy sauce
salt and pepper
½ cup fish stock or chicken
    stock (homemade or canned)
¼ cup chopped scallions

1. Blend cornstarch with sherry.

2. In a wok or skillet over high heat — or an electric skillet set at 370 degrees — saute the shrimp in 2 tablespoons oil for about 2 minutes. Don't overcook. Remove and reserve.

3. Add the remaining 1 tablespoon oil to the skillet. Add garlic and ginger, saute a few seconds, add water chestnuts, cabbage, peppers, and peapods. Cook, tossing or stirring. Add soy sauce, a pinch of salt, pepper, stock, and scallions. Continue to toss and cook until peapods are cooked but still firm.

4. Stir cornstarch-sherry mixture and add to hot pan, cook, stirring a minute. Add sauteed shrimp, cook 2 minutes, tossing to heat. Serve immediately, with rice.

Serves 4. Approximate nutrition information per serving: Calories 345; protein 35g; fat 14g; carbohydrates 19g; sodium 1480 mg.

Shrimp Remoulade

Remoulade is a well-known French preparation, basically a mayonnaise made with mustard and garnished with capers, parsley, gherkins, chervil, and tarragon, and finished with anchovy essence or anchovy paste. In New Orleans cooking, the sauce was transformed into something more emphatic. In Chef Paul Prudhomme's Louisiana Kitchen, *Prudhomme gives a recipe for remoulade containing egg yolks, oil, celery, green onions, parsley, horseradish, lemon with its rind, bay leaf, creole and prepared mustards, ketchup, Worcestershire sauce, white vinegar, Tabasco sauce, minced garlic, sweet paprika, and salt, all worked in a blender. The following version is less emphatic in flavor, but still in the New Orleans tradition.*

Creole mustard, available in specialty shops and better grocers, is made with brown mustard seed and is a whole grain mustard. You may also use a moutarde de Meaux *or one of the German whole grain brands. Whole grain mustards are now being made in California also. Since this dish is served cold, it may be prepared ahead. If the dish is to be served as a first course salad, use ½ pound of shrimp, but use the same amount of the other ingredients.*

1 pound cooked peeled shrimp
1 head of soft-leaf lettuce

FOR SAUCE:
2 tablespoons creole mustard or
   other coarse-grained mustard
2 tablespoons paprika
¼ cup minced onion
½ cup minced celery heart

1 teaspoon salt
freshly ground black pepper
½ cup olive oil
¼ cup minced scallions
¼ cup lemon juice
¼ cup minced fresh parsley
Tabasco or Louisiana hot sauce
   to taste

1. In a large mixing bowl, combine mustard, paprika, onion, and celery. Season with salt and pepper. Add oil slowly, while whipping with a wire whisk, as in making mayonnaise. Combine remainder of ingredients except shrimp, mixing thoroughly.

2. Add well-drained shrimp. Mix, cover with plastic wrap, and chill in the refrigerator 2 hours or more for flavors to marry.

3. Set out a bed of lettuce and mound the shrimp remoulade in center. Alternately, prepare individual salad plates with a bed of lettuce and divide shrimp remoulade among them.

Serves 4. Approximate nutrition information per serving: Calories 435; protein 31g; fat 30g; carbohydrates 12g; sodium 930 mg.

Maine Shrimp Scampi

The double cooking of this dish might not seem necessary, but it is if you are using Maine shrimp. Small Northern shrimp exude a great deal of moisture for their size and dry out quickly. The frying helps them to retain moisture and gives a crisp, nutty quality to the finished shrimp as an added bonus. Try it and you may not want to cook your Maine shrimp scampi any other way. You may either deep-fry the shrimp or fry them in a skillet containing at least 2 inches of oil.

With either method, do not overcook the shrimp; they are tiny and cook quickly.

1½ pounds peeled raw Maine shrimp (2 cups, about 6 ounces per person)	½ teaspoon salt
	freshly ground black pepper
½ cup milk	juice of ½ lemon
flour for dusting	¼ cup minced fresh parsley
⅓ cup butter	vegetable oil for frying
1 large or 2 small garlic cloves, minced	lemon wedges

1. Pat shrimp dry with paper towel. Dip shrimp in milk and drain them. Dredge in flour, shake to remove excess.

2. Heat oil for deep frying to 360 to 370 degrees.

3. In a skillet, melt ⅓ cup butter. When the foam subsides, add garlic and stir a moment. Add shrimp, salt, and black pepper, and saute, tossing, to crisp, about 2 minutes. At the last moment, squeeze a half lemon over the shrimp. Remove.

4. Deep fry the shrimp in hot oil just until crisp. Drain on paper towels and dust with minced parsley.

5. Serve at once with lemon wedges.

Serves 4. Approximate nutrition information per serving: Calories 495; protein 43g; fat 31g; carbohydrates 10g; sodium 850 mg.

Peapods Stuffed with Shrimp

This simple preparation makes a light first course. To make it, you will need a small Chinese steamer or a folding steamer insert in a pot.

Much of the preparation for this dish can be done early, leaving the steaming for the last minute.

¼ pound peeled raw shrimp
1 tablespoon soft butter
1 teaspoon minced fresh ginger
1 tablespoon minced fresh
   mushrooms
1 tablespoon minced red bell
   pepper

1 tablespoon minced scallions,
   including some green
1 teaspoon lemon juice
salt and pepper to taste
12 to 16 snow peapods — 3 to 4
   per person, depending on size
lemon-butter

1. Mince shrimp almost to a puree. Use a knife, not a food processor or blender, as you want to retain some texture.

2. Mix all ingredients, except peapods, with minced shrimp.

3. Set water for steaming to simmer.

4. Split raw peapods open on the concave side and either pipe mixture in with a decorator bag or push it in with a demitasse spoon.

5. Place filled peapods into steamer rack and set over simmering water. Steam for 2 minutes; you want the peapods to be cooked, but quite firm.

6. Arrange the filled peapods pinwheel fashion on individual salad plates. They may lie on their sides. Serve them warm, not hot.

7. Use warm lemon-butter as a sauce.

Serves 4. Approximate nutrition information per serving: Calories 175; protein 8g; fat 15g; carbohydrates 4g; sodium 380 mg.

Shrimp Athena
∎∎
FROM 57 RESTAURANT, BOSTON

The 57 Restaurant in Boston's Park Square is noted for its steaks, roast beef, chops, and veal, but seafood is not an also-ran in this stately dining room located adjacent to a Howard Johnson Hotel. This dish has its genesis in the little restaurants that crowd the Athenian port of Pireus, from which the patriarch of the family that owns the hotel and restaurant complex undoubtedly sailed for America many years ago.

The secret of this dish is the handling of the feta cheese. First, make every effort to buy fresh feta cheese, still moist and somewhat briny in flavor. Dried-out cheese will provide only a pallid reflection of the piquant sparkle the dish should have. Add the cheese at the last moment so that it will have begun to melt when the dish is served, but still should show chunks of cheese in the dish.

2 pounds raw shrimp (16 to 20 count)	1 tablespoon dry basil or 2 tablespoons fresh
¼ cup olive oil	½ teaspoon salt
1 clove garlic, minced	½ teaspoon pepper
½ medium onion, chopped	1 level teaspoon sugar
⅓ cup sherry	½ pound feta cheese cut into chunks
2 cups canned plum tomatoes	dash of Tabasco
¼ cup tomato puree	
1½ tablespoons dry oregano	

1. Shell and devein the shrimp.

2. Saute garlic and onions in olive oil until transparent. Add sherry, simmer a few minutes to reduce. Add plum tomatoes, tomato puree, oregano, and basil. Simmer lightly for 10 minutes. Add salt, pepper, and sugar.

3. Add shrimp and saute about 4 minutes until they change color. Add the cut-up chunks of feta cheese. Cook until the shrimp is done and the cheese is heated through. Correct the seasoning. The cheese should not be completely melted when you serve this dish.

Serves 4. Approximate nutrition information per serving: Calories 580; protein 65g; fat 27g; carbohydrates 10g; sodium 1620 mg.

Acorn Shrimp

■■

Here's a one-dish meal in the New England tradition — or the autumn tradition anywhere on the East Coast, really. Acorn squash, shrimp, breadcrumbs, and grated cheese give body to this flavorful dish, while diced vegetables add color.

½ pound peeled raw shrimp	½ cup green pepper, in ¼-inch dice
1 tablespoon parmesan cheese	½ cup red pepper, in ¼-inch dice
3 tablespoons fresh breadcrumbs	
2 acorn squash	
1 teaspoon oil	2 tablespoons butter
salt and pepper	¼ cup chopped toasted almonds
½ cup onion, in ¼-inch dice	

1. Combine parmesan cheese and breadcrumbs and reserve.

2. Preheat oven to 400 degrees.

3. Cut squash in half horizontally and take a slice of skin off the bottom of each half so that the squash will stand upright without tipping. Remove the seeds, and leave the pulp.

4. Season with salt and pepper. Drizzle ¼ teaspoon oil into each squash. Place squash cut-side up on a lightly oiled, ovenproof baking pan and bake 25 to 30 minutes or until the squash is done. Allow to cool.

5. Lower oven temperature to 350 degrees.

6. Carefully remove pulp from each half of squash, leaving a wall ¼- to ½-inch thick. Mash pulp and place in a small saucepan over low heat to evaporate most of the moisture.

7. Saute onion and peppers in 1 tablespoon butter only until soft, but not yet picking up color.

8. Chop the shrimp and add it to the vegetables in the saute pan. Add almonds. Continue to cook 1 to 2 minutes. Do not overcook the shrimp. Remove from the heat. Off the heat, blend in the remaining 1 tablespoon butter and add the squash pulp. Mix well and correct the seasoning.

9. Return the mixture to the squash shells, top each with the cheese and breadcrumb mixture, and bake 12 minutes; in the 350-degree oven.

Serves 4. Approximate nutrition information per serving: Calories 290; protein 20g; fat 13g; carbohydrates 29g; sodium 360 mg.

Shrimp à la Hongroise

FROM CAFE BUDAPEST, BOSTON

There is no more romantic restaurant anywhere than Edith Ban's Cafe Budapest. This elegant lady is in the tradition of hard-working, uncompromising women who have created restaurants of great character by sheer determination against difficult odds.

Edith Ban can stir up thirty gallons of savory sauce or sweat a bag of onions to a golden rich sweetness at the drop of a necessity, and in the kitchen she can be as demanding a taskmaster as any chef. She can stretch a strudel dough until its thin elasticity defies the laws of physics and kitchen science. This is an aspect of Edith Ban that few of her customers have ever seen. To most she is the tall, slender, handsome woman draped in dramatic white — and only white — designer gowns that set off her classic European features.

If one is to define the food at the Cafe Budapest it probably should be termed Hungarian-Continental, but that is only a category. What it really is is in the unique style of Edith Ban, food with good taste that is seasoned with a bit of drama and embellished with tempered flair.

4 pounds peeled raw shrimp (16 to 20 count)
8 medium sweet green bell peppers
2 medium sweet red bell peppers
2 cups diced onions
1 cup rendered chicken fat
1 teaspoon crushed hot red pepper flakes
2 diced tomatoes, 1 cup or a little more
6 large cloves garlic, pureed
1 tablespoon tomato paste
2 tablespoons sweet paprika
2 cups chicken stock, homemade (preferred) or canned
salt to taste
pinch of sugar

1. Cut tops off red and green peppers and remove stems, pulp, and seeds. Chop pulp and usable portion of tops; reserve. Cut peppers vertically in half, and then into ⅜-inch slices. Reserve.

2. Saute onions in chicken fat until they are transparent. Add crushed red pepper flakes, chopped pulp and tops from peppers, and diced tomatoes, and saute over medium heat until the pepper tops are soft but not mushy.

3. Add garlic and tomato paste and cook for several minutes longer; the fat will rise to the top. Reduce the heat to the lowest setting, sprinkle the paprika on the fat, and cook, stirring. Do not allow the paprika to burn. The color should change to a brilliant red as the paprika is incorporated.

4. Add chicken stock and stir. Bring the ingredients back to a simmer, then add pepper slices, salt, and sugar. Simmer for only 5 minutes, or until peppers are *al dente*. Correct the seasoning.

5. Add shrimp to sauce, and simmer until they are done, approximately 5 to 7 minutes. Garnish with additional chopped fresh raw green and red pepper if you like.

6. If you serve this as a main course, you'll need 3 cups of cooked rice as an accompaniment.

Serves 24 as a first course or 12 as entree. Approximate nutrition information per serving of entree: Calories 440; protein 40g; fat 20g; carbohydrates 23g; sodium 780 mg.

Shrimp Croustade

In this recipe, dinner rolls are hollowed out, as they are for Shrimp Rarebit on page 330, and filled with a highly flavored shrimp mixture. You will want to eat it with a knife and fork.

Rolls should be white, round, dinner-type rolls, crisp-crusted with smooth seamless bottoms and sides, and soft interiors. If the rolls are seamed, they are likely to leak. Since they should be served hot, just before they are filled they should be toasted in the oven, unless you have a small electric broiler.

1 pound peeled raw Maine or
    other tiny shrimp, whole
4 dinner rolls
2 large red bell peppers
1 tablespoon butter
½ cup dry sherry
1 teaspoon salt
2 to 3 turns freshly ground black
    pepper

½ cup heavy cream
¼ cup soft, not melted, butter
2 tablespoons horseradish,
    freshly grated if available, or
    bottled
juice of ⅓ lemon, about 1½
    tablespoons

1. Cut off the top portion of each roll and remove most of interior to form a basket. You will want to create a cavity of about ¾ cup, so the amount of top you remove will depend on the size and shape of roll. Leave a thick shell.

2. Over an open flame, under the broiler, or in a hot oven, char whole red peppers until the entire skin is blackened. Remove and place in a brown paper bag and allow to steam with their own heat for 10 minutes. Remove and peel the skins under running water. Remove stems, split peppers open, remove seeds and white membrane, and roughly cut to make 1 cup. Set aside.

3. In a skillet, melt 1 tablespoon butter, add shrimp, sherry, salt, and pepper while tossing lightly. Cook just until tender — don't overcook.

4. Strain pan liquids into a clean, small, wide skillet or pan. Reserve the shrimp, cover, and keep warm. Keep the original skillet for the last operation.

5. Reduce the liquids by half. Add ½ cup cream and reduce by ⅔. You should end up with about ½ cup liquid.

6. In the work bowl of a food processor, puree the red pepper. Add the cream-stock reduction and ¼ cup soft butter, and puree until smooth.

7. Put the puree into the original skillet. Heat, add horseradish, and reduce the sauce until it is thick enough to coat a spoon heavily.

8. Add the shrimp and lemon juice and heat through. Correct the seasoning.

9. Preheat oven or a small toaster oven to 375 degrees. Toast rolls in oven so that they are lightly colored and hot. Place the shrimp mixture in the rolls just as they come from the oven.

10. Serve hot, accompanied with asparagus tips or spears and lemon butter.

Serves 4. Approximate nutrition information per serving: Calories 450; protein 33g; fat 28g; carbohydrates 19g; sodium 1060 mg.

Shrimp San Remo

This dish is marvelous either for company or family dinners. While the custard filling resembles a quiche, it eliminates the need for pastry and is quickly prepared. The bread that holds the custard is more substantial in texture than a pie shell or pâté brisée, and the combination of basil and the sun-dried tomatoes of San Remo (available in cans or jars) is a happy, traditional flavor combination.

The procedure is basically the same whether you use a whole loaf as recommended or individual servings in rolls. The large loaf makes a better presentation, however, and it can easily be cut and served at table.

Use a round loaf of bread, a French boule; or an Italian or Portuguese round loaf, or make individual loaves, using a bulkie roll, kaiser rolls or similar breads. The bread may be a day or two old. The interior must be soft. The bread must be crisp-crusted with smooth bottoms and sides and have no cracks or deep creases that are likely to cause leaks. (A little of the custard might leak, no matter how careful you are, but it should seal while it bakes.)

½ pound peeled raw Maine or
    Gulf shrimp
1 round loaf bread; 6 to 8 inches
    in diameter, 4 inches thick
¼ chopped onions
½ tablespoon butter

TO MAKE CUSTARD:
2 cups light cream
3 egg yolks
1 whole egg
½ teaspoon salt

pinch of white pepper
grating of fresh nutmeg

1 tablespoon minced fresh basil
1 ounce (about 4) sun-dried
    tomatoes, coarsely chopped
1 whole sun-dried tomato and
    another cut in ¼-inch
    lengthwise strips to be used
    for garnishing
⅓ cup diced Swiss or gruyère
    cheese

1. Slice off top ¼ to ⅓ from loaf or rolls, depending on their thickness. Pull out most of the soft interior, leaving a ½-inch-thick shell. Set aside.

2. Saute onion in butter until transparent but not taking on color. Reserve and allow to cool.

3. Preheat oven to 375 degrees.

4. Make custard: In a bowl, mix cream, egg yolks, whole egg, salt, white pepper, and nutmeg.

5. Bake hollowed bread (or rolls) 3 minutes, just until slightly toasted.

6. Smear the interior of the bread with some of the custard, using a pastry brush. Return the loaf to the oven for 2 to 3 minutes until the custard sets. This will help seal your loaf and prevent it from becoming over-soaked from the filling.

7. Place the toasted loaf on a cookie sheet.

8. Arrange the shrimp, basil, chopped sun-dried tomatoes, and cheese in the bottom of the loaf and pour the custard mixture over them.

9. Place the whole sun-dried tomato on top of the custard in the center and radiate thin strips of tomato around it, sunburst fashion.

10. Bake 20 to 25 minutes, or until the custard is set. Serve immediately with a green salad.

Serves 4. Approximate nutrition information per serving: Calories 690; protein 23g; fat 50g; carbohydrates 40g; sodium 460 mg.

Shrimp Custard in Avocado

Raw avocados often are used in combination with shrimp, but in this recipe you hollow the avocado shell, stand it upright on its broad end, and replace the pulp with chopped shrimp. The buttery pulp is combined with a rich custard flavored with sherry and tomato and poured back into the avocado shell to be baked. The result is that you dip into an avocado with a crisp top crust on a soft and mellow custard to get at the tender shrimp at the bottom.

This recipe may be made a few hours ahead, through step 5, and the final steps done closer to serving time.

¼ pound raw Maine shrimp, or
    8 medium raw Gulf shrimp
    (about 26 count), with shells
2 tablespoons butter
½ cup dry sherry
1 minced shallot
1¼ cups half and half

1 tablespoon tomato paste
1 teaspoon salt
pinch of pepper
4 medium avocados, firm and
    not too ripe
2 eggs plus one yolk

1. Peel shrimp and reserve shells.
2. Saute shrimp in 1 tablespoon butter over medium heat just until

they turn color and "set." Don't overcook. Reserve, and when they have cooled, cut the shrimp into ½-inch pieces if necessary.

3. In a skillet, saute the shrimp shells in the remaining 1 tablespoon of butter, cooking until they brown slightly (don't darken too much or they will get bitter).

4. Remove the pan from the heat for a moment and add the sherry. Place the pan back on the heat and cook a minute (be careful it does not flame), then add shallot, half and half, tomato paste, salt, and pepper. Simmer 10 minutes over medium heat.

5. Remove from heat and pass the mixture through a fine strainer, pressing down on the shells with a spoon to extract the juices. You should have 1½ cups of liquid. Allow it to cool.

6. Meanwhile cut one-third off the top (narrow end) of each avocado, and a thin slice off the bottom or broad end (so that the fruit will stand on its end without tipping). Reserve the slices you trim from avocados, as you may need them later. With a demitasse spoon or small melon baller, scoop out the pulp and pit from avocado, making certain you don't puncture the skin. Coarsely chop the pulp you have removed.

7. Place the reserved shrimp and about half the avocado pulp into a bowl and toss lightly to mix. Divide the mixture among the avocado shells, filling each ¼-to ½-full.

8. Mix two eggs and 1 yolk together with a fork and then mix them with the cooled, strained cream mixture. Correct the seasoning.

9. Preheat oven to 375 degrees and set a kettle of water to simmer.

10. Lay enough aluminum foil into an ovenproof baking dish so that you can crumble and mold it to hold the filled avocados firmly upright. Stand the avocado shells on the foil. If needed, you may use the slices taken from the avocados as wedges to help steady them. Add the egg-cream mixture to filled avocado shells.

11. Add simmering water to the pan to a depth of 1 inch and bake 20 minutes. The finished custard should have a crust on top. Let them rest for a few minutes before serving.

Serves 4. Approximate nutrition information per serving: Calories 625; protein 12g; fat 56g; carbohydrates 22g; sodium 460 mg.

Classic Shrimp Charles

FROM JIMMY'S HARBORSIDE RESTAURANT, BOSTON

Jimmy's Harborside is a Boston landmark. The story is that Jimmy's began as a seven-stool restaurant on the edge of the Boston Fish Pier many years ago, when haddock was seven cents a pound, and people in the fish trade were the only regular customers.

James Doulos took this small restaurant to the top of the heap in Boston, where it became a mecca not merely for tourists and suburbanities, but also for the city's shakers and movers of business, government, and commerce. The following dish is named for Jimmy's son, Charles, who now operates the restaurant.

1 pound shrimp (15-and-under count), peeled and deveined	1 teaspoon minced fresh parsley
2 teaspoons oil	½ teaspoon salt
2 cloves garlic, minced	¼ teaspoon freshly ground black pepper
1 medium onion, chopped	1 tablespoon butter
1 1-pound can stewed tomatoes	¼ pound feta cheese, in strips
4 chopped mushrooms	½ x 1 x ¾-inch

1. Heat oil in a skillet. Add garlic and onion and saute until golden brown. Strain juice from tomatoes into skillet. Finely chop tomatoes and add to skillet. Simmer about 15 minutes until sauce thickens. Add mushrooms and simmer 5 minutes more. Add parsley, salt, and pepper. Remove from heat.

2. Preheat oven to 400 degrees.

3. Coat a shallow casserole with 1 tablespoon of butter. Butterfly the shrimp to form a pocket, place strips of feta cheese into shrimp, and arrange in casserole.

4. Pour tomato sauce over them and bake in the preheated oven for 20 minutes.

Serves 3. Approximate nutrition information per serving: Calories 385; protein 45g; fat 17g; carbohydrates 13g; sodium 1020 mg.

Shrimp Rarebit

As all quiches trace their lineage to an early model first made in Lorraine, France, all rarebits have their antecedents in the one called Welch, which features melted cheese flavored with mustard and beer or sherry and other ingredients, with or without an egg for body. A rarebit, what the English call a savory, is usually served hot on toast points.

Our rarebit follows the same general style, but we add shrimp to the cheese mixture, sharpen the flavors, and use a toasted roll to hold it all and to make a more substantial dish. The roll is a substitute for the croustade in French culinary preparations. It was a loaf baked to the size and shape desired, trimmed of crust, and hollowed out to hold a filling. For our use, the rolls are perfect and save baking. They should be white, round, dinner type, crisp-crusted with seamless bottoms and sides, and soft interiors.

1 pound raw Maine or Gulf shrimp (16 to 20 count)
4 small, hard-crusted dinner rolls with soft interiors
1 12-ounce bottle ale or beer
¼ cup celery, cut in ¼-inch dice
¼ cup carrots, cut in ¼-inch dice
¼ cup shallots, cut in ¼-inch dice
½ teaspoon black peppercorns, cracked
¼ teaspoon dried thyme
6 parsley stems
¼ teaspoon dry mustard
pinch cayenne
pinch white pepper
1 tablespoon Worcestershire sauce
10 to 12 ounces grated sharp cheddar cheese (1½ cups)

1. Cut off the top quarter or third of each roll and remove most of the interior to form a basket. How much you remove will depend on the size and shape of the roll. Create a cavity of about ¾ cup or so; leave a thick shell, as described for shrimp Croustade, page 300.

2. Place beer, celery, carrots, shallots, cracked peppercorns, thyme, and parsley stems in a saucepan and simmer for 15 minutes.

3. Strain liquid into a clean saucepan and return to the heat. When the liquid boils, add the unpeeled shrimp, return to a boil, and cook 2 minutes on high heat. Remove shrimp with a slotted spoon and let them cool. (Larger shrimp may take 4 minutes or more depending on their size.)

4. Over medium-high heat, reduce the liquid in the saucepan to ⅓ cup.

5. While the liquid reduces, peel shrimp and reserve. Discard shells.

6. Add mustard, cayenne, white pepper, Worcestershire sauce to the reduced sauce. Stir to combine.

7. Melt grated cheese over low heat.

8. Stir the beer mixture into the cheese, combine well, add the shrimp, and cook for 3 minutes, stirring so the mixture won't stick.

9. While the shrimp cooks, toast rolls lightly. Divide the shrimp and cheese among 4 hot dinner rolls. Serve hot.

Serves 4. Approximate nutrition information per serving: Calories 630; protein 50g; fat 30g; carbohydrates 40g; sodium 1170 mg.

Mollusks

*"It is unreasonable and unwholesome in all months
that have not an r in their name to eat an oyster."*
— William Butler, "Dyet's Dry Dinner"

*"Let's sing a song of glory to Themistocles O'Shea
who ate a dozen oysters on the second day of May."*
— Stoddard King, "The Man Who Dared"

Scallops in Zucchini Boats

Clams

■

There are two major considerations when dealing with clams. First, all clams can be and are eaten raw. Overcooking, therefore, is a prime fault in preparing them. When it is raw, the clam is as tender as it is ever going to be. Heat will toughen it, so don't overdo the cooking, whatever form your dish takes.

Secondly, because they live in mud and sand, clams must be well washed — unless you enjoy the grind of grit in your food. Wash them thoroughly in cold running water, scrubbing shells with a brush, a piece of burlap, or terry or another rough cloth.

If you have time, you can soak them in salted water (¼ cup of salt to a gallon of water; 1 tablespoon to a quart) for several hours to help purge them. Some authorities suggest stirring a cup of cornmeal or flour into the water to make purging more efficient. Professional clam diggers disapprove of this method, since the cornmeal itself will probably not be purged when you eat the clams and will adversely affect their flavor. Further, cornmeal will not have sufficient time to cook even when clams are steamed or deep-fried, and raw cornmeal won't help the flavor.

There are three varieties of clam of interest to East Coast diners. The softshell clam, usually called "steamers," the quahaug (pronounced co-hog) or hardshell clam, and the razor.

The Razor Clam

Not well known nor much used unless you live within smell of the ocean, razor clams are difficult to capture and highly perishable.

The razor, or "racer" as it is sometimes known along the coast, is a narrow, slender clam, four to eight inches long, with a thin, sharp shell. Its brownish-gray rubbery body usually protrudes from both ends of its shells, which gape permanently. Its name comes from its resemblance to the straight razors used by barbers and men of an earlier generation. The edges of its shell are almost as sharp as a razor; many amateur diggers have learned the hard way that you can't tug at a razor half-buried in sand. The clam is not only a speedy digger, but its "foot" is an incredibly strong anchor. These characteristics, plus an extremely brittle shell, make it difficult to gather the oblong bivalve without damaging it.

Only rarely are they used in restaurants or sold in fish markets, though they are sometimes marketed alive in the shell close to where they have been dug. Among connoisseurs of clams, however, the razor is highly regarded. The *Wall Street Journal* published a story last year about razor clam diggers in Alaska whose production was sold in Oregon and Washington at up to $9 a pound.

If you get a chance to sample some, try them in chowders. They are also good — raw or barely cooked — in salads, especially in a salad containing squid, conch, crabmeat, and the like. They can also be deep-fried like "steamers."

Softshell Clams

Softshell clams are best steamed or fried. Generally they are steamed in nothing more than plain water; the resulting broth is used to swish the clams in to remove any traces of sand before dipping them in melted butter and eating. You can enrich the broth by adding onion, parsley stems, a whole peeled garlic clove, and/or a chunk of linquica (Portuguese sausage) or pepperoni to the water before steaming the clams.

Any leftover broth should be strained for use in cooking. It can be frozen. It is an excellent quick stock that can be used in many dishes (see the section on Stocks and Fumets, page 28). Don't use spicy sausage in the broth if you plan to use the broth in a sauce, as it will be too strong.

Bottled clam juice is also available and is useful in recipes. Most of what is sold is labeled "Clam Broth" and has been diluted with water. "Clam Juice" is undiluted clam broth, and therefore is stronger. "Clam Nectar" is an evaporated and concentrated product and is the strongest of the three.

New Englanders discovered a long time ago that softshell clams (*Mya arenaria* is the Latin name) make excellent fried clams, and they are still considered fine enough eating to be included on many American restaurant menus in the Northeast. Evaporated milk as a wash and cornmeal as batter is the normal way to handle them.

As with nearly all shellfish, softshell clams should be alive when you steam or fry them. A live clam will retract its black siphon or neck when it is touched — if the clam is limp and lifeless and doesn't react, you don't want it.

For some, the bellies of *Mya arenaria* present a problem in eating. Steamed and fried clam purists insist that they should be eaten, but many diners discard them. They tend to be both soft and mushy and gritty. Since clams dine only on innocuous diatoms, the belly is as perfectly edible as the rest of a sound clam taken from unpolluted waters. It's a matter of taste.

Quahaugs

As A. J. McClane points out in *The Encyclopedia of Fish Cookery*, the original Latin name of the quahaug or hardshell clam was *Venus mercenaria*, or "money conscious goddess of love." The name has been changed to *Mercenaria mercenaria*, but the original name had pertinence. Venus, after all, was born in the sea and arrived on a seashell (the scallop, to be sure, but a seashell nevertheless). The quahaug shell was the black or purple wampum of the American Indian, and was the dearest wampum. White wampum, from the conch and other shellfish, also was used, but was not so highly esteemed. The name quahaug is from a Wampanoag Indian name.

The quahaug, like the softshell clam, is found from the Arctic to Cape Hatteras. The quahaug prefers a salty bed, while the softshell likes its surroundings low in salinity, such as in places like Chesapeake Bay, which is fed by freshwater rivers. You can find chauvinistic argument for the superior merit of the quahaug from Cape Cod, Narragansett Bay, Long Island's Great South Bay, and other repositories, but all are equally good if fresh. It is variously called a hardshell clam and a chowder clam as well as a quahaug.

All states where commercial digging is permitted have a minimum size that may be taken to assure reseeding of clam beds. Quahaugs traditionally have been divided into three categories by size. In recent years, purveyors have added a fourth, primarily for the restaurant trade. The sizes are: little neck, 2 inches or less, 450 to 460 to a bushel; cherrystone, 3 inches or less, 300 to 325 to a bushel; chowders, 4 inches or more, 125 to a bushel; and top neck, which is the new category. It falls between the little neck and the cherrystone. Although both little necks and cherrystones are eaten raw on the halfshell, some diners find a cherrystone too large. The top neck provides a smaller size, but at less than the premium price demanded for little necks. They come at about 180 to a bushel.

The little neck, named for Little Neck Bay, Long Island, is a quahaug that is three years old; the top neck about four, and the cherrystone about five years old. The cherrystone gets its name from Cherrystone Creek, Virginia. Top neck is a term without historical or geographical derivation.

Quahaugs larger than a cherrystone are lumped together as chowders. They also are called surf clams, (sand) bar clams, sea clams, skimmers, and just quahaugs. Almost three-quarters of the clams harvested in the United States are this clam. Too large for eating raw on the shell, they are usually chopped, minced, or ground. These clams are also what you are most likely to get as preminced clams sold in fish markets. Minced clams are often used not only in chowders and fritters, but also for baked stuffed quahaugs, red and white clam sauce for pasta, and similar recipes. A lot of clams are canned as minced clams.

Gatherers of surf clams go out after storms, when the large quahaugs are thrown up from their resting places. Those people who have a bountiful catch often use only the tenderest part of the clam, the adductor muscle, which resembles a sea scallop.

The larger surf clams tend to have yellow flesh, which is not a drawback when the clam is batter-fried or combined with many other ingredients. When softshell clam beds were decimated in some areas during and immediately after World War II, enterprising purveyors discovered that the big clams could be cut into strips for frying; today a lot of fried clams are made from such strips.

A different sub-species of quahaug — the ocean, black, or mahogany quahaug — is taken in deep water of 45 to 300 feet. It is brought in by dredges and landed primarily in Middle Atlantic and New England ports. Also, occasionally after a northeast storm these clams are likely to be torn loose from the seabed and tossed ashore on exposed beaches. Its meat is dark and it is used in the same manner as the surf clam.

Preparing Clams

Whenever taking raw clam meats from their shells, do so over a large pan or bowl to collect whatever liquid the clams yield. The liquid should be strained through a double thickness of dampened cheesecloth and then put to use in cooking.

The razor clam, with shells that don't quite close and with its body extending from both ends, is so easy to open that professional shuckers often use a flattened spoon rather than a knife to do the job.

The softshell clam is best handled with a dull clam knife, but it is rather easy to slide the knife above the protruding neck and into the clam between the shell and flesh. After the top portion has been separated, the knife can be slid between the meat and shell on the underside to completely separate the meat from the shell. The veil covering the siphon, or neck, is then given a diagonal slash from base toward tip and slipped off. The clam meat is rinsed in clam broth or water to remove sand and patted dry before being dipped in batter for frying.

Hardshell clams are more difficult to shuck. The operation requires a stiff-bladed clam knife. For the novice, a glove on the hand holding the clam (the left hand if you are right-handed) is also probably a necessity. A staunch rubber glove would be better than a cloth of some kind, since a cloth would absorb the clam's natural juices that you will want to save.

Much has been written about how to open a quahaug, but be assured the job is not an easy one. One edge of the clam is rounded; it is the part that opens. The other edge is a kind of hinge that keeps the shells together.

Think of the clam inside the shell as a chunk of meat with two suction cups (the adductor muscle) holding the shells together. The suction cups hold tightly; they are the lock that secures the hinged shells. Your job is to sever these suction cups at the point they are attached to the shell. You must get a knife between the shells and then get the tip of the blade against the top shell so that you can scrape it forward to cut the suction cup loose. The clam will open; you can repeat the operation easily on the bottom shell and the meat will fall free.

To begin, hold the clam in your left hand with the hinge pointed toward your wrist. The pointed hinge should be lodged against the heel of your hand. Cup the clam in that fashion and bring the sharp edge of the clam knife to the cleft in the rounded part of the clam. You are trying to find the small gap between the two shells. Catch the blade of the knife in this gap, using the two middle fingers of your left hand on the dull side of the blade to steady and guide the knife. Rather than trying to jab the knife between the two halves of the shell with the force of your right hand, think of the operation in terms of squeezing the blade between the shells with the middle fingers of your left hand.

If you find the gap, the blade will enter partway. You can then force it in farther, twisting it so that the front end of the knife, rather than just the leading edge, is into the shell. Raise the tip of the blade within the clam so that it is against the top shell, otherwise you might slice the meat in half. By sliding the knife forward, you will sever the adductor from the shell. Twist the knife after the cut has been made to further widen and separate the shell. Now it will be easy to pry off the top shell and cut the bottom of the adductor muscle free. Drop the meat into a sieve over a pan to collect the meat and juices. The entire clam is edible.

An easier method of opening hardshell clams is to put them into a freezer for several hours or overnight just as they come from the fishmonger. When you wash them, the shells will open slightly; making shucking much easier. All shellfish are easier to shuck when they are well chilled, which is one reason shellfish bars in good restaurants keep their offerings packed on ice.

For raw clams on the halfshell, only the first half of the above operation is performed. The top shell is removed and discarded, and the meat is loosened, but not removed from the bottom shell to make eating easier. The job is done carefully so that the liquid in the shell remains, keeping it moist and briny-flavored. Clams on the halfshell are normally served on ice or at least well chilled. Just be certain that they are not allowed to dry out.

Steaming clams, whether softshell or hard, is an operation similar to steaming mussels. For a normal serving for four people, use ¼ cup or more of water in a pan large enough to hold the clams. Fit with a tight cover and set over high heat. When steam begins to escape, protect your hands from the heat and shake the pan with a tossing motion, holding the cover down tightly. This will guarantee that clams that are wedged in tightly will open. Steamed clams should all open within 5 to 7 minutes after water begins to steam, but it may take as long as 10.

Cooking clams is done with the same caution as applies to cooking other shellfish: Raw, they are as tender as they are ever going to be, so don't cook longer than necessary. In most cases this will mean just heating through. As with other shellfish, any that fail to open during steaming or cooking should be discarded.

In a dish such as clams casino, the quahaug is treated as a clam on the halfshell and left whole, though some cooks prefer to chop it if it is large. The flavoring ingredients (bacon, minced sweet pepper, and seasoned breadcrumbs) are placed atop the meats before the clams are broiled just until the bacon is cooked.

For chowders, fritters, and the like, quahaug meat sometimes is ground, but grinding destroys not only texture but flavor as well. Clams should be chopped with a knife for just about every use.

Clams in the shell most often are purchased at retail by the count, by weight, or by quantity (quarts or gallons). Minced clams are sold by the pound or by quantity (pints or quarts). As a guide when purchasing larger quantities for a crowd: Three 12-quart buckets of clams in the shell equal a bushel, three bushels make up a barrel.

Generally, six to eight littleneck clams, shucked, make one serving. For steamed clams, allow one quart unshucked clams per serving. Eight quarts of clams in the shell make about one quart, shucked. Two dozen cherrystones, allowing for size variations, will yield about 1½ cups of meat and about 3 cups of juice. Two cans (6½ to 7 ounces each) of minced clams are equal to about three dozen hardshell clams, chopped.

Quahaug Pie

This is a recipe of many variations, since it was a standby of early Atlantic seaboard cooking wherever clams were found. Our version is fairly straightforward. It makes a 10-inch pie, a wedge of which makes a substantial main course.

To make the pie, you will have to bake the bottom crust "blind," by placing something into the uncooked shell to keep it from rising while it bakes. Kitchen foil is the handiest material. Crumple a large wad of foil and lay it into the shell so that it fills the shell. Some bakers use rice, beans, or similar dry ingredients — or pellets made for the purpose. Remove the foil or other filling after baking.

Although this, like most pies, is best hot from the oven, you can make it a day ahead; it will keep. The crust will undoubtedly get a little soggy as it waits. Allow it to cool after baking and keep it in the refrigerator. Rewarm before serving. Or, you can prepare the pastry and the filling and not put them together until just prior to baking the pie.

CRUST:
3 cups flour
1½ teaspoons salt
⅔ cup soft, not melted, butter
2 egg yolks
10 tablespoons cold water

FILLING:
2 cups chopped quahaugs, drained
6 small potatoes, peeled
¾ pound raw bacon
1 cup chopped onions
salt, pepper, and cayenne to taste

1. Make crust: Sift flour onto a flat surface. Make a well in the center. Add the soft butter to the center of the well in small pieces. Add egg yolks, salt, and a small amount of water to the well. Using your fingertips, incorporate all the ingredients. Slowly draw the flour into the center, until the mixture looks like coarse cornmeal. Sprinkle with additional water as necessary to form a smooth ball. When all the flour is incorporated, the ball should be soft but not sticky. Wrap in plastic and chill for 30 minutes.

2. Lightly flour a flat surface and roll out the dough for the bottom of the pie. It should be about 1½ inches larger in diameter than a 10-inch pie plate. Set it into the pie plate. Chill it, as well as the pastry for the top crust.

3. While the dough is "resting," parboil the peeled potatoes in salted water. Drain the potatoes and, when cool enough, cut into a small, rough dice, to make about 2 cups.

4. Chop the bacon into approximately one-inch squares. Place in a

large frying pan or skillet and cook gently until it exudes most of its fat. Remove, and leave about ½ cup fat in the pan. Add onions and cook gently over a low flame until translucent and soft, not browned. Add salt, pepper, and cayenne pepper to taste. The mixture should be fairly piquant. Allow to cool. When cool, add potatoes and drained chopped quahogs and toss gently. Correct the seasoning.

5. Preheat oven to 425 degrees. Remove the bottom crust from the refrigerator, and prick it with a fork. Bake it "blind" for 12 to 15 minutes. Lower the oven temperature to 350 degrees.

6. Add the cooled filling to the pie shell. Wet the edge of shell with milk or water. Roll out the top piece of dough and lay it over the pie shell. Trim the excess and crimp the edges. Bake it at 350 degrees for 30 to 40 minutes or until golden brown.

7. Allow the pie to rest at least 30 minutes before cutting it into 6 wedges and serving.

Serves 6. Approximate nutrition information per serving: Calories 1340; protein 29g; fat 103g; carbohydrates 73g; sodium 1800 mg.

Clam Chili

When we first thought of trying to make a chili with clams instead of meat, the idea seemed far-fetched. After we had made the following recipe we were glad we had experimented. The dish is good and would be savory and satisfying on a cold day.

As with most chilis, this one improves the longer it sits. It can be reheated. Add a bit of clam broth or water if it dries out. The direction to cook the clams for one hour is not an error. This amount of cooking is necessary to develop the flavors. If they are minced, they won't be tough and chewy.

Because the strength of chili powder varies greatly and weakens as it ages, it is difficult to determine exactly how much is needed to suit a particular palate. Please your own palate, but begin with the quantity we give to play it safe. Minced canned clams may be used in this recipe.

20 ounces minced raw clams
⅓ cup clam juice
1½ cups coarsely diced onions
1 cup diced celery
2 tablespoons oil
2 medium tomatoes, peeled,
    seeded, diced to make about
    2 cups, or 2 cups of canned
    Italian plum tomatoes, diced
1 cup water
½ teaspoon cumin
3 cloves garlic, minced
3 tablespoons chili powder

½ teaspoon salt
5 to 6 ounces of dried red kidney
    beans, soaked and cooked, or
    1 pound canned red kidney
    beans with their liquid

OPTIONAL GARNISH:
1½ tablespoons minced onion
1½ tablespoons shredded cheese
    (Monterey Jack or sharp
    cheddar)
fresh or canned whole or minced
    green chilies

1. Collect the clam juice as you open the clams, and measure ⅓ cup. If you need more, use bottled clam juice.

2. Saute onions and celery in oil until soft and barely colored. Add tomatoes and cook 1 minute. Add minced clams, broth, water, cumin, garlic, and chili powder.

3. Cook, covered, at a low simmer for 1 hour. Add beans during the last 15 minutes and continue to cook covered.

4. Correct seasoning. You may need more salt, garlic, cumin, or chili powder.

5. Serve in chili or soup bowls. Pass raw onion, cheese, and chili peppers as a garnish, if desired.

Serves 4. Approximate nutrition information per serving: Calories 420; protein 35g; fat 15g; carbohydrates 33g; sodium 430 mg.

Clam Risotto

◼◼

Risotto is not merely an Italian manner of serving rice, it is as different in style from the traditional American — or for that matter, Oriental — way with rice as chicken cacciatore is from chicken velvet.

In making risotto, a cook strives to keep every grain separate; if the grains lump together it is not risotto. Secondly, the rice is cooked much firmer than is rice as we traditionally eat it. Al dente *is as operative a phrase with risotto as with pasta.*

To help them achieve the quality they seek, Italian cooks use native Arborio rice that effectively retains starch, making it easier to keep the grains separate.

If you can't find Arborio rice, substitute domestic short-grained rice, which, while not the same thing, is the closest to it in this country. Mussels may be substituted for clams in this recipe, but they should be kept whole.

This dish is hearty enough to function as a complete lunch with a green salad.

24 cherrystone or 32 little neck clams	1 cup fish stock (see White Wine Fumet, page 30) or homemade or canned chicken broth
¼ cup dry white wine or water	
2 to 3 thin onion slices	
1 garlic clove	freshly ground black pepper to taste
3 to 4 parsley stems	
4 cups clam juice	1 tablespoon minced fresh parsley
3 tablespoons butter	
1 tablespoon olive oil	2 tablespoons grated parmesan cheese
1¼ cups raw Arborio rice	

1. Wash the unshucked clams for cooking as described at the beginning of this section.

2. Place in a pot ¼ cup wine (or water), onion slices, garlic clove, and parsley stems. Cook 10 minutes and add the clams. Steam just until the clam shells gape; do not overcook. Remove clams, set aside, and keep warm.

3. Strain the broth through a double thickness of dampened cheese-cloth. Measure, and add bottled clam juice to make 4 cups of liquid.

4. Remove clam meats from shells and chop. Discard shells.

5. Melt 1 tablespoon butter in a large skillet and add the olive oil. Add rice and stir to coat. Add 1 cup clam broth and ½ cup fish stock or chicken broth and bring to a boil, stirring.

6. Lower the heat to a slow simmer. Season with pepper and continue

to cook, uncovered, stirring frequently. As the liquid is absorbed, add the rest of the fish stock, and then begin adding clam broth ½ cup at a time, making certain that all the liquid is absorbed and the rice is glistening but nearly dry before adding more. The rice may absorb only 2½ to 3 cups of the clam broth or it may absorb it all. Stop adding broth when the rice doesn't absorb any more. The cooking up until this point should take about 15 minutes and the rice should be about ¾ cooked. The dish should be moist at this point, but not soupy.

7. Add the clams and minced parsley, and cook at a slow simmer until the rice is done to the *al dente* stage. Add a tablespoon or 2 more of clam broth if the risotto is dry; it should glisten moistly. Add the final 2 tablespoons butter and parmesan cheese and blend well.

8. Serve on individual warmed plates. Pass pepper mill and additional grated parmesan cheese.

Serves 4. Approximate nutrition information per serving: Calories 475; protein 28g; fat 19g; carbohydrates 46g; sodium 640 mg.

Fried Clams

When the definitive work on American cooking is finally written, Howard Johnson will be remembered as the man who popularized the fried clam. It is pure Americana — a shellfish that can be eaten as a finger food in the casual style that Americans like best. Before the orange roofs began spreading out from their Massachusetts birthplace, the fried clam was strictly a coastal regional dish. Howard Johnson gave it widespread fame, and, prior to the invasions of pizza parlors and McDonald's, it became one of the Atlantic coast's best known take-out foods. Dwindling resources and high prices have cut into its availability, but it remains good eating of the unfussy kind.

You can use softshell clams or strips cut from surf clams, depending on what your fish market has available. Purists eschew the strip. It is customary when using softshell clams to use the belly as well as the rest of the flesh, but you may discard the bellies if you prefer.

The ratio of oil to food is important in deep-frying. Too much food in too little oil is counterproductive. It is better to deep-fry in two or three batches than try to do them all at once.

Use fresh oil. Keep oil clean by skimming loose food particles after every batch is fried. Make certain that oil returns to 360 to 370 degrees before frying a new batch.

This recipe is sufficient for 4 dozen clams, enough for 4 diners to have 1 dozen each.

4 dozen chilled, shucked, softshell clams, or the equivalent in stripped meats
½ cup evaporated milk, chilled

FLOUR MIX:
2 cups cornmeal

½ cup all-purpose flour
½ teaspoon salt
⅛ teaspoon pepper

oil for deep frying
tartar sauce (page 43)
lemon wedges for garnish

1. To achieve the ultimate crispness, the evaporated milk and the clams must be very cold. Keep them in the refrigerator until the last moment.
2. Mix flours, salt, and pepper.
3. Drain clams well on paper towels.
4. Dip clams in milk. Drain, dredge in flour mixture, and shake off the excess.
5. Deep-fry the clams in hot oil (360 to 370 degrees) until crisp.
6. Drain on paper towels; serve with tartar sauce and lemon wedges.

Serves 4. Approximate nutrition information per serving: Calories 625; protein 23g; fat 32g; carbohydrates 59g; sodium 550 mg.

Clams Basilico

Clams oreganato is an appetizer course that is popular in restaurants featuring southern Italian cooking. It has the simplicity of clams casino. This recipe substitutes fresh basil leaves for the dried oregano.

This is a quick appetizer or first course that requires little time and work once the clams have been opened and arranged on the halfshell. You can prepare the clams several hours ahead, through step 3, and keep them covered with plastic wrap in the refrigerator. Moisten with a drop or two of broth and bake.

The finished dish should be moist — neither powdery dry, nor pasty wet.

16 to 24 quahaugs
1 garlic clove, minced
2 tablespoons minced fresh basil
1 tablespoon minced fresh
    parsley

¼ cup fine fresh breadcrumbs
1 tablespoon olive oil

1. Use 6 clams per person if clams are little necks; use only 4 if they are cherrystones. Shuck the clams and catch their juices. If cherrystones are quite large you may want to halve or quarter the meats to make them easier to eat. Leave meat on the halfshell. Reserve and strain ½ cup clam juice.

2. Line a baking pan with foil, crumbling it so that you will be able to set the clams into the foil without their tipping.

3. Combine remaining ingredients, including ½ cup reserved clam juice, and mix well. Add more clam juice if needed. Top the clams with the mixture. Set clams onto foil.

4. Preheat the broiler. Slide the baking pan under hot broiler about 4 inches from flame until the top of each clam is barely browned. Serve hot. The clams also may be baked in a 400-degree oven.

Serves 4. Approximate nutrition information per serving: Calories 135; protein 13g; fat 5g; carbohydrates 10g; sodium 250 mg.

Warm Clam Salad

We combined clams with ingredients usually found in the home to create a different method in which to serve the popular bivalve.

12 cherrystone clams
8 medium-small new potatoes
¼ cup olive oil, plus 1
    tablespoon oil
2 tablespoons minced shallots
freshly ground black pepper
1½ tablespoons lemon juice
1 teaspoon minced chives
¼ cup diced sweet green bell
    pepper

¼ cup diced sweet red bell
    pepper
⅛ teaspoon Tabasco or other
    hot sauce
1 tablespoon minced fresh
    parsley
salt to taste
lettuce

1. Scrub the potatoes well, but do not peel. Set to cook in lightly salted water. Cook until done, but still fairly firm. Drain well and leave in pot in which they cooked to dry from their own heat. When ready to use, slice them ¼- to ⅓-inch thick. They should still be warm.

2. Shuck the clams, chop the meats into a rough dice, and reserve and strain their juices.

3. Saute the shallots in 1 tablespoon olive oil until transparent, but not yet picking up color. Add clams, reserved clam juice, and black pepper, and cook 1 minute. Don't overcook. Remove clams with a slotted spoon, cover, and keep warm.

4. Return the pan containing shallots and clam juice to heat — you might have as much as ¼ cup — and reduce to 2 to 3 tablespoons. Mix it with ¼ cup olive oil, lemon juice, chives, diced peppers, Tabasco, and minced parsley. Toss well. Carefully fold in the potatoes and clams so that the potatoes are not crumbled. Correct the seasoning. (Don't oversalt, as the clams may be salty.)

5. Serve on lettuce leaves while still warm.

Serves 4. Approximate nutrition information per serving: Calories 365; protein 11g; fat 18g; carbohydrates 40g; sodium 250 mg.

Clams in Black Bean Sauce

The sauce for this dish should be well flavored, unctuous and thick, almost syrupy. Wash clams well and place them in pot ready for steaming before you begin making sauce. You can stop momentarily halfway through the sauce-making to steam the clams, and then finish the sauce, so that both will be hot when served. (If you are going to use the broth acquired from steaming the clams in making the sauce — instead of using fish or chicken stock — you will have to steam clams first and then keep them warm until ready to serve.)

Measure and prepare all the ingredients ahead of time, and keep them on hand, ready for use, so that the actual cooking time will be very brief. The fermented black beans, oyster sauce, and rice wine are sold in Chinese markets.

With cherrystones, this recipe will serve 6 as an appetizer in a Western-style meal or 4 if used in a Chinese meal with 3 or 4 other dishes.

36 little neck or 24 cherrystone clams
1½ tablespoons fermented black beans
1 or 2 tablespoon peanut oil
3 tablespoons shao hsing (Chinese rice wine) or dry sherry; or use 2 tablespoons white wine with 1 tablespoon dry gin
2 cloves garlic, minced
2 tablespoons minced fresh ginger
1½ cups fish stock (see White Wine Fumet, page 30) or homemade or canned chicken broth; or use broth from steaming clams

3 tablespoons oyster sauce
1 tablespoon light soy sauce
½ teaspoon sugar
1½ tablespoons cornstarch dissolved in 3 tablespoons water
2 stalks scallions, sliced thinly crosswise, white portion with some of freshest green parts
few sprigs of coriander, optional

1. If the fermented black beans are packed in salt, wash them well. It is best to rinse them quickly in a sieve, followed by a 15- to 20-minute soak in tepid water. A final rinse under cold running water will rid them of salt, but not any flavor.

2. Place 1 tablespoon peanut oil in a small hot skillet or wok (or 2

tablespoons if you're planning to use the clam broth). Add 1½ tablespoons black beans and mash thoroughly with a fork. Add rice wine or sherry, garlic, and ginger. Cook over high heat 2 or 3 minutes, stirring constantly. Stir in stock or broth, oyster sauce, soy sauce, and sugar. Remove from heat while you steam the clams.

3. Scrub clams well. Steam in ½ cup water 6 to 7 (up to 10) minutes, shaking occasionally, until all the clams are open. (Use 1½ cups water if you are going to use clam broth in sauce.) Do not separate the meat from shells. Drain, cover, and keep warm.

4. Return the sauce to the heat and bring it to a simmer. Stir the cornstarch mixture to make sure it is thoroughly combined, then add it to the pan, and stir until thickened.

5. Set clams in their shells on a warmed deep platter, with their open sides facing up. Pour the sauce over them, and sprinkle with scallions and optional sprigs of coriander. (Although the coriander sprigs are optional, they make a considerable difference.) Serve immediately.

Serves 4. Approximate nutrition information per serving: Calories 125; protein 12g; fat 2g; carbohydrates 14g; sodium 940 mg.

Mussels

The edible or blue mussel found from Canada to the Carolinas is not originally native to our shores. It is thought to have reached America by hitchhiking a ride on the hulls of vessels sailing into the Colonies from Europe. The migration was easy enough since mussels, like oysters, begin life as free-swimming "spat" before they find a home and begin to grow their shells. Once they established themselves, they became bountiful. Bound together in colonies with their seaweed-like anchor threads, they cling to rocks, seawalls, pilings — almost any surface that lies in the zone between high and low tide.

Despite their abundance, mussels traditionally have failed to win the popularity in this country that other mollusks, such as the clam and scallop, have enjoyed. By and large the mussel's popularity in the United States has been confined, in the past, to ethnic groups from the Mediterranean, where it has been part of the cuisine for at least 700 years — though there is evidence that it was eaten in southern France before that region became Roman Gaul. Southern Europe may find the shiny blue-black bivalve captivating, but it is equally cultivated in Holland and Belgium, and in nineteenth-century Great Britain, mussels were something of a rage.

Just how ignored the mussel has been in the American larder can be garnered from the fact that as recently as 1976, a mere 3000 tons were cultivated in the United States while France was raising more than 45,000 tons, and consuming that much more again in wild varieties.

Finally, today the mussel is enjoying a boom in popularity. It is finding its way more and more into the home kitchen. It appears on menus of the simplest as well as the most sophisticated restaurants — in soups hot and cold; in salads; stuffed, sauced, paired with other seafood; as a garnish and as the main event. Most frequently it is featured in the classic *Moules Marinière* — that aromatic French brew of mussels with white wine, shallots, and parsley.

The growth in popularity makes sense. The mussel is much more adaptable in recipes than is the clam — which, even its most devoted enthusiasts would agree, is best eaten raw on the halfshell. The tan yellow-orange meat of mussels is sweeter than other bivalves; and mussels are less expensive than the others. They are sleek bundles of good nutrition, being 12-percent protein, low in fat, and rich in vitamins, minerals, and trace elements.

One can obtain mussels year round, but they are at their best from September to May, as the oyster is. They spawn during the warm months and, though edible, are likely to be less than perfect in texture at that time, being thin and watery, much like lobsters in the softshell stage. Mussels take about three years to grow to 2 inches in length.

In New England, it is fairly easy to gather wild mussels. One should observe several precautions, however, when gathering them. First, mussels prefer harbors and estuaries as a habitat. Such locations tend to be the first to suffer from pollution, so make certain you are harvesting in a safe area. If in doubt, check with local authorities or avoid areas that might be contaminated. Secondly, take only those mussels that are firmly attached to an anchorage. It is also wise to avoid mussels that in warm weather are exposed to long periods of low tides and hot sun. Obviously, one does not take mussels during Red Tide emergencies.

While mussels can be and are eaten raw in many cultures, they are always served cooked in this country.

The overriding consideration for eating mussels is to first make certain that they are alive, whether you have gathered them yourself or purchased them. A live mussel will always keep its shells closed, or will close them when handled. You test for this by holding the mussel between your thumb and forefinger and squeezing gently, pushing the top shell forward with your finger and the bottom shell backward with your thumb, as though trying to slide one across the other. Shells of live mussels will not move. Discard any that do move. Also discard any that are inordinately heavy; they are likely to be filled with mud or sand. Even if the mussel within is alive, you will never completely remove all the muck, a little of which can ruin a dish.

Cleaning the mussels is your next task. Give each one an initial washing, then remove their beards (the strong filaments, or byssus), which served to anchor the mussel to its lodging place. The easiest way to do this is to grasp the beard between your thumb and a dull knife blade and give it a tug to pull it free. Scrape or pull away any that remains. Some enthusiasts leave the beards on, ignoring aesthetics in favor of the flavor they feel the beards add to a mussel broth. They are also handy for dipping the mussels into hot drawn butter.

Each mussel then must be scrubbed to remove all traces of mud and clinging grass. Scales and barnacles do not have to be removed, especially when the shells are not going to be served. Use either a stiff brush or a soapless scouring pad of either plastic or metal under cold running water. A piece of burlap also will do.

It's a good idea to soak de-bearded and scrubbed mussels for an hour or so in cold water to help eliminate sand trapped in the shells. Two or three changes of water are beneficial. Lift the mussels from the water bath gently, so that you leave the sand behind. Some cooks suggest soaking the mussels in water with flour, cornmeal, or oatmeal to help purge them; but if this is not purged also, it will remain raw through the cooking and affect the flavor. Unless the mussels are unusually sandy, this is generally unnecessary. If you do use this technique, do not leave the mussels in such a bath more than 2 hours unless the water is salted (¼ cup salt to a gallon of water), or you are likely to asphyxiate them.

Normally, mussels are cooked over high heat. They should not be overcooked or they will shrink and toughen. Do not submerge mussels in liquid as you cook them — the water that adheres to them is usually enough to create steam — though you may want to add a cup or more of liquid to make a broth or sauce. Cook them in a covered pan and shake the pan every 2 or 3 minutes so that no shells are trapped in such a way as to prevent their opening. Usually 6 to 7 minutes is sufficient to cook a quantity for four. The larger in circumference the pan, the more efficient the cooking. Whenever possible, select a pan that will hold all the mussels as nearly in one layer as practical. Discard any mussels that refuse to open.

As with all broth obtained from steaming or poaching seafood, you should always consider straining the liquid and storing it in the refrigerator or freezing it for future use.

As an appetizer, 10 to 12 average mussels per person should be sufficient; use 20 to 24 for a main course. When buying mussels, it helps to know that there are about 1 dozen large, or 15 medium, mussels to the pound. Figure on 1½ to 2 pounds per person for a main-course dish of mussels cooked in the shell; 4 pounds will yield about 50. Mussels are usually sold at retail by the quart. One quart equals 1½ to 2 pounds, or about 18 to 24 mussels.

Moules Marinière

Historically, this is a simple recipe, uncluttered with anything but the simplest ingredients, as homely and good as New England clam chowder. And, like a clam chowder, it not only does not need the added embellishments and fillips some people might add, but is made less honest and good by their addition. Resist the temptation to add bay leaf, thyme, flour, egg yolks, or whatever else some misguided kitchen kibitzer might suggest.

In a French country home this mussel dish would be served with the mussels still in the shells — and no forks or spoons. A set of hinged mussel shells makes perfect tongs to lift the hot meats from the remaining broth-soaked shells or to capture those that have escaped into the steaming broth. And an empty shell is a perfect scoop to get at the last spoonful of broth.

Choose a cooking pot large enough to leave plenty of room for the mussels to open and expand. If they are crowded or packed too tightly, some of the mussels will not open.

1 gallon of mussels, scrubbed and de-bearded	1 tablespoon minced shallots
2 tablespoons minced fresh parsley	4 tablespoons butter
	freshly ground white pepper
1 cup dry white wine	juice of ½ lemon, 1 tablespoon

1. Place 1 tablespoon parsley, wine, shallots, 2 tablespoons butter, and 3 turns of pepper in a large cooking pot. Bring the ingredients to a boil, add the cleaned mussels, cover, and cook over high heat, shaking the pot and tossing the mussels several times to ensure that they open.

2. When all the mussels have opened, transfer them to a serving bowl, cover, and keep warm.

3. Strain the liquid, if desired, through a double thickness of dampened cheesecloth into a small saucepan, reduce by ⅓, remove from heat, and whisk in the remaining 2 tablespoons butter.

4. Add the lemon juice and pour the sauce over the mussels. Sprinkle with remaining tablespoon of parsley. Serve immediately.

Serves 4. Approximate nutrition information per serving: Calories 329; protein 34g; fat 17g; carbohydrates 10g; sodium 774 mg.

Billi-Bi

CREAM OF MUSSEL SOUP

Technically, this dish belongs in the soup chapter, but because the mussel meats from a billi-bi are the basis for many other dishes (only the mussel broth is used in the billi-bi), we are placing it here. We use the mussel meats in several of the following dishes.

The recipe is said to have been created in the 1920s by a chef named Louis Barth at Maxim's in Paris for an American client named William Brand. Brand's last name initial (B) and first name diminutive (Billy) became the name of the dish. Whatever its origins and for whomever it was named, it is a magnificent soup served either hot or cold. It is more quickly made than most soups, yet it has a deep, sustained flavor that lingers.

If you want, the mussels can be eaten with a little melted butter just as they emerge from the pot, rather than holding them for other uses. The Billi-Bi broth also can be used as a stock as clam broth is, though the flavor obviously will be different.

If Billi-Bi is to be served cold, it can be made up to 6 hours before it is to be served. It also can be made sometime ahead and be reheated, but it will lose its freshness if it is held too long.

4 pounds (approximately 2 quarts) of mussels, cleaned and scrubbed	½ teaspoon dried thyme or one sprig of fresh thyme
1 cup dry white wine	3 tablespoons butter
2 minced shallots	2 turns freshly ground white pepper
4 parsley stems, coarsely chopped	2 cups heavy cream
½ crushed bay leaf	2 egg yolks

1. In a large non-corrosive kettle, place white wine, shallots, parsley, bay leaf, thyme, butter, and pepper, and cook over low heat for 5 minutes, stirring once or twice to blend well. Add mussels, cover, and bring to a boil. Shake and toss once or twice. Steam for 6 to 7 minutes to make certain all the mussels have opened. Discard any that remain closed. You probably will need to cook the mussels in batches so that they are not crowded in the pot.

2. Remove the mussels carefully with a skimmer so as to disturb the sediment in the bottom of the pan as little as possible. Reserve the mussels. Ladle the broth in the pan (there should be about 1½ cups) through a fine

sieve lined with a double thickness of dampened cheesecloth. Stop before all the broth is poured to avoid pouring out any sand and grit.

3. In a saucepan, bring the broth to a boil. Reserve 2 tablespoons of heavy cream and add the rest to the broth. Bring it back to a boil. Reduce the heat to the lowest setting.

4. In a small bowl or cup mix together the egg yolks and reserved 2 tablespoons cream. Pour some of the hot liquid into the yolk mixture, stir well to incorporate all the egg, and return it to the cream-broth mixture in the saucepan. Keep it over low heat until it is slightly thickened. Do not allow the soup to boil again. Correct the seasoning. You may want to add a little salt.

5. Serve it hot, or refrigerate to serve it cold.

6. A few cooked mussels, after being removed from their shells, can be added to the soup as a garnish, though this is not traditional. Use leftover mussels in recipes that follow.

Serves 6. Approximate nutrition information per serving: Calories 455; protein 16g; fat 40g; carbohydrates 9g; sodium 460 mg.

Mussels with Snail Butter

The same Burgundian-style butter that is used with snails works equally well with mussels. See the recipe for Beurre d'Escargot, *page 69.*

1. Steam the mussels, or use those from Billi-Bi. Leave the meats in the bottom half of the shell. Cover with escargot butter and slide under a broiler just until hot. This makes a delicious appetizer.

Approximate nutrition information per mussel: Calories 50; protein 2g; fat 4g; carbohydrates 1g; sodium 130 mg.

Fried Mussels

■□

Mussels fry up beautifully, retaining their briny moistness beneath the crisp skin created by batter-frying. Steam the mussels open, or use those from Billi-Bi. We prefer to first marinate the steamed mussels before dipping them in batter for frying. Serve these mussels as an appetizer, or double the recipe for dinner.

1 cup steamed mussel meats

MARINADE:
juice of ½ lemon
1 tablespoon oil

½ teaspoon salt
pinch of white pepper
½ tablespoon minced fresh
  parsley

1. Marinate mussel meat for 15 minutes to 1 hour in the marinade made from the other ingredients, tossing occasionally. Then dredge in one of the following coatings before frying.

COATING I:
flour for coating
1 egg
1 tablespoon water

salt and pepper to taste
1 cup fresh breadcrumbs

vegetable oil for deep frying

1. Dredge marinated mussels in flour to coat thoroughly, shaking off excess.
2. Make egg wash with egg, water, salt, and pepper.
3. Dip mussels in egg wash, drain, and dredge in breadcrumbs. Pat to make crumbs adhere. Chill a few hours before frying the mussels.
4. Deep-fry the mussels at 370 degrees until golden brown. Serve at once with lemon wedges.

Serves 4. Approximate nutrition information per serving: Calories 255; protein 11g; fat 20g; carbohydrates 8g; sodium 630 mg.

COATING II:
¼ cup condensed milk
¼ cup yellow cornmeal
salt and pepper to taste

vegetable oil for deep frying

1. Dip mussels in condensed milk. Drain.
2. Dredge mussels in cornmeal seasoned with salt and pepper. Pat so

that flour will adhere and shake to remove excess. Chill.

3. Deep-fry the mussels at 370 degrees until golden brown. Serve at once with lemon wedges.

Serves 4. Approximate nutrition information per serving: Calories 310; protein 11g; fat 20g; carbohydrates 21g; sodium 580 mg.

Cold Mussels Ravigote

This is a good way to use the mussels remaining from Billi-Bi. You will need 1 cup of mussel meat. If you are buying fresh mussels in the shell, you will need one quart. This dish may be made 6 to 8 hours before it is to be served.

1 cup mussel meat (steamed as for Billi-Bi)
½ cup homemade mayonnaise (see page 42)
2 tablespoons mussel broth
1 tablespoon minced shallots
1 tablespoon chopped capers
1 tablespoon minced sour gherkins
½ tablespoon minced fresh parsley or chervil
½ teaspoon Dijon mustard
salt and pepper to taste
lettuce

1. Mix all the ingredients except the mussels and the lettuce with the mayonnaise. Add cooked whole mussels, blend gently but thoroughly. Refrigerate, covered, until thoroughly chilled. The ravigote is best if it is made an hour ahead of time, but it may be kept for 6 to 8 hours.

2. Arrange a bed of lettuce on a small platter and mound ravigote in center, using pimientos, tomatoes, or another suitable garnish around perimeter. You also may serve each portion on a lettuce leaf on individual plates.

3. Alternately, do not mix the mussel meat with the sauce. Place a bit of the sauce in the bottom of a reserved mussel shell, drop in a mussel, and add another dab of sauce on top. Chill thoroughly. Serve as an hors d'oeuvre.

Serves 4. Approximate nutrition information per serving: Calories 260; protein 9g; fat 23g; carbohydrates 4g; sodium 600 mg.

Eclade de Moules

This is a seaside mussel bake from an Atlantic region of France, the Charente-Maritimes, a neighbor of Cognac.

This is the same kind of recipe, not gourmet or stylish, but as casual and rustic as an authentic clambake with the same wonderful real flavors — and a lot less work.

The authentic New England clambake, in which a pit is dug on a beach and filled with stones to serve as a kind of oven, is a fun — but laborious — way to capture the briny ocean taste in food. The following recipe achieves the same results on a smaller scale, but adds a resinous whiff of pine to the meaty moistness of fresh mussels.

The recipe was provided by Lylianne Benoit, one of France's great female chefs, who, with her husband, operates a restaurant called Le Soubise in a town by that name. The recipe is often used there — where mussels and pine are plentiful — on seashore family picnics.

The procedure is simple enough, you merely arrange mussels on some driftwood, cover with clean, dry, pine needles, and ignite the needles, allowing them to burn until the mussels are ready — adding fresh needles as needed to complete the cooking.

The whole point is to keep the mussels wedged against one another so that they do not open, but instead, steam with their own moisture within their shells. When you remove the mussels from the formation, the healthy ones will gape open. Discard those that do not.

If you can pick your own mussels from clean beds near the spot where you are going to bake them, so much the better. Of course, you can take all the ingredients to the backyard and have your Eclade de Moules there.

20 or so mussels per person	lemon wedges
a bushel of dry pine needles	melted butter
a plank or planks	

1. Wash and de-beard (if desired) the mussels, scrubbing them clean with a brush or rough cloth and seawater. If you have time, allow them to soak for as long as you can in seawater that is as clear and clean as you can find. This is not necessary, of course, if your mussels are extremely clean and recently plucked from a nearby bed.

2. Use any unpainted board or driftwood for this operation, but not plywood. The strong glues used to hold the veneers together might impart a

disagreeable taste and undoubtedly are not something you would want to eat.

3. Soak the wood in water for at least 30 minutes.

4. As the wood soaks, collect dry clean pine needles. You will need a bushel of needles for 6 to 8 people.

5. Place the mussels on the board so that the part that will open when they are cooked is facing down and the hinged side is up—you don't want the ash from the pine needles falling into the moist mussels. Also, the edges of the part of the shells that open are thin and brittle and are likely to burn.

6. Arrange the first 4 mussels in the form of a cross, pointed ends touching — hinge up — they should stand without falling. Use small stones, or nails, if necessary. Set the next 4 mussels within the formed cross, wide ends innermost this time. The 8 mussels should brace each other and you then can proceed to add more mussels, wedging them against the first 8 and fanning out in a widening circle until all the mussels are used.

7. Top the mussels with 2 inches of pine needles and ignite. As the fire dies down, add more needles. Six or 7 minutes of this, and your mussels should be ready. Test one. Cook more as needed. When they are done, serve them hot, passing wedges of lemon and melted butter for dipping.

Approximate nutrition information per serving: Calories 160; protein 25g; fat 4g; carbohydrates 6g; sodium 500 mg.

Moules à la Poulette
■□

If you would prefer a rather easy mussel dish that is more luxurious than the above Marinière, Moules à la Poulette is the one to try. Silky and suave, enhanced with egg and cream, it is incomparably good. Its basis is the Marinière recipe, with a minor change.

To serve it as an appetizer, allowing 10 to 12 mussels per person, you will need 2⅔ to 3 quarts of mussels. To serve as an entree, allowing 18 to 20 mussels per person, you will need a gallon. Often, for this recipe, the mantle, or darkened edge that circles the mussel meat, is removed for appearance after the mussels have cooked.

Remove the opened mussels from Marinière broth and reserve while you make Poulette sauce.

We included two variations of the recipe, one with a mustard accent; one with curry.

1 gallon mussels, scrubbed and de-bearded	5 tablespoons butter
	freshly ground white pepper
2 tablespoons minced fresh parsley	3 tablespoons flour
	1 egg yolk
1 cup dry white wine	½ cup heavy cream
1 tablespoon minced shallots	1 tablespoon lemon juice

1. Preheat oven to 225 degrees. Cook mussels in a large pot with 1 tablespoon parsley, wine, shallots, 2 tablespoons butter, and 3 turns of pepper. Remove the mussels when all of them have opened, place them into a deep platter in which they will be served; cover with a kitchen towel wrung out in hot water, and place in the preheated oven. (Alternately, you may wish to serve mussels on the halfshell in individual soup bowls, which will make a more attractive presentation. They also will be easier to eat. In which case, arrange the steamed mussels on halfshells in the soup bowls in which they are to be served. Arrange them in a circular pattern and cover each bowl either with a dampened dishtowel or several layers of dampened paper towels. Place in a 225-degree oven to keep warm while you make the sauce.)

2. Strain the cooking liquid through a double layer of dampened cheesecloth, and return it to the cooking pot.

3. In a flat dish or small bowl, mix together well the remaining 3 tablespoons butter, softened, with 3 tablespoons flour, using a fork. This is called a *beurre manie* in French cooking parlance and is a handy thickening agent.

4. In another bowl, beat the egg yolk and cream lightly with a fork until they are well mixed.

5. Return the pot with the strained mussel juices to medium heat and bring it to a boil. Add *beurre manie* and stir with a wire whisk, allowing it to cook for 2 minutes. Add 2 or 3 tablespoons of the hot liquid to the yolk-cream mixture, mix well, and pour this into the mussel juices, stirring constantly. Heat without boiling. Remove from the heat, add lemon juice, and correct the seasoning.

6. If you are serving mussels on the halfshell in individual soup bowls, ladle some of sauce into each mussel and pass the additional sauce in a bowl. If serving mussels on one large deep platter, ladle the sauce over the mussels. In both cases, sprinkle with the remaining tablespoon of minced parsley and serve immediately.

Note: You can vary this dish by accenting its flavor with mustard or curry.

Add 2 tablespoons of grainy Dijon mustard (*moutarde de Meaux*) to the pan after you have incorporated the yolk-cream mixture. Stir and heat, but do not boil, and then proceed with the recipe. The mustard will provide a different texture as well as flavor. You may use 2 tablespoons of a smooth Dijon-style mustard if you prefer not to have the grainy texture.

Alternately, mix ¾ to 1 tablespoon of prepared or homemade curry powder with 2 tablespoons of water. Add it to the pan before mixing in the *beurre manie* so that its flavor will be well infused. Proceed with the recipe. The exact amount of curry you use will vary depending on the strength of the curry powder and how you prefer the dish. Taste after the addition of ¾ tablespoon and correct with about ¼ tablespoon at a time until the flavor meets with your approval.

Serves 4. Approximate nutrition information per serving: Calories 595; protein 38g; fat 39g; carbohydrates 26g; sodium 988 mg.

Mussels Tempura

Tempura is often prepared with shrimp or squid, but it is also an excellent way to prepare mussels. The following batter ahderes well and gives the delicate, lacy kind of crisp exterior so prized in Japanese tempura dishes. Japanese cooks like to chill their tempura batter, which serves to thicken it. Pastry flour will work best in this recipe, but you can use all-purpose flour. This recipe makes enough batter for 4 appetizer servings.

Vegetables dipped in the same batter are a nice accompaniment to mussels. String beans, carrots, eggplant, fresh mushrooms, and zucchini work well. You may blanch vegetables like string beans and carrots first, depending on how crisp you like your vegetables. Cut the vegetables into julienne strips — carrots and string beans would be in finer julienne than eggplant and zucchini — dip in batter, and fry. Japanese chefs often substitute very thin but wide slices of carrots and zucchini in their tempura dishes. Double the batter recipe if you plan to serve vegetables, too.

Serve the tempura with our sweet and sour sauce (page 63), or make our tempura dipping sauce below. It calls for several Oriental ingredients, which are available in Oriental markets, and, nowadays, in many supermarkets. Dashi is a clear stock made with kelp and dried bonita shavings. Mirin is a sweet thick rice wine (you can approximate it by cooking equal parts of granulated sugar and sake — or even sherry or white wine — to make a syrupy blend that is similar in flavor). Daikon is the white Japanese icicle radish.

40 raw mussel meats (1-1½ quarts)

BATTER:
½ cup pastry or all-purpose flour

½ cup cornstarch
1 teaspoon salt
¼ teaspoon baking soda
1 egg, beaten
1 cup ice water
oil for frying

1. Sift flour, cornstarch, salt, and baking soda into a mixing bowl. If using all-purpose flour, sift it twice by itself, before sifting it with the other ingredients.

2. Add egg and ice water and beat lightly. Blend well, but do not be afraid to leave small lumps of undissolved flour, just as you might in a pancake batter. Chill. Occasionally, stir the batter while using it to prevent settling.

3. Heat at least 2 inches of vegetable or peanut oil in an electric skillet or deep fryer set at 360 to 370 degrees. Dip mussels into batter and immedi-

ately drop into hot oil. Fry a few pieces at a time — don't crowd. They should cook to a light brown in only a minute or two. Serve immediately with Tempura Dipping Sauce.

Tempura Dipping Sauce

1 cup double-strength dashi
⅓ cup Mirin
1 tablespoon light soy sauce

pinch of sugar
½ cup shredded daikon
1 tablespoon grated fresh ginger

1. Warm dashi, Mirin, soy sauce, and sugar in a small pan.
2. Remove from heat and stir in daikon and ginger. Serve in individual bowls. It makes enough dip for 4 to 6 diners.

Serves 4. Approximate nutrition information per serving of tempura without sauce: Calories 355; protein 20g; fat 18g; carbohydrates 28g; sodium 950 mg.

Cold Curried Mussels
with Rice Pilaff

This recipe is another way to use up leftover mussels after making Billi-Bi. Or, if you are buying fresh mussels in the shell, you will need to buy one quart and steam them. The amount of curry given is for one of an average strength and age. You may need more or less depending on how assertive and spicy you prefer curry dishes.

This dish may be made 6 to 8 hours before it is served. It is generally used as an hors d'oeuvre, but if you wish, you can turn it into a delicious dinner entree by doubling the recipe and serving it with Rice Pilaff.

1 cup steamed mussel meat
1 teaspoon curry, your favorite
    mix or a prepared powder
½ cup homemade mayonnaise
    (see page 42)

2 tablespoons minced shallots
2 tablespoons mussel broth
lettuce

1. Mix curry, mayonnaise, shallots, and broth. Add the cooked whole mussels, blend gently but thoroughly. Correct the seasoning. Refrigerate,

covered, until well chilled. It is best if it is made an hour ahead of time, but it may be kept for 6 to 8 hours.

2. You may arrange a bed of lettuce on a small platter and mound the curry in the center, using pimientos, tomatoes, or another suitable garnish around the perimeter. Serve with rice pilaff.

3. Alternately, do not mix in the mussel meat. Place a bit of sauce in the bottom of a reserved shell, drop in a mussel, and add another dab of sauce on top. Chill thoroughly. Serve as an hors d'oeuvre.

Serves 4. Approximate nutrition information per serving: Calories 255; protein 9g; fat 23g; carbohydrates 3g; sodium 330 mg.

Rice Pilaff

4 tablespoons butter	2¼ cups chicken or beef stock,
1 cup converted rice	fish fumet, or water
¼ cup minced onions	salt and pepper to taste

1. Preheat oven to 350 degrees. Melt 2 tablespoons of butter, add onions, saute until transparent, add rice and stir and cook over low heat until rice becomes milky in color. Add liquid, bring to a boil, cover with buttered parchment paper, and then with a pot cover.

2. Bake for 18 to 20 minutes in oven. Remove cover, dot with 2 tablespoons of butter in small pieces. Re-cover and let stand off heat for 10 minutes more.

3. Fluff rice with a fork to separate grains before serving. Add salt and pepper to taste.

Serves 4. Approximate nutrition information per serving: Calories 300; protein 7g; fat 13g; carbohydrates 39g; sodium 570 mg.

Oriental Mussels

This curry-based dish has several variations and several ways to serve it.

The recipe as we give it makes an assertive curry. If you prefer yours with less fire and tang, reduce the curry powder by half (to 2 tablespoons). For a richer curry sauce, double the heavy cream to 2 cups and allow it to cook longer — reduce by about half — to thicken the cream. The richer version also may be tempered by reducing the proportion of curry, but the extra cream also will soften the effect somewhat.

For those who prefer their curry to make an incendiary statement, the preparation may be made without the addition of cream at all.

Alternately, you may remove the mussel meats from their shells entirely, adding them back to the broth to heat through just before serving. The best method of serving the dish in such a case would be to set the cooked mussels into the center of a rice ring — what the French call en turban.

4 quarts mussels	1 cup dry white wine
4 tablespoons butter	1 bay leaf
1 cup chopped onions	2 turns fresh black pepper
1 teaspoon crushed garlic	1 cup heavy cream
¾ cup celery in ¼-inch dice	¼ cup chopped chutney
1 cup peeled, cored, diced apples	2 tablespoons minced fresh
4 tablespoons curry powder	parsley
½ cup peeled, seeded, chopped	salt
fresh or Italian plum canned	
tomatoes	

1. De-beard, scrape, and wash the mussels and reserve.

2. Saute onions in butter until soft and transparent, but not colored, in a saucepan or pot large enough to hold mussels. Add garlic, celery, and apples, and sprinkle with curry powder. Blend well over medium heat, and add the tomato, white wine, bay leaf, and pepper. Cook 15 minutes over low heat.

3. Raise the heat to medium, add the mussels, cover and cook, tossing occasionally, until they open. Remove from the heat and take the mussels from the broth.

4. Remove one shell so that the meat rests in the other. Arrange the mussels in a circular pattern on individual serving dishes; cover with a kitchen cloth wrung out in hot water and keep warm, or set into a warm, 225-degree oven. Discard the excess shells.

5. Return the broth to medium heat and reduce until it is thick enough

to coat a spoon. Add heavy cream and cook 5 minutes. Remove bay leaf, add chopped chutney, cook 2 minutes more. Correct the seasoning (add salt only after tasting), and ladle hot mixture over mussels.

6. Garnish with minced parsley and serve at once.

Serves 6. Approximate nutrition information per serving: Calories 661; protein 37g; fat 41g; carbohydrates 39g; sodium 920 mg.

Stuffed Mussels Provençal

This recipe is capable of infinite increases. We have made it as an appetizer for more than 40 diners. It works well as the only appetizer or, for contrast, can be paired with one that is mild and subtle, such as Salmon Tartare, page 210. The mussels can be stuffed up to 4 hours ahead and held in the refrigerator. They should be brought to room temperature before being slid under the broiler or baked in a 400-degree oven. For large groups, the mussels can be set on separate trays and served in batches, guaranteeing hot hors d'oeuvres with a minimum of last-minute effort.

You can make this recipe from scratch, but it is an excellent way to use mussels remaining after making Billi-Bi, since that recipe does not use the meats and this one does not need the stock.

24 mussels on halfshell	½ cup fresh breadcrumbs
2 tablespoons finely chopped almonds or walnuts (optional)	½ cup peeled, seeded, squeezed, and chopped fresh tomatoes
1 large clove of garlic, or 2 small	½ cup soft butter
2 tablespoons minced fresh parsley	⅔ teaspoon salt
	½ teaspoon black pepper

1. If not using mussels from Billi-Bi, steam fresh mussels in ¼ cup water in a covered pan just until they open, shaking the pan often so that none are packed in so tightly they cannot open.

2. When mussels have opened — discard any that fail to do so — separate the shells so that the meat is left in one half of the shell. Loosen the meat

in the shell and set all the halfshells onto an ovenproof serving tray. Cover and keep warm.

3. If you prefer the flavor and textural interest of the optional nuts, put them into the work bowl of a food processor or into a blender, and work them to a rough crumb. Measure that you have 2 tablespoons of nuts. Remove.

4. In the food processor or blender, work garlic, parsley, and breadcrumbs until blended. Add the tomato, soft butter, salt, and pepper. Work until smooth, scraping down the sides of the work bowl with a rubber spatula once or twice. Mix in nuts.

5. Top each mussel on the halfshell with some of this mixture.

6. Either cook at once or hold in refrigerator until needed, as described above.

7. Preheat oven to 400 degrees or preheat broiler. Slide the tray of mussels under the hot broiler or into the oven just long enough to heat through. Serve immediately.

Serves 4. Approximate nutrition information per serving: Calories 300; protein 9g; fat 26g; carbohydrates 7g; sodium 815 mg.

Oysters

The oyster's first recorded cultivation is attributed to the Romans at Brundisium (Brindisi) at least 2000 years ago, but wild oysters had passionate adherents long before that. This marine bivalve mollusk has provided sustenance and pleasure to humans since earliest times.

And the passion has never really abated. Eastern American Indians were as fond of the oyster as were Roman emperors, Casanova, Louis XIV, and Diamond Jim Brady.

There are some 300 types of oysters in the world, but less than a dozen species are to be found in commercial circulation. All the best oysters are bred and raised in special beds. Some are born and live their early life in one area, and are then moved to another area to continue their growth and improve their flavor.

In the western Atlantic, the oyster is found from Nova Scotia to Venezuela, in the Caribbean, and along the Gulf of Mexico. Its natural European range is from Norway to Morocco. In Britain it is referred to by its species, by its birthplace, and in other ways, but its source appears to be the most common method of designation. Thus, there are Whitstables and Royal Whitstables, Helfords, Colchesters, and Pyefleets.

In France, the Belon, from Brittany, has long been highly rated. And today, in Blue Hill, Maine, the Belon is being cultivated by an American firm that has brought the seed from France.

Which may or may not mean anything when applied to *Crassostrea virginica* — the American East Coast or Chesapeake Bay oyster, which presumably has been around for centuries, as large and fat now as before.

United States oysters generally are ranked as small, medium, and large. The only nomenclature applied to United States Atlantic oysters is to indicate where they came from. The list is endless and all have their unrelenting boosters. A.J. McClane comes down hard for the Indian River oyster of Florida in *The Encyclopedia of Fish Cookery.*

"The best of all for my palate. . ." he exclaims. "It is without peer."

". . . the best oyster in the world is the Wellfleet oyster. It is very salty, yet its meat is sweet and gamey; it is not at all flabby and squishy like estuarine oysters which gorge themselves on too much fresh water," Howard Mitcham proclaims just as passionately in *Provincetown Seafood Cookbook.*

In spite of McClane and Mitcham, don't expect to run down to your local fishmonger to find either of these choices awaiting your arrival. Both are in such limited supply that it is lucky if they can satisfy local demand. And fish markets don't always know precisely where their oysters come from, anyway.

Don't despair, however. The United States is the world's largest producer of oysters, and there are plenty from other localities to go around.

Natural oyster beds occur at all depths along tidal shorelines. The bivalves prefer salty ocean water diluted with freshwater from rivers and estuaries. Brackish waters of 3- to 18-percent salinity make an oyster very comfortable, but his growth is rather slow in such a medium.

Cultivators of the oyster help him find a home by providing oyster, scallop, and other seashells, stones, tiles, bamboo branches, and other supports. These may be strewn about the bottom of bays (Chesapeake Bay, for example) or suspended on cords from floating racks (Cape Cod).

When the oysters have grown to sufficient size, they might be moved to other areas higher in salinity and richer in minerals, both to "fatten" (much like steers moved from open range to feed lots) and to improve their flavor. In doing this, oyster farmers must devise a means to keep the oysters secure from their predators, protected from rough water, and away from other dangers.

In warmer waters (bayous, in Gulf states), depending on food and other local conditions, an oyster may grow to market size in a year or so. In colder surroundings (Chesapeake Bay), unaided by man, it may take 2 to 3 years, and in truly cold climates (Cape Cod or Maine) it may take 4 or 5 years. Man can speed up the process in the latter two cases by selective "planting" of the bivalve.

The salinity as well as the mineral content of the water and the quality of available food are determining factors in the flavor of the oyster.

As with other shellfish, oysters should be taken from unpolluted waters, and this fact is virtually assured with cultivated oysters.

Oysters are high in vitamins and minerals, especially iodine, copper, iron, and zinc.

There are two questions concerning the oyster that are raised whenever the bivalve comes up in conversation. The first is whether or not it is safe to eat oysters in a month that does not contain an R (May, June, July, and August). The second is whether or not the oyster is an aphrodisiac.

It is perfectly safe to eat oysters in months without an R, but it is not likely to be rewarding. Oysters spawn during this period, which causes certain chemical and physical changes that make the meat less palatable. The flesh takes on a milky appearance and the flavor drops to bland or worse.

The oyster is not an aphrodisiac, at least no one involved in recent research has claimed as much. The quantity of zinc in its flesh is relatively high, however, and some researchers have held that zinc is or can be a regulator of hormonal balance. What they seem to be saying is that while eating oysters won't make you more virile, it might help to bring you closer to what your normal virility might be if you were sub-par. Whether true or not, oystermen appreciate the continuation of such discussions.

They also don't mind if we think we might someday find a pearl in an oyster we're eating. Fact is, the edible oyster can grow a pearl of sorts — a dull calcareous mass that is of no value, unlike the pearl of the pearl oyster. It is interesting to note, however, that out of 35,000 pearl oysters, only 21 or so gem pearls are found.

Oysters are marketed fresh in the shell; as shucked meats chilled in containers; frozen shucked meats; smoked and then canned in oil; fresh meats packed in brine and canned; dried (primarily in Oriental markets); and in soups, stews, and bisques either canned or frozen.

The best way to enjoy an oyster is on the halfshell. Fresh. Just opened. Kept on ice. Well chilled. An oyster on the halfshell should be eaten within minutes of opening. An oyster lover needs no ketchupy, sticky sweet, or spicy hot glop for a truly prime specimen. Don't mask the briny flavor; take it neat. Or with just a squeeze of lemon juice and a turn of freshly milled black pepper.

Before they are shucked, oysters should be washed well, scrubbing with a brush if necessary. Never submerge oysters, or any shellfish, in plain water for too long or they will suffocate. Many find the idea of shucking an oyster intimidating. It need not be.

An easy method is used by many oyster fishermen. They use a beer can opener. They slip the pointed end between the shells at the hinge and pry up. The oyster usually opens with an easy snap. A screwdriver will work nearly as well.

Regardless of color or shape, oysters generally have one shell that is rounder or deeper than the other. When opening oysters keep the rounder or more cup-shaped shell on the bottom. This will guard against spilling the oysters' liquor. You will want to save as much of the liquor as possible whether you are going to eat them on the half shell or use them in a cooked recipe.

This is another shellfish that frequently suffers from overcooking. In fact, you should not think in terms of "cooking" oysters at all. Think in terms of merely firming them up with heat and they will remain tender and moist. Regardless of the method used, heat just until the edges begin to curl, and the bivalves will remain as succulent as when on the halfshell.

Shucked oyster meat may be frozen if you find yourself with an abundance. As with all shellfish, however, they do lose quality in freezing. Use them within 2 months.

One dozen oysters yield about 4 ounces of meat and ⅔ to ¾ cup of liquid. Six oysters on the halfshell are considered an adequate pre-dinner course, though some people can eat a dozen. In prepared dishes, especially those such as our oysters wrapped in spinach, 4 oysters is a good first course, but 10 to 12 would be better as a main course. One quart of undrained, shucked oysters makes about 6 servings.

Oyster Croustade

This recipe, with its oysters, spinach, and Pernod, is reminiscent of oysters Rockefeller, but the appearance is totally different.

A croustade originally was a rectangle of bread, trimmed and hollowed out to take a filling. To make the preparation easy, we suggest in place of the croustade one of the many rolls available in bakeries or made at home. Just make certain that the roll you select is smooth-bottomed without creases or seams, fairly thick-crusted, and without breaks. Also, follow our suggestions for toasting and baking the empty roll to eliminate the chances of the custard leaking from the roll before it sets.

8 raw oysters in the shell

CUSTARD:
2 cups half and half
6 egg yolks
2 whole eggs
salt and pepper to taste
pinch of nutmeg

FILLING:
fresh leaf spinach, enough to make 4 cups shredded
1 tablespoon butter
½ clove garlic, minced
salt and pepper to taste

4 rolls, with crisp crust and soft interior
½ teaspoon Pernod or Ricard (optional)

1. Shuck the oysters over a fine strainer or dampened double thickness of cheesecloth set over a bowl to catch the juices. Reserve the oysters in a bowl.

2. Pour the oyster liquor into a 2-cup measure; add half and half to make 2 cups liquid.

3. Preheat oven to 375 degrees. In a bowl, combine yolks, whole eggs, salt, pepper, nutmeg, and half and half combined with oyster liquor. Mix well and reserve.

4. Cut off the top ¼ to ⅓ of rolls. Scoop out interior, leaving about a ⅜-inch shell. Toast the hollowed rolls in an oven until they just pick up color, about 3 minutes. Remove and brush the interior with some of the custard mixture. Return to the oven for another 3 minutes to set the custard as a seal.

5. Remove ribs and coarse part of the spinach, wash well, and drain. Shred into chiffonade strips about ¼-inch wide to make 4 cups.

6. Melt the 1 tablespoon butter in a skillet, add the spinach, garlic, salt, and pepper, and saute until the spinach is tender.

7. Place the rolls on a flat sheet pan or cookie sheet.

8. Put two oysters into each roll. Top with the spinach mixture, equally divided among the rolls.

9. Add the optional Pernod or Ricard to custard mixture and blend. Ladle some of the custard into each roll. All the custard mixture will not fit into the rolls the first time around. Wait a moment and continue to ladle custard into the rolls until all or nearly all of it has been absorbed and the rolls will not absorb more.

10. Bake in the oven until the custard has set all the way through, but is still tender — 15 to 20 minutes, depending on the size of rolls.

11. Serve as a luncheon entree.

Serves 4. Approximate nutrition information per serving: Calories 490; protein 20g; fat 29g; carbohydrates 39g; sodium 770 mg.

Oysters Wrapped in Spinach

This recipe is an excellent first course because you can prepare the dish up to 6 hours in advance of serving and reheat at the last minute. Bay scallops may be substituted for oysters.

24 raw oysters in the shell	1 teaspoon minced fresh ginger
fresh leaf spinach, enough for 24 good leaves	¼ cup diced mushrooms
5 tablespoons butter	2 tablespoons ground almonds or other nuts, optional
1 tablespoon minced shallots	

1. Wash and pick over the spinach, and cut away the tough ribs.

2. Blanch the spinach for 10 seconds in simmering salted water and immediately refresh it in cold running water. Select best leaves and lay out flat on paper towels. Blot these, but do not dry them thoroughly; you want the leaves to be slightly moist to make them easier to fold. Reserve.

3. Shuck the oysters over a fine strainer or dampened double thickness of cheesecloth set over a bowl to catch the juices. Reserve ½ cup of the liquor.

4. Melt 1 tablespoon butter in a skillet and add shallots, ginger, and mushrooms. Cook them until soft and tender, but not yet picking up color.

5. Add the reserved oyster liquor; bring to a boil. Lower heat, add the oysters, and poach just until they curl. Remove the oysters with a slotted spoon and drain well. Reserve and keep warm.

6. Reduce the liquor until it is thick enough to coat a spoon heavily, stirring throughout. Add 4 tablespoons butter off the heat, whipping it in well to fluff. Correct the seasoning. Add almonds, if using, and mix in well. Allow the sauce to cool enough so that you can perform the next step.

7. One by one, dip the oysters into the sauce with your fingers, picking up some of the solids. Lay the coated oyster on a spinach leaf and wrap it. Continue with all the oysters, placing 6 of each in a circle, seam-side down, on 4 small, ovenproof serving plates. Put the plates in the refrigerator for up to 6 hours until ready to use. Chill the remaining sauce.

8. Preheat oven to 250 degrees. Place the plates holding the oysters in the oven to warm through while you warm the sauce.

9. Serve the oysters with a bit of the warmed sauce spooned over them.

Serves 4. Approximate nutrition information per serving: Calories 416; protein 33g; fat 21g; carbohydrates 22g; sodium 225 mg.

Oysters in White Wine in Puff Pastry

■ ■

This is a rich, suave dish. You may use your own favorite recipe for puff pastry or purchase it already made, which will save hours of work. Many supermarkets now carry frozen puff pastry and it works well. Follow the package directions for handling.

The pastry will be easier to cut if it is quite cold, but not frozen.

As an hors d'oeuvre: Make 24 individual pastry cases approximately 1½ by 2½ inches. After baking, open as you would a book and make a depression with your thumb in one side. Place one oyster in each.

As a first course: Make six pastry cases 2 x 3 inches. With the tip of a knife, before baking, score the pastry case with a ¼-inch border all around each puff, to create a basket effect. Do not go through the pastry; merely score the top. Place 4 oysters in each.

As a main course: Make four pastry cases 4 x 4 inches. With the tip of a knife, before baking, score the pastry case with a ¼-inch border all around each puff, to create a basket effect. Do not go through the pastry; merely score the top. Place 6 oysters in each.

Reheat puff pastry cases for a few minutes in a 250-degree oven just before filling to crisp them.

Bay scallops may be substituted for the oysters.

24 oysters, shucked over a bowl	1 cup white wine
1 sheet puff pastry at least 16 x 20-inches, ⅛-inch thick	liquor from oysters (about 1⅓ cups)
1 egg	pinch of pepper
1 tablespoon water	2 egg yolks
2 tablespoons butter	¼ cup soft butter
2 tablespoons shallots	2 tablespoons lemon juice

1. Mix 1 egg with 1 tablespoon of water and brush it on the sheet of pastry to glaze it. Cut it to the desired shapes. Score a border around the edges of the larger pastry cases. Rechill until ready to bake.

2. Preheat oven to 400 degrees. Bake the pastry cases 10 to 12 minutes, until golden brown and fairly dry. Open the smallest cases as you would a book. Reserve.

3. Saute shallots in 2 tablespoons butter over low heat until soft and transparent, but not yet colored.

4. Add wine, oyster liquor, and pepper. Boil for a few seconds, then lower the heat.

5. Add the oysters and poach them just until their edges curl — think in terms of firming the oysters, not cooking them. Remove the oysters with a slotted spoon, and reserve, covered, to keep warm. Reduce the liquid in which you poached the oysters to approximately ½ cup.

6. Place egg yolks in a small bowl and pour in a few tablespoons of the reduced hot oyster cooking liquid and stir.

7. Add this to the remainder of the reduced liquid, place it over a flame tamer or in a large skillet with water, and cook, stirring throughout, until it is thick enough to coat a spoon heavily. Do not boil. Remove from heat and whisk in soft butter and lemon juice. Whip well. Correct the seasoning.

8. Preheat oven to 250 degrees. Drain oysters well — there should be no moisture that might thin the sauce — and add to sauce. Stir gently.

9. Return puff pastry to oven to warm. Then, spoon the oysters with the sauce into the pastry cases, spooning on the additional sauce. If you are making the smallest size, place a single oyster in one half of the open pastry "book," and place the other half on top. For larger sizes, make a slight depression, if necessary, in each pastry case and spoon in either 4 or 6 oysters with some of the sauce.

10. Serve immediately.

Serves 4 as main course, 6 as first course, 12 as appetizer.

As 12 servings: Approximate nutrition information per serving: Calories 230; protein 13g; fat 14g; carbohydrates 14g; sodium 170 mg.

As 6 servings: Approximate nutrition information per serving: Calories 455; protein 26g; fat 27g; carbohydrates 27g; sodium 340 mg.

As 4 servings: Approximate nutrition information per serving: Calories 685; protein 39g; fat 41g; carbohydrates 41g; sodium 520 mg.

Periwinkles

A periwinkle is a mollusk, a small sea snail with a conical or round, whorled shell, which may be black, brown, gray, or orange. There are about 300 species of periwinkle, but most are too small to eat. The periwinkle most often eaten in this country is about 1 inch in diameter. It has been eaten by Europeans and native Americans since prehistoric times.

The periwinkle — or simply, "winkle" — lives in fresh or ocean water, but, like many shellfish, prefers brackish waters with a mixture of sea and fresh water. It has gills adapted to breathe air and therefore is found in intertidal zones both in and out of the water clinging to pilings, rocks, wharfs, boat hulls, and anything else it can get a grip on. The creature lives within its shell and is covered at its opening with a hard lid, the operculum, for protection.

The operculum can be easily removed by hand before cooking, although it falls off readily when cooked. After cooking, the meat may be picked out of the shell with a hat pin, a toothpick, or the point of a small knife. Many users go to great lengths to "open" the shell from the closed end. Some clip away the small point on the backside of each periwinkle with snipping pliers before cooking. One fancier we know holds the pointed end of each periwinkle against the side of a grinding wheel to accomplish the same thing. This is done more to assure the complete immersion of the sweet meat in whatever the periwinkle is cooked, than to assist in removal of the meat.

Periwinkles are consumed in northern Europe; they even used to be roasted in the shell and sold on London streets. In this country consumption is confined mostly to ethnic groups, especially Asians. Periwinkles in black bean sauce are a time-honored Chinese preparation, and Japanese, Thais, Vietnamese, and other Oriental cultures all have recipes for them. The periwinkle is now becoming grander, according to Alan Davidson in *North Atlantic Seafood* and is often served as an *amuse-gueule* in luxury restaurants on the European continent. In Ireland, he states, they may end up in a sauce made by boiling carragheen moss in milk.

Periwinkles generally are sold in ethnic markets close to the shore. You also can pick your own, but, as with all shellfish, they must come from unpolluted waters. Those found on pilings, wharfs, hulls, and rocks within harbors are best left alone.

Wash periwinkles in several changes of water. Stir vigorously to make certain all the sand is dislodged. Don't pour the water out of the pan, but lift the periwinkles out so that the sand is left behind.

You may remove the operculums by hand — they peel away easily with a small paring knife — or cook the periwinkles in salted water, in which case most of the lids will fall away by themselves. Cook periwinkles only 3 to 4 minutes if they are going to cook further in a sauce, and up to 7 minutes if no further cooking is required. Many cooks cook them only 3 to 4 minutes.

There are several ways that periwinkles can be prepared. Mostly they are a steamed-clam, corn-on-the-cob kind of food that is best enjoyed at a casual meal with a group.

Simply boiled, they can be served with melted butter for dipping. They can be cooked, taken from their shells, and tossed with butter, sauteed garlic, lemon juice, salt, and pepper, and served on rice and pasta. They are excellent in black bean sauce, and in southern Italian dishes they are normally simmered in variously flavored marinara sauces.

We present them as a stuffing for mushroom caps below and in a sauce for pasta on page 427.

Periwinkles come about 100 to the pound, give or take a dozen, depending on size. In the shell, a pound is about 2 cups. A pound in the shell will yield about 4 ounces of meat.

Mushroom Caps Stuffed with Periwinkles

This recipe is sufficient for 4 persons as an hors d'oeuvre or first course.

1 pound periwinkles	3 tablespoons fresh breadcrumbs
½ teaspoon salt	¼ teaspoon salt
16 large mushroom caps with stems	4 turns of freshly ground black pepper
¼ cup soft butter	1 clove garlic, finely minced
1½ tablespoons chopped almonds	1 teaspoon cognac or brandy
1 tablespoon minced fresh parsley	

1. Wash periwinkles thoroughly. Place them in a pan, barely cover with water and add ½ teaspoon salt. Bring to a boil and cook 3 to 4 minutes. Stir the periwinkles vigorously with a wooden spoon to loosen the operculum over the periwinkles' opening. Place the pot with the periwinkles under running cold water, stirring all the time. This will further remove the lids, and most will float away with the agitation.

2. Drain the periwinkles. With a small, sharply pointed knife, toothpick, or hat pin, remove the meat from periwinkles. It is easy to catch the front edge of the flesh and lift the meat out just as you would do with an escargot, or land snail. The anchor of a periwinkle is not too fastly secured.

3. Remove the mushroom stems and reserve the caps. Mince four or five stems finely to make about ¼ cup.

4. Combine butter, almonds, ¼ cup of minced mushroom stems, parsley, breadcrumbs, pepper, salt, garlic, and cognac; add periwinkles and blend well.

5. Preheat oven to 400 degrees. Stuff mushroom caps with the mixture. This may be refrigerated for a few hours until you're ready to complete it. Set in a 400-degree oven for 10 minutes or until the top of the stuffing is nicely browned.

Serves 4. Approximate nutrition information per serving: Calories 155; protein 5g; fat 14g; carbohydrates 3g; sodium 560 mg.

Scallops

■■

A bivalve mollusk, the scallop is well known along the Atlantic seaboard since it is found in various species from Iceland to the Gulf of Mexico.

It has a rounded, hinged shell of brown, black, white, yellow, red, or orange with radiating ribs that end in an orbed undulating edge. Through the centuries, its sunburst beauty has inspired artists, wood carvers, and a major petroleum company, among others. Its flesh has inspired gourmets for centuries.

It was a symbol for religious pilgrims headed for the shrine of St. James at Compostella, Spain. The French name for scallops — *Coquilles Saint-Jacques* — commemorates the association. In *Madame Prunier's Fish Cookery Book*, the late proprietor of the famous Paris and London seafood restaurants recounts an early Christian legend of how the association between the Apostle and scallops came to be. When the body of St. James was being taken from Joppa to Galicia by ship, she wrote, it passed a tiny village, on the beach of which a wedding party was gathered. As the ship passed, the bridegroom's horse bolted and plunged deep into the sea. The ship stopped and the horse and rider materialized beside it. The saint's disciples on board explained that it was St. James, whose body was on the ship, who had saved the bridegroom's life. The bridegroom was converted, eventually went ashore, and converted the wedding party, too. When he first re-emerged from the sea, "both his dress and the trappings of his horse were covered with scallop shells; and therefore the Galicians took the scallop shell as the sign of St. James."

There are two principal scallops that come to the American table. The most abundant is the sea scallop. It is found from Labrador to New Jersey, but is most plentiful off the coast of Maine. Its shell grows to 5 inches across, and they can run as large as 5 or 6 to a pound. The average, however, is 20 to 50 sea scallops per pound. Sea scallops are available more or less year round.

The bay scallop is much less numerous. It is found in three commercially valuable subspecies from Cape Cod to the Gulf of Mexico. The bay scallop is best from October to February. In New England it also is known as the Cape scallop. It also is smaller than the sea scallop, running about 90 per pound. At their freshest best, the scallops differ somewhat in flavor. The sea scallop has more of a fresh sea flavor, is more briny, and is seemingly "leaner." Bay scallops are nuttier, richer, and sweeter. While the bay scallop has generally obtained high prices at market and is generally regarded as the "gourmet's scallop," there are many who prefer the somewhat sharper flavor of the sea scallop. Except for a few recipes (stuffed scallops, for example, where the larger sea scallop must be used), their use is interchangeable; flavor preference and/or price being the determining factors.

A third scallop, the calico (or southern bay), is a deep-water species that is found in rather abundant quantities off Georgia and Atlantic Florida. It is small, similar to the bay scallop, and has been growing in importance in recent years. It is more frequently found in markets today. It is beginning to compete with bay scallops because it can be sold at lower prices. Its flesh is milky white with tan or gray blotches.

Unlike other bivalves that cling to a fast-hold or dig into mud or sand, scallops live freely in the water and move about in zigzag skips as though jet-propelled. They do this by forcefully snapping their shells together. A single large adductor muscle and an elastic ligament are what manipulate the shells. It is this milky white-to-pearly gray adductor muscle that we eat in this country, though the entire content of the shell — like that of the clam — is edible. When we refer to scallops as food, we are referring to the muscle.

In Europe, the orange colored roe is considered as great a delicacy as the scallop itself. Creative chefs in America today are beginning to seek out sources of scallops with their roe, and the practice is sure to grow. The roe resembles the more familiar coral of a lobster.

Generally scallops are more highly perishable than other shellfish because they cannot close their shells tightly and begin to deteriorate soon after being taken from the water. Therefore, they are immediately shucked, and we never see the whole scallop in the market.

In choosing fresh scallops, look for those that are cream-colored, not chalky white. Many dealers soak scallops for a time in freshwater. This increases their bulk and whitens them, but dilutes their flavor.

Scallops are delicate and tender; overcooking toughens them and evaporates their moisture. Cook them in liquid just until they firm up. Cook bay scallops no more than 4 minutes if you are poaching or steaming them; give sea scallops no more than 5 minutes.

Sauteing or pan-frying scallops requires only a minute less for each variety. The best advice is to dry scallops thoroughly before you saute or pan-fry them. Dredge them in a flour batter and place them in a hot pan with butter and oil. Toss and roll them 3 or 4 minutes and serve hot on warm plates.

To deep-fry breaded or floured scallops, cook only until the exterior takes on a light brown color. The shriveled mahogany scallops one gets in inferior restaurants are always overcooked.

Scallops also broil up well. In this instance also, too many restaurants overcook them and then set them swimming in a pool of melted butter that drowns whatever flavor might have been left. A mere 3 or 4 minutes, 2 inches or so from the heat of a preheated broiler will turn out perfect scallops.

One pound of raw scallops makes 3 or 4 servings.

Scallops aux Noix

This recipe is simplicity personified and wonderfully flavorful. Preparation and cooking time is about 15 minutes.

1 pound scallops, cut in half or quarters if large	½ cup fresh breadcrumbs
⅓ cup soft butter	1 tablespoon lemon juice
2 tablespoons minced shallots	¼ cup chopped walnuts
2 tablespoons minced scallions	½ teaspoon salt
	pinch of freshly ground pepper

1. Preheat oven to 425 degrees.
2. Mix all the ingredients thoroughly.
3. Place in a casserole or individual scallop shells and bake 5 to 6 minutes. Remove from the oven and slide under the broiler until nicely browned.
4. Serve immediately.

Serves 4. Approximate nutrition information per serving: Calories 330; protein 29g; fat 21g; carbohydrates 5g; sodium 780 mg.

Navarin of Scallops

The Larousse Gastronomique *specifically recommends that the word* nava- rin *not be used for shellfish or poultry preparations, that it should be re- served in its classical meaning for a stew or ragout of mutton or lamb with vegetables. But in modern culinary parlance, the word is often broadened to include seafood of all kinds, and we take that more liberal view.*

This is a one-pan dish in which the vegetables contrast with the scallops in color, flavor, and texture. Use a large skillet or saute pan with a cover. The finished dish should be neither soupy nor dry, but moist with a liquid thick enough to coat a spoon heavily.

Sea scallops are preferred in this dish because they can stand up to the strong flavors of the other ingredients.

12 to 16 ounces sea scallops
white turnips
celery stalks
carrots
zucchini
12 tiniest pearl onions, or ½ cup
      coarsely chopped onions
1 tablespoon butter
1 cup clam juice
1 cup dry white wine

1 small bay leaf
⅛ teaspoon dried thyme
2 tablespoons tomato puree
1 clove garlic, minced
½ teaspoon salt
pepper
1 cup sliced mushrooms
1 tablespoon minced fresh
      parsley

1. If scallops are large, cut them crosswise into thick slices.

2. Cut turnip, celery, carrots, and zucchini into wedges about 2 inches long. You may use these vegetables this way but for a more attractive ap- pearance, you should "turn" those that lend themselves to it into rounds or ovals the shape and size of an olive. Melon ballers of various sizes and shapes work well if you don't want to trim the vegetables with a knife. You should have a cup of each cut-up vegetable.

3. Saute either the whole pearl onions or the chopped onions 1 minute in 1 tablespoon butter. Add the turnip, celery, and carrots and saute them until they wilt, without having picked up color.

4. Add clam juice, wine, bay leaf, thyme, tomato puree, garlic, salt, and pepper. Toss, cover, and cook over low heat for 15 minutes.

5. Add zucchini and mushrooms, toss, cover, and cook for 10 minutes longer.

6. Add scallops and cook for 5 minutes, covered. Remember to keep the heat low throughout the cooking and to shake the pan occasionally. If

the sauce is runny, remove the vegetables and scallops and reserve while you reduce the liquid.

7.   Add parsley and blend. Remove the bay leaf and correct the seasoning.

8.   Serve in soup bowls. Boiled parsley potatoes, traditional accompaniment for a navarin of lamb, would be an excellent choice with this dish.

Serves 4. Approximate nutrition information per serving: Calories 245; protein 31g; fat 5g; carbohydrates 20g; sodium 690 mg.

Seviche Cape Cod

Originally a Chilean or South American dish for fish, Seviche is now part of international cuisine. It is pieces of raw fish "cooked" in a marination, most often of lime juice, though other citrus is sometimes used. In this respect, a seviche cooks similarly to the way Japanese sushi is "cooked" by swishing it in soy sauce.

Some authorities assert that the dish was born in Polynesia, but the voyage of Thor Heyerdahl's Kon Tiki *seems to indicate that trans-Pacific traffic in pre-history went the other way. In any event, the Polynesians did use citrus and/or coconut milk to achieve the same result.*

In our New England version, tiny bay scallops are substituted for the fish and the traditional chilies are omitted. Whole cranberries are used to bring color and a new fresh, tart flavor to the dish.

½- to ¾-pound bay scallops, about 48
1 tablespoon minced shallot
½ cup fresh lemon or lime juice
1 tablespoon minced chives, or minced scallions
2 tablespoons olive oil
1 tablespoon cognac
¼ teaspoon salt

white pepper to taste
1 cup whole cranberries
¼ cup dry white wine or vermouth
1 tablespoon distilled white vinegar
1 teaspoon sugar
½ cup water
salt and pepper

1.   Wash, drain, and dry scallops.
2.   Combine shallots and lemon or lime juice in a bowl with chives,

olive oil, cognac, salt, and pepper. Add the scallops and toss. Place all the ingredients in a glass baking dish and allow the scallops to marinate for 2 hours, turning occasionally.

3. Meanwhile, poach whole cranberries in white wine, white vinegar, sugar, ½ cup water, salt, and pepper for 10 minutes. Pick out a dozen or so still-whole berries to use as a garnish and set them aside. Cook the remaining berries 10 minutes more, mashing and crushing them to release as much color as possible.

4. Strain the liquid through a fine-meshed sieve, again mashing the cranberries with a spoon to extract as much color as possible. Discard cranberries.

5. Reduce the liquid over high heat to about ¼ cup. Let it cool, then add it and the reserved whole cranberries to the scallop marinade and toss. Continue marinating to complete the 2 hours.

6. If you plan to serve this dish as an appetizer, cut 4 lemons or limes crosswise in half and remove the pulp. Take a thin slice from the bottom so that the fruit will stand without tipping. Place 6 scallops in each hollowed-out half, dressing the top with a tablespoon of the marinating liquid and a few of the whole cranberries for color.

7. For a light luncheon main course, serve a dozen scallops to each person, arranging the scallops on a leaf or two of romaine or bibb lettuce, topped with the liquid and cranberries. The scallops also may be served on small bamboo skewers.

Serves 4 as main course, 8 as appetizer. Approximate nutrition information per serving for 4: Calories 215; protein 27g; fat 9g; carbohydrates 7g; sodium 430 mg.

Scallops in Puff Pastry

You may use your own favorite recipe for puff pastry or purchase it already made, which will save you work. Many supermarkets now carry frozen puff pastry and it works well. Follow package directions for handling. The pastry will be easier to cut if it is quite cold, but not frozen. Rechill the pastry if you are not going to bake it immediately.

In this dish you fill pastry with a scallop mixture and make small turn-

over-like cases that are baked. If bay scallops are not available, you may use larger sea scallops cut into quarters.

You can make the filling several hours ahead and hold it in the re-frigerator.

½ pound bay scallops
2 tablespoons minced shallots
¼ cup butter
salt and pepper to taste
1 cup vegetables — carrots, leeks, celery — in fine julienne, about 2 inches long

1 8 x 16-inch sheet puff pastry, ⅛-inch thick
1 egg yolk
1 tablespoon of water

1. In a skillet or saute pan, saute shallots in butter until transparent but without color. Add scallops, salt, and pepper. Cook the mixture over low heat, stirring often, only until the scallops firm up, about 3 minutes. Remove scallops and set them aside.

2. In the juices remaining in the skillet, simmer the 1 cup mixed vegetables until cooked but still *al dente*, allowing the juices to reduce and thicken at the same time. Most of the liquid should evaporate. Off the heat, add the scallops and toss with the vegetables. Allow the mixture to cool. Chill until you are ready to finish the preparation.

3. Lay the puff pastry out and cut it into eight 4 x 4-inch squares. (Chill until you are ready to complete the preparation.)

4. Preheat oven to 400 degrees.

5. Arrange the pastry squares so that one point of the square is facing you. Place about 2 tablespoons of the mixture slightly below the center of each square, spreading it out toward either side. Fold the square in half, corner to corner, to make a triangular turnover-shaped package. Moisten the edges of the two bottom sides of the pastry with water, so that the top flap will stick to the bottom. Crimp the edges to seal.

6. Lightly mix the egg yolk with the tablespoon of water to make an egg wash. Glaze the top of the triangles with the egg wash. Score the top of the triangles lightly in a crosshatch pattern with a knife and place on a buttered baking sheet.

7. Bake 12 to 15 minutes until the pastry is nicely browned and puffy.

8. Serve two turnovers to each diner as an entree; one for lunch. Serve with sauteed zucchini julienne or a baked stuffed tomato.

Serves 4 for dinner, 8 for lunch. Approximate nutrition information per turnover: Calories 540; protein 23g; fat 38g; carbohydrates 25g; sodium 1050 mg.

Les Coquilles Saint-Jacques à la Vapeur Crème d'Estragon

■

FROM MAISON ROBERT, BOSTON

This recipe for fresh steamed scallops in cream sauce with tarragon is another recipe created by Chef Pierre Jamet at Maison Robert.

1½ pounds medium-sized sea scallops	1½ cups heavy cream
1 tablespoon fresh minced tarragon	1 stick (¼ pound) butter, cut in 5 pieces
4 finely chopped shallots	salt and pepper
1½ cups dry chablis	¼ teaspoon fresh thyme

1. Pour wine into a saucepan with shallots and tarragon. Bring to a boil and reduce until all the wine evaporates. Add heavy cream, and reduce again until slightly thickened.

2. Add butter, one piece at a time, stirring with a wire whisk until incorporated. Add salt and pepper to taste and set aside.

3. Place scallops in a skillet with enough water to just cover them. Add thyme. Bring the water to a boil and remove the scallops from the water immediately. Do not overcook.

4. Coat serving plates with the cream sauce and place scallops on top.

5. Serve with cooked fresh spinach.

Serves 4. Approximate nutrition information per serving: Calories 750; protein 42g; fat 59g; carbohydrates 12g; sodium 900 mg.

Evergreen Scallops

COQUILLES SAINT-JACQUES CRESSONNIÈRE

The amenable scallop accommodates itself to a multitude of preparations with flavorable results. Try this quick alternative to the more frequently encountered dish called Coquilles Saint-Jacques in this country.

1 pound scallops	2 bunches watercress
2 tablespons minced shallots	1 cup heavy cream
1 tablespoon butter	salt and pepper to taste
½ cup dry white wine	

1. In a saucepan over medium heat, saute shallots in butter until they are transparent, without any color.

2. Add wine, scallops, salt, and pepper. Cover and cook gently over low heat for 4 to 5 minutes depending on the size of the scallops. Do not overcook. Remove the scallops from the pan with a slotted spoon, cover, and keep warm.

3. Meanwhile, wash the watercress thoroughly by dipping the bunches several times into clear cold water and shaking off the excess. Pick off the leaves, selecting 1 cup of the best.

4. Add the watercress leaves to the pan and reduce until the liquid is nearly evaporated, leaving a puddle of about 1 tablespoon. Add cream and reduce until it will coat a spoon. Correct the seasoning.

5. Add the cooked scallops, heat through, and serve in warmed individual serving plates or scallop shells.

Serves 4. Approximate nutrition information per serving: Calories 379; protein 28g; fat 27g; carbohydrates 4g; sodium 503 mg.

Scallops in Pernod

The flavor accent for this dish is Pernod, an anise-flavored 90-proof spirit that is reminiscent of absinthe (now prohibited in most countries). It has a light yellow-green color that turns milky when mixed with water, and a sharp, pronounced aroma. The dominant note is licorice. Its flavor can overpower other ingredients, so use it gingerly. Ricard, a similar French product, may be substituted for the Pernod.

1 pound scallops	pepper to taste
2 tablespoons minced shallots	½ cup dry vermouth
¼ cup butter	2 cups heavy cream
1 cup sliced fresh mushrooms	1 tablespoon Pernod or Ricard
pinch of saffron, about	1 tablespoon minced fresh
⅛ teaspoon	parsley
1 teaspoon salt	

1. Saute shallots in butter until soft, but not yet picking up color. Add scallops, mushrooms, saffron, salt, pepper, and dry vermouth. Cover and simmer 3 minutes; do not overcook. Remove the scallops and mushrooms with a slotted spoon and reserve. Cover and keep warm.

2. Bring the liquid to a boil, add cream, and reduce until it is thick enough to coat a spoon. Add any liquid that has drained from the reserved scallops and continue to reduce the sauce if necessary.

3. Remove the sauce from heat, add the Pernod or Ricard, and correct the seasoning. Add the cooked scallops and mushrooms, and heat through.

4. Serve, sprinkled with a bit of parsley, on individual plates.

Serves 4. Approximate nutrition information per serving: Calories 270; protein 28g; fat 16g; carbohydrates 3g; sodium 840 mg.

Scallop Salad

This recipe will serve four as a first course; two as an entree. It makes an admirable meal opener because it can be made in the afternoon and chilled until just before it is served, allowing the cook to concentrate on the rest of a dinner. The mayonnaise can be made a day ahead.

1 pound sea scallops, thickly sliced
1 cup dry white wine
2 tablespoons minced shallots
½ cup finely diced celery
½ teaspoon salt
pepper to taste
1 tablespoon plus 1 teaspoon minced fresh basil
½ cup mayonnaise, homemade, preferably with olive oil (see page 42)
1 teaspoon lemon juice
salt and pepper to taste
½ small, sweet red pepper, in fine strips
1 head soft lettuce, shredded
6-12 rings of fresh sweet red pepper

1. Cook shallots and celery in wine until tender. Add scallops, salt, pepper, and 1 teaspoon basil. Cook, covered, 4 minutes. Remove scallops with a slotted spoon and allow them to cool. Then, cover and put in the refrigerator.

2. Reduce the remaining pan juices to 1 to 1½ tablespoons, and no less. (This reduction must thin the mayonnaise as well as flavor it.) Allow it to cool.

3. In a small bowl, add the reduction to the mayonnaise, mixing it in with a whip. Stir in lemon juice, remainder of basil, salt, and pepper. Add the strips of red pepper for color, mix, and add the scallops, mixing again to coat. Refrigerate for at least an hour for the flavors to meld. Correct the seasoning.

4. Distribute the salad over the shredded lettuce. Decorate with fresh rings of red pepper.

Serves 4. Approximate nutrition information per serving: Calories 360; protein 29g; fat 24g; carbohydrates 8g; sodium 890 mg.

Scallops in Zucchini Boats

■■

When garden zucchini are maturing profusely, one can tire of them if they are always served in the same way. That is the time to scoop out some thick zucchini rounds and stuff them with scallops. A topping of breadcrumbs, a quick bake, and your zucchini will take on new dimensions.

8 ounces bay scallops (or sea scallops cut in quarters)
2 unpeeled zucchini, 2 to 3 inches in diameter
7 tablespoons melted butter
2 tablespoons minced fresh parsley

1 tablespoon minced fresh coriander leaves (or fresh basil, thyme, tarragon, or dill)
salt and pepper to taste
⅔ cup fresh breadcrumbs

1. Cut scallops if necessary. Cut the zucchini in crosswise pieces, about 1½ inches long. With a melon baller or a small spoon, scoop out a well in each round of zucchini, leaving a wall about ⅛-inch-thick on the sides and slightly thicker at the bottom.

2. Combine scallops, 2 tablespoons butter, parsley, coriander, salt, and pepper. Toss well.

3. Fill the hollowed-out zucchini pieces with the mixture.

4. Mix 4 tablespoons butter and breadcrumbs, tossing to coat evenly.

5. Pat the breadcrumbs on top of each filled zucchini round.

6. Preheat oven to 375 degrees. Using the remaining 1 tablespoon butter, grease a baking dish to hold the zucchini and bake 10 minutes. Serve immediately.

Serves 4. Approximate nutrition information per serving: Calories 280; protein 15g; fat 21g; carbohydrates 7g; sodium 570 mg.

Steeped Scallops
■■
COQUILLES SAINT-JACQUES À LA NAGE

This recipe demands homemade fish stock, richly flavored, robust, and fresh. The stock should be well skimmed and as clear as possible. It can be made a day ahead and chilled so that the sediment settles; you can ladle off the top clear liquid before making this dish. You cannot use clam juice or another substitute, for the dish will lack luster and not be worth the effort. If you don't wish to make a real fumet, don't attempt the dish.

1 pound scallops
1 cup fish stock (see White Wine Fumet, page 30)
1 cup white wine or dry vermouth
1 large carrot
1 large stalk celery
1 large leek

salt and pepper
¼ cup fresh tomatoes, peeled, seeded and diced ¼ inch
12 flat or Italian parsley leaves, or 2 small dill sprigs
1 recipe beurre blanc (see page 64)

1. Cut carrot, celery, and leek in thin julienne strips, about ¼-inch wide by 3 inches long.
2. Bring fish stock to a boil, add wine, and reduce to about 1¼ cups, skimming occasionally. Lower the heat to simmer.
3. Cook vegetables in simmering stock for 4 minutes. Put the carrots in first, after 1 minute add the celery, and after 2 more minutes add the leeks and tomatoes. Season lightly with salt and pepper. Taste. With the concentrated stock and vegetables, the savor will be what the French call *de haut gout,* "of high taste," indicating the depth of flavor you seek.
4. Add the scallops and 1 dozen parsley leaves (no stems; select nice leaves), and bring to a boil. Cover the pot, remove it from heat, and correct the seasoning. Allow the ingredients to poach in the liquid for just 5 or 6 minutes off the heat.
5. Make 1 recipe for beurre blanc.
6. Divide the scallops, parsley, and pan juices among 4 preheated soup bowls, and serve immediately. Pass the beurre blanc.

Serves 4. Approximate nutrition information per serving, without beurre blanc: Calories 235; protein 35g; fat 6g; carbohydrates 9g; sodium 610 mg.

Scallops with Green Hollandaise and Whole Radishes

The green hollandaise called for in this recipe can be used in almost any other preparation where hollandaise is needed and the green color would be advantageous. The radishes are a wonderful counterpoint of color and flavor to this dish and the cooking softens their bite.

20 ounces sea scallops	GARNISH:
1 recipe for Green Hollandaise (page 54)	1 recipe for steamed radishes

1. Make the hollandaise and keep it warm.
2. Cut the scallops into 2 or 3 crosswise slices.
3. Blanch them in 2 tablespoons lightly salted water for 3 or 4 minutes or until they have firmed. Don't overcook. Drain immediately.
4. Place a pool of warm hollandaise in the center of individual serving plates and arrange scallops in the pool. Arrange a border of radishes around each plate.

Steamed Unpeeled Whole Radishes

Radishes bought in a supermarket in plastic bags and without stems are not suitable for this dish. You need radishes with their green stems that are usually sold by the bunch. The red of radishes fades to pink when cooked and "hot" radishes lose their bite.

2 bunches of radishes (you will need 4 to 6 radishes per portion, depending on size)	½ cup water
	1 tablespoon salt
	1 tablespoon butter

1. Trim the green stems 1 to 1½ inches long. Remove the root tips, and wash the radishes.
2. You can make this garnish even more attractive by slicing the radishes almost all the way through so that they will spread into a fan shape when they cook.
3. Place radishes in a pan with the water and salt and cook over low heat, 5 to 7 minutes, or until tender. Drain. Return to cooking pot, add butter, and toss to coat evenly.

Serves 4. Approximate nutrition information per serving: Calories 605; protein 35g; fat 50g; carbohydrates 4g; sodium 1090 mg.

Scallops and Shrimp Saute with Fresh Pear and Tarragon

FROM GAZELLE RESTAURANT, QUINCY, MASSACHUSETTS

Here is another dish created by master chef Bank Szerenyi of the Gazelle Restaurant. The recipe requires four bosc pears, three to be used in the sauce, and the fourth to be used as garnish. Peel that fourth pear, cut it into quarters, and core. In each quarter, cut thin sections lengthwise from the wide portion almost to the stem, but do not cut through. When you set it on the serving platter, spread it out to resemble a fan.

1 pound bay scallops
1 pound raw shrimp (16 to 20 count), peeled, deveined, and butterflied
flour for dusting
¾ cup clarified butter (see page 71)
3 bosc pears, peeled, cored, cut in ½-inch dice
7 large sprigs of fresh tarragon, or 1 teaspoon dried
salt and freshly ground white pepper to taste
½ cup dry vermouth
4 tablespoons freshly squeezed lemon juice
1 cup heavy cream
1 bosc pear, peeled, cut in quarters, cored, and fanned

1. Lightly flour shrimp and scallops.
2. Preheat saute pan with clarified butter.
3. Saute shrimp and scallops together for approximately 2½ minutes.
4. Meanwhile, chop the leaves of 3 sprigs of tarragon. Add chopped tarragon (or dried tarragon) and diced pear to the seafood. Warm through.
5. Season with salt and white pepper to taste.
6. Deglaze the pan with dry vermouth.
7. Add lemon and cream, reduce for 2 minutes, until liquid will coat a spoon. Correct seasoning.
8. Place on individual serving plates, garnish with the four sprigs of tarragon, and pear fan.

Serves 4. Approximate nutrition information per serving: Calories 890; protein 57g; fat 60g; carbohydrates 29g; sodium 880 mg.

Scallop-Stuffed Leeks

Every cookbook should quote Jean Anthelme Brillat-Savarin, eighteenth century French gourmet, politician, and author of La Physiologie de Gout *("The Physiology of Taste"), at least once. Now is the time to cite one of his aphorisms; it applies to this recipe. Said Brillat-Savarin, as translated by M.F.K. Fisher: "He who plays host without giving his personal care to the repast is unworthy of having friends to attend it."*

This recipe requires a certain amount of patience. The technique is not difficult but it does take time. The appearance and layers of flavor of the finished dish make it all worthwhile.

The patience comes in getting the leeks ready. The first eleven steps can be done ahead of time, however, with final cooking just prior to serving.

Your goal in preparing the leeks is to end up with double-thick, hollow tubes that you can stuff. They neither have to be the same circumference nor the same length, but they must be of two layers with no splits or holes.

1 pound sea scallops, washed, dried, chilled	2 small stalks celery, finely julienned
3 or 4 medium-sized leeks	1½ cups fish stock (see White Wine Fumet, page 30), or water seasoned with ½ teaspoon salt
1 small carrot	
1 small red pepper	
2 egg whites, chilled	
salt and freshly ground white pepper to taste	8 tablespoons fish stock or clam juice
1½ sticks butter	4 tablespoons dry vermouth
2 small carrots, finely julienned	

1. Wash leeks. Cut them 5 inches long by cutting off the bottom knob and keeping at least some of the green part of each leek. Gently but firmly, force the inner portions of leek up from the bottom; you will have to push up and ease the inner portions out, much like removing a calendar from a mailing tube, leaving you with hollow tubes of 2 layers of leek. Separate all inner layers in the same way; you want to end up with 8 tubes, each consisting of 2 layers. Use any extra leek for another purpose. Wash well in cold running water, but handle tubes carefully to avoid splitting them. Drain.

2. Dice the carrot and red pepper very fine, about ⅛-inch, to make 2 tablespoons of each. Blanch in a strainer in lightly salted water. Drain, blot dry on paper towels, and chill.

3. Work the chilled scallops through a food mill. You also may use a food processor, but the texture will be better if a food mill is used. If you use

a food processor, use an off-on pulse so that you do not overwork the scallops, but just get them smoothly broken down.

4. Using a rubber spatula, scrape the processed scallop meat into a stainless steel or glass bowl sitting in a larger bowl with ice. Add the 2 chilled egg whites, and work the scallops and egg whites with a rubber spatula to incorporate thoroughly. Fold in salt, white pepper, and the reserved carrot and pepper. Place the mixture in the refrigerator until ready to use.

5. Saute the julienned carrots and celery in 2 tablespoons butter, covered, over low heat. Cook them *al dente*, but do not allow them to color. Reserve.

6. Bring 1½ cups stock or water to a boil.

7. Using a pastry bag or small spoon, tightly stuff each leek tube with the scallop mixture. Again, handle the leeks carefully so as not to split them. Set the filled leeks aside.

8. Using 2 tablespoons butter, coat a shallow, ovenproof casserole or other pan large enough to hold all the scallop-stuffed leeks comfortably in one layer. Place the stuffed leeks into the pan and pour the boiling liquid gently into the pan until the stuffed leeks are covered. Simmer gently for 12 minutes.

9. With a skimmer or a slotted spoon remove the leeks and immerse them in cold water. Drain them on paper towels.

10. Cut the leeks into ¾-inch-thick rounds — you must use a very sharp serrated knife to keep from breaking or tearing the tender leeks. A tomato knife should be perfect.

11. Butter 4 individual ovenproof casseroles (using ½ tablespoon butter for each), and arrange rounds of stuffed leeks within. Leave the center area open. You should get 10 to 12 rounds into each casserole. Place 1½ tablespoons butter, 2 tablespoons fish stock, clam juice or water, 1 tablespoon dry vermouth, and one-fourth of the julienned carrots and celery into the center of each casserole. Cover with buttered foil or parchment. Refrigerate until you're ready to cook.

12. Preheat oven to 375 degrees while you bring the casseroles back to room temperature. Bake, covered, for 12 minutes. Serve hot.

Serves 4. Approximate nutrition information per serving: Calories 540; protein 34g; fat 38g; carbohydrates 14g; sodium 1650 mg.

Squid

Let's face it, it's rather difficult to fall in love with a dye-squirting, literally jet-propelled marine animal that has two flexible arms, eight tentacles, a cigar-shaped body with steering fins attached, and whose very name — squid — sounds squishy. Even its scientific class name is a put-off: *Cephalopod*, meaning "head-footed," so named because the feet (arms?) (legs?) (tentacles?) sprout from its head.

Restaurants have gotten around the imagery of the name with growing success by calling the squid by a foreign name, *calamari*.

In spite of what most people think about the squid (or its cousins, the cuttlefish and octopus, themselves relatives of the more benignly viewed snail, clam, and oyster), it is loved in Japan and the Mediterranean.

And why not? The squid is 80-percent edible, without the external shell that other mollusks have. Its flesh, unless in the hands of an incompetent cook, is as tender as, and flavored similarly to, that of the scallop, and is easier to get at than that of the oyster, quahaug, or whelk. It is lean, and with 19-percent protein, about as nutritious as anything from the sea. Its tube-like body had to have been designed by some heavenly architect solely to be filled with something delicious.

On top of all that, the squid is an underutilized species. There are a lot more out there than the 10 to 20 percent that man is estimated to harvest.

Even the ink sac can be used. In many cultures, but most notably in Spain, the ink is used to flavor and color a sauce in which the squid is served. The sauce has a mild, almost sweet flavor that surprises most first-time tasters. The usual comment is that it does not taste anything like what they expected.

Buy a whole fresh squid, 6 to 7 inches long, including the body and tentacles. Plan on one or two per person, depending on appetite, and whether it is to be stuffed or cut up in a stew or fried. Some fish dealers will clean or partly clean the squid for you.

Separate the head and tentacles as one piece from the body of the squid by pulling them apart. A long mantle will come out with the head. Separate the head and the mantle from the tentacles, cutting through just below the knobby, bony protusion under the eyes. Remove the "pen" (a cartilaginous transparent rudimentary shell) from inside the body, and the ink sac, and discard. The body should be totally empty; wash it inside and out.

Retain the tentacles, and discard the head and mantle. Wash the tentacles and bodies of the squid under running water, rubbing away the purplish skin with your fingers. The wings, or side flaps, may be easily pulled ·off. Save these, along with the tentacles, either to use in a stuffing or to add to the chopped body meat. The squid should now be as white as a scallop. Don't worry if some of the purplish color of the skin remains along the edges.

If the squid is to be stuffed, leave the body whole, and chop the tentacles and wings and use them in the stuffing.

If the body is not to be stuffed, cut it into crosswise rings about ½-inch wide; cut the tentacles and wings into 1-inch pieces unless they are very small. The same procedure is followed for fried squid.

Refer to the drawings on pages 374 and 375 for information on preparing squid for cooking.

Sauteing, pan-frying, or deep-frying squid follows the same procedures as for cooking other fish. You only want to firm and color the squid, whether it is whole or in pieces. Dredge it in flour, batter, or breading and fry at 370 degrees just until it is crisp and brown.

We tested cooking squid by poaching for various lengths of time from 10 seconds to 5 minutes. We found that rings cut from fresh squid bodies were at their best when they were poached in simmering water for 1½ to 2 minutes. Longer poaching toughened them.

Where squid is stuffed or cooked in a stew-like fashion, we found that 5 to 6 minutes, or up to 10 to 12 minutes, depending on the stuffing, was the best cooking time for the squid. In that short period, however, some stuffings would be uncooked, but with more time the squid grows tougher and more rubbery. When the stuffed squid is allowed to stew longer — 50 to 60 minutes — it begins to soften again.

In addition to the following recipes for squid, there is a recipe for Squid with Pasta on page 423.

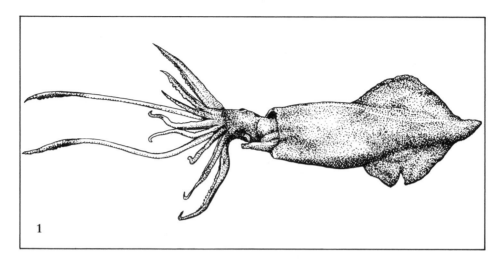

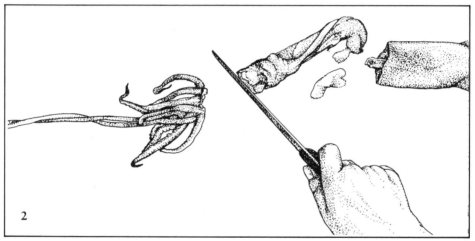

HOW TO PREPARE SQUID FOR COOKING

1. A whole squid before it has been cleaned.

2. Pull the head and tentacles apart from the body. A long mantle will come out with the head. Cut the tentacles apart from the head and mantle at the bony knob just below the eyes.

3. Remove the "pen" from the body.

4. Remove the purple skin from the body. The wings have been pulled off the body and may be saved, along with the tentacles, for use.

5. For some recipes you will need to slice the body into crosswise rings about ½-inch wide.

3

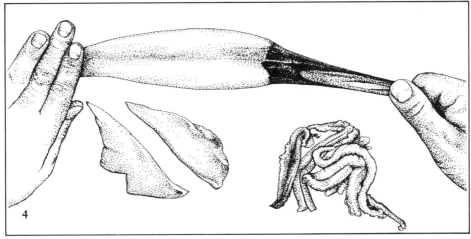

4

5

Chopped Squid in Marinara Sauce

The chopped squid in this recipe is cooked in a marinara sauce that is enhanced with red wine and additional flavorings. If you prefer just a hint of garlic flavor, leave the garlic cloves whole. For a more emphatic flavor, mince them. If ripe native tomatoes are available, use 2 cups, peeled, seeded, and chopped.

2 pounds squid, cleaned and cut up
2 tablespoons olive oil
2 cloves garlic
⅛ teaspoon red pepper flakes (optional)
½ cup chopped onions
1 cup dry red wine

2 cups imported canned peeled plum tomatoes
½ tablespoon dried basil
1 teaspoon dried oregano
1 teaspoon salt
freshly gound pepper
1 tablespoon minced fresh parsley

1. In a saute pan over medium heat, saute garlic in oil until it is browned. You may either discard the whole cloves or leave them in the dish. If using minced garlic, cook only until it is softened.

2. Add red pepper flakes if using them. The amount is variable, but this dish should not be hot; a light tang is all you want. Stir for a moment, add chopped onions and cook until the onion and garlic have begun to pick up color, but do not burn. Add all the other ingredients but the squid and minced parlsey, and cook for 20 minutes.

3. Add squid and cook at a bare simmer for 4 minutes, or until it is cooked but tender. Correct the seasoning.

4. The squid may be served with or without pasta. Serve, sprinkled with parsley.

Serves 4. Approximate nutrition information per serving: Calories 250; protein 25g; fat 10g; carbohydrates 15g; sodium 940 mg.

Squid Salad with Vegetables

Prepare this salad at least 2 hours before you plan to serve it to allow the flavors to develop and meld. Serve it, if you wish, as a summer lunch dish.

24 ounces cleaned squid (about 2 pounds whole uncleaned)
½ cup broccoli flowerettes, or ½ cup watercress
fresh parsley to make 3 tablespoons minced
fresh basil, to make 1 tablespoon minced
1 small clove garlic
½ cup carrots, cut in batons ⅜-inch wide by 1½ inches long
¼ cup sliced celery
½ cup zucchini, cut as carrots
½ cup snow peapods, cut in thirds on bias
1 teaspoon salt
freshly ground black pepper
4 tablespoons good olive oil
2 tablespoons red wine vinegar
½ cup chopped onions
½ cup julienned sweet red bell pepper
4 to 6 romaine leaves (optional)

1. Trim and wash the cleaned squid. Separate the tentacles and wings and chop them. Reserve the whole bodies and chopped parts.

2. Separate broccoli in flowerettes. (Or, separate watercress into leaves and set aside.) Mince the parsley, basil, and garlic clove together.

3. Cook the carrots, celery, and broccoli in boiling salted water for 2 minutes. Add the zucchini and peapods and blanch for 1 minute longer. Drain, cool, and reserve.

4. Poach the squid in simmering salted water for 2 to 3 minutes. Remove, drain, and cool. When cool, cut the bodies into ¼-inch rings.

5. Place salt, pepper, olive oil, and vinegar into a salad bowl with garlic-parsley-basil mixture, and stir well. Add the cooked squid with the cooked carrots, celery, broccoli, zucchini, and peapods, and raw onions and sweet pepper. Add raw watercress leaves if you are not using broccoli. Toss. Correct the seasoning. Chill at least 2 hours.

6. Serve on a bed of romaine lettuce or simply on chilled plates.

Serves 4. Approximate nutrition information per serving: Calories 315; protein 31g; fat 15g; carbohydrates 13g; sodium 1090 mg.

Scallop-Stuffed Squid in Red Wine Sauce

These stuffed squid can be served alone in Red Wine Sauce, or be served with ¾ to 1 pound of pasta. The sauce may be made in advance.

8 whole squid
8 ounces sea scallops
1 recipe for Red Wine Sauce (page 61)
2 tablespoons butter
4 slices bacon, chopped
1 tablespoon minced shallots
¾ cup diced mushrooms

1 tablespoon minced fresh parsley
1 clove garlic, crushed
½ teaspoon salt
few turns of freshly ground pepper
¾ cup fresh breadcrumbs

1. Make the sauce.
2. Clean and wash the squid. Cut off tentacles, pull the wings free, and chop. Reserve the chopped meat and the whole bodies.
3. Blanch scallops in butter just until firm. Remove and chop coarsely while still warm. Reserve.
4. Render bacon in skillet, add shallots and mushrooms, and saute until the moisture in the mushrooms has been evaporated and the mushrooms are well browned.
5. In the same skillet with the mushrooms, saute scallops and squid pieces for 2 to 3 minutes. Add parsley, garlic, salt, and pepper. Stir and cook until the moisture has evaporated. Add breadcrumbs. Allow to cool.
6. Preheat oven to 375 degrees.
7. Stuff the 8 squid bodies with the scallop mixture with a teaspoon; don't pack them too tightly as the stuffing will expand in cooking. Seal the end with skewers or toothpicks.
8. Put half the red wine sauce in an ovenproof casserole or pan. Place the squid in the sauce, and cover with the rest of the sauce. Cook 6 to 7 minutes in the preheated oven.

Serves 4. Approximate nutrition information per serving: Calories 275; protein 32g; fat 9g; carbohydrates 16g; sodium 920 mg.

Neapolitan Stuffed Squid
in Light Marinara Sauce

8 squid
1 recipe for light marinara sauce
   (see page 58)
1 tablespoon minced onion
1 garlic clove, finely minced
2 tablespoons oil
salt and pepper to taste
1 cup fresh breadcrumbs

1 ½ tablespoons minced fresh
   parsley
2 tablespoons grated parmesan
   cheese
1 tablespoon dried basil or
   oregano
8 pitted black olives, chopped

1. Make the sauce in advance, if you wish.

2. Clean and wash squid and prepare for stuffing. Chop tentacles and wings and reserve for use in the stuffing.

3. Saute the onion and garlic in the oil until they are soft but not browned. Add the chopped squid, salt, and pepper, and cook, stirring, for 2 minutes. Add breadcrumbs, stir, and cook over low heat 2 or 3 minutes more.

4. Allow the mixture to cool in a mixing bowl. Add parsley, parmesan cheese, basil or oregano, and olives, mixing well. Correct the seasoning. Mixture should not be too dry. If it is, add up to 2 tablespoons oil.

5. Stuff the squid bodies with mixture, but leave the stuffing loose as it will expand in cooking. Secure the end with skewers or toothpicks.

6. Simmer squid in sauce over lowest heat for 10 minutes. Serve 2 per person with sauce. Stuffed squid also may be served over or with ¾-pound cooked spaghetti.

Serves 4. Approximate nutrition information per serving of squid: Calories 320; protein 29g; fat 13g; carbohydrates 21g; sodium 690 mg. Approximate nutrition information per serving of sauce: Calories 75; protein 2g; fat 4g; carbohydrates 9g; sodium 440 mg.

Squid-filled Gnocchi Pie

Americans do not use farina with anywhere near the regularity that it is enjoyed in much of Europe. The Italian version, little curled pieces of poached dough, called gnocchi, served with various sauces, is only occasionally seen in Italian restaurants and on home tables here. The French make half-dollar rounds with farina and then bake them with butter and cheese. It is relatively easy to handle and is a good way to work starch into a meal, because of its unobtrusive adaptability to other ingredients.

This recipe calls for marrying farina with squid in our Red Wine Sauce. You may use the entire recipe to make a rectangular farina shell that will hold about 1 quart of filling, or 4 individual servings of a half-pint each.

The trick to making mixtures such as farina, cornmeal, polenta, and the like is to stir well so that the ingredients do not stick to the bottom of the pot or clump together.

1 pound squid	2 egg yolks
2 cups milk	5 tablespoons butter
salt	1 cup grated parmesan cheese
white pepper	1 recipe Red Wine Sauce
nutmeg	(page 61)
1 cup farina	

1. Wash, clean, and chop the squid into bite-sized pieces.

2. Bring milk to boil in a heavy pot or a 4-quart saucepan with salt, white pepper, and nutmeg. Stirring, pour in the farina all at once, and lower the heat immediately. Stir continuously while the mixture bubbles. Cook 6 minutes or until the farina is very thick. Remove it from heat and add the egg yolks while the mixture is still hot, stirring well. Add parmesan and 4 tablespoons butter, and stir well.

3. Butter a sheet of wax paper and lay it, buttered-side up, on a cookie sheet. Pour the mixture onto it and spread with a spatula or with your hand dipped in oil or water. Spread to a uniform ½-inch thickness.

4. Cover with another sheet of buttered wax paper and allow it to cool thoroughly. You may chill it, but the resulting dough is likely to become rather brittle and difficult to work with. Room-temperature dough will be more pliable.

5. Make the recipe for Red Wine Sauce, simmer it for 45 minutes instead of 30 minutes to make it a thicker consistency.

6. Preheat oven to 375 degrees.

7. You will need a deep-dish plate or another deep ovenproof mold

that will hold at least 1 quart. With the remaining tablespoon of butter, coat the sides and the bottom of the dish and line it with ⅔ of the dough, leaving a margin of extra dough around the sides. Force dough well into the corners of the dish.

8. Lay the chopped squid into the bottom of the pie and cover it with sauce.

9. Top it with remaining dough, and press the edges together to seal.

10. Bake 30 minutes. Serve hot, directly from the plate.

Serves 4. Approximate nutrition information per serving: Calories 625; protein 40g; fat 36g; carbohydrates 36g; sodium 1210 mg.

Squid Stuffed with Ricotta in Mushroom Cream Sauce

This recipe is a different way to serve stuffed squid. The creamy sauce marries well with the ricotta stuffing.

8 squid

FOR STUFFING:
1½ cups ricotta
½ cup chopped mushrooms
⅓ cup minced fresh parsley
½ teaspoon salt
5 or 6 turns freshly ground black
    pepper
2 tablespoons grated parmesan
    cheese
pinch freshly grated nutmeg
1 egg

FOR SAUCE:
½ cup fish stock (see Quick
    Fumet, page 33)
1½ cups heavy cream
¼ cup minced fresh mushrooms
½ teaspoon salt
freshly ground black pepper to
    taste
pinch freshly grated nutmeg
2 tablespoons butter
2 tablespoons grated parmesan
    cheese

1. Clean and wash squid and prepare for stuffing. Chop tentacles and wings and reserve for use in the stuffing.

2. Lightly mix the chopped squid with all the stuffing ingredients, ex-

cept the egg. When well combined, correct the seasoning. Add the egg, and again mix lightly. Stuff the mixture into squid bodies. Don't pack too tightly as the stuffing will expand in cooking. Seal end with skewers or toothpicks. Refrigerate until ready to cook.

3. Make sauce: In a wide heavy saucepan, reduce the fish stock to ¼ cup. Add cream, mushrooms, salt, pepper, and nutmeg. Cook, reducing the sauce to 1½ cups.

4. Add butter and cheese and simmer to heat through.

5. Preheat oven to 375 degrees.

6. Place half of the sauce in the bottom of an ovenproof casserole or pan large enough to hold the 8 stuffed squid. Place the squid on the sauce, and cover with the rest of the sauce. Cover loosely with foil. Bake 7 to 8 minutes, turning once or twice.

7. Serve 2 squid per person with some of the sauce. Pass pepper mill and additional parmesan cheese.

Serves 4. Approximate nutrition information per serving of squid: Calories 470; protein 23g; fat 36g; carbohydrates 11g; sodium 510 mg. Approximate nutrition information per serving of sauce: Calories 275; protein 2g; fat 29g; carbohydrates 2g; sodium 240 mg.

Soups

*"A proper fish chowder should marinate on the
back of the stove for an hour or more while the ingredients
become thoroughly familiar with one another."*
— Old Yankee cooking instructions

Navarin of Scallops

Soups

To earlier generations, soups were, with bread, the indispensable food. They were a one-pot dish; more often than not, a one-dish meal. They could be fashioned in a multitude of ways with a myriad of ingredients. They were most often eminently digestible and nourishing beyond reckoning, since everything was right in the pot and nothing got away. A liquid or semi-liquid food that could be served hot or cold, as the season dictated; thin, thick, clear, with or without other preparations added. They could be creamed or pureed or made into a chowder or a thick *potage*.

And best of all, in the days or wood- or coal- or peat-burning stoves, they cooked for free, often simmering soup all day at the back of the stove to extract sustenance from bones and flesh that would give it up no other way.

We modern humans, in this country at least, relegated what Alice found wonderful in Wonderland to an insipid snack most often taken from a can or a paper package.

But soups still can be the warming, cheering dishes they have been through the millenia. If you want to enjoy real soup, make one of the eleven we offer here and prove that our ancestors knew more than we do.

When the law meets
culinary tradition in a chowder

The court, "in the light of a hallowed tradition," was not "inclined to tamper with age old recipes. . . ."

The case was simple enough: A women was seeking damages because a bone in a fish chowder that she had eaten in a restaurant had stuck in her throat.

"This is a case which by its nature evokes earnest study not only of the law but also the culinary traditions of the Commonwealth which bear so heavily upon its outcome," Justice Paul C. Reardon of the Supreme Judicial Court of Massachusetts stated in a preamble to the decision without dissent, as he steered a course through culinary, historical, and legal shoals in an entertaining and literate style.

The 1964 case had come before the state's highest court on a series of appeals. The facts were clear:

"... about 1 p.m. the plaintiff entered the Blue Ship Tea Room operated by the defendant.... This restaurant, which the plaintiff characterized as 'quaint,' was located in Boston on the third floor of an old building on T Wharf which overlooks the ocean.

"The plaintiff, who had been born and brought up in New England (a fact of some consequence), ordered.... Presently, there was set before her 'a small bowl of fish chowder' ... The fish chowder contained haddock, potatoes, milk, water, and seasoning. The chowder was milky in color and not clear. The haddock and potatoes were in chunks (also a fact of consequence).

"She agitated it a little with a spoon and observed that it was a fairly full bowl.... It was hot when she got it ... (she) stirred it in an up-and-under motion. She denied that she did this because she was looking for something, but it was rather because she wanted an even distribution of fish and potatoes.

"She started to eat it, alternating between the chowder and crackers which were on the table.... She ate about 3 or 4 spoonfuls then stopped. She looked at the spoonfuls as she was eating. She saw equal parts of liquid, potato, and fish as she spooned it into her mouth. She did not see anything unusual about it. After 3 or 4 spoonfuls she was aware that something had lodged in her throat because she couldn't swallow and couldn't clear her throat by gulping, and she could feel it.

"This misadventure led to two esophagoscopies at the Massachusetts General Hospital, in the second of which ... a fish bone was found and removed. The sequence of events produced injury to the plaintiff which was not insubstantial.

"We must decide whether a fish bone lurking in a fish chowder, about the ingredients of which there is no complaint, constitutes a breach of implied warranty under applicable provisions of the Uniform Commerical Code.

"The defendant asserts that here was a native New Englander eating fish chowder in a 'quaint' Boston dining place where she had been before; that (fish) chowder, as it is served and enjoyed by New Englanders, is a hearty dish, originally designed 'to satisfy the appetites of our seamen and fishermen'; that '(this) court knows well we are not talking of some insipid broth as is customarily served to convalescents.' "

Justice Reardon then cited various cookbooks, authors from Nathaniel Hawthorne to Daniel Webster and precedents in law to explain the court's decision.

"Chowder is an ancient dish preexisting even 'the appetites of our seamen and fishermen.' The word 'chowder' comes for the French 'chaudière,' meaning a 'cauldron' or 'pot.' In the fishing villages of Brittany ... 'faire la chaudière' means to supply a cauldron in which is cooked a mess of fish and biscuit with some savoury condiments, a hodgepodge contributed by the fishermen themselves, each of whom in return receives his share of the prepared dish. The Breton fishermen probably carried the custom to Newfoundland, long famous for its chowder, whence it has spread to Nova Scotia, New Brunswick, and New England.

"The recitation of ancient formulae [recipes] suffices to indicate that in the construction of chowders in these parts in other years, worries about fish bones played no role whatsoever. This broad outlook on chowders has persisted in more modern cookbooks. 'The chowder of today is much the same as the old chowder. . .' (*The American Woman's Cook Book*).

"It is not too much to say that a person sitting down in New England to consume a good New England fish chowder embarks on a gustatory adventure which may entail the removal of some fish bones from his bowl as he proceeds.

"We are not inclined to tamper with age-old recipes by any amendment reflecting the plaintiff's view of the effect of the Uniform Commercial Code upon them.

"We are aware of the heavy body of case law involving foreign substances in food, but we sense a strong distinction between them and those relative to unwholesomeness of the food itself. e.g., tainted mackerel, and a fish bone in a fish chowder.

"In any event, we consider that the joys of life in New England include the ready availability of fresh fish chowder. We should be prepared to cope with the hazards of fish bones, the occasional presence of which in chowders is, it seems to us, to be anticipated, and which, in the light of a hallowed tradition, do not impair their fitness or merchantability.

"While we are buoyed up in this conclusion by Shapiro v. Hotel Statler Corp. (a California case), in which the bone which afflicted the plaintiff appeared in 'Hot Barquette of Seafood Mornay,' we know that the United States District Court of Southern California, situated as we are upon a coast, might be expected to share our views. We are most impressed, however, by Allen v. Grafton, where in Ohio, the Midwest, in a case where the plaintiff was injured by a piece of oyster shell in an order of fried oysters. Mr. Justice Taft . . . in a majority opinion held that 'the possible presence of a piece of oyster shell in or attached to an oyster is so well known to anyone who eats oysters that we can say as a matter of law that one who eats oysters can reasonably anticipate and guard against eating such a piece of shell.'

"Thus," Justice Reardon concludes, "while we sympathize with the plaintiff who has suffered a peculiarly New England injury, the order must be. . . .

"Judgement for the defendant."

Little Neck Soup

Try a steaming bowl of these clams on a cold and drizzly night. Pick up the clams on the way home and you can be enjoying the soup with evening news.

If fresh tomato is truly ripe and red, use it. If it is a pale winter version, you can still use it, but fortify it by using 1 tablespoon of tomato paste mixed with ¼ cup water or tomato juice. Otherwise use 2 whole tomatoes from a can of imported Italian peeled plum tomatoes. You may substitute ½ cup of the liquid from canned tomatoes for the tomato juice in the recipe.

32 little neck or 24 cherrystone clams in shell	freshly ground pepper
6 tablespoons olive oil	1 tablespoon freshly squeezed lemon juice
2 whole, peeled cloves of garlic	¼ cup white wine
1 small fresh tomato, peeled, seeded, and chopped	2 tablespoons minced fresh parsley
½ cup tomato juice	1 teaspoon dried basil

1. Thoroughly wash clams, but do not open. Leave the meat in the shell.

2. Pour olive oil into a pot large enough to hold clams. The pot should have a well-fitting cover. Add garlic cloves and brown. Discard garlic.

3. Add clams in shell, tomato, tomato juice, pepper, lemon juice, white wine, parsley, and basil.

4. Cover pot and steam clams until they open (about 7 to 10 minutes). Hold the cover down tightly and shake the pan so that all the clams open. Discard any that fail to open.

5. Ladle everything into deep soup bowls. The clams should be in a liquid that is not exactly a soup and not exactly a sauce, more like our Navarin of Scallops.

6. Pass crusty bread to accompany soup.

Serves 4. Approximate nutrition information per serving: Calories 339; protein 20g; fat 22g; carbohydrates 15g; sodium 410 mg.

Seafood Matzo Ball Soup

According to Jewish tradition, matzo originated at the time Moses led the people of Israel out of bondage in Egypt. They left so hurriedly they carried with them an unleavened bread dough that had not risen, flour mixed with water. When they tasted some that had baked in the hot desert sun, they realized it was palatable. Matzo has been made ever since and is used in the Jewish feast of Passover that commemorates the Exodus. It is a flat cracker about ⅛-inch thick made from fine white wheat flour and water, similar to a water biscuit.

Matzo meal is ground and used with egg to bake blintzes, in gefilte fish, to coat foods to be fried, and to make dumplings for soup, usually a rich chicken broth. The matzo meal for that dish is normally mixed with egg yolks, chicken fat, hot chicken broth, ginger, salt, and pepper, and sometimes grated onion and potato flour. The matzo balls are often cooked in the chicken broth in which they will be served.

Use any firm white fish, or a variety of fishes: cusk, hake, ocean perch, sea bass, tilefish, monkfish, pollock, cod, or haddock. You also may use some scallops, oysters, mussels, or clams. An ounce or two of shark, swordfish, or tuna mixed in will provide a bit of silky oil film that would enrich this soup in the manner of one made with chicken stock.

You can get this soup ready through step 4 and then finish it closer to the time it will be served.

1½ cups, or 8 to 10 ounces mixed seafood

FISH STOCK:
3 to 4 pounds fish trimmings, etc. (see fish stocks, page 28)
1 carrot, chopped
½ stalk celery, chopped
½ cup leek trimmings
2 whole fresh tomatoes cut in pieces
½ cup chopped onion
pinch of saffron (about ⅛ teaspoon)
freshly ground white pepper

MATZO BALLS:
½ cup matzo meal
1 teaspoon salt
2 tablespoons melted fat (butter is fine, chicken fat traditional)
2 eggs, slightly beaten
2 tablespoons concentrated fish stock

FOR GARNISH:
½ leek
½ stalk celery
½ carrot
¼ cup peeled, seeded, chopped fresh tomato
1 tablespoon minced fresh parsley

1. Make 2 quarts of stock: Set fish trimmings, carrot, celery, leek, tomato, onion, saffron, and pepper in water to cover and cook for 30 minutes. Strain and return liquid to pot and reduce to 1 quart of stock. Set aside.

2. Remove ¼ cup of stock and place it in a small wide pan over medium-high heat. Reduce to 2 tablespoons to be used in making matzo balls.

3. Begin matzo balls: Mix salt and matzo meal together in a small
bowl. Mix fat, eggs, and 2 tablespoons water or cold concentrated stock
together in another bowl and add matzo meal. Stir to incorporate. Cover
the mixing bowl and place in the refrigerator for 20 minutes or more.

4. Make matzo balls that are about 1 inch in diameter, by rolling pieces
of matzo mix between the wetted palms of your hands. Place completed
balls on a flat plate; you should have about 2 dozen matzo balls.

5. Set a 2- or 3-quart pot of salted water to simmer. Hold the plate of
matzo balls over the pot of simmering water. Gently pour water over the
balls with a ladle until they firm up. They should then easily roll off the plate
into the water. Bring the pot to a bare simmer, cover, and cook 30 to 45
minutes. With a slotted spoon, remove the matzo balls from the cooking
water and set them aside.

6. Meanwhile, cut the half leek, half stalk of celery, and half carrot into
fine julienne strips. Set aside.

7. At this point, you may hold the ingredients in the refrigerator for
several hours, if you wish, until 10 minutes or so before serving time.

8. Heat the fish stock, and add the julienned vegetables and chopped
tomato. Allow to simmer 1 minute. Add the mixed seafood and parsley.
Add the matzo balls to the stock. Correct the seasoning. When the vegetables are done to your liking, probably 5 or 6 minutes, the dish is ready.

Serves 4. Approximate nutrition information per serving: Calories 234;
protein 18g; fat 10g; carbohydrates 19g; sodium 770 mg.

Clams Germiny

◻

Potage Germiny *is a standard dish in the French repertoire. It is made with egg yolks mixed with cream, butter, consomme, and shredded sorrel.*

In this dish clams are suffused in a light saffron-flavored custard.

The recipe requires sorrel, but if it's not available you may substitute romaine cut the same way, with ribs removed and a few drops of lemon added to increase the acidity.

You can prepare this recipe through step 3 several hours in advance of serving, and then conclude the preparation just prior to serving.

36 little neck clams	2 cups washed, shredded sorrel
3 cups clam juice	6 egg yolks
⅛ teaspoon saffron	1 cup heavy cream
1 tablespoon plus 2 teaspoons butter	

1. Wash and scrub clams well. Shuck clams and chop meat fine. Keep chilled. Save their juice; if necessary, add enough water to make 3 cups.

2. Combine clam juice, shallots, and saffron in a skillet and heat to a simmer. Cook about 3 minutes. Set aside.

3. In a separate skillet, melt 2 teaspoons butter, add shredded sorrel over low heat, and "sweat" it, while stirring, until tender.

4. At the last minute, mix yolks and cream in a bowl. Warm the clam juice, and add a ladle or two of it to the egg-cream mixture and stir to warm the yolks.

5. Stir warmed yolk mixture into broth and cook for 4 minutes, stirring constantly. You are making a thin custard so you will have to watch it carefully; it should not boil.

6. Strain, add 1 tablespoon butter, and heat. Add chopped clams and sorrel and heat through. Correct seasoning.

7. Serve immediately. Cheese straws would be a good accompaniment.

Serves 4. Approximate nutrition information per serving: Calories 430; protein 18g; fat 35g; carbohydrates 10g; sodium 320 mg.

Cream of Fish Soup

You may use any raw, lean fish for this recipe, mixed or all of one kind.

1 pound raw boneless, lean fish	2 cups white wine
1 cup chopped onions	1 large pinch saffron
1 cup chopped leeks	½ teaspoon dried thyme
1 tablespoon olive oil	2 bay leaves
2 cups seeded and chopped fresh tomatoes or canned Italian plum tomatoes	1 teaspoon salt
	⅛ teaspoon pepper
1 dozen parsley stems	1½ cups heavy cream
2 garlic cloves, crushed	1 tablespoon Pernod or Ricard
½ cup chopped celery	garlic croutons
2 cups fish stock (see White Wine Fumet, page 30)	

1. In a 6-quart stock pot, saute onions and leeks in oil until soft but not browned. Add tomatoes, parsley stems, garlic, and celery, and continue to cook for 2 minutes. Add fish stock, white wine, saffron, thyme, bay leaves, salt, and pepper. Simmer 20 minutes and add fish. Raise heat and boil rapidly for 5 minutes — you want the fish to break up.

2. Put the ingredients through a food mill or work in batches in a food processor.

3. Return to the pot, add cream, and reheat, cooking for a few minutes. Pass through a colander or large-mesh strainer; you don't want a soup that is too smooth, because the texture that the fish and vegetables impart is desirable in this soup.

4. Return the soup to the cleaned pot and bring it to a boil. Lower heat to a bare simmer and add Pernod or Ricard. Correct the seasoning.

5. Serve with garlic croutons. (To make croutons, slice fresh bread and toast; rub with a split clove of garlic. Butter if you wish.)

Note: The soup can also be made with cooked (poached) fish. If so, be careful if you're using fish with small bones, as they can pass through a strainer into the soup. Large bones in fish such as halibut will add to the soup's flavor.

Serves 4. Approximate nutrition information per serving: Calories 365; protein 23g; fat 21g; carbohydrates 21g; sodium 840 mg.

Bluefish Soup

This recipe will work just as well with mackerel.

8 ounces skinless bluefish fillet,
    in bite-sized pieces
4 slices bacon, diced
1 tablespoon butter
½ cup chopped onion
1 quart of fish stock (White
    Wine Fumet, page 30) or use
    half water, half clam juice, or
    plain water
2 cups chopped celery (save
    1 tablespoon of leaves)

pinch of dried thyme
½ teaspoon salt
3 to 4 turns freshly ground
    pepper
1 cup heavy cream
½ cup peeled, seeded, and diced
    tomatoes
1 tablespoon minced fresh
    parsley

1. Fry bacon in butter in a thick-bottomed 4-quart saucepan or stock pot to render the fat. When bacon is crisp, remove half of it, blot on paper towels, and reserve. Leave bacon fat and the other half of the bacon in the pan.

2. Add onion to pan and saute until lightly browned. Add fish stock or other liquid, celery, thyme, salt, and pepper. Simmer, covered, 30 to 35 minutes, or until celery is tender.

3. Place contents of pan into work bowl of food processor, in two batches if necessary, and work until smooth.

4. Return to pan and bring to a boil, then lower heat to simmer, and add cream. Cook over low heat 5 minutes. Add tomatoes and parsley and then fish. Simmer 3 to 4 minutes, and correct the seasoning.

5. Ladle the soup into individual soup plates or into a soup tureen. Add bacon bits and celery leaves as garnish.

Serves 4. Approximate nutrition information per serving: Calories 739; protein 49g; fat 52g; carbohydrates 20g; sodium 1790 mg.

Bluefish Chowder

Whole biscuits or common crackers were used traditionally to thicken a chowder. Some cooks today use flour, which will give a raw-dough taste if not cooked through. We use bread, which is already a cooked product.

8 ounces of bluefish, cut in
    ½-inch dice
1 tablespoon butter
2 tablespoons minced, washed
    salt pork
¾ cup chopped onion
½ cup chopped celery
1 quart fish stock (see White
    Wine Fumet, page 30) or use
    half water, half clam juice, or
    plain water

¼ teaspoon dried thyme
½ bay leaf
½ teaspoon salt
pinch of pepper
1½ cups good crusty bread,
    French or Italian, cut in
    ¼-inch dice
1½ cups half and half
1¼ cups potatoes, cut into
    ⅜-inch dice

1. In a thick-bottomed 4-quart saucepan or stock pot, melt butter, add salt pork, and fry it until crisp. Add onion, and saute until it is soft and transparent, but not yet taking on color. Add celery, cover with fish stock or other liquid, and add thyme, bay leaf, salt, and pepper. Cook for 10 minutes.

2. Soak diced bread in ½ cup cream about 15 minutes.

3. Add bread and all the cream to pot. Stir well and bring to a boil, then simmer for one minute to break down the bread. Don't overcook, as you don't want to lose the bread's texture entirely.

4. Add potatoes and cook 12 to 15 minutes, or until tender.

5. Add fish, bring to boil, and simmer 2 more minutes. Correct the seasoning. Serve immediately.

Serves 6. Approximate nutrition information per serving: Calories 700; protein 50g; fat 41g; carbohydrates 34g; sodium 1725 mg.

Lobster Bisque

Boiled lobster enjoys great popularity as a dish to be enjoyed at home, especially as a special occasion dish. Most people discard the "empty" bodies, however, which is wasteful. Lobster bodies can make a delicious bisque at a fraction of the cost of using whole lobster.

When eating a whole boiled lobster, few take the time to remove the meat from the small walking legs, or to clean out the body meat well. Small morsels of meat, found at the last joint between the body and legs, are perfect for garnishing a rich, creamy bisque. It is time consuming, but it is worth the effort to pick over the lobster bodies a second time to make sure they are totally clean, and reserve the bits of meat. Discard the stomach sac.

Then, to extract the full flavor of the boiled lobster shells, break them up by hand and grind them through a meat grinder (large hole disk) or chop them in a food processor, one at a time. The carapace, or large shell, while not yielding much flavor, does provide a great deal of coloring. It can be used whole if breaking it smaller is too much trouble.

This recipe is dedicated to Francine and Emile Surel.

6 lobster bodies	1 bay leaf
3 tablespoons butter, plus ¼ cup for roux	1 clove garlic, crushed
1½ cup diced onions	2 quarts water
1 cup diced carrots	¼ cup flour
1 cup diced celery	3 tablespoons cognac
2 cups dry white wine	1 cup heavy cream
½ cup tomato paste	⅛ teaspoon, or less, cayenne
salt and pepper to taste	pepper
sprig of fresh thyme or ¼ teaspoon dried	

1. Melt 2 tablespoons butter in a large pan. Add diced onions and carrots and saute until onions are transparent.

2. Add ground lobster bodies, diced celery, white wine, tomato paste, salt, pepper, thyme, bay leaf, garlic, and 2 quarts of water. Bring to a boil and simmer for 1 hour.

3. Strain broth through a fine sieve, pressing down with a spoon in order to extract all liquid from shells and vegetables. Strain again through a double layer of dampened cheesecloth or clean towel. Return pot to heat and reduce liquid to 1 quart.

4. Melt ¼ cup of butter in a saucepan, add flour, stir, and cook over low heat for approximately 10 minutes.

5. Add the reduced broth, stirring well with a wire whisk, and bring to a boil. Simmer for 5 minutes. Strain once more through a double layer of dampened cheesecloth. (This may be held up to 12 hours, refrigerated, before completing.)

6. Add cream and cayenne and reheat.

7. In another pan, melt the remaining tablespoon butter, add reserved lobster pieces, and saute for a few minutes. Add cognac to warm, ignite, and shake until flame dies.

8. Add the reduced bisque. Correct seasoning and serve hot in warmed bowls.

Serves 6 generously. Approximate nutrition information per serving: Calories 350; protein 4g; fat 29g; carbohydrates 20g; sodium 140 + mg.

Crab Bisque

For this recipe use live blue crabs, or other available crabs. If live crabs are unavailable, you can use whole crabs that have already been boiled or steamed by your fishmonger. You will lose some of the essential flavor, however. Canned or frozen crabmeat cannot be used.

Prepare crabs for cooking by cracking them and removing stomach sac and spongy gills (see section on crabs, page 254). Do not remove the meat. Crack the walking legs, and collect the creamy parts.

6 small crabs
3 tablespoons butter
1 tablespoon oil
¼ cup plus 2 tablespoons brandy
1 cup diced onions
¾ cup diced carrots
¾ cup diced celery
1½ cups dry white wine
1½ cups fish stock (see White Wine Fumet, page 30) or water
7 to 8 parsley stems

2 small or 1 large cloves garlic
¼ teaspoon thyme
1 bay leaf
2 cups diced tomatoes, or 1-pound can ground peeled tomatoes
1 teaspoon salt
½ teaspoon freshly ground black pepper
1 cup heavy cream
pinch of cayenne
1 tablespoon butter, optional
1 tablespoon flour, optional

1. Preferably in a long-handled skillet, saute crab parts, including claws, chopped walking legs, body parts, and their creamy "butter" in 1 tablespoon of butter and 1 tablespoon oil. Toss and heat for a minute or so, then remove from heat to add ¼ cup brandy. Return to heat, warm, and ignite. Toss until the flame goes out. Remove from heat and reserve.

2. In a 6-quart, deep, non-corrosive saucepan, melt 1 tablespoon butter and saute onions, carrots, and celery until tender. Toss in the brandy-flamed crab and cook for 2 minutes over medium heat, mashing crab shells with a long-handled cooking spoon, or, better, a potato masher.

3. Add wine and fish stock and heat. Then add parsley stems, garlic, thyme, bay leaf, tomatoes, salt, and pepper.

4. Simmer uncovered for 30 minutes, occasionally mashing crab.

5. Strain through a coarse sieve or colander, mashing ingredients with a spoon to extract maximum flavor. Measure — you should have 3 cups of liquid — and return to clean pot. (If you do not have enough liquid, add bottled clam juice.)

6. Add cream and simmer 10 minutes. Add cayenne, cook 1 more minute.

7. Strain into a clean pot through a fine sieve, rubbing ingredients with a rubber spatula to extract maximum flavor.

8. Add 2 tablespoons brandy, bring to a boil, correct the seasoning, and serve hot with common crackers.

9. If a thicker bisque is desired, mix thoroughly 1 tablespoon soft butter with 1 tablespoon flour. Stir it into the bisque and bring it to boil before serving.

Serves 6. Approximate nutrition information per serving: Calories 408; protein 20g; fat 29g; carbohydrates 16g; sodium 853 mg.

Mussel Chowder

This is a chowder that follows traditions all the way back to those chaudières of France that were brought to the New World. If you prefer a richer chowder, use heavy cream.

Choose small mussels if you can, as they work better in chowders. You can make large mussels smaller if you like, by pulling free the mantle, or dark band of flesh that rims each mussel. This also may be done for appearance.

1½ quarts mussels, cleaned and scrubbed
2½ cups water
3 tablespoons finely diced or grated salt pork
½ cup finely chopped onion
2 tablespoons flour

1 cup potatoes, peeled and cut into ⅜-inch dice
¼ teaspoon dried thyme, or one sprig of fresh
salt and pepper to taste
1 cup half and half

1. Place mussels in a large kettle and cook, covered, with 2½ cups water 6 to 7 minutes until the mussels are opened. Holding cover down tightly, shake pan occasionally to make sure that all mussels open. Remove mussels with a skimmer. Discard any that failed to open.

2. Strain broth through a double layer of dampened cheesecloth. Reserve.

3. Allow mussels to cool before removing from shell. Remove mantle, if desired.

4. In a heavy pan or skillet, fry salt pork until lightly browned. Add chopped onion, saute a few minutes, add flour and stir well. Slowly add broth, blending until it is smooth, then add potatoes, thyme, salt, and pepper. Cover and cook over low heat until potatoes are tender, about 10 to 14 minutes.

5. Add the cooked mussels and bring to a boil. Then lower the heat and add cream; heat thoroughly, but do not boil. Correct the seasoning and serve.

Serves 6. Approximate nutrition information per serving: Calories 225; protein 12g; fat 14g; carbohydrates 11g; sodium 520 mg.

Oriental Soup

This soup is hearty, filling, and flavorful. For authenticity as well as variety, we suggest you use noodles made from mung beans, variously called "bean thread noodles," "cellophane noodles," or "Chinese vermicelli." They must be soaked 30 to 60 minutes in cold water and then heated and dropped into soup, in which they should cook 4 to 5 minutes.

You may substitute Chinese flour noodles, also called Chinese flour vermicelli. They are parboiled until nearly done, drained, and added to soup to finish cooking for 6 to 8 minutes. You can use Western-style noodles if you prefer them or if you can't find the others.

You will need 16 ounces of boneless fish or seafood. It may be all of one type, but for the sake of variety we suggest the following mixture: 4 ounces Maine shrimp (if larger shrimp are used, cut in half); 4 ounces scallops; 4 ounces squid; and 4 ounces lean, white, firm fish.

In a soup like this, or in any delicate fish, you should use light soy sauce. The heavy, black soy sauce available everywhere would overwhelm this soup.

1 pound boneless fish, in bite-size pieces	1½ cups fish stock (see White Wine Fumet, page 30 or Quick Fumet, page 33)
½ cup dry black mushrooms	½ cup Chinese rice wine
3 ounces Chinese noodles	3 tablespoons light soy sauce
4 ounces bean curd or tofu, optional	½ teaspoon curry powder
2 teaspoons minced garlic	1½ cups chopped cabbage
1 teaspoon minced fresh ginger	¼ cup chopped scallions
1 tablespoon peanut oil	1½ cups chopped bok choy

1. Wash the mushrooms and soak in ¼ cup warm water, 20 to 30 minutes. Remove stems and cut mushrooms in quarters. Reserve. The minced stems, if not too tough, and soaking water also may be reserved and added to the soup.

2. Prepare noodles as described above.

3. Cut the bean curd or tofu into 2 pieces about 3 inches square and 1 inch thick.

4. In a 6-quart stock pot, saute garlic and ginger in peanut oil until soft but not colored.

5. Add the fish stock to the pot and bring it to a boil. Add rice wine, soy sauce, and curry. Add cabbage and mushrooms and simmer for 4 minutes. Add seafood and scallions. Simmer for 3 minutes and add bok choy and

noodles. Simmer 5 to 6 minutes more, or until vegetables and seafood are cooked to your liking. Add tofu if using it and cooked rice noodles. Heat and serve in warm bowls.

Serves 6. Approximate nutrition information per serving: Calories 256; protein 26g; fat 8g; carbohydrates 17g; sodium 1100 mg.

Lobster Consomme

This clear broth is an excellent way to begin a special meal. It is light, yet potent in flavor, a savory way to whet your appetite without being filling.

You can use the bodies of lobsters whose meat you plan to use another way. Or, it is often possible to obtain bodies from dealers who cook them to sell lobster meat out of the shell.

The consomme may be served with a garnish, if desired. Use one or more of the following: strips of blanched carrot or leek, diced cooked lobster meat, or a sprig of fresh dill. Or you can use our recipe for small monkfish sausages (page 145), or Chef Jasper White's Lobster Sausages (page 278).

This consomme can be prepared a day ahead and kept chilled. Bring it to a boil before serving.

FOR STOCK:
6 lobster bodies
2 quarts water
2 cups dry white wine
1 cup diced onion
¾ cup diced carrots
½ cup diced celery
4 tablespoons tomato paste
3 whole tomatoes
½ teaspoon thyme leaves
1 bay leaf
12 parsley stems
2 crushed cloves garlic

2 tablespoons salt
1 teaspoon cracked pepper

FOR CLARIFICATION:
4 egg whites
½ cup water
½ cup coarsely chopped parsley
½ cup diced tomatoes
¼ teaspoon dried tarragon (or ½ teaspoon fresh)

2 tablespoons brandy

1. Place all the stock ingredients in a stock pot, bring to a boil, reduce heat, and simmer gently for 1 hour. Skim occasionally. Strain, cool, and refrigerate overnight.

2. When removing the stock from the refrigerator the next day be careful not to disturb the sediment. Remove any fat or scum on surface. Pour or ladle the stock gently into a stainless steel pot, making sure you leave the sediment in the pot. A consomme must be perfectly clear.

3. Mix egg whites, water, parsley, tomatoes, and tarragon in a stainless steel bowl. Beat until foamy. Bring the stock to a boil, add it slowly to the egg white mixture, stir, and return to the original pot. Bring to a boil, and then let it simmer gently for 25 minutes.

4. Do not disturb the foam that rises to top. Ladle consomme through a strainer containing 3 layers of dampened cheesecloth or a fine linen dishtowel.

5. Hold in refrigerator. When ready to eat, return consomme to burner and heat. Correct the seasoning and add 2 tablespoons brandy.

6. Serve in heated soup bowls with any of the indicated garnishes, if desired.

Serves 6. Approximate nutrition information per serving, including garnish: Calories 106; protein 10g; fat 1g; carbohydrates 14g; sodium 2260 mg.

New England Clam Chowder

It is a shame how maligned this traditional New England dish is even on its home grounds. It is served up as thick as porridge, often tasting of uncooked flour. It is flavored with paprika, bay leaves, thyme, coriander leaves, and every other imaginable herb and spice. It is turned golden with butter — or worse, margarine. More often than not, it is an unholy insult to the frugal, sensible Yankee housewives who warmed many a winter's night with a heaping bowlful served with nothing more imposing than common crackers.

If ever there were a dish that called for restraint on the part of the cook, this is it. Resist the impulse to "do something" to make it better. You can't. You shouldn't. You mustn't. The only substitution that you should consider is butter for the salt pork if you don't want to use salt pork for any reason.

Use steamed softshell clams or minced raw quahaugs. You can often buy fresh, minced sea clams from fish dealers. These should be your second choice. And if you cannot possibly find fresh clams, you will need two 6½-to-7 ounce cans of minced clams for this recipe. Reserve the juice that comes with them and increase its quantity, if necessary, with bottled clam juice.

1½ cups chopped clams	3 small potatoes, diced (2 cups)
3 tablespoons finely minced, washed salt pork	2 pints half and half
	salt
1 small onion, minced (about 5 tablespoons)	pinch white pepper
	1 tablespoon butter, optional
1¼ cups clam broth	

1. Render salt pork in a soup pot over medium heat until cracklings are lightly browned. (You can remove cracklings if you prefer, but they are a part of the traditional dish.)

2. Add minced onion and cook over low heat until onion is soft and transparent but not browned. Add clam broth. Stir and add diced potatoes and simmer, uncovered, until potatoes are tender, about 10 to 14 minutes. Liquid will reduce slightly.

3. Add half and half and heat thoroughly, but do not boil. Add salt and pepper to taste. Simmer for 2 minutes and add chopped clams. They do not have to cook; just heating them through will guarantee their tenderness. Correct the seasoning.

4. You may add a pat of butter just before serving if you want added richness.

Serves 4. Approximate nutrition information per serving: Calories 520; protein 11g; fat 40g; carbohydrates 27g; sodium 750 mg.

Fish Farinaceous

*"Fish stuffing for pasta
is not a recent invention of* nuova cucina . . ."
— Guiliano Bugialli, *Foods of Italy*

**Scallop-Stuffed Squid
in Red Wine Sauce with Linguine**

Fish Farinaceous

Rice, pasta, farina, cornmeal, and other such products have long been favorites with cooks. Their neutral flavor marries well with most other foods, sauces, and gravies; and yet their identity is not lost. They absorb much of what they are combined with, extending the flavor. They can add greatly to the volume of a dish without destroying it. They get a starch into every dish. They are inexpensive. They can be used in a multitude of sizes and shapes and can be used with fillings. No wonder cooks like them.

In recent years, creative chefs and restaurateurs have applied their talents to pasta — fettucini, ravioli, and other forms in new and different combinations.

Here are Fish Farinaceous recipes to add to your personal repertoire.

Egg Pasta

PASTA ALL' UOVO

The basic formula for homemade egg pasta such as fettucini is 1½ cups of flour to 2 large eggs with a bit of salt. This makes a fairly rich egg pasta. It makes enough pasta for 4 to 6 persons, depending on the other ingredients in a dish. For 2 to 3 persons, you would use ¾ cup of flour and 1 egg; for 8 persons, increase the flour to 1¾ cups and use 3 eggs.

Some cooks use a teaspoon of oil instead of water, others claim oil toughens the dough while making it more silky. Some cooks omit the liquid entirely. After you have experimented with a batch or two using oil and using water, you will know the texture you prefer. The liquid is somewhat variable as it helps to balance the difference between flour on a dry day as opposed to flour on a humid day. When dealing with such small amounts, however, it is not critical.

You can increase the amount of the recipe to make more pasta, but only 1 tablespoon water (or 1 teaspoon oil) is used when recipe is doubled.

Using a food processor eliminates the tedious chore of hand kneading, but we also give instructions for making the dough by hand in step 7 below.

1½ cups all-purpose flour	1 tablespoon water or 1
¼ teaspoon salt	teaspoon oil
2 large eggs at room temperature	

1. Place flour and salt in the work bowl of a food processor. Pulse the machine in quick bursts to mix. Now pour the eggs through the feed tube and process 10 to 15 seconds or until the mixture resembles coarse meal.

2. Add the water or oil and process in bursts until the dough forms a ball that pulls away from the sides of the work bowl. Stop immediately.

3. Remove the dough, divide it into 4 pieces and flour each piece. While rolling the first piece, cover the others with a damp towel so that they do not dry out.

4. Run one piece of dough through the widest opening of the rollers on a pasta machine 4 or 5 times until the pasta has gained some elasticity and loses its creases. Flour and fold the pasta in half or thirds after each run through the rollers. Now proceed to run the pasta through the subsequent, ever-narrowing openings until you have a length of smooth pasta, about the thickness of a dime for fettucini and similar styles.

5. If the pasta becomes unmanageably long during the rolling, just cut it in half or thirds. If the pasta seems moist or sticky during the rolling, dust it with flour between rolls. Use the cutting rollers of the machine to obtain

the shape you want, or roll up well-floured dough like a jelly roll and cut it crosswise with a knife into the width you prefer.

6. Scatter the fresh cut pasta onto a clean kitchen towel and allow it to dry at least 15 minutes before cooking. It can dry for up to 3 or 4 hours if necessary.

7. Alternately, mix salt and flour on a dough board. Make a well in the center of the flour and add the lightly beaten eggs with the water or oil. With your fingers, work a bit of the flour into the egg, mixing and incorporating a little of the flour at a time until all of it is absorbed and you have a rather sticky ball of dough. Flour the board and begin kneading the dough, dusting the board with flour if the dough gets sticky. Work for 10 minutes, cut dough in fourths, and then proceed to roll it to the thickness of a dime, with a rolling pin. Dust it frequently with flour if it begins to get sticky. Cut as desired.

Cooking Hints

Whether the pasta is fresh or dried, 4 to 6 quarts of water for 1 pound of pasta is the best ratio for cooking it. The water should be boiling furiously when the pasta is added. Unless you have dietary reasons for not using salt, add 1 tablespoon to the cooking water before adding the pasta. Jack Denton Scott, in his book on pasta, argues that salt should be added to cooking water immediately prior to the pasta otherwise the salt will form sharp-smelling hydrochloric acid. We have never tested his idea, nor do we know why the little acid that might result would hinder the flavor or texture (or a diner's health), but, following Pascal's philosophy, we choose to believe and add the salt at the last moment. Many cooks do not feel the precaution is necessary. Some cooks add a few drops of oil to the cooking water to prevent the pasta from sticking while it cooks. Since most pasta should be dropped into rapidly boiling water and be stirred for the first half minute of cooking, and occasionally thereafter, we do not add oil. But if it makes you feel more secure, add it.

With filled pasta, which would be likely to break up if the boiling or stirring were too vigorous, adding a few drops of oil is more necessary.

Really fresh thin pasta, such as fettucini and other noodles, can cook within 30 seconds to a minute. Slightly thicker pasta will take up to 2 minutes. As pasta dries, its cooking time increases. Dried commercial pastas usually take 6 to 8 minutes; some dried macaroni takes 10 to 12; and we have sampled some non-machine-dried styles from Italy made from unusually hard flour that took 30 to 35 minutes to cook.

Filled pastas, such as ravioli, cappelletti, or tortellini, can cook as quickly as 3 minutes if made with extremely thin dough, but generally 6 to 8 minutes is average.

Begin timing not when you put pasta into water, but when the water returns to a boil.

The only real way to know when pasta is ready is to taste it as it cooks — though this is rather difficult for styles that cook in less than a minute. Don't depend too much on counting the minutes that pasta has cooked. Use time only as a guide, and begin testing pasta after it is half-cooked by biting into a strand. It should be firm, without tasting "doughy"; it should be cooked through, not powdery white at the very center, nor soft or mushy. This is al dente.

If pasta is going to be tossed with a hot, soupy sauce, it will not only continue to cook from its own heat, but also will cook a bit more in the sauce. In such cases remove the pasta from the cooking water slightly underdone.

When pasta has finished cooking drain it immediately. You do not need to rinse it. Some cooks like to place a little butter in the still hot pot in which it cooked, return the pasta to the pot, add another dollop of butter, and toss, before mixing the pasta with sauce. The butter slows down the rate at which the pasta will absorb a sauce.

Serves 4. Approximate nutrition information per serving: Calories 200; protein 8g; fat 3g; carbohydrates 33g; sodium 960 mg.

Green Pasta

■■

PASTA VERDE

Use green pasta when a green color would be attractive.

1 tablespoon, about 3 ounces,
   cooked fresh spinach leaves
   (about 7 ounces raw)
⅛ teaspoon salt

1½ cups all-purpose flour
1 large egg at room temperature
1 teaspoon oil

1. Drain cooked spinach thoroughly and squeeze it dry, using paper towels if necessary.

2. Place the spinach in work bowl of a food processor and mince it fine. Remove and set aside.

3. Rinse and wipe the bowl, add salt and flour and turn the motor on and off once.

4. Add the egg to the spinach and mix with a fork. Turn on the machine and add the egg-spinach mixture through the feed tube and process 10 to 15 seconds until the texture resembles coarse meal. Add oil and run the motor in bursts until a ball of dough forms. (It is best to omit water from the pasta recipe when spinach is used.) Remove and proceed as above.

Serves 4. Approximate nutrition information per serving: Calories 190; protein 8g; fat 2g; carbohydrates 35g; sodium 1120 mg.

Linguine with Clams and Fresh Tomatoes

This dish was prepared by Jean Jacques Paimblanc during a weekend at the Long Island summer home of Pierre Franey when native tomatoes, fresh basil, and freshly dug clams were available.

The unique aspect of this dish is that the linguine are only partly cooked in water and then finish cooking in clam juice, to absorb the flavor of the clams.

24 cherrystone clams
4 tablespoons olive oil
2 tablespoons minced garlic
4 cups diced fresh tomatoes
⅛ teaspoon hot pepper flakes, or more to taste
freshly ground black pepper to taste

1 pound packaged linguine (number 8)
⅓ cup butter
18 fresh basil leaves
salt to taste
grated parmesan cheese, optional

1. Shuck clams and reserve juice. Chop clams into ½-inch pieces.
2. Heat oil in a saucepan, add garlic, tomatoes, red pepper flakes, and black pepper. Cook 5 to 10 minutes, or longer if tomatoes have a lot of liquid.
3. Add chopped clams, bring to a simmer, and turn off heat.
4. Meanwhile, bring 2 quarts salted water to a boil.
5. Add linguine to water and cook for 6 minutes. Drain, but save 1 cup of cooking water.
6. Bring reserved clam juice to a boil and add partly cooked linguine. Cook until *al dente,* 2 to 6 minutes longer, depending on pasta. All or almost all of the liquid should be absorbed by the pasta.
7. Add the clams and tomatoes and blend. Add the butter and basil leaves. If the mixture seems too dry, add part or all of the reserved cup of pasta cooking water. Correct the seasoning. Serve on a hot platter. Pass the grated cheese.

Serves 4. Approximate nutrition information per serving: Calories 1110; protein 30g; fat 62g; carbohydrates 102g; sodium 310 mg.

Tortellini with Smoked Salmon and Vodka

You can either make or buy the tortellini for this recipe. If you are buying them, purchase the dried or fresh cheese-filled kind, not those with pork, chicken, or veal. If you make your own, they should be made before you begin the sauce. They can be cooked and held in cold water in the refrigerator for several hours.

You do not have to buy prime slices of salmon as you would for serving the salmon sliced as an hors d'oeuvre. You can save money by purchasing trimmings of smoked salmon or lox.

¼ pound smoked salmon or lox trimmings	1 cup vodka
6-ounce box tortellini (or use recipe below)	freshly ground black pepper
½ tablespoon butter	2 cups heavy cream
	freshly grated parmesan cheese

1. If using commercial tortellini, cook them in salted water for half the time recommended in the package directions. They should be cooked very firm *al dente*. (If using homemade tortellini, follow the directions below.) Drain the cooked tortellini and reserve in cold water.

2. Cut salmon into pieces about ½-inch wide and 1 to 2 inches long. Trim away any dark meat. Use these trmmings plus as much more as needed to obtain 1 tablespoon, finely minced, with which to begin sauce.

3. Melt ½ tablespoon butter over low heat in a large, heavy saucepan. Add the finely minced tablespoon of smoked salmon and a few grinds of black pepper and allow to stew for a minute or two. Add vodka, reserving 1 tablespoon to finish sauce.

4. Raise heat to medium-high and reduce vodka to about 2 tablespoons. The salmon may begin to disintegrate.

5. Add 2 cups cream and reduce to about half over medium-high heat. The sauce should be thick enough to coat a spoon.

6. Drain tortellini well (water will thin the sauce too much) and add to the sauce. Cook over medium-low heat until the tortellini are tender. Add smoked salmon pieces and the reserved tablespoon of vodka. Cook for 1 minute more to heat the salmon through. Correct the seasoning; the sauce may need salt.

7. Serve in soup bowls, pass freshly grated parmesan cheese and a pepper mill.

Making Tortellini

Tortellini are nothing more than tiny filled turnovers of pasta dough with the edges pulled together like the ends of a kerchief.

Follow the recipe for making egg pasta using 1½ cups of flour and 2 eggs.

Roll out the dough in strips 12 to 18 inches long, about 3 inches wide, and with the thickness of a dime. Tortellini are usually made from circles of dough 1½ to 2 inches in diameter, but if you have never made them before, it is wiser to make them larger until you get the knack. After all, you are not trying to prove you are a professional tortellini maker; you merely want to make something that will taste good.

Use a cookie cutter or some other method to make rounds of dough 2 to 3 inches in diameter. Put about ¾-teaspoon of filling just below the center of each round, moisten the edges, and fold the dough over to form a half-moon. Wrap the half-moon around your finger, or use a dowel of some kind, and press the ends together.

Tortellini Filling

1 to 2 ounces finely minced smoked salmon or lox trimmings
1 teaspoon butter
1 teaspoon minced shallot or onion
1 tablespoon minced fresh parsley

8 ounces ricotta cheese
¼ cup freshly grated parmesan cheese
freshly ground black pepper
pinch freshly grated nutmeg
1 whole egg, beaten lightly with fork

1. Melt butter in a small skillet, add shallot or onion, and saute until soft, but not browned. Allow to cool.

2. In a bowl, mix shallot or onion with parsley, add salmon or lox and ricotta, and mix well with a wooden spoon. Add parmesan cheese, 2 or 3 turns pepper, and a pinch of nutmeg, and blend again. Correct the seasoning. Add the beaten egg and mix.

3. Make and fill tortellini according to directions above.

4. Cook for 3 minutes in salted water. Drain well and spoon into the hot vodka-cream sauce to continue cooking for a further 4 to 5 minutes so that they will absorb additional flavor from the sauce. Test for doneness.

Serves 4. Approximate nutrition information per serving: Calories 830; protein 25g; fat 63g; carbohydrates 40g; sodium 1820 mg.

Ravioli Dough

Filled pastas such as ravioli, cappelletti, and tortellini are sometimes intimidating to amateur cooks. Yet the procedure requires no more dexterity or kitchen acumen than sealing a filling within pie crusts. One or two experiences are all that is needed to get the hang of it.

4½ cups all-purpose flour	1 tablespoon water or 1
6 large eggs at room temperature	teaspoon oil
½ teaspoon salt	

1. In the work bowl of a food processor, proceed as in making egg pasta until you have a large ball of dough. Divide it into 4 sections, flour them, and keep 3 pieces covered with a kitchen towel while you roll one section.

2. If using a machine, roll through widest setting of rollers 4 or 5 times and then keep reducing thickness of pasta until you get to the thinnest setting on your machine and you have strips at least 2 inches wide and 12 to 18 inches long. Do the same with the remaining 3 pieces of dough.

3. If rolling out the dough with a rolling pin, roll it a shade thicker than a dime. Cut the strips 2 inches wide and 12 to 18 inches long.

4. It is better to make lengths of dough shorter, as they are easier to work with, but too many short lengths might take too long for you to fill and seal; the dough might become too stiff before you have finished.

5. Lay out one strip in front of you on a flat surface. Since your ravioli are to be about 2 inches square, place about 1 teaspoon of filling every 2 inches, centered, along the strip. Moisten the edges around each teaspoon of filling with water on a pastry brush. Cover with another strip of dough of the same width and length and press the dough firmly together between and around the fillings.

6. Trim the edges of the strip square with a zig-zag pastry wheel and cut between each ravioli. Seal the edges of each individual ravioli with the tines of a fork or pastry crimper.

7. Alternately, some cooks find it easier and quicker to cut their strips of dough 4 inches wide and 12 to 18 inches long. These strips are creased in half along their length and the filling is placed every 2 inches on one side of the crease. The dough is then moistened and the other half is folded over the filling and pressed firmly together with the bottom dough. Cutting and crimping then proceeds as in the first case. Use whichever method works best for you.

8. Place ravioli in one layer onto a floured baking sheet or sheets so

that they don't touch. It will help them to dry for 15 minutes or so while you boil the water for cooking. If you are going to cook them immediately, you do not have to refrigerate them. Otherwise, refrigerate the filled ravioli up to 6 hours. They also can be frozen, but they should be used in a day or two.

9. Bring 6 quarts of water to a rolling boil. Add 1 tablespoon salt to water just before adding ravioli. Allow water to return to a boil, but don't let it boil furiously. The ravioli will not stick together if you use sufficient water, but you may add a half-teaspoon or so of cooking oil as a precaution. Cook ravioli 3 or 4 minutes after they have risen to the surface. Drain thoroughly.

10. You also can cook the ravioli a day ahead. To keep them for 24 hours: Cook the ravioli just until they rise. Drain and cool. Reserve, covered with a wet towel, in the refrigerator. Don't crowd them or they might stick together. Reheat in simmering salted water.

Note: If the filling is very moist, ravioli and other filled pastas must be cooked soon after they are filled, or the dough will become soggy. Ricotta, a common filling, is likely to vary from very moist to very dry. If it seems too wet, place it in a strainer lined with a double thickness of cheesecloth to drain away some of the liquid. You can do the same with any filling that seems too moist before you fill the pasta.

This recipe makes 24 to 30 ravioli, depending on the size.

Serves 4. Approximate nutrition information per serving: Calories 592; protein 24g; fat 10g; carbohydrates 99g; sodium 1155 mg.

Shrimp Ravioli

1 recipe for ravioli

5 ounces raw shrimp, minced
10 ounces fresh spinach
1 tablespoon butter

1 teaspoon minced fresh ginger
1 garlic clove, mashed
salt and pepper to taste
Beurre Blanc Vert (page 66)

1. Thoroughly wash the spinach. Remove stems. Blot the leaves dry with paper towels, and mince until they are almost a puree.

2. Saute the minced spinach in butter until the moisture is nearly evaporated. Add ginger and garlic and continue to cook until the spinach is dry.

3. In a mixing bowl, add shrimp to the cooked spinach and toss. Season to taste.

4. Fill and seal the ravioli as described above, using about 1 teaspoon of filling in each.

5. Cook the ravioli as described on pages 412 — 413. Make Beurre Blanc Vert, and serve.

Serves 4. Approximate nutrition information per serving without sauce: Calories 682; protein 34g; fat 13g; carbohydrates 103g; sodium 1455 mg.

Clam Ravioli

1 recipe for ravioli

FILLING:
1 cup chopped raw clams
2 tablespoons soft butter
¼ cup minced onion
1 tablespoon finely minced salt
    pork or prosciutto
salt and pepper to taste
1 teaspoon minced fresh parsley
pinch of dried thyme

SAUCE:
1 cup clam juice
1 clove garlic, mashed
1 tablespoon minced fresh
    parsley
1 tablespoon butter

1 tablespoon grated parmesan
    cheese

1. Make dough for ravioli.

2. Make filling: If using salt pork, first render it with 1 tablespoon butter. Otherwise, saute onion with 1 tablespoon butter until transparent, but not colored. Add clams, prosciutto, salt, pepper, parsley, and thyme. Toss for a minute over medium heat. Remove from heat and allow to cool.

3. Drain liquid, if any, and reserve for sauce. Add the remaining 1 tablespoon soft butter and incorporate. The butter should act as a binder. Correct the seasoning.

4. Fill and seal ravioli, using about 1 teaspoon of mixture in each. Cook as described on pages 412 — 413, just until ravioli rise to the top of the cooking water. Allow ravioli to rest while you make the sauce.

5. Make sauce: Heat clam juice together with any liquid drained when making the filling. Add garlic and parsley. Allow the sauce to reduce by about ¼ — you should have ¾ cup remaining. Add 1 tablespoon butter and blend. Correct the seasoning.

6. Preheat oven to 350 degrees. Place 2 tablespoons of sauce in individual ovenproof casseroles. Or use one large ovenproof baking dish and pour all but 4 tablespoons of sauce on the bottom. Add ravioli and pour the rest of the sauce on top. Sprinkle with parmesan cheese. Bake 10 minutes; shake once or twice while cooking to keep ravioli moist. Serve immediately.

Serves 4. Approximate nutrition information per serving: Calories 727; protein 31g; fat 19g; carbohydrates 105g; sodium 1545 mg.

Scallop Ravioli

1 recipe for ravioli

FILLING:
8 ounces scallops; 1 cup in small
    dice
1 tablespoon butter, plus 1
    teaspoon
1 cup mushrooms in small dice
¼ cup heavy cream
1 tablespoon minced shallots

SAUCE:
clam juice or fish stock (see White
    Wine Fumet, page 30)
1 tablespoon minced shallots
¼ cup dry white wine
4 tablespoons butter

1. Saute mushrooms in 1 teaspoon butter until all moisture is evaporated. Add cream and reduce it until it is as thick as mayonnaise.

2. Saute shallots in 1 tablespoon butter until they are soft, without having changed color. Add scallops and cook firm, about 2 minutes. Drain pan juices and reserve.

3. Mix scallops with mushroom-cream mixture. Correct the seasoning. Fill ravioli, using about 1 teaspoon of filling. Cook the ravioli in boiling, salted water. Drain and keep warm.

4. Make sauce: Add white wine and 1 tablespoon shallots to the reserved pan juices. Add fish stock or clam juice to make ¾ cup. Reduce by half or until it is thick enough to coat a spoon.

5. Whip in the 4 tablespoons butter, a small piece at a time, making sure each piece is incorporated before adding another. Correct the seasoning. Serve ravioli napped with sauce.

Approximate nutrition information per serving: Calories 855; protein 37g; fat 31g; carbohydrates 102g; sodium 1500 mg.

Crabmeat Ravioli

You may substitute our Tomato Sauce for Seafood Ravioli (page 60) for the sauce given here.

1 recipe for ravioli

FILLING:
4 ounces crabmeat
1 tablespoon butter
1 tablespoon minced onion
3 tablespoons minced celery
2 tablespoons minced sweet red
   pepper
¼ cup chopped walnuts
salt and pepper

SAUCE:
¾ cup tomato concassée (see
   page 59)
½ cup tomato juice or liquid
   from canned tomatoes
½ cup fish stock or clam juice
   (see White Wine Fumet, page
   30)

2 tablespoons freshly grated
   parmesan cheese

1. Saute onion, celery, and red pepper in 1 tablespoon butter until the onion is transparent but not colored. Remove from heat. Add walnuts, and salt and pepper to taste. Then add crabmeat and toss gently.

2. Fill ravioli with mixture and cook in boiling, salted water, just until they rise to the top of the cooking water.

3. Preheat oven to 350 degrees. Make sauce: Thin the ¾ cup of tomato concassée with tomato juice or liquid from canned tomatoes and fish stock; bring to a boil, and cook 2 or 3 minutes. Correct the seasoning. Put half of the sauce on the bottom of a large casserole. Set the drained ravioli into the casserole and cover with the remaining sauce. Sprinkle the top with parmesan cheese.

4. Bake 15 minutes, serve hot.

Serves 4. Approximate nutrition information per serving without sauce: Calories 690; protein 48g; fat 31g; carbohydrates 156g; sodium 2340 mg.

Smoked Trout Ravioli

1 recipe for ravioli

FILLING:
1 smoked trout
1 tablespoon minced fresh
    parsley
salt and pepper to taste
1 tablespoon soft butter
1 hardboiled egg, peeled and
    chopped

SAUCE:
1 cup heavy cream
salt and pepper to taste
pinch ground nutmeg
1 teaspoon horseradish

1. Skin trout and flake the flesh from the bone, being careful to remove all small bones. Crumble into small pieces.

2. Combine trout flesh with parsley, salt, and pepper, and mix well. Work in soft butter and chopped egg to bind the mixture. Correct the seasoning.

3. Use about 1 teaspoon of the mixture to fill each ravioli. Seal, and cook in boiling, salted water, just until they rise to the top of the water.

4. Make sauce: Place all the ingredients into a wide saucepan and reduce to about ¾ cup, until it is thick and coats a spoon heavily. Correct the seasoning.

5. Preheat oven to 350 degrees. Place half of the sauce on the bottom of a large casserole — or divide among individual casseroles — lay in ravioli, cover with remaining sauce, and bake 15 minutes.

Serves 4. Approximate nutrition information per serving: Calories 967; protein 40g; fat 43g; carbohydrates 102g; sodium 3165 mg.

Shrimp and Sun-dried Tomatoes with Pasta

½ pound small shrimp
1 small head broccoli
1 tablespoon chopped onion
1 clove garlic, minced
1 cup sun-dried tomatoes
about 4 tablespoons olive oil

1 cup fish stock, shrimp cooking
   water, or bottled clam juice
salt and pepper to taste
½ pound pasta shells,
   approximate size of shrimp
   and broccoli

1. Cook shrimp in boiling water only until they change color. Drain, peel and reserve. Reserve the cooking water, if desired, for use in step 6.

2. Trim broccoli into flowerettes approximately the same size as pasta shells. Blanch until they are still quite firm — about half their cooking time. Drain and reserve.

3. Cook shells for half the recommended time on package. Drain and hold in cold water. Drain well before step 6.

4. Drain the oil from the sun-dried tomatoes. Measure the oil and add enough olive oil to make 8 tablespoons. In a 12-inch skillet, saute onion in the oil until soft and transparent but not picking up color. Add garlic and saute 2 minutes more.

5. Cut the tomatoes into ½-inch dice. Put them into a small skillet and saute for about 5 minutes over very low heat in the oil that clings to them. Add them to the garlic and onion, then add the broccoli and toss until heated through, about 3 minutes.

6. Meanwhile, bring fish stock, clam juice, or shrimp cooking water to a boil in a large saucepan. Add the pasta and cook until almost done. Add tomatoes and broccoli, season to taste with salt and pepper, and allow to simmer for 3 minutes.

7. Add shrimp and toss everything to heat. The dish is ready when the pasta is cooked *al dente*. Serve immediately.

Serves 4. Approximate nutrition information per serving: Calories 690; protein 32g; fat 39g; carbohydrates 53g; sodium 690 mg.

Lasagne di Magro

FROM ROMAGNOLI'S TABLE, BOSTON

The Romagnolis, Margaret and Franco, are as well known outside of Boston as they are within the city that is home to their restaurant. Romagnoli's Table has been one of the most popular eating places in Faneuil Hall Marketplace since it opened. The couple adapted the recipes and ideas of their well-received educational television show to a commercial enterprise — and made it work. Romagnoli's Table features the regional foods of Italy, and on a given day one is likely to find on the menu the elegance of Milan, the richness of Bologna, the exuberance of Rome, and the spiciness of Naples.

The following dish is from the region of the Italian Riviera, where a seafood lasagna would provide a hearty, though still light, Lenten dish.

Lasagne di magro is a lasagna using fish, white sauce, and mushrooms instead of the more common meat sauce and ricotta or, as is done in much of Italy, meat sauce and white sauce. This recipe is the great-great-grandchild of a Ligurian Lenten recipe. In adapting it for special restaurant use, they have used North Atlantic fish most of the time. When fresh salmon is available, it is a must.

14 ounces boned salmon (save trimmings)
16 ounces cod fillet (save trimmings)
8 ounces peeled raw shrimp

FISH STOCK:
1 celery stalk with leaves
1 large carrot
1 small onion
2 basil leaves
10 parsley stems
¼ cup dry white wine or 2 tablespoons white wine vinegar
6 cups water
1½ teaspoons salt
shrimp peels, fish trimmings (head, tails, and bones)

BESCIAMELLA:
8 tablespoons butter
12 tablespoons unbleached all-purpose flour
½ teaspoon freshly grated nutmeg
½ teaspoon ground white pepper
2 tablespoons chopped flatleaf parsley
1 quart hot fish stock
7 tablespoons butter
2 anchovies
12 ounces sliced mushrooms
⅛ teaspoon white pepper

12 sheets (8 x 6 inches) fresh green (spinach) pasta

½ cup fresh breadcrumbs
¼ cup grated parmesan cheese

1. Make stock: Place all ingredients in a large saucepan or stainless steel stockpot and bring to a boil. Lower heat and simmer about 1½ hours.

2. Strain broth through double- or triple-layered cheesecloth and reserve for poaching fish and making besciamella.

3. Poach each of the three kinds of seafood separately in the fish stock — about 1 minute each just to firm. Remove to a platter. The fish should be almost ready to flake but not cooked through. The shrimp should have just turned color. Measure 1 quart of the fish stock.

4. Make besciamella: Melt the butter in a saucepan. Stir in the flour and stir and cook until smooth. Continue cooking and stirring over medium heat, add the nutmeg and pepper, and then pour in the reserved hot fish stock in a steady stream. Cook and stir for 3 minutes longer. Remove from heat, stir in the parsley, and taste for salt as well as to make sure that the flour has cooked thoroughly. (If not, return to medium heat for a minute or two.) Place plastic wrap over the surface and allow to cool.

5. In a small saucepan, melt 3 tablespoons butter, stir in the anchovies and add the mushrooms. Cook 3 minutes or until the anchovies have more or less dissolved and the mushrooms have given up their moisture. Season with white pepper to taste and set aside.

6. Half-cook the pasta sheets and allow to drain on the side of a colander or on clean kitchen towels.

7. Using 2 tablespoons butter, coat a lasagne pan (approximately 9 x 13 x 3 inches) and dust it with breadcrumbs. Reserve excess breadcrumbs.

8. Place 4 pasta sheets in a single layer to cover the pan bottom, meeting at the center and coming up a bit at each end.

9. Cover this layer of pasta with morsels of cod interspersed with the shrimp.

10. Dot the cod/shrimp with besciamella and cover with 2 sheets of pasta.

11. Spread about half the mushrooms over the pasta, dot with besciamella, and cover with 2 more sheets of pasta.

12. Make a layer of salmon, flaked into ½-inch bits, and cover with dabs of besciamella, and 2 sheets of pasta.

13. Make a layer of the remaining cod, salmon, and shrimp. Dot with besciamella and cover with the last of the pasta sheets. Tuck in the ends and sides of the pasta with the point of a knife, leaving a sort of smooth, flat look.

14. Make a topping of the remaining mushrooms and put the last of the besciamella over this, dotting it around. Sprinkle with the remaining breadcrumbs.

15. Melt the remaining 2 tablespoons butter and dribble it back and

forth over the breadcrumbs. Sprinkle with the parmesan cheese. Refrigerate for several hours, if you wish.

16. Bake at 350 degrees for 1½ hours. Remove from heat and let rest about 15 minutes before serving. Cut into squares and serve on warmed dinner plates.

Serves 8 to 10. Approximate nutrition information per serving, based on 8 servings: Calories 825; protein 58g; fat 43g; carbohydrates 50g; sodium 840 mg.

Shrimp and Pasta Pesto

Shrimp, America's most popular seafood, is combined here with one of Italy's most popular pasta sauces, the basil-scented, unctuous green garlic sauce known as pesto.

1½ pounds peeled raw Maine shrimp, or other shrimp
1 recipe for Pesto Sauce (page 62)
¾-pound linguine or similar pasta

2 tablespoons butter
salt to taste
pinch of pepper
parmesan cheese

1. Make the pesto sauce.
2. Set 4 to 6 quarts of water to boil for pasta.
3. Saute shrimp in 2 tablespoons butter just until cooked, about 3 or 4 minutes, seasoning lightly with salt and pepper. Don't oversalt. Remove the shrimp from the heat.
4. Meanwhile, add 1 tablespoon salt to the rapidly boiling water. Add pasta, stir for a minute or two to prevent sticking, and cook to the *al dente* stage. Drain well.
5. While the pasta cooks, toss the warm shrimp in a large serving bowl with about 1 tablespoon of pesto. Add the drained pasta to the shrimp in the bowl, add 2 tablespoons more of pesto, and toss thoroughly.
6. Serve immediately, passing remaining pesto. Provide grated parmesan cheese, salt, and a pepper mill at the table.

Serves 4. Approximate nutrition information per serving: Calories 815; protein 65g; fat 18g; carbohydrates 99g; sodium 1210 mg.

Squid with Pasta

■■

4 medium squid
1½ cup sliced fresh mushrooms
2 tablespoons oil
1 large clove garlic, minced
2 cups fresh tomatoes, peeled,
    seeded, diced; or 2 cups
    canned whole Italian plum
    tomatoes, mashed
salt and pepper to taste
8 whole fresh basil leaves, or 1
    tablespoon dried

1 tablespoon minced fresh
    parsley
⅛ teaspoon ground red pepper
    flakes
¼ cup chopped black olives
1 pound fettucini or other egg
    noodles
1 tablespoon butter

1. Separate tentacles and wings from squid bodies and cut up. Cut bodies in rings about ¼-inch thick. You should have 1½ cups of squid. (See pages 372 — 375 for general information on squid.)

2. Saute mushrooms lightly in 1 tablespoon oil. Add garlic and tomatoes, salt, pepper, basil, parsley, and ground red pepper flakes, and stew 5 minutes. Add olives.

3. Meanwhile, saute squid about 4 minutes in a separate skillet in 1 tablespoon oil over medium-high heat. Don't overcook; the pieces should barely pick up color.

4. Add squid to tomatoes and cook 1 minute longer.

5. At the same time, cook pasta *al dente* in 4 to 6 quarts salted water. Drain and set in a warmed serving bowl with 1 tablespoon butter. Toss. Add squid sauce, toss, taste, correct seasoning, and serve.

Serves 4. Approximate nutrition information per serving: Calories 595; protein 25g; fat 13g; carbohydrates 101g; sodium 1170 mg (based on canned tomatoes).

Seafood in Angel Hair Nests

This recipe is an adaptation of two recipes created by chef Michael Fitouzzi when he was at the Palace Restaurant in Manhattan. At that time, the restaurant claimed to be the most expensive restaurant in the world. While the dish uses three high-priced seafood items, their quantities are not great. The dish would be elegant for a dinner party, without being too demanding of time or cooking technique.

The dish is capable of infinite expansion, but don't double the sauce ingredients. Add 1 cup cream and 1 tablespoon finishing butter for each doubling of seafood. The seasonings may need some adjustments, but these can be made at the last minute.

If you are making the recipe for more than 4, don't use the bird's nest. Handling more than 4 hot, cooked bird's nests can be awkward. Set straight angel hair pasta in a circular fashion on each serving plate. You may use the lobster tomalley (liver) in this dish — it will give the dish a more intense lobster flavor — but we found the greenish-gray cast unattractive and its flavor too assertive. So, reserve it for another use, or spread it on plain crackers and use as an hors d'oeuvre.

You may substitute white turnip for the celery if you like; its flavor will be more neutral.

1 chicken lobster (preferably a female with coral)	1 cup dry white wine
½ pound small shrimp (if large cut in half, crosswise)	2 cups heavy cream
	½ teaspoon salt
½ pound sea scallops, cut in half or quarters	pinch of white pepper
	½ pound of homemade or commercial angel hair pasta, wound in bird's nest fashion (4 nests, 3 to 4 inches across)
1½ tablespoons butter	
2 tablespoons water	
⅓ cup julienned leeks	
⅓ cup julienned carrots	1 tablespoon salt for pasta cooking water
⅓ cup julienned celery	¼ cup soft butter
1 tablespoon minced leek, white part only	

1. At least 4 hours ahead of time, or the night before, boil the lobster. Cook about 10 minutes; don't overcook. Cool. Cook shrimp, if they are not already cooked. Cool, peel, and cut in half, if necessary. Reserve the whole unshelled lobster and shrimp in the refrigerator in plastic wrap, if storing overnight.

2. At least 2 hours before serving, remove the lobster meat from the

shell. Cut it into sizes similar to the scallops. If the lobster has coral or roe, remove it, and chop into peppercorn-sized pieces. Reserve it and the lobster meat in 2 separate bowls.

3. In 1 tablespoon butter and 2 tablespoons water, sweat the julienned leeks, carrots, and celery, covered, until cooked, but still firm.

4. In a 4- to 6-quart, heavy, wide, thick-bottomed saucepan, melt ½ tablespoon butter over low heat. Add the minced leek and cook for a minute or so to soften. Add the white wine and reduce until only about 2 tablespoons of liquid remain — about 10 minutes cooking time over medium heat. Add cream, salt, and pepper and reduce by half, which might take as long as 15 minutes.

5. As the cream reduces, boil about 4 quarts salted water for cooking the pasta. A small, deep roasting pan is best, for the bird's nests will expand both in width and height. You will want the water to cover them.

6. Timing is critical in cooking the pasta — it should be ready about 1 minute before the seafood and sauce are. You don't want the seafood to overcook, or the pasta to cool, dry, and stick together. Fresh homemade angel hair pasta can cook in 20 seconds; dried commercial pasta will take about 10 minutes (follow package directions). Test it as it cooks.

7. When the water is rapidly boiling, add 1 tablespoon salt. Place the bird's nests gently into the water and cook *al dente*. Make sure that the pasta remains totally submerged as it expands. Don't overcook, as the pasta will continue to cook in the seafood and sauce.

8. When the cream is reduced by half and is thick enough to heavily coat a spoon, add scallops, lobster, and shrimp and cook 2 minutes. Add the cooked julienned vegetables, bring the mixture to a boil, remove the pot from the heat, and add ¼ cup soft butter, a bit at a time, stirring to incorporate. Correct the seasoning.

9. Meanwhile, remove the bird's nests from the cooking water with a flat skimmer or large slotted spoon. Drain them very well — water will thin the sauce — and place one in the center of each of 4 heated serving plates.

10. Ladle the seafood, vegetables, and sauce onto the bird's nests, making certain everyone receives some of each kind of seafood and vegetable. Sprinkle the chopped lobster coral on each dish and serve immediately.

Serves 6. Approximate nutrition information per serving: Calories 980; protein 43g; fat 65g; carbohydrates 53g; sodium 1530 mg.

Spaghetti with Clams and Butter

Linguine with clam sauce has become a ubiquitous American dish — at least in many urban centers. For every admirer, there are an equal number whose palates rebel at the garlic-ladened sauce, often intensified by the addition of anchovies. If you are among the latter, try this gentle version of clam sauce with spaghetti.

1 pint minced clams with their liquor
7 tablespoons butter
1½ tablespoons minced fresh parsley

¾ to 1 pound linguine
freshly ground black pepper

1. Melt 6 tablespoons butter in a saucepan.

2. Add clams and their liquid and cook over low heat for 4 or 5 minutes. You don't want to cook the clams, merely heat them through and blend their flavor with that of the butter.

3. Cook pasta *al dente* in 4 to 6 quarts salted water, and drain. Put it back in the pot and toss with the remaining tablespoon butter. Toss again with clam mixture and place in a warmed serving bowl.

4. Serve and pass the pepper mill.

Serves 4. Approximate nutrition information per serving: Calories 665; protein 27g; fat 20g; carbohydrates 93g; sodium 1250 mg.

Periwinkles with Pasta

You can use this sauce with any form of pasta, but the shells we suggest are likely to capture some periwinkles and sauce within them, making eating not only easier but more enjoyable. Refer to pages 352 and 353 for general information about periwinkles.

½ pound periwinkles in shell
2 tablespoons butter
½ cup celery, diced
     approximately size of
     periwinkle meat
1 cup mushrooms, diced like
     celery
½ cup pecans or walnuts,
     chopped to size of celery

¼ cup sherry, a medium-dry
     amontillado, or medium-dry
     madeira or dry marsala
1 cup heavy cream
salt
1 pound pasta shells about size
     of periwinkle meats
1 tablespoon butter
freshly grated parmesan cheese

1. Wash periwinkles well. Boil 7 minutes, barely covered with water seasoned with ½ tablespoon salt, and stir vigorously to loosen the operculum over the periwinkles' opening. Drain.

2. With a small, sharply pointed knife, toothpick, or hat pin, remove the meats from the shells over a bowl to catch the juices. Reserve meats together with any juices. (Refrigerate, if you wish, until you're ready to finish cooking.)

3. Saute celery in 1 tablespoon butter until nearly soft; add mushrooms and saute for 3 minutes, tossing. Add chopped nuts, toss, then add wine and juices from periwinkles.

4. Cook for another minute, add cream and bring to a boil. Cook just long enough to thicken the cream. Turn off the heat, cover and keep warm.

5. Cook pasta *al dente* in 4 to 6 quarts of salted water. Drain. Place ½ tablespoon butter in the bottom of the pot the pasta was cooked in. Return the pasta to the pot, add remaining butter, and toss.

6. Reheat the sauce, add periwinkles, and cook 30 seconds. Place the pasta shells in serving bowl, pour on the sauce, and toss well.

7. Serve and pass grated parmesan cheese.

Serves 4. Approximate nutrition information per serving: Calories 820; protein 20g; fat 41g; carbohydrates 93g; sodium 860 mg.

Pierre Franey's Spaghetti and Clams Cooked in Foil

Pierre Franey devised this recipe for his "60-Minute Gourmet" column in the New York Times *two years ago. We give it here for 2 persons, as he originally printed it. Since it is excellent for a crowd, we also give a variation suitable for 20 to 24 persons.*

36 little neck clams, the smaller the better
1 cup tomato and anchovy sauce below

salt to taste if desired
½ pound spaghetti
freshly grated parmesan cheese (optional)

1.   Prepare tomato and anchovy sauce. Fifteen minutes before it is done, preheat the oven to 500 degrees. Bring water to boil with salt to taste for cooking spaghetti.

2.   Open clams and reserve their liquid. There should be about 1 cup of clam juice and slightly less than ¾ cup of clams. If the clams are large, chop them. Discard shells.

3.   Line a baking dish with a double layer of wide, heavy-duty aluminum foil, leaving the ends free.

4.   Drop spaghetti into boiling water and cook exactly 5 minutes. Drain immediately.

5.   Meanwhile, bring clam broth to boil.

6.   Place spaghetti onto the center of the foil. Add the simmering tomato sauce and clam juice and pour the clams on top. Seal foil tightly all around. Place the dish in the oven and bake exactly 10 minutes.

7.   Carefully open the package and transfer its contents to a hot platter or hot soup bowls. Serve with parmesan cheese on the side if desired.

Tomato and Anchovy Sauce

4 cups canned imported tomatoes with liquid
¼ cup olive oil
1 tablespoon finely minced garlic
1 teaspoon dried, crushed oregano

½ teaspoon dried hot red pepper flakes
⅓ cup finely minced parsley
2 teaspoons anchovy paste
2 tablespoons capers
1 tablespoon cognac

1. Put tomatoes in a saucepan and cook down until they are reduced to 2 cups.

2. Heat oil in a heavy saucepan and add garlic. Cook briefly without browning. Add reduced tomatoes, oregano, pepper flakes, parsley, anchovy paste, and capers, stirring often from bottom. Stir in cognac.

3. The recipe yields about 2 cups. Leftover sauce will keep well for a week or longer if it is kept tightly sealed in the refrigerator. It also can be frozen.

Serves 2. Approximate nutrition information per serving: Calories 699; protein 32g; fat 20g; carbohydrates 106g; sodium 1150 mg.

Adaptation for a crowd

The same recipe, enough for 20 to 24 people, follows. In the sauce, canned anchovies were substituted for the anchovy paste; ¼ cup red wine was added for flavor and tomato paste was added for body. A bit of minced onion was added and the oregano omitted. The clams were chopped fresh surf clams with their liquor.

The procedure for preparing the dish is basically the same with a couple of adjustments. You should use a separate pot for each 2 to 2½ pounds spaghetti. The roasting pan in which you place the foil must be large — the larger the better. The aim is to get the sauce to cover the spaghetti fairly evenly and the pasta should not pack down during the short cooking time. The sauce should be hot when added to this large a quantity of spaghetti.

The 3 cups of clam juice were reduced to about 2 cups. If there is not that much liquor from your chopped clams, add bottled clam juice to make the 3 cups.

The sauce preparation is somewhat different. The 12 cups of tomatoes were not reduced by half, but rather, to about 9 cups.

8 cups chopped clams
6 pounds spaghetti
3 cups clam juice, reduced to
    2 cups

SAUCE:
12 cups canned imported
    tomatoes with liquid,
    reduced to 9 cups
¼ cup olive oil
2 teaspoons dried hot red pepper

3 tablespoons minced garlic
2 cans flat fillets of anchovies,
    drained
½ small minced onion, about 2
    tablespoons
3 tablespoons tomato paste
¼ cup red wine
3 tablespoons capers packed in
    vinegar, drained
⅔ cup minced fresh parsley

1. Refer to the recipe above for the preparation of the dish.

2. Heat oil in large saucepan, add red hot pepper, stir a moment, then add garlic, and stir and cook to soften. Add anchovies and cook until they have nearly disintegrated. Add onion and cook until soft; the anchovies should have fully disintegrated at this point

3. Add tomato paste and stir with a wooden spoon to dissolve; add wine and simmer for a minute. Add capers along with tomatoes and parsley. Bring to a boil and let cook for about 30 minutes.

Serves 20 - 24. Approximate nutrition information per serving: Calories 610; protein 30g; fat 5g; carbohydrates 110g; sodium 560 mg.

Pasta with Fish and Artichokes

Normally artichoke pieces are simmered in water before being used in recipes. This recipe calls for raw artichoke bottoms to be cut into strips and then sauteed, a procedure that offers texture contrast and different flavor.

20 ounces sole fillet(s)	¼ cup milk
4 large raw artichokes	flour for dusting
4 tablespoons butter	¼ cup oil
salt and pepper	2 tablespoons lemon juice
1¼ cups sliced fresh mushrooms	1 tablespoon minced fresh
4 ounces prosciutto or ham,	parsley
sliced thinly and then into	¾-to-1 pound fettucini
strips	

1. Cut the fish into ⅜-inch strips about 3 inches long.

2. Cut off the stem and trim the leaves from the artichokes until you get to the soft innermost part. Remove the choke in the center, and cut the bottoms into strips of the same size as fish.

3. Melt 1 tablespoon butter in a skillet on low heat and saute the artichoke pieces until they are nearly cooked through, tender, but still firm. This should take 10 to 15 minutes; don't rush this step. Season them lightly with a pinch of salt and pepper.

4. When they are done, add sliced mushrooms, and saute, tossing, for 1

minute. Add prosciutto, toss just to combine, and reserve off the heat, covered.

5. Combine milk with salt and pepper to taste in a small bowl. Put flour into a flat dish. Dip the fish in the milk, drain, and dredge in the flour, patting it on so that it adheres well. Shake to remove the excess.

6. Heat ¼ cup oil in a skillet that is large enough to fit all the fish in one layer. When the oil is hot, add the fish and fry it quickly until it is nicely browned on both sides. Remove and set aside for a moment while you drain the skillet.

7. Heat 1 tablespoon butter in the skillet and add the combined artichokes, ham, and mushrooms, and fish. Add lemon juice, toss to warm, and correct the seasoning. Toss once more with parsley.

8. Meanwhile cook fettucini *al dente* in 4 to 6 quarts salted water. Drain and set into a warm bowl with 1 tablespoon butter in it. Top with another tablespoon of butter and toss again. Add the fish and artichoke mixture, toss it gently so that you don't mash the fish, and serve immediately.

Serves 4. Approximate nutrition information per serving: Calories 855; protein 49g; fat 26g; carbohydrates 104g; sodium 1320 mg.

Seafood Couscous

Couscous is the French term for a North African dish. There, a cereal grain, which is about the size of a peppercorn and similar to the hard durum grain — semolina — of the best pastas, is used. The grain is steamed over water or broth or a stew of lamb, chicken, or even meatballs. The grain is placed in a perforated steamer set over a special stew pan called a couscousier *in French.*

The use of fish instead of meat or fowl is within the traditions of the dish, since seafood is often used in coastal North Africa and other places to which couscous has emigrated.

Our recipe uses packaged instant couscous, which will prove to be more than adequate. You can, of course, make your own by your favorite method if you wish. The cinnamon called for in some recipes for couscous should not be used in this dish.

We used tilefish, monkfish, scallops, shrimp, and mussels — a total of about 5 or 6 ounces of seafood for each serving. You could use cod, haddock or other lean fish, but we recommend you do not use flounder, which is too fragile and will fall apart. Use all one kind or a mixture. You may use little neck or cherrystone clams, or lobster meat.

The traditional accompaniment with couscous is a fiery sauce, harissa, variously made with dried hot peppers, garlic, cumin, caraway seeds, coriander, and olive oil. We provide the recipe for a less complicated version.

You can substitute sliced yellow squash, cut-up acorn squash, or artichoke hearts for the zucchini.

You can use chick peas that have been soaked and cooked, although canned chick peas will do. One cup of raisins, plumped by soaking in water, can be substituted for the chick peas if you prefer; or use both.

8 sea or bay scallops
4 medium raw, peeled shrimp
4 to 8 mussels, scrubbed and de-bearded
16 ounces of fish

FOR COUSCOUS:
2 cups instant couscous
2 cups water
1 teaspoon salt
3 tablespoons butter

2 tablespoons olive oil
1 cup coarsely chopped onions
½ cup chopped sweet green pepper
½ cup chopped sweet red pepper
2 cups fresh tomatoes, peeled, seeded and diced, or canned imported plum, with liquid, diced

1 cup carrots, cut in walnut-sized pieces
1 cup turnips, similarly cut
1 cup coarsely chopped leeks
1 cup celery, in 2-inch pieces
1 quart of fish stock (see White Wine Fumet, page 30)
2 tablespoons minced garlic
½ teaspoon crushed hot red pepper flakes
½ teaspoon dried thyme
2 small bay leaves
1 cup thickly sliced zucchini
1 cup cooked or canned chick peas
salt and pepper to taste

harissa (optional)

1. Make couscous: Bring water to boil with salt and 1 tablespoon of butter. Add instant couscous all at once. Stir, cover, and allow to stand off the heat until water is absorbed. Add remaining 2 tablespoons butter, stir it into couscous, cover, and keep warm until ready to serve.

2. Saute onion in 2 tablespoons olive oil until soft but without color. Add peppers, saute a minute, add tomatoes, carrots, turnips, leeks, celery,

fish stock, garlic, red pepper flakes, thyme, and bay leaves, and simmer 30 minutes. Add zucchini or another soft vegetable, and cooked chick peas. Cook 5 minutes, add mussels. Cook 5 minutes, add fish, shrimp, and scallops, cook 5 minutes more. Correct the seasoning. Remove the bay leaves.

3. Use large soup bowls. Place a serving of couscous in one side of the bowl and ladle a portion of vegetables and fish into the other side. Moisten with pan juices, using it all.

4. A good substitute for the traditional harissa can be made by combining ½ cup of cooking liquid and 1 teaspoon crushed red pepper flakes, and simmer it for 10 minutes. You can use more or less pepper, according to taste. Pass, allowing diners to season their couscous according to their own taste.

Serves 4. Approximate nutrition information per serving: Calories 954; protein 88g; fat 39g; carbohydrates 66g; sodium 2490 mg.

Appendix

*"There are as good fish in the sea
as ever came out of it."*
— English proverb

Shark Brochettes

Seafood for the Table

━

While there are fishermen who are cooks and cooks who are fishermen, there are not many who have intimate first-hand knowledge of a wide range of fish and other seafood. (While it might be equally true that there are also very few who know whether their steak came from a Texas Longhorn or Black Angus steer, the knowledge in the case of beef appears less compelling. Many are put off from cooking or eating a fish simply because they are unfamiliar with it, but the same persons are likely to cook or eat a steak without a thought to its name.)

Before one can cook a fish, one must obtain it. And to get it you have to know the name. Aside from the nomenclature used by the scientists, and sport and commercial fishermen — not to mention wholesalers and retailers — there are regional or local names that obstinately hang in there to confuse and present an obstacle to your getting what you want. What is the poor cook to do when he looks for a monkfish and finds it may be called an angler fish, goosefish, lotte, devil fish, sea devil, or frog fish — or bellows fish and allmouth as well. And the cod is not a fish, but a whole family of fishes, of which the Atlantic cod is only one of about a dozen members that are important commercially. Yet just about everyone orders "cod" in a fish market, including ichthyologists, fishermen, and cooks.

There are 240 commercial species of fish and shellfish now marketed in the United States. Cod, haddock, salmon, ocean perch, halibut, flounder (soles), tuna, whiting, red snapper, and catfish (in the Southern states) represent more than eighty percent of the catch. In the following alphabetical listing of fish and shellfish, we are not trying to cover the entire range of seafood, merely those that are most often available at retail or might be brought home from a fishing excursion. They are found from the Florida Keys to the Gulf of Maine. Freshwater fish also are included. This list will help you know more about fish you may need to substitute for the fish we use in our recipes.

African Pompano: One of the pompanos that is occasionally found north of its tropical and semitropical Atlantic habitat. A fish with high oil content.

Albacore: A tuna.

Alewife: In the same family as the herring, but more closely related to the shad. An anadromous fish that lives most of its life in the sea and returns to freshwater to spawn.

Anchovy: Rarely seen fresh in this country, though abundantly available along Atlantic Coast. Canned flat and rolled fillets of anchovies are used primarily as a garnish and flavoring agent. The flesh is white in fresh anchovies; the more familiar red of the canned anchovy is the result of curing.

Angler Fish: A monkfish.

Atlantic Cod: The leader of the cod family.

Atlantic Salmon: The only native salmon of the Atlantic.

Bass: A name that covers many unrelated fish in American waters. What the French call *bar* or *loup* is a bass or sea bass, but on this coast the name can refer to groupers, striped bass, giant sea bass, and, most frequently, the black sea bass.

Bigmouth Buffalo: A member of the freshwater suckers and a native primarily of the lower Mississippi and its tributaries. It is medium oily with white flesh and delicate flavor. There are also black and smallmouth buffalo.

Black Bass: These freshwater fish are not related to either the black sea bass nor the striped bass and cannot be interchanged with them in recipes. They are not true bass, but members of the sunfish family. They are extremely lean with delicate texture and flavor. There are several members, including smallmouth, largemouth, red eye, and spotted.

Blackfish: See tautog.

Black Sea Bass: See chapter on sea bass.

Blowfish: See puffer.

Bluefin: A tuna.

Bluefish: See chapter on bluefish.

Bluegill: Like the crappie and pumpkinseed, a small, medium-fat freshwater sunfish.

Bonito: A tuna.

Bream: Bream or brim is a name applied to sunfish. Do not confuse it with sea bream.

Brook Trout: See chapter on trout.

Bullhead: A catfish.

Burbot: A freshwater member of the cod family.

Butterfish: Like the bluefish and mackerel, this small fish has a high fat content. Running only 10 to 12 inches long, butterfish are deep-bodied and light-meated. They are best treated in ways similar to mackerel.

Carp: A freshwater fish that is as ancient as China, where it was pond-cultured before the birth of Christ. Its fat content is moderate. Its flesh is best in winter, and because of its bottom feeding, best when taken from clear flowing waters.

Catfish: There are 28 species of catfish in the United States including the black, brown, flat, green, spotted, and yellow bullhead. A freshwater fish, it is taken from ponds and streams, and catfish farming is a big industry in the South. It has a moderate fat content and must be skinned before cooking.

Chain Pickerel: A medium-fat fish with good flavor. As with the pike, its bone structure can present problems to the novice. Best used for frying.

Chub: A whitefish.

Clam: See chapter on clams.

Cod: See chapter on cod.

Conch: Pronounced "konk," a gastropod mollusk found primarily south of Cape Hatteras, but important for food only in South Florida, the Bahamas, and the Caribbean, where it is made into chowders, fritters, and salads. The flesh is similar to that of a mild clam, though sweeter. It is handled similarly to whelks.

Crab: See chapter on crab.

Crappie: A sunfish.

Croakers: Another name for the drums.

Cunner: A wrasse, related to the tautog, though smaller and bonier. Found from Newfoundland to Chesapeake Bay. Medium to low fat content. Its flesh is tasty and perhaps best pan-fried.

Cusk: A cod.

Dab: A flounder.

Dogfish: One of the edible sharks.

Dolphin: The fish, not the mammal, which is a porpoise. Mostly tropical, but as with many tropical fish can be found in warm seasons riding the offshore Gulf stream far north of its usual haunts. The meat is sweet, moist and large-flaked. Favored in Hawaii, where it is known as mahi mahi.

Drum: These fish, also called croakers, are mostly found in southern waters, although one member of the family, the red drum, channel bass, or redfish, is much used south of New Jersey as a chowder fish. The drums include the Atlantic croaker or hardhead, black drum, northern and southern kingfish. Similar fish would be the tautog, cunner, wolffish, silver perch (yellow tail), spot (lafayette), and northern goatfish (a mullet).

Eel: A catadromous freshwater fish, going from the rivers to the ocean to spawn. Its flesh is oily and sweet and, when properly cooked, tender. It has good nutritional value. It is excellent when smoked. The usual method of cooking eels is pan-frying, most often as cross-cut sections or steaks, but it is amenable to broiling, steaming, and baking. Many authorities consider frying the least satisfactory way to cook it because it requires relatively long cooking. Its flesh is much firmer than that of other fish. It must be skinned before it is cooked.

Eelpout: Another name for the burbot, or freshwater cod. Also a name for the oceanpout.

Flounder: The major western Atlantic flatfish. See chapter on the flat fishes.

Fluke: The summer flounder.

Goosefish: The monkfish.

Grayfish: The spiny dogfish of the Atlantic.

Grayling: A freshwater fish, a Salmonoid, that prefers fast flowing streams. Mountain Whitefish, Chub, Arctic or Montana Graylings are all related. Medium-fat, it is treated like a trout when small; as salmon trout when larger.

Grouper: A southern and tropical fish, a member of the sea bass family that includes the hinds. Deep-bodied; a lean, white-fleshed fish with a tough skin similar to that of sea perch. The grouper does not have floating ribs (the bones that extend down from the backbone and around the sides of most fish), so it fillets well. It seldom is found north of Cape Hatteras. Low fat content.

Grunt: A fish primarily of Florida and south, to Brazil, but a few — the pigfish and white grunt — venture as far north as Chesapeake Bay. As might be expected, they make a grunting sound. They are small fish with soft, finely flaked flesh.

Haddock: A member of the cod family.

Hake: A member of the cod family.

Halibut: A flatfish, and a true flounder.

Herring: Among the most important food dishes of the Atlantic. It has long been an imported commercial species along the East Coast. In Maine and New Brunswick, juvenile herring are canned and marketed as sardines. The fish is about 6 percent fat and rather oily, so it is a prime candidate for pickling and smoking. It is found in many commercial versions, including kippers, Matjes herring, Rollmops, and Bloaters. Fresh herring has a tasty flesh, fried or grilled, but it rarely is available.

Hogfish: A wrasse of tropical and semitropical water, abundant in the Florida Keys. Its flesh is white and firm. Hogfish is also another name for the pigfish, which is a different species.

Jack: Although they occur as far north as Massachusetts, the jacks are essentially warm water fish. The pompano is a jack, but in a class by itself; the rest of the family is not important as a food fish in the United States. Some members contain a great deal of red muscle that is best eliminated.

John Dory: A large, ugly flat fish, extremely thin and compressed vertically when viewed head-on. The head and viscera can make up as much as two-thirds of the fish. The American variety differs from the European. The European fish's flesh is firm, finely flaked, and delicately flavored; the American slightly less so on all counts. It is not as abundant here as it is in Europe; in recent years, American chefs have been importing the fresh fish by air both from Europe and New Zealand.

Lake Trout: See chapter on trout.

Lobster: See chapter on lobster.

Lotte: The French name for monkfish.

Mackerel: See chapter on mackerel.

Marlin: Similar to the swordfish, there is both a white and blue marlin; the white is considered the better food fish. Related to the spearfish and sailfish. Considered a game fish rather than table fish, but it is good broiled or smoked. It is somewhat leaner than swordfish.

Monkfish: See chapter on monkfish.

Mullet: See chapter on mullet.

Muskellunge: The largest of the freshwater pike of northern rivers and ponds, the "muskie" can range from 10 to 30 pounds.

Mussel: See chapter on mussels.

Norway Haddock: An ocean perch.

Ocean Catfish: The wolffish, highly regarded in Europe, but not yet appreciated here. A fine food fish.

Ocean Perch: See chapter on sea perch.

Ocean Pout: The ocean pout (or eel pout) found in the Atlantic looks like an eel. The flesh is white and sweet tasting. Do not confuse with the freshwater burbot, which often goes by the name eel pout.

Oyster: See chapter on oysters.

Perwinkle: See chapter on periwinkles.

Permit: A southern fish, larger than its relative, the pompano, and not as fine eating.

Pickerel: A freshwater fish similar to pike.

Pigfish: A grunt. Also called hogfish, but the true hogfish is another species.

Pike: A freshwater fish of northern rivers and ponds with greatest abundance in Canada. Its preponderance of small bones is probably its greatest drawback as a food fish, because the white flesh is sweet and firm. Fish marketed as yellow pike and blue pike are not pike at all, but perch, and are really walleye.

Pollock: A member of the cod family.

Pomfret: A European name for the butterfish.

Pompano: One of the jacks, a fish of southern waters much admired as a game fish. The demand for it is great and it is usually expensive. The southern season runs from October to May, but a great deal of pompano is sold frozen. It has high oil content and is best baked, broiled, grilled, or smoked.

Porgy: See chapter on porgy.

Puffer or Blowfish: Also known as the swellfish, globe fish, sea squab, and in Japan, the *fugu*, this is a fish to avoid. It can be deadly. Its skin, liver, gonads, and intestines are all toxic.

Quahaug: A hardshell clam.

Ray: Also known as skate. See chapter on skate.

Redfish: Also known as rosefish. Common names given to fish are often confusing. The redfish and rosefish are prime examples. The sea perch is often called redfish or rosefish, but so is the red drum.

Red Snapper: A fish of southern and tropical waters, snappers are sought by consumers in many fish markets in the country where it is always expensive. It has medium-low fat content and is usually marketed at from 4 to 6 pounds. It can be baked, broiled, poached, or stuffed.

Rockfish: The name "rockfish" is used for striped bass in the Chesapeake Bay area, where they spawn. However, with the exception of the ocean perch, all United States rockfishes are found in the Pacific.

Rosefish: See redfish.

Salmon: See chapter on salmon.

Sardine: Young of many small fishes are sold as sardines — herring, sprats (brisling sardines), pilchards, and others. Most of the domestic sardines sold in this country are from the Gulf of Maine. Fresh sardines are not easily found.

Sauger: A perch, related to the yellow pike or walleye and the blue pike.

Scallops: See chapter on scallops.

Scrod: A young cod or haddock.

Scup: Another name for porgy.

Sea Bass: See chapter on sea bass.

Sea Bream: The porgy or scup.

Sea Perch: See chapter on sea perch.

Sea Robin: An ugly fish with "legs" that it uses to walk across the sea bottom looking for its dinner. Its unattractive appearance helps to keep it from being a human dinner very often. It is usually sold in fillets that can be sauteed, broiled, deep-fried, or poached. Its firm white flesh is medium fat and its flavor is delicate.

Sea Slug: What the French call *beche de mer*. Also known as sea cucumber and trepang in the Pacific. A sausage-shaped gastropod without a shell, 6 inches to more than 3 feet long. In this country, it is food for the Chinese community who purchase it dried and use it after long soaking.

Seatrout: See chapter on seatrout.

Sea trout: When written as two words, an anadromous brown trout.

Sea Urchin: There isn't much demand for these "sea porcupines" in this country, although they are popular in the Mediterranean and Japan. The edible portion of a sea urchin is the male gonad and female roe; both are eaten and both are generally lumped under the name roe or ovaries. The roe is soft with a briny sharpness, and can be eaten with a spoon, or as a spread on bread.

Shad: The American shad is a Clupeoid, a family of fishes that includes the sprat, herring, sardine, and alewife. An anadromous fish, the shad lives most of its life in the sea and returns to freshwater to spawn. Pollution and dams nearly wiped out the shad, but now it is beginning to make a comeback. The female shad, laden with eggs and ready to spawn, is considered a prime springtime delicacy.

Sheepshead: A porgy, although a freshwater drum goes by the same name.

Shrimp: See chapter on shrimp.

Silversides: See whitebait.

Skate: See chapter on skate.

Smelt: An important and popular fish for generations. Smelt are usually sold fresh from 5 to 8 inches long and 6 to 10 to the pound. While they can be broiled or baked or grilled over charcoal, the preferred method for most enthusiasts is to pan-fry or deep-fry them. Some people liken the smelt's flavor and aroma to cucumbers or violets.

Snapper: Generally refers to the red snapper, though juvenile bluefish also are called snappers.

Snook: Of greatest interest nowadays to sports fishermen. Prefers a habitat of low salinity, such as the mangrove swamps of Florida. More important as a tablefish in Central and South America. The white flesh is medium fat, and finely flaked with a sweet delicate flavor. It is best in smaller specimens.

Sole: In this country, on either coast, most often a flounder. See chapter on flat fishes.

Spot: A member of the drum family, primarily a pan fish brought home by anglers. Soft flesh, low in oil, but it tends to be parasitized. Also known as the Lafayette.

Squid: See chapter on squid.

Sturgeon: Most frequently encountered as a smoked product, and as such, an excellent appetizer. A fish that is best cooked in ways one would cook a swordfish or mako shark.

Striped Bass: A prized sportfish, it is usually marketed in lengths between 18 and 24 inches. It is olive green with dark stripes running down its back. The meat is slightly oily, white, and flaky. A seasonal fish, its population has declined to the point that the twelve states near where stripers are fished, plus the federal government, are seeking to adopt coastwide measures to protect it.

Sucker: A freshwater fish often marketed in smaller sizes. The flesh is white, firm, and sweet, and can be substituted in recipes for carp.

Sunfish: Small fish for small boys. This freshwater family includes the bluegills, crappies, and pumpkinseeds of ponds and lakes that are easily taken by fishermen. A good pan fish when there is enough meat. It can be deep-fried and eaten like corn on the cob.

Swordfish: See chapter on swordfish.

Tautog: Also called blackfish. The tautog, a wrasse, prefers rocky shorelines as it ranges in inshore waters from Nova Scotia to Cape Hatteras. It is most abundant from Massachusetts to Delaware. A dark, dull gray appearance, plump body, and thick lips are its distinguishing characteristics. The tautog averages about 3 pounds but can weigh as much as 25. Its firm white meat is excellent in chowder as the flesh does not shred or flake easily. Medium-low fat content.

Thresher: A shark.

Tilefish: See chapter on tilefish.

Triggerfish: Although a reef-dwelling tropical fish, one of the two species — the queen triggerfish — occasionally gets as far north as Massachusetts. Its excellent, firm white meat has a low fat content and is usually compared to frogs legs in flavor and texture. It can be substituted for monkfish. The ocean triggerfish tends to remain in warmer waters of the western Atlantic.

Trout: See chapter on trout.

Tuna: See chapter on tuna.

Turbot: One of the flatfishes. This is strictly a European fish that is rarely seen in the western Atlantic, though occasionally one will show up on East Coast docks. Pronounced "tur-bow" by the French and many food people, it is more often referred to as "tur-butt" by East Coast fishermen.

Walleye: Though its more common market name is yellow pike, it is not a pike, but a perch. Other members of the family are the blue pike and the sauger.

Weakfish: See chapter on seatrout.

Whelk: A marine mollusk with a single, convoluted shell; a gastropod like the snail, periwinkle, slug, or limpet, with a broad muscular organ of locomotion. It is not in the same family as the conch. There are three species of whelk in this country that are table food; the waved whelk, which exists as far south as New Jersey; the knobbed whelk that gets to northern Florida, and the channeled whelk to Texas. Sold primarily in Italian neighborhoods as scungilli, it has a thick shell and its meat is tough. It must be tenderized before cooking, either by pounding, par-boiling, or grinding. It is used with other seafood in cold salads, in marinara sauce, and in chowders. Whelks are handled much like periwinkles and the meat is more easily removed than that of the conch.

Whitebait: Although this is often spoken of as a fish, it is a dish of fish that contains a mixture of immature fish such as small herring, silversides, anchovies, and the like, dusted with flour and fried.

Whitefish: A freshwater fish, related to the salmon and the trout, though its flesh is white. Lake whitefish, found from New England westward to Minnesota and northward to Arctic Canada, is more popular in the Midwest than on the Atlantic seaboard. In this country, it is — with carp, suckers, and walleye pike — one of the three main fishes used in making *gefilte fish*, though on the East Coast, cod, haddock, or halibut may be substituted when freshwater fish are not readily available.

Whiting: A member of the cod family.

Wolffish: The ocean catfish.

Fish Substitution Guides

◘

The following guides help categorize fish that are intended for the table. Thus, if you live in the South and don't have access, say, to whiting for a recipe, you can check these guides to learn what fish you can substitute for the whiting. We have included both northern and southern species in these listings, as well as freshwater fish, though trout are the only freshwater fish specifically included among our recipes. Along the East Coast other freshwater species are more likely to be taken home by an angler than a shopper, and we include them should that happen to be your luck. Some of the ocean fish listed are also likely to be found mostly at the end of a sports fisherman's line.

In general, you may substitute any fish within a category for another in the same category so long as the cut of fish is the same. Obviously you won't always be able to substitute a thick fillet from a large roundfish for a small flatfish fillet, especially if the recipe calls for the fillet to be rolled. Nor will a thick halibut steak substitute for a fillet that is to be deep-fried.

A second caution is that while these guides are generally correct, they are still only guides. Seasonal variations, sex, the temperature of the water in which an individual fish has lived, its diet, and whether it has recently spawned or is about to, can all influence texture, flavor, and other qualities of the flesh.

The guide based primarily on flavor is based on one prepared by the National Marine Fisheries Service. The categories proceed from lightest in color and flavor to the darker and more flavorful. The terms "light," "delicate," and "very light" are relative.

It is interesting to note that fish that swim constantly are likely to have better flavor than fish that laze about. This is one reason why a fast and constantly moving bluefish has more flavor than a flounder, which spends a lot of time resting on the bottom. This also accounts for the difference between a brook trout and a lake trout. There are other factors, including diet, that affect flavor.

Refer to these guides before buying fish so that you will know what alternatives you have if you have decided you wish to prepare a specific dish. Your dealer can help you in making a selection, but he will be more certain of what to give you if you can name two or three fishes that would be suitable.

Firm or Soft: A Guide to Fish Flesh

I. Firm Fleshed

Moist: Halibut, monkfish, tilefish, red snapper, porgy, or scup, pompano, grunt, permit, northern kingfish (a small drum), and the dolphin (the fish, not the mammal, which is a porpoise). Freshwater: Black Bass and its cousins among freshwater sunfish, the crappies, bluegill, pumpkinseed and rock bass; freshwater drum (sheepshead), burbot.

Oily: Atlantic salmon, tuna, butterfish, smelt, eel, bonito. Freshwater: trout, landlocked salmon.

Dry: Swordfish, mako shark, striped bass, black sea bass, tautog (blackfish), hogfish, grouper, sheepshead (a porgy). Freshwater: Lake whitefish, (trout), perch, pike, yellow perch or walleye, muskellunge or muskie (because of diet and other factors, some of these might be included among soft-fleshed fish at times).

II. Soft Fleshed

Moist: All flounders except halibut, mullet, whiting (silver hake), bonefish, seatrout (ocean catfish), southern kingfish, rockfish or striped bass. Freshwater: Northern pike, pickerel, perch, lake whitefish, trout.

Oily: Atlantic mackerel, Spanish mackerel, tinker mackerel, herring, bluefish, smelt.

Dry: Atlantic cod, cod tongue and cheeks, haddock, shark's fins, cusk, pollock, hake, salt cod, finnan haddie, stockfish.

Light or Pronounced: A Guide to Fish Flavor

I. White Meat, Light Delicate Flavor
    Cod, cusk, halibut, summer flounder, yellowtail flounder, witch flounder. Lake whitefish.

II. White Meat, Light to Moderate Flavor
    Winter flounder, American plaice (long rough dab; sand dab), spotted seatrout, whiting, red snapper, tilefish, wolffish (ocean catfish), seatrout, butterfish. Catfish, sauger.

III. Light Meat, Very Light Delicate Flavor
    Sea bass, grouper, tautog, white sea bass, Atlantic sturgeon, smelt. Brook trout, rainbow trout, walleye, crappie.

IV. Light Meat, Light to Moderate Flavor
    Monkfish, ocean perch, scup, pollock, drum, croaker, sheepshead, pompano, striped bass, swordfish, shark, mullet, crevalle jack, eel, Atlantic salmon, coho salmon, skate. Lake sturgeon, northern pike, burbot, carp, lake trout.

V. Light Meat, More Pronounced Flavor
    Atlantic mackerel, King mackerel, Spanish mackerel, redeye mullet, juvenile bluefish (snapper).

VI. Darker Meat, Light to Moderate Flavor
    Black sea bass, ocean pout, adult bluefish, chinook and red (sockeye) salmon.

Seafood and Nutrition

In 1980, Americans ate 14 pounds of fish per capita, compared to 150 pounds of meat and 63 pounds of poultry. The ratio is changing, however, as concern grows about diet in general and cholesterol in particular.

Fresh seafood has no chemical preservatives, flavorings, or additives. (Note, however, that some seafood, notably shrimp, minced clams, and some processed fish fillets, fresh or frozen, is given a dip in phosphates to retain the moisture that would escape through drip loss.) Fresh seafood is one of the few natural foods on the market today. It is naturally high in protein and low in fat. Seafood contains more polyunsaturated fats than saturated fats. There is evidence that polyunsaturated fats found in fish help to reduce cholesterol levels.

Fish are low in calories, at least compared to many other foods we eat. Eel, with 230 or so calories in a 3.5 ounce serving, ranks highest, but it is still considerably below a T-bone steak, which has 397 calories in 3.5 ounces. Hake and cod, with between 75 to 80 calories for the same portion, are among the lowest in caloric content. The difference among fish is an attribute of their fat content.

Food (per 100 grams)	Calories	% Protein	% Fat	% Carbohydrates
Beef (retail, raw)	263	13.5	30	0
Pork (various, raw)	311	16	27	0
Chicken (all, raw)	124	22	3.3	0
Fish				
(lake trout)	168	18	10	0
(halibut, raw)	100	21	1.2	0
Milk (whole)	66	3.5	3.7	4.9
Eggs (raw, whole)	163	13	12	0.9

Sodium

Saltwater fish have no more sodium in their flesh than freshwater species.

Brined and smoked fish have higher sodium contents and usually are not recommended for those on restricted diets. As a general rule, however, all species of fresh fish are lower in sodium than is beef.

The following chart gives a comparison of the sodium content of various foods and seafood. This listing, drawn from various sources, is not intended to be a definitively correct list for those whose sodium intake is medically restricted; such persons should base their diets on a physician's advice. This list is merely to help the average consumer understand the average amount of sodium in some foods.

Seafood	Amount	Sodium
Bluefish, baked with butter	3 ounces	123
Cod, broiled with butter	3 ounces	93
Flat fish baked with butter	3 ounces	201
Haddock, breaded, fried	3 ounces	158
Mackerel, raw	3 ounces	40
Salmon, broiled with butter	3 ounces	99
Trout (lake), raw	3 ounces	67
Clams, raw, hardshelled	3 ounces	175
Clams, raw; softshelled	3 ounces	30
Lobster, boiled	3 ounces	212
Mussels, raw	3 ounces	243
Oysters, raw	3 ounces	113
Scallops, raw	3 ounces	217
Shrimps, raw	3 ounces	137

Other Food	Amount	Sodium
Beef, veal	3 ounces	75
Lamb, pork	3 ounces	75
Ham (cured)	3 ounces	675
Bacon	1 slice	675
Corned beef	4 ounces	1970
Frankfurter	1 whole	540
Bologna	1 slice	390
Chicken	3 ounces	75
McDonald's Big Mac	1	1500
Butter, salted	1 tablespoon	140
Butter, unsalted	1 tablespoon	1
Chicken bouillon cube	1 cube	950
Salt, table	1 teaspoon	2000

Seafood and Wine

Seafood and wine go together, both in the pan and at table.

Throughout this book we recommend that you cook with a dry white wine. Which wine? The first choice is always the wine that you will drink with the dish. This is easy to do when you will make the dish and eat it within an hour or two. But if the time span is longer, or if the wine is a rather expensive one that you don't wish to have sitting in the refrigerator too long after opening, you can use any good quality wine. Some professional chefs prefer dry vermouth, both because its higher alcohol acts as a preservative keeping the wine fresh, and because it is already flavored.

A recipe cannot be helped by an inferior wine — find a good label that you like and stick with it. We do not recommend the "cooking wines" sold in supermarkets. Such wines have salt in them that is likely to confuse the flavor balance of your dish. Be careful in buying so-called "jug" wines. Many are slightly sweet, and are not as good in cooking as truly dry wines are.

For almost all seafood dishes, a white wine is the perfect accompaniment. White wines tend to be higher in acid than red and it is the resulting tartness that makes them the best partners for fish. Some dishes, however, are better with a dry rosé or even a light red wine. Whatever the color, wine's natural acidity and other attributes are perfect for cleansing the palate and preparing it for the next bite.

While one can make general observations about which wine goes with which fish or shellfish, such matchings are not the last word. Personal tastes aside for the moment, the sauce or accompaniments more often than the seafood will determine which wine would best suit the moment. A delicate white wine would not stand up to our Salmon in Geneva Sauce, for example.

Wine, of course, can be merely what one is going to drink with a dish — or it can elevate the dish to a higher gastronomical plane. A serving of oysters on the halfshell with any crisp white wine is excellent fare, but oysters with a top-of-the-line French Grand Cru Chablis from an excellent vintage is in a class by itself.

Sometimes a lean, crisp wine is used to counterbalance the richness of a dish; sometimes the wine goes along with the dish: An herbaceous Sauvignon Blanc with an herbaceous dish. Our recipe for Flounder with

Cider and Apples might be served with a Chardonnay or a Mosel, for example. The hints of apple in the wine would echo the flavors of the dish. The apple, in turn, would accent the fruit of the wine. Some might find the redundancy not to their liking and choose a Fumé Blanc for its crispness and contrasting flavor. (And still another might bypass wine and drink cider — but we wouldn't mention that.)

The problem of matching wine with food can get more complicated. An individual wine will not always be exactly the same as it was the previous year. Even a wine of such long-understood characteristics as French Chablis can loose some of its flinty edge when the weather does not cooperate. Chardonnays in California range from lean, crisp, almost austere, to big, oaky, buttery, full-bodied monsters. And wineries are known to switch around as they seek the perfect character and style for their grapes. Complicated, to be sure, but that is why the wine lover loves wine — for its infinite variety.

We have divided wines into seven categories below. Admittedly they are arguable categories since wine cannot be categorized so easily. But the breakdown should be a helpful start if you are trying to decide which wine to serve with which seafood.

The white wines progress from everyday table wines to the lightest and then up to the biggest and fullest. Some wines appear in several categories because they are made in several styles, or because they will be different in a light year from a "normal" year, and different still in the very best years.

One final word of advice about white wine: Most Americans serve it too cold.

Simple white wines, those in category 1 below, and sparkling wines, should be served no colder than 39 degrees. The best vintage Champagne should be between 46 and 52 degrees. Most other white wines should be served between 43 and 50 degrees. Better California Chardonnay and Sauvignon Blanc should be served from 48 to 54 degrees, and the best white Burgundies from France should be served between 54 and 57 degrees. Most light reds that can tolerate chilling should be served between 48 and 57 degrees.

Wines For Our Recipes

Mousse preparations: Chardonnay, especially with rich sauces.

Flat Fish: Categories 1 and 2 offer many acceptable wines. The Sole with Seedless Grapes would probably be best with a fruity Chenin Blanc, while the Fish with Fennel would marry well with a Muscadet or Chardonnay. Halibut with Tomato Mousseline needs some crispness, a Fumé Blanc, Sancerre, or Muscadet. Halibut Terrine with Aspic needs an herbaceous wine such as one from the Loire or a California Sauvignon Blanc.

Cod Family: Dry wines without excessive acid generally would work well; category 1 and 2 wines. Graves, Entre-Deux-Mers or Muscadet and Fumé Blanc (also called Sauvignon Blanc, the names are used interchangeably). No wine with Fish with Pickled Vegetables. A hot Curried Hake calls for beer, but a mild version might team well with a sweet German Spätlese Riesling.

Salt Cod: This fish usually requires a steely, dry white such as Chablis or Muscadet; or a wine from category 1. Alsatians are specialists in sauerkraut and teaming that with salt cod provides an excuse to try one of their Gewürztraminers or Rieslings; beer might prove best for such a strongly flavored dish.

Monkfish: No wine with Monkfish Marsala. A light commune Burgundy, Côtes du Rhône, *cru* Beaujolais or whatever red wine you used in making it is needed for the *Civet de Lotte*. For the rest, fuller wines from categories 3 and 4.

Porgy: Muscadet.

Sea Bass: Wines from categories 1 and 2 will work well.

Sea Perch: No wine with Sea Perch à la Grecque. Try Chenin Blanc or Sauvignon Blanc with Sea Perch with Cucumber; Chardonnay, white French Burgundy, or Sauvignon Blanc with the next few. Categories 1 and 2 generally work well with Sea Perch.

Sea Trout: For these recipes, French Chablis, Muscadet.

Tilefish: White Burgundy or Chardonnay from California would team with Tilefish à l'Orange as would other choices from category 4, but garlic and black olives need a crisp wine from category 2 or 3.

Bluefish: The generous use of lemon in the baked bluefish recipe calls for a citrus-like Loire wine or a California Sauvignon Blanc. The fish needs assertive wines — Hermitage Blanc, big Burgundies, oaky Chardonnays.

Mackerel: Gravad would respond well to the sweet spiciness of a Gewürztraminer from Alsace or California that is late-picked. Otherwise, a crisp wine from category 3, or Vinho Verde.

Salmon: There are many who swear by light red wines like Beaujolais for salmon. The combination works for some, especially if the salmon is poached in a red wine. For Potted Salmon, a Vouvray *sec* or Chenin Blanc; Seafood Tartare needs a crisper wine from category 2. For the Salmon with Sorrel Sauce, a Sauvignon Blanc or Burgundy or Chardonnay from category 4. Salmon with Hazelnut Coating would marry with the nutty flavors of a Meursault or other big Burgundy. Generally stay with bigger wines in 3 and 4.

Trout: Chardonnay, Riesling, especially Mosel, and wines similar in style to a Mâcon.

Shark: Fuḿe Blanc, Sancerre, Mâcon; category 2.

Swordfish: Similar wines.

Tuna: For Braising Pan Tuna, Beaujolais and similar light red wines, especially for the red-meated fresh tunas. Otherwise wines such as Mâcon and dry Chenin, or Vouvray *sec*.

Crab: Chardonnay, Pouilly-Fumé, Sauvignon Blanc.

Lobster: For Homard à l'Americaine, a Mersault or Pouilly-Fuissé. Wines from category 4, generally, but Lobster of the Sun would not marry well with wine.

Shrimp: Creole and Remoulade dishes could be served with dry rosé and Stir-Fried Shrimp with Gewürztraminer, but in general choose from category 3 and 4. Shrimp San Remo's sharp sun-dried tomatoes and bread could be paired with a light red such as Beaujolais or Zinfandel, but Fumé Blanc and other category 2 wines with crispness also will work. Shrimp rarebit calls for beer.

Clams: Chili, and most other clam recipes, could be served with a light red, a dry rosé, or, if you like yours especially fiery, beer. A light Zinfandel would complement the sweet peppers in the Clam Salad.

Mussels: Muscadet, Mâcon, Fumé Blanc, and other wines in category 2 are good choices. The curry, if you prefer it fiery, would call for beer; otherwise a Spätlese Riesling. No wine would be served with Tempura. Mussels Provençal needs either an assertive crisp wine from category 2 or 3 or a Rosé of Provence.

Oysters: Chablis for the Oysters in Spinach; though a Burgundy or Chardonnay would marry with all the dishes.

Scallops: Category 1, 2, and 3 wines, though a fuller wine from category 4 would better serve Scallops in Puff Pastry.

Squid: Most of the dishes call for a light red from category 6, though some find Zinfandel heightens the fishy flavor too much. For the Stuffed Squid in Mushroom Cream Sauce, Orvieto or Italian Chardonnay.

Soups: Hot and cold liquids generally do not marry well with wine. A dry Sherry, such as a *fino* or dry *amontillado* or a *Sercial* or *Verdelho* Madeira is sometimes served with consommes and bisques. With creamy soups or chowders, an Alsatian or California Riesling could be tried. A dry rosé, light Zinfandel, or Côtes du Rhône Blanc would serve the Little Neck Soup as well as any.

Fish Farinaceous: Shrimp Pesto, crisp Sauvignon Blanc, Muscadet, and similar category 2 wines. Most recipes will marry with category 1 and 2 wines, except the Smoked Trout Ravioli, which needs a wine like a Riesling *Kabinett*, Pinot Blanc, or Sancerre. A fruitier dry Sylvaner or dry Chenin Blanc would be better with the Pasta, Fish and Artichokes. Shrimp, Broccoli and Sun-Dried Tomatoes would pair well with a Bardolino, Valpolicella, French Beaujolais, or Gamay Beaujolais.

The Wines

The description "crisp" is relative to other wines in the category, but not necessarily true in every case.

Category 1, dry to off-dry everyday wines: Portuguese Vinho Verde, French Entre-Deux-Mers, Gros Plant du Pays Nantais, Soave (the crisper wines); Australian, Hungarian and Yugoslavian Rieslings; Rieslings and Chardonnays from Chile and Argentina, and some of the simpler, softer, and less expensive wines that appear in the next category. California "jug" wines. These are inclined to have a touch of sweetness or mellowness. Also, German *Tafelwein* (the driest style) and some Liebfraumilch. Also many inexpensive, proprietary wines (house brands) from almost all the world's winegrowing regions.

Category 2, dry, light-bodied wines: Mâcon Blanc, dry white Graves (crisp), simple dry Vouvray, Beaujolais Blanc, Côtes-du-Rhône Blanc, Macon-Villages, Mâcon Viré, Muscadet (crisp), Sylvaner or Riesling from Alsace, German Kabinett-style wines, Pinot Grigio, Italian Chardonnays, Verdicchio, Frascati (crisp), Galestro, Lugana, Orvieto (secco), Italian Chardonnays, Pinot Bianco, Pinot Grigio, Soave Classico, Trebbiano, Fendant, some white Spanish wines, California Chenin Blanc, Sauvignon Blanc (if not aged in oak) also called Fumé Blanc (crisp), dry Gewürztraminer and Rieslings from both Alsace and California, and some California Chardonnays. Vidal Blanc, a hybrid grown east of the Rockies to New England, also would be in this category.

Category 3, dry medium-bodied wines: Bourgogne Aligoté, White Graves (crisp), simpler French Chablis including *premier cru* in lighter vintages (crisp), Côte-de-Beaune commune wines, Pouilly-Fuissé, Pouilly-Fumé, Alsatian Riesling and Sylvaner, Saint-Véran, Sancerre (crisp), white Châteauneuf-du-Pape, Fiano d'Avellino, Gavi, California Riesling, some California Chardonnays, Sauvignon Blanc, or Fumé Blanc (crisp); Seyval Blanc and Ravat, two other French-American hybrids grown outside California.

Category 4, dry full-bodied, complex wines: French *Grand Cru* Chablis, chateau-bottled Graves, the best white Burgundies of France (Meursault, Puligny-Montrachet, Chassagne-Montrachet, Corton-Charlemagne), Hermitage Blanc, Condrieu, Chateau Grillet, Savennières, Alsatian Gewürztraminers and Rieslings *Reserve* and *Reserve Personnelle*, many California oak-aged or barrel-fermented Chardonnays and Sauvignon Blancs, German *Kabinett* and Spätlese wines of lighter vintages, Greco di Tufo.

Category 5, dry to off-dry rosés: Tavel, Cabernet d'Anjou, Castel del Monte, Grenache, some Zinfandels from California.

Category 6, light red wines: Beaujolais, Beaujolais-Villages, lighter *cru* Beaujolais such as Saint-Amour, Brouilly, Fleurie, Chiroubles; Bordeaux Superior in lighter vintages, Borgueil, Chinon, Corbières and other Midi wines, Côtes de Beaune commune wines, Côtes-du-Rhone, Côtes-de-Ventoux, all nouveau-style wines, Bardolino, Valpolicella, Italian Merlot, Cabernet del Friuli, Cerasuolo, dry Lambruscos, Dolcetto d'Alba, Grumello and Inferno; Blauburgunder; Gamay, Napa Gamay, Gamay Beaujolais and some Zinfandels.

Category 7, off-dry wines: California wines labeled "Chablis," "White Table Wine," or some form of "Mountain White"; French Colombard, Chenin Blanc, white Zinfandel and Pinot Noir Blanc are made in both dry and off-dry styles. All California "late harvest" wines are sweet to varying degrees and more suited for dessert. Riesling and Sylvaner, especially if labeled Spatlese, and likely to reveal some degree of sweetness. Vouvray *demi-sec* is, and Gewürztraminer can be, sweet. Orvieto is seen in a sweet, *abboccato*, style.

Fish Kitchen ABCs

This glossary is intended to give a full explanation of culinary terms and foods that we have used in this book.

Acidulated water: Cold water with vinegar or lemon or lime juice added. It is used to prevent discoloration of peeled fruits and vegetables that brown when exposed to air. Also used to firm various ingredients, such as fish roe.

Al dente: Italian for, literally, "to the tooth." The term refers to the way pasta, rice, or vegetables should be cooked so that they are firm to the bite.

Anchovy paste: The addition of anchovy flavor can add a robust flavor to a dish. If the flavor of mashed anchovy fillet is not assertive enough, use anchovy paste. You can buy it or make it. Mash together a half can of flat anchovy fillets and a small clove of garlic.

Aspic: A jelly produced by mixing the stock of fish, meat, or fowl with gelatin.

Baste: To moisten and flavor while roasting or baking, usually with the pan juices, butter, or a liquid such as wine or fat.

Baton: A piece cut about 2½ inches long and about ¾-inch square, as in a vegetable.

Bay leaf: An herb. It is used in cooking, but is removed before serving in all but a few preparations — such as a pâté. The reason for this, other than the fact that it is tough, is that it has sharp spines along its margin, which can do real harm if swallowed.

Bind: To cause a mixture to hold together by adding, folding, or beating in egg, butter, sauce, or a thickening agent as the "binder."

Bisque: A thickened, creamy soup, originally of shellfish. Today the term is also applied to other forms of such a soup.

Blanch: To immerse an ingredient in boiling or simmering water to retain color and to firm; to scald momentarily. If the aim is to retain color, say, in spinach, the vegetable is blanched for about 10 seconds and then immediately submerged in cold water.

Blend: To mix ingredients until well combined and smooth.

Bouquet garni: A bundle of herbs used in a preparation, especially of stock and soup, and then removed before serving. A basic bouquet consist of a bay leaf, a sprig of thyme, and a few sprigs of parsley. Almost anything can be added that the cook feels will improve flavor. Make it by tying fresh herbs with string, or wrapping the herbs in cheesecloth or putting them in a tea infuser made with stainless steel wire mesh. In some cases, where celery is called for, it is simpler to enclose the herbs within two pieces of celery stalk that are tied together. If the string is left long and tied to the pot handle, it can be removed easily.

Braising: Also called pot roasting. To brown in fat first and then cook slowly in a covered casserole or pot, such as a Dutch oven.

Broth: A thin soup, or the water in which fish, meat, poultry, or game have been cooked.

Butter, compound or savory: Butter that is whipped or worked with a flavoring or flavorings. Anchovy, garlic, and crayfish butters are frequently made, as well as butters using almost any herb. The butter is rolled up and slices are taken from the roll as needed.

Butterfly: To cut an ingredient, such as shrimp or fish, almost in half so that when it is flattened the two halves resemble butterfly wings.

Capers: The flower buds of a tropical shrub, often packed in salt or vinegar. They have a peppery taste and are used with fish dishes and in sauces. Use those packed in vinegar. The small ones marked "nonpareille" are considered the best. If you buy capers packed in salt, wash and drain them before using.

Caviar: The best of the roe, or eggs, of fish. Caviar is from the sturgeon, a freshwater fish of primitive characteristics, which grows to enormous size, up to 2000 pounds or more. Federal regulations prohibit the use of the word caviar alone on the label unless it is truly from sturgeon roe. The word "malossol" in relation to caviar means lightly salted, up to 4 to 6 percent of the finished weight. The size of caviar eggs varies from pea-sized down to that of a peppercorn. Generally black or gray, the eggs also can be shades of yellow, dark green, and brown.

Caviar, Salmon: Not caviar in the true sense. It is made from the eggs of the chum salmon found in the American Northwest and in western Canada. The eggs are large, nearly transparent, red, pink, or orange-red; the flavor is salty, but the roe have delicacy and a flavor different from that of sturgeon caviar.

Caviar, Poor Man's: Not caviar at all, but a dish made with eggplant.

Chiffonade: Finely cut vegetable strips used to garnish soups, but also may apply to greens such as lettuce used as a bed or in a salad.

Chop: To cut ingredients ¼-to-½-inch in size so that they will add texture to a dish.

Chop, coarsely: To cut ingredients from ½-to-¾-inch in size.

Clarify: To make a liquid limpid and free of sediment. Stocks and consommes are frequently clarified by the use of egg whites and eggshells.

Coriander: An herb. Fresh coriander somewhat resembles flat-leaved (Italian) parsley; it can be found in Oriental markets as "Chinese parsley" and in Latin markets as "cilantro."

Cornstarch: Corn milled as an extremely fine white powder that is used to thicken liquids.

Crabmeat, artificial: A new product that contains about 85 percent fish (pollock), 12 percent crab or crab extract, and a binder. It is dyed red or orange on one side to simulate crabmeat.

Cube: A ½-inch cube would be about right when no specific size is given, but cubes can be anything from ⅜-inch up.

Curing: To preserve meat, fish, and other foods with salt or by drying or smoking.

Curry: A powder made from a blend of herbs and spices, usually at least four or five. It is usually mustard yellow, a color that comes from the turmeric often used in preparation. You can purchase it or make it. A typical simple curry might contain coriander, cumin, turmeric, ginger, and mustard seed, all ground and blended.

Deep-fat fry or deep-fry: To cook in hot fat, about 360 degrees, that is at least 3 inches deep.

Deglaze: Deglazing dissolves caramelized meat or seafood and juices accumulated during the cooking process. This recovered food is frequently used as the basis for or the enhancement of soups, gravies, and sauces.

Devil: Usually means to combine with hot or spicy seasoning or sauce. Mustard and cayenne pepper are two common ingredients in deviled dishes.

Dice: To cut an ingredient ⅛-to-¼-inch in size, but it may vary.

Drawn butter: Melted butter; sometimes clarified butter. In lesser restaurants it may be a combination of margarine and butter.

Dredge: To coat with a dry ingredient: flour, cornmeal, breadcrumbs, and/or cornstarch. Fish is often dredged before it is fried.

Duxelles: At its simplest, minced fresh mushrooms simmered in butter. A more complicated version would be minced ham, mushrooms, shallots, and herbs simmered in butter, and used to flavor soups, sauces, stuffings, and the like.

Escallop: A slice of fish or meat, without bones or skin, that is thinner than a medallion.

Fish smell: Sometimes in handling seafood, your hands are left with a "fishy" smell. Rub them with a wedge of fresh lemon.

Flute: To make a decorative edge on a pastry shell; to cut fruits, vegetables, and other foods in a decorative manner.

Fold: To combine, usually two different mixtures, by turning over gently to prevent air from escaping. Beaten egg whites or whipped cream often are folded into other mixtures, usually to lighten them by incorporating air.

Food processor blade: All recipes in this book require only the steel blade of the food processor.

Forcing bag: A forcing or pastry bag is made of strong cloth or plastic and fitted with various nozzles or tubes. It is used for filling and stuffing an ingredient into another, for piping a border, and for decorating.

Fumet: In this book, a concentrated fish stock used to give body and flavor to a dish, especially sauces.

Garnish: Any addition to a dish that improves the appearance and flavor. Also used as a verb, to garnish.

Gelatin: Made from boiling parts of meat and bones; a jelling agent. It is softened in cold water, which it always must be, and added to hot broths. When cooled it forms a gel. A package of commercial gelatin usually contains 1 ounce or 1 tablespoon, sufficient for 2 cups of liquid.

Gherkins: Small cucumber pickles, either sweet or sour. Also called cornichons.

Grate: To cut into small pieces using the smallest holes of a grater. What you do to fresh parmesan cheese.

Half-and-half: A mixture of cream and milk.

Julienne: Fine julienne would be the size of a toothpick or wooden match. This size would do for vegetables such as carrots, turnips, and celery. Julienne without further definition might be a little thicker than fine julienne.

Kosher salt: Also called coarse salt. It is often preferred in cooking because its larger grains adhere well and make a dish taste saltier. It also is used, as we have done, to encase fish or other foods to be baked, and as a bed for tipsy foods such as bivalves on the halfshell.

Medallion: A coin- or medal-shaped slice of boneless fish or meat cut on a 45-degree angle to give more cooking surface.

Mince: Mince is what one usually does to parsley, garlic, or fresh ginger root. It means to cut the ingredient very small, into pieces 1/8-inch or less in size, so they do not add texture to a dish.

Mirepoix: A French vegetable and herb combination used to flavor dishes and sauces. Most often, 1 carrot, 1 onion, 3 sprigs of parsley, a bay leaf, and a healthy pinch of thyme sauteed in butter for about 4 minutes.

Noisette: A French butchery term for a round slice of meat cut from the fillet, rib, or leg of lamb or mutton. Also a small round of beef or veal, not less than 2 ounces. We use it for salmon. The word also can mean flavored with or made with hazelnuts; a sauce made with hollandaise; potatoes cut to resemble a hazelnut and then fried in light brown butter. *Beurre noisette* is butter cooked until the color of hazelnut.

Pan-fry: To fry with a small amount of shortening; the opposite of deep-fry.

Papillote: A French term for paper cookery. Also refers to fancy paper shapes and ruffles used to cover the ends of chop bones.

Parboil: In parboiling, the aim is to cook partway, so the ingredient is held in boiling or simmering water longer than it is in a blanching procedure, but not so long as in a boiling procedure.

Parchment: Kitchen parchment paper is a translucent, heavy, parchment-like paper used to line or cover pans. In many cases, kitchen foil will work just as well. To cut it to cover a round dish to be baked: Cut a square of parchment or foil slightly larger than the round dish. Fold the square in half and then in half again. Refold at least twice more until you have a triangular shape that looks like a child's paper airplane. Measure the radius of the dish: Hold the folded paper over the dish so that the point is at about the center. Cut the paper where it touches the outside rim of the dish. Unfold; you should have a roughly cut circle that covers your container. Butter half of the circle. Fold the unbuttered half onto the buttered half and place in the refrigerator until needed. Unfold and lay onto ingredients to be baked, buttered-side down.

Parsley: Fresh parsley leaves are often used minced, to sprinkle over a dish. Some people recommend discarding the stems, but we use them in stocks, soups, and sauces. They add considerable flavor. Six to twelve parsley stems are adequate for most preparations.

Pepper: Whether black or white, pepper loses it volatile oils quickly. Get a pepper mill and grind your peppercorns fresh, not only for better flavor, but in that way you can be sure that you are not getting pepper that has been adulterated or "cut" with less expensive ingredients. Or, crack peppercorns by placing them in a clean dishtowel and cracking them with a heavy instrument.

Pickle: To preserve, usually in brine, but other mediums also are used. Some fish is pickled by merely salting and allowing it to remain in the liquid that it produced.

Planking: A style of baking, broiling, or outdoor grilling where fish or meat is placed on hardwood.

Poach: To cook food in a liquid that is just barely simmering.

Preheat: An oven should always be brought to cooking temperature before food is placed into it. This is especially true with fish, which requires such short cooking. It would dry and toughen otherwise.

Puree: To grind or mash to a paste in a food processor or blender, or by forcing through a food mill. For small quantities a mortar and pestle may be used.

Reduce: To boil a liquid rapidly, uncovered, thus reducing its volume by evaporation. With a sauce or gravy, this not only thickens the liquid, but also concentrates and increases the flavor. Reducing is a good way of dealing with diluted pan juices, for it avoids the addition of flour or another thickening agent, which would tend to mask flavor. A wide pan speed the process when reducing; a heavy pan helps avoid burning or scorching. When acid is present, as in tomatoes, wine, vinegar, and citrus juices, a non-corrosive pan should be used.

Refresh: To immerse hot vegetables in ice water to set the color and flavor. The food is then drained and added to a dish or reheated in a sauce or butter.

Render: To melt solid animal fat by heating it slowly in a pan. Salt pork, bacon, and lard are often rendered before being used in a dish.

Roast: To cook in dry heat, as in an oven.

Roe: The mass of eggs in the ovarian membrane of female fish or the gonad of the male fish, known as milt. The eggs are known as hard roe, the milt as soft roe. The roe of sturgeon, shad, lumpfish, white fish, carp, mackerel, halibut, tuna, cod, haddock, mullet, flounder, salmon, and herring all are eaten. The roe of sturgeon is known as caviar. The less expensive roe of some fish, especially salmon, lumpfish, tuna, and gray mullet, often are substituted for caviar. Some of these are artificially colored — black or gray — to simulate caviar. To buy roe, look for those that are intact, clean, and uniform in color.

Round, turn: Vegetables such as carrots, turnips, zucchini are sometimes cut into round or olive shapes, either with a paring knife or a melon baller.

Roux: A kind of cooking paste, usually made with equal parts of butter and flour, that is used as a thickening agent. Roux are pale blond (a white roux) to caramel (a brown roux), depending on the time they have cooked.

Score: To make shallow patterned cuts on the surface of foods, either to tenderize, to prevent curling, or for decoration.

Season: To add salt, pepper, herbs, and/or spices to a preparation to flavor it. Food should be tasted and seasoning corrected by the cook before it has completed cooking, and certainly before it is served.

Shred: To shred an ingredient you would cut it by using the largest holes on a kitchen grater. To shred lettuce or similar ingredients, you would either tear it with your hands or slice it into ribbons with a knife — about 1/3-inch wide in most cases. Fish and seafoods such as crabmeat can also be shredded by tearing.

Simmer: To heat a liquid to just below a boil. The liquid should palpitate rather than boil. A simmering liquid technically is at 195 degrees.

Skim: To remove anything floating on top of a liquid. Skimming is especially important in making fish stocks and soups.

Smoke: To preserve meat or fish by drying it slowly in the smoke of a fire. Aromatic or fragrant smoke is preferred. Foods may be hot- or cold-smoked.

Snip: What you do to chives. You can cut them, but the job is more quickly done with scissors.

Stew: To cook long and slowly in liquid.

Stir: To mix with a circular motion.

Stir-fry: The Chinese method of flash-frying in a circular pan called a wok.

Sweat: A method of cooking in simmering butter.

Toss: To turn food by tossing it in the air (to some extent). Usually applied to the tossing of a salad in a bowl. Chefs also often toss foods they are sauteing so that they will cook evenly.

Unmold: To remove food from a container, especially a decorative mold. Gelatin and fatty dishes like pâtés can be unmolded by immersing the mold in hot water briefly.

Vegetables, as garnish: There are times when you will want the vegetables used as garnish for a dish to be uniform in appearance. As an example, consider our Monkfish with Zucchini and Yogurt on page 158. Trim the ends of the zucchini, but do not peel. Cut crosswise into thick rounds 2 or 3 inches long. Stand each round on end and cut into lengthwise wedges ½- to ⅜-inch thick on the skin side, the point coming to the center of the zucchini. In this way, each piece will get the same portion of seeds and skin and each will be of uniform size. After cooking, arrange the zucchini pieces on the plate spread like the ribs of a fan with all the skin sides facing in the same direction. Voila, an attractive presentation instead of something ordinary. The procedure will work well with other vegetables and fruit, such as cucumber, summer squash, apple, and pear.

Vegetables, sauteing: When sauteing mushrooms, onions, or similar vegetables you want to brown, keep them in one layer in the pan. If the pan is too small, heat won't strike the vegetables evenly and they will sweat, evaporating and wasting moisture and flavor. Cook in two batches if necessary.

Vinegars: There are three major types of vinegar generally put to use in the kitchen. White vinegar serves a purpose in making fruit vinegars, and in some preparations where its sharpness is needed, but in general it does not have much character. For most culinary uses, red or white wine vinegar is the best. These may be flavored with herbs and other ingredients, though most professional cooks generally prefer to add the herb to the cooking for a measured result. Cider vinegar also may be used in specific cases; it has more character than white vinegar.

Whip: To beat quickly, using a whisk, electric beater, fork, or other instrument.

Work: To knead or mix. In cooking, work generally applies to foods such as dough and pastry.

Zest: The colored part of a citrus fruit rind. When using it in cooking, take only the colored section. The white pith that lies just beneath it is bitter.

Weight and Volume Equivalents

Weight:

1 gram	= 0.035 ounces	
1 kilogram	= 2.21 pounds	
1 ounce	= 28.35 grams	
1 pound	= 453.59 grams	= 16 ounces
⅓ pound	= 5 ⅓ ounces	
½ pound	= 8 ounces	

Volume:

1 gallon	= 16 cups	= 4 quarts	= 128 ounces	
1 quart	= 4 cups	= 2 pints	= 32 ounces	= 946.4 milliliters
1 pint	= 2 cups	= 16 ounces		
1 cup	= 16 tablespoons	= 8 ounces	= 237 milliliters	= 2 decaliters
½ cup	= 8 tablespoons	= 4 ounces	= 118 milliliters	= 1 decaliter
¼ cup	= 4 tablespoons	= 2 ounces	= 59 milliliters	
1 tablespoon	= 3 teaspoons	= ½ ounce	= 14.8 milliliters	
1 teaspoon	= ⅓ tablespoon	= 4.9 milliliters		

Index of Illustrations

Index

*For specific seafood, not found in this Index, please refer
to Seafood for the Table in the appendix.*

About the Authors

Jean-Jacques Paimblanc, an acclaimed professional chef, has practiced his culinary skills in such renowned establishments as the Savoy Hotel in London, Maxim's in Paris, and Le Pavillon in New York. A friend and colleague of Pierre Franey and Jacques Pépin, he began his career as an apprentice at La Mère Brazier, a famed three-star restaurant in Lyon, the gastronomic capital of France.

Anthony Spinazzola, a dedicated amateur chef, was Boston's first, and for several years only, restaurant reviewer. In fifteen years he covered over one thousand restaurants for *The Boston Globe*. He now serves as the *Globe's* food and wine critic and has also acted as editor of both the paper's magazine and its Sunday edition.